CLOSE-UP:

THE CONTEMPORARY

DIRECTOR

General Editor: Jon Tuska

Associate Editor: Vicki Piekarski

Research Editor: David Wilson

The Scarecrow Press, Inc.
Metuchen, N.J., & London
1981

Library of Congress Cataloging in Publication Data
Main entry under title:

Close-up.

  Includes filmographies and index.
  1. Moving-picture producers and directors--United
States--Biography. I. Tuska, Jon. II. Piekarski,
Vicki. III. Wilson, David, 1942-
PN1998.A2C547   791.43'0233'0922   80-23551
ISBN 0-8108-1366-1

Copyright © 1981 by Jon Tuska

Manufactured in the United States of America

TABLE OF CONTENTS

ACKNOWLEDGMENTS

In addition to the directors whose career studies appear in this book, and who so generously gave of their time in interviews with the respective authors, the editors wish to extend special thanks to several people in the motion picture industry who assisted them in various ways: Joe Abruscato and Patricia Hibbets of Columbia Pictures Television, Stanley DeCovnic of Twentieth Century-Fox Film Corporation, Allen Green of Films, Inc., Ray Swank of Swank Motion Pictures, Bill Becker of Janus Films, Bob Burriss of Warner Brothers Non-Theatrical, Adrian Weiss of Weiss Global Pictures, Henry Sapirstein of United Productions of America, and Bart Farber of United Artists Television.

The Editors

INTRODUCTION

This is the third, and last, book in the three-volume Close-Up on the Cinema series. The career studies contained in it, when combined with those in Close-Up: The Contract Director and Close-Up: The Hollywood Director, constitute a broad spectrum of perspectives on film directors of all kinds, covering a wide range of genres, specialties, and classics in American filmmaking over the last seven decades.

No one is more acutely aware than I am of the vast number of fine motion picture directors whose careers have had to be omitted due to limitations in space imposed by a series confined to three books which sought for both depth of coverage and the broadest possible representation from all areas of filmed entertainment. I would propose, therefore, that the series be judged, not on the basis of who was excluded, but rather on the inclusions and how thoroughly and vividly this cross-section has been handled in terms of their over-all careers, the results they hoped to achieve, the difficulties with which they had to contend, and the themes with which they have been preoccupied.

Nor do I feel it out of place to reflect for a moment on what it was, precisely, that I had in mind three books ago when I set out on this project and to what extent my thinking has been modified by subsequent experience. C. G. Jung comments in an essay titled "Die Lebenswende" that 'niemand tritt ins Leben ohne Voraussetzungen. Diese Voraussetzungen sind gelegentlich falsch, sie passen nicht auf die äusseren Bedingungen, denen man begegnet. Oft handelt es sich um zu grosse Erwartungen oder um Unterschätzungen der äusseren Schwierigkeiten oder um unberechtigten Optimismus oder um Negativismus. Man könnte eine lange Liste von all jenen falschen Voraussetzungen herstellen...." [No one enters upon life without assumptions. These assumptions are occasionally false, not arising from external conditions which

1

one encounters. Frequently it is a question of too great an
expectation or an underestimation of external difficulties or
an unjustified optimism or negativism. One would be able to
reconstruct a long list of all these assumptions...." Die
Dynamik des Unbewussten, Vol. VIII, Gesammelte Werke,
Rascher Verlag, 1968.]

I am not about to embark on a list of all my incor-
rect assumptions about life, but I should perhaps mention a
few which affected this series. I did not realize, going in,
that there was so little interest in film directors among
Americans outside the few elitist and variously subsidized
cinema magazines. The opposite was and remains true of
Europe, in terms of not only contemporary directors but
also directors of the innumerable silent and vintage sound
films programmed on European television. Roman Polanski,
I fear, has received far more exposure in the American news
media for his recent personal indiscretions than he could ever
hope to achieve as a result of his professional work as a filmmaker; and this coming fast on the heels of his notoriety for
having been married to Sharon Tate.

I suspect that one reason why so little attention continues to be paid to film directors in the United States is
that the American television culture has become accustomed
to overlooking individual merit on the basis of performance
or artistic achievement. The popular idols of the day are
"created" through publicity campaigns and need possess no
inherent merit whatsoever. Gulf & Western, the giant oil
conglomerate, as part of its empire to manipulate public
opinion owns Paramount Pictures, Simon & Schuster Publishers, and Pocket Books, Inc. This media syndicate can nom-
inate an inferior novel, have Simon & Schuster contract to
publish it, sell motion picture rights to Paramount, and have
Pocket Books pay out a huge sum for paperback rights by
simply transferring money from one set of books to another--
without it ever leaving corporate hands. Independent book
clubs witnessing this can commit large sums for book club
rights, which will underwrite the syndicate even if it does
poorly on the book and yet be assured of making a profit
because the public, exposed to a plethora of prepublication
publicity--to say nothing of the continued exposure through
the movie version on a network movie of the week and, later,
in syndication--will want to buy the book.

There is an arresting moment in François Truffaut's
FAHRENHEIT 451 (Universal, 1966). In a society where

books are outlawed, there exists a village of outcasts, far
from the well-policed cities, where each man and each woman commits to memory the entire contents of one book so
that, even if all copies of it are seized and burned, its text
still will not be lost to mankind. Near the end of the film
one of these outcasts remarks that it should be kept in mind
that behind each book there is a man, an individual human
being who cannot be permitted to vanish without a trace.

Behind every film to an extent, and behind contemporary films in particular, there are many men, but perhaps
none so important as the director. By saying this I am not
"taking back" anything I wrote in the Introduction to Close-
Up: The Contract Director, merely seeking to clarify it.
There is in connection with every film usually one guiding
personality who shapes the character of the final product.
In former times, this guiding personality may have been the
executive producer as often as it was one of the producing
studio's contract directors arbitrarily assigned to direct the
film, but more recently it has been the big-name star who
was in a position to tell both the producer and the director
what to do. When Andrew V. McLaglen was hired to direct
a John Wayne picture--and he has directed several--Wayne,
and not McLaglen, would personally oversee every set-up,
camera angle, the lighting, sound, action, and dialogue delivery.

On the other hand, even the collaborative effort between a director and a producing company on one side and
the screenwriter and the players on the other is today often
undermined, at least in television production with series like
The Life and Times of Grizzly Adams, by the circumstance
that every scene, before it is even drafted in script form,
has been pre-tested for audience reaction via a specially
programmed computer that is presumably able to measure
and predict emotional response. Those scenes which do make
it to the script stage are again pre-tested aurally before random audiences in supermarkets. This information--reactions
to words, phrases, ideas, moods, plot sequences, clothes,
types of dwelling--is then resubmitted to the computer for
further analysis. The subsequent print-outs are then con-
densed into brief reports and distributed to the director,
story editor and writers, forming a set of absolute guide-
lines. According to Grizzly Adams' producer, Charles E.
Sellier, Jr., whose Sunn Productions has also produced some
twenty-six money-making theatrical movies by using this system, "We select only high-test stories and we eliminate any

negatives our audiences consistently dislikes [sic]." (TV
Guide, Jan. 28-Feb. 3, 1978.)

With such a powerful onslaught of conglomerate-created
or computer pre-tested popularity, backed by money seeking
with the greatest possible assurance to make more money,
Americans are reduced to being entertained as common de-
nominators and are forced into a mass collectivization process that would attempt to do nothing less than deny them the
one thing that once was characterized as the raison d'être
for the American experiment: the infinitely precious independence of the individual human soul. This shouldn't surprise us too much, since as long ago as Alexis de Tocque-
ville the American need for conformity in all things was discerned as our single most vicious national impulse.

If these reflections appear to have taken me rather
far afield from the subject at hand, let me say: not at all--
I am merely outlining the distance run in this series. The
first book dealt with the individual efforts of film directors
to infuse their distinctive personalities into corporate cinematic creations, in open conflict with the studio bureaucracy,
the mediocre nature of the stories and plots they were supposed to bring to life, and the unsophisticated audiences their
films were intended to entertain. From this, in the second
volume, we passed into a transitional period where individual-
ism and the personality of the director could for brief moments enjoy total independence. In this third volume we are
dealing with directors who are confronted not only by producing companies in many cases owned or controlled by the opin-
ion-forming conglomerates but even with the more awesome
foe of mass audiences whose most intimate responses have
been the object of on-going efforts at measurement and pre-
diction.

It was undoubtedly a false assumption on my part to
think that in the time it has taken to assemble these books
there might arise in the United States an interest in who directs a film which would compare with that in who stars in
it or the pre-tested suitability of its plot-line, but there are
a few favorable indications of just such a trend developing.
Accordingly, I have retained my commitment throughout all
three volumes to include only those career studies which concentrate on an individual director's personality. A director's
personality is important, I feel, because it cannot but influence the outcome of his work. For me the individual human
being remains the measure of all things in his life. Yet I
do not wish to confuse an interest in the personality of a

director with the objective fact of his film work. I only
claim that, ideally, both should be given stress in a career
study.

   To find writers capable of accomplishing this dual perspective hasn't been easy. I made another erroneous assumption upon embarking, one that I came to recognize only much
later and after much travail. Although cinema history was a
relatively unexplored region in 1969, given over chiefly to a
nostalgia wave when I founded Views & Reviews magazine,
there was every reason, it seemed at the time, to expect its
rapid maturation to follow a fresh and unique course--because
film itself is unique--and not a course derived from other dis-
ciplines such as literary analysis, aesthetics, or psychoana-
lytic dream interpretation. Prior to that time this is the
path that several film critics and cinema historians had opted
to follow. They insisted on treating film as if it were a
novel, a painting, or a neurotic dream. I couldn't regard
these practices as an advance in any way over those newspaper and magazine reviews of new films which rely solely
on the subjective emotional responses of the reviewer, or
those very early "pictorial history" compilations which, if
they didn't actually stoop to quoting trade reviews, did little
more than substitute the compiler's subjective opinions for
an anthology of reviewers' comments.

   I grant that the experience of a film, and one's response to it, is a very individual and eccentric emotional
reaction, to be applauded surely, as we must applaud anything at all individual in our collectivized world, but scarcely
worthy for that reason alone to be called film criticism or
cinema history. Pauline Kael's opinions about new films,
like William K. Everson's opinions about old films, are just
that, opinions, with which we can agree or disagree, which
we can quote or forget, as is our inclination; but they have
nothing to do with film critique or history.

   My objectives in publishing Views & Reviews magazine
were carried over when I undertook to edit the Close-Up series: to bring together a series of critical and informed essays that would unite the talent and resources of a number
of film historians, both established and novitiate, so as to
provide the reader interested in the cinema with writing of
an exceptional nature, factual, intelligent, and human. It
was also my hope by this means to lay a firmer foundation
for film criticism and cinema history in the future.

   I was, as I have said, dissatisfied with the manner

in which writers seemed to be lost and muddled in their approaches to film. The most common, and to my mind the
least effective, way of dealing with the subject in the 1960s
was to borrow the abortive techniques of literary analysis.
Even when these "film analysts" were willing to concede
C. G. Jung's point that a work of art is an objective psychic
fact and not, as the Freudians maintain, a neurotic distortion
of a peculiar and repressed personality, they still regarded
film the way literary analysts regarded literature. The literary analyst assumed much the same posture as an arm-
chair detective. Like Edgar Allan Poe's C. Auguste Dupin,
the literary analyst preferred the seclusion of his dark rooms
to the bright sunlight of the external world; he would spend
time ruminating about what an event might possibly mean and
what had conspired to produce a certain effect.

In "The Mystery of Marie Roget," Poe has Dupin solve
a murder from the confines of his study merely by perusing
and analyzing newspaper accounts of the tragedy. Ever since
Poe, there has been a plethora of detectives who amuse us by
making all manner of deductions about characters involved in
the commission of a crime by means of a series of fantastic
speculations about how such persons might be expected to act
in a given set of circumstances. I do not know what the
reader's reaction has been to detective stories of this kind,
but it was my experience while writing The Detective in Hollywood (Doubleday, 1978), for which I had to read an assort-
ment of detective fiction and watch countless detective films,
that the explanation offered by the author, supposedly revealing the logic behind all the startling and macabre events he
had narrated, was by far the most far-fetched, the most
clumsy, and the most disappointing aspect of the entire plot.

Perhaps because literary analysts behaved in a similar
fashion, their results were also disconcerting. They would
select a novel, retell its story-line in boring detail, re-intro-
duce the reader to its characters, and then set about analyzing these characters in depth, informed at all times by dis-
ciplines wholly alien to the novelist, consulting with Freudian
psychology, Marxist ideology, Christian theology, folklore,
or making endless references to characters in other novels
which the author of the book being analyzed probably hadn't
read. Armed with these observations, these analysts would
next proceed to elucidate the novel under examination, which
is to say they would advise us what the novel really meant
and what it was the author was really driving at when he
wrote it.

It was depressing to me to find that motion pictures, so early in their history, when they were taken seriously at all, were subjected to film analysis with a similar methodology. After all, literary analysis and the "teaching" of literature had significantly contributed in the United States to the lamentable fact that a very small percentage of the American population reads books, despite nearly universal education. The "teaching" of literature spurred publishers to flood campus bookstores with student aids for use in "learning" what literature was all about. The upshot was that students no longer needed to read the novels but could instead rely on plot synopses reducing chapters of a given novel to a paragraph and elaborate footnotes referring to the various literary interpretations by legions of analysts of what those chapters of the novel, or the novel as a whole, could be said to "mean." Literature was no longer something we read for pleasure; indeed, as laymen, as readers, we weren't even qualified to read it without these study guides, because there was presumably a difference between what the author said and what he meant!

Only readers who love books as much as I do would have been as saddened as I was by what had happened to literature in the United States. We didn't need the fire engines, sirens blaring, rushing to burn a cache of books found hidden somewhere, as in FAHRENHEIT 451; the analysts had destroyed literature far more effectively by completely discouraging the impulse to read. I didn't want to see this deplorable practice stifle yet another popular art. Take as an instance what happened to Alfred Hitchcock. American professors and literary analysts mercilessly latched onto him. If this subtle form of abuse had a beginning, it was probably with Eric Rohmer and Claude Chabrol, who claimed in their book Hitchcock (Editions Universitaires, 1957) that thanks to Hitchcock's early exposure to Jesuit schools, the director was deeply imbued with the moral outlook of Roman Catholic theology. Their book sought to demonstrate how each Hitchcock film carries a Catholic message about the nature of man and the nature of sin.

Once Hitchcock departed London for Hollywood, English critics tended to dismiss him as a commercial hack until Raymond Durgnat published a series of interpretive essays about his films in Films and Filming in 1970, which he expanded to book length for The Strange Case of Alfred Hitchcock (Faber & Faber, 1974). Durgnat took exception to the French Catholic school but still insisted on a theological orientation. "For

Chabrol and Rohmer," Durgnat wrote, "Hitchcock's vision is impregnated by a Roman Catholicism the severity of whose morality evokes Jansenism. This severity may, however, have reached Hitchcock by a different route. Jansenism is the result, in French Catholicism, of the Calvinist influence, and Hitchcock's sense of a blind, implacable, cruel, yet, somehow, just, providence may well have come to him via the influence, in the British middle classes, of that Puritanism which is the English version of Calvinism." (Films and Filming, April, 1970, and, in expanded form, The Strange Case of Alfred Hitchcock.)

François Truffaut did the intelligent thing: he conducted exhaustive personal interviews with Hitchcock. He questioned Hitchcock about this supposed moral philosophy, Calvinist or Catholic, and was told by Hitchcock: "... My love of film is far more important than any considerations of morality." (Hitchcock, by François Truffaut, Simon & Schuster, 1967.)

You might think such an unequivocal statement would be sufficient, but it wasn't. Robin Wood, in his book Hitchcock's Films (Barnes, 1969), swept aside everything Hitchcock had said to Truffaut in 1967, or elsewhere, with the observation: "I used to find maddening Hitchcock's refusal to discuss his work with interviewers on any really serious level; I have come to admire it. It seems so much in keeping with the character of the films themselves that their creator should be such a delightfully modest and unassuming man who makes no claims for his art outside the evidence of his films." But this was not to be construed to mean that Wood himself was willing to limit himself to the "evidence of the films." This is how Wood worked it: he provided his reader with a summary of a plot and then speculated on the possible motivation of the characters, more often than not asserting his findings rather than finding his assertions in the films.

One brief instance should be enough. In SUSPICION (RKO, 1941), based on Frances Iles' novel Before the Fact, Hitchcock had a story to his liking, about a young, inexperienced, and unattractive woman who marries a worldly socialite who has no money and decides to murder her for her inheritance. The RKO management felt Cary Grant ill-suited to the role if it would actually call for him to murder Joan Fontaine, playing his wife, so they forced Hitchcock to alter the ending. In the release version Fontaine is the victim of paranoia and Grant, although a liar and a bounder, has no

intention of murdering her. Wood didn't choose to contrast
the film with the novel--in the novel the husband murders his
wife and, even though she knows it while it's happening, she
drinks the poison anyway. What Wood did do was conduct an
analysis of characters who appear neither in the film nor in
the novel. "She is irresistably attracted to the man," he
wrote of Fontaine, "who represents glamour and reckless,
carefree abandon; but he represents also a total rejection of
everything her family background and upbringing has stood
for: subconsciously, she wants him to be a murderer."

     The emphasis belongs to Wood. He never told us what
dialogue or what scene showed the viewer that Fontaine wanted
Grant to be a murderer. It was merely an analysis of Fontaine's portrayal which, according to Wood, would tend to
heighten our appreciation of the film. How it was supposed
to be able to do this, having nothing really to do with the
film, he did not say. When I recently saw SUSPICION again
at a re-issue theatre in Los Angeles, the audience laughed
at the right times, and was transfixed by suspense at the
right times, so the picture works as well today as it did in
1941 and can be enjoyed without having our appreciation heightened by transforming the characters into persons they are not
and never were intended to be.

     I felt there must be an alternative approach to dealing
with a director's oeuvre other than film analysis, which introduces too many notions extraneous to the director or his films,
or merely a holding forth with opinions illustrated with stills
from a director's films, or the auteur theory which, in many
cases, could not apply to the directors whose careers were
to be studied. Although an admitted auteuriste, Andrew Sarris in his book of perceptive, albeit brief, glimpses of the
director's particular art, The American Cinema (Dutton, 1968),
came closest to what I had in mind, but I wanted to go one
step further, to approach each director in terms of portrai-
ture. If the director was still alive, I felt the author should
talk to him, and never dismiss everything he had to say about
his films as irrelevant. Because of the attrition rate among
directors, more than one final interview appears in this series. Where the director could not be interviewed, the next
best thing was to evoke his personality from conversations
with those who knew and worked with him. I also thought it
preferable in every case to explicate the background of a director's films and thus to recreate the environment in which
his common themes and professional techniques were grounded,
rather than giving plot synopses in detail.

Since my conception of how to treat film history and
how these career studies should be written was new, I believed that every essay should be new. It was a painfully
erroneous assumption on my part to presume that the task
of commissioning career studies would be an easy one. I
have been quite often a "standing-offer man," to use a term
from the career study of Douglas Sirk in Close-Up: The
Hollywood Director. I have been deceived in every way imag-
inable, told by potential contributors week after week for
months that "it's in the mail." One author from New York
City, after volunteering an essay, finally after a year had
his girl friend tell me that the situation was hopeless, that
he was sitting in a corner, his hands between his legs, sob-
bing inconsolably because his wife was divorcing him. Mono-
nucleosis, a mother-in-law's suicide, leaving writing for the
real estate business, inexplicable but debilitating headaches,
sudden love affairs, trying to get me to set up an interview
with a noted director so the would-be contributor could present him in person with a screenplay he had been unable to
peddle elsewhere--I must have heard all the usual excuses,
and some that were rather extraordinary. But what does it
matter? At last the series has been completed and now it
must stand or fall on its own merits.

It would be misleading and unfair to enumerate the
difficulties I have had without stressing at the same time how
pleased I have been with many of the excellent contributions .
to this series. It is always easier to complain than to give
proper credit, yet, in this instance, credit is perhaps more
in order than expressions of annoyance. I marvel at the results contributors have been able to achieve in their career
studies. I spent time with Bob Altman in Palm Springs while
he was shooting 3 WOMEN (20th-Fox, 1977) and, as articulate as I found him to be, there is about his cinematic oeuvre
an insight into what America is all about, so penetrating and
unsettling that it cannot be approached, much less compre-
hended, through an ordinary interview or even an examination
of his films. David Wilson, by a necessarily circuitous route,
was able to make Altman's vision intelligible and yet multi-
dimensional. I know he accomplished this by treating the
milieu around Altman so that there is a continuous refractive
process where cause and effect become indistinguishable, as
if Altman and his milieu were inseparable, and I admire what
he has done because I could not have done it. In a sense,
too, in this volume more than in any of the others Los Angeles has become a character--Los Angeles as it is today,
dismal as a river bottom in the Bayou country, infested with

snapping, money-eating piranha fish, malodorous with dope,
congested sexuality, smog, automobile exhaust, where poverty
is a capital sin, and Jesus freaks rub shoulders with all the
other spaced-out losers and degenerates of a generation that
was born and perhaps reached maturity without ever seeing
the mountains through the brownish silt hanging, as it does
over the San Fernando Valley, like a giant cloud over their
lives, a generation born burned-out, to which the smell of
decay is as natural as the claustrophobic skyline.

None of this is intended as a diatribe against Los Angeles. Ross Macdonald, the detective story writer, once told
me that everything good and bad starts in California, and then
moves East. His intention in his Lew Archer novels is to be
critical of Southern California. I think he is right. If we
aren't aware of what has happened in Southern California, it
might very well move East, which would not be desirable ...
at least, I don't think so, any more than Bob Altman thought
so in producing WELCOME TO L.A. (United Artists, 1977).

Thanks to Vicki Piekarski, the female point of view
has also been well-represented. I have always felt there is
much to be learned from what women have to say, more in
fact in my experience than I have ever been able to learn
from men. Vicki's career study of Sydney Pollack, along
with those by Jacoba Atlas of George Roy Hill and Bella
Taylor of Martin Scorsese in the present volume, stand
as a vital counter-balance in a world too long shaped, possibly even corrupted, by an exclusively male bias. Although
when I began this series, Vicki was my secretary/companion,
that is no longer true at its close. The Westerns: An Encyclopedia of Western Fiction, Film, Radio, and Television,
which will be appearing from McGraw-Hill in 1981, is only
the first of what I am sure will be many projects which Vicki
will conceive independently from me, but which grew out of
her editorial duties here. I owe to everyone, those I have
mentioned as well as the many whom I have not, my deepest
gratitude for always having given their best.

Let me take an editor's prerogative and conclude with
a remark or two about my own contributions. My personal
concern has long been, and I suppose will long remain, this
business of living, of finding one's way in the world. I am
therefore inclined to place more than usual emphasis on just
how a man has lived, what he may have learned, what he
never foresaw, and how much life itself diminished him. Whatever I have had to contribute to cinema history, then, has

been told necessarily in terms of the personalities and experiences I have encountered along the way.   Perhaps the reader
will recall how Friedrich Klein, in that most beautiful short
novel by Hermann Hesse, Klein und Wagner, was accustomed
to carrying a volume of Schopenhauer with him on his travels
and how, once, he opened the book at random and read:
" 'Wenn wir auf unsern zurückgelegten Lebensweg zurücksehn
und zumal unsre unglücklichen Schritte, nebst ihren Folgen,
ins Augen Fassen, so begreifen wir oft nicht, wie wir haben
dieses tun, oder jenes unterlassen können; so dass es aus-
sieht, als hätte eine fremde Macht unsre Schritte gelenkt.' "
[When we look back on our life as we have lived it and above
all at our steps where they faltered, and their consequences,
fastening it all before our eyes, it is often inconceivable that
we were able to do this or omit doing that; so that it appears
as if a strange force had directed out steps.   Gesammelte
Dictungen, Vol. III, Suhrkamp Verlag, 1958.]   This zurücksehn, looking backward, has concerned me most of all, but
never in isolation, never without looking forward with equal
intensity toward the future.

I have never written anything by assignment, only what
I have chosen by conscious design to write.   In dealing with
the directors about whom I have provided career studies, I
haven't been guided solely by my liking for their films, but
also by my liking for them as people.   It might be said of
me, on this account, that I therefore lack objectivity and im-
personality.   I don't mind this criticism, because true objectivity is always questionable in criticism--it is often merely
a matter of human personalities and experiences--and imper-
sonality has never been my purpose; rather, I have sought the
unique, often incomprehensible, sometimes even profound individual human soul.   Only when that is the object of study
are we confronted by those depths which Heraclitus once
called an expanse without measure.   That expanse, frequently
fashioned out of prolonged suffering, certainly from blunder-
ing through life as all of us do, crowned occasionally by
achievement, besieged by failures too numerous and probably
too painful to count--that expanse is the counterbalance we
all need to hold precious against the demons which perpetually
torment us, the baseless assumptions leading us into inevitable
error, the illusions which we create for ourselves.   In the
best films there is a confrontation with life, accomplished at
times with poetry, at others with emotional electricity, that
can be as insubstantial as a shadow on a sunny day, as brutally frank as the barbed-wire of a concentration camp, and,
for all that, nonetheless liberating because in truth the artist
is still the only free man.

Looking back, I have been at work for five years, on and off, on this series, and I am astonished, in terms of all the interviews I have conducted in that time, how little film criticism and film history have taken milieu into account. I have tried, to the extent I have been able, to make milieu a more significant component of my own career studies in this book. In my opinion, at any rate, it goes a long way toward explaining the atmosphere of many of the films produced by those directors with whom I have dealt. Looking forward, I can only hope that all of the career studies in these three books, taken as a composite, will make a definite and positive contribution to the way film is regarded in our time.

Jon Tuska

Los Angeles, California
1978

KEY TO FILM CHECKLISTS

P: Production Company

D: Director

C: Cast

ft. /m.   footage/running time

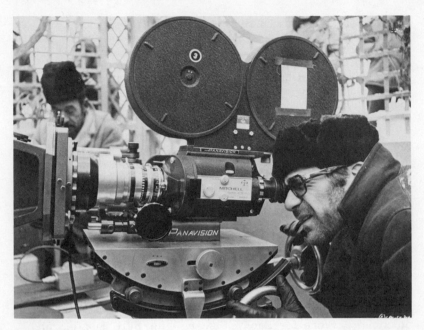

Chapter 1

SYDNEY POLLACK

by Vicki Piekarski

Sigmund Freud was fond of quoting Conrad Ferdinand Meyer: "Ich bin kein ausgeklügelt Buch. Ich bin ein Mensch mit seinem Widerspruch." [I'm not a well-rounded book. I'm a man with his contradiction.]

Sydney Pollack is just such a man; the highly skeptical philosophy developed in his films over the last twelve years stands in direct contradiction to his personal way of life. He once said in an interview: "... I do not understand why

Above: Sydney Pollack checks camera angle for a scene in CASTLE KEEP (Columbia, 1969). Photo courtesy of Eddie Brandt's Saturday Matinee.

I have done any particular film, or what I have done with
the material involved.   I have a great wife and family [one
son and two daughters].   I have some good friends.   I think
of myself as a happy person, yet only one of the eight films
[ten as of 1978] I have made has a happy ending.   Maybe my
unconscious is at work.   Perhaps I am more pessimistic
than I think that I am. "

Pollack became interested in the theatre while attend-
ing South Bend High School in Indiana, where he grew up.
Eldest son of a pharmacist, Pollack was born on 1 July,
1934 in Lafayette, Indiana; he has one brother and one sister.
Upon graduation Pollack headed for New York, at the age of
seventeen, and once there enrolled at Sanford Meisner's
Neighborhood Playhouse, where he was a drama student for
two years.   Meisner, who influenced Pollack greatly, asked
Pollack to stay on as his assistant and he did so for five
years until 1960, an apprenticeship which no doubt helped
Pollack's ability to work well with, and understand, actors
when he began his directorial career.   While coaching other
actors, Pollack himself acted in both the theatre and in television.   Among the plays Pollack performed in were Harold
Robbins' A Stone for Danny Fisher, with Zero Mostel, and
Christopher Fry's The Dark Is Light Enough, with Katherine
Cornell and Tyrone Power.   He married Claire Griswold,
one of his former drama students, in 1958.

John Frankenheimer, who was one of the earliest directors to make the transition from television to films, directed Pollack in several Playhouse 90 entries, including two
Hemingway adaptations, "For Whom the Bell Tolls" and "The
Snows of Kilimanjaro. "   It was one of many fortuitous meet-
ings for Pollack.   Frankenheimer asked Pollack to be his
dialogue director on THE YOUNG SAVAGES (United Artists,
1961)--Pollack had just finished serving a two-year stint in
the Army.   The cast of THE YOUNG SAVAGES featured
Burt Lancaster, Shelley Winters, and Telly Savalas, all of
whom Pollack would work with subsequently in his own films.

Frankenheimer and Lancaster encouraged Pollack to
stay in Hollywood and he began directing television episodes,
the first of which was a Shotgun Slade entry, a syndicated
Western series.   Also, about this time Pollack landed an
acting job (his only feature film performance) in a Korean
war film, WAR HUNT (United Artists, 1962), directed by
R. Denis Sanders, in which newcomer Robert Redford made
his first film appearance.   It was another fortuitous meeting:

Pollack and Redford have remained close friends and have, so far, collaborated on four film projects.

Among Pollack's television credits are episodes of Chrysler Theatre, The Naked City, The Defenders, and fifteen episodes of Ben Casey, one of which, "A Cardinal Act of Mercy," was nominated for five Emmy awards, including best direction (stage actress Kim Stanley was awarded the Best Actress Emmy). Pollack was nominated twice more for an Emmy for his directorial achievements in television and won the award for Outstanding Directorial Achievement in Drama for "The Game," a Bob Hope Presents Chrysler Theatre entry. Before turning to film direction, Pollack directed a play at UCLA called P. S. 193, which was very successful, and also prepared the American version of THE LEOPARD (1963), starring Burt Lancaster. He directed his first film in 1965.

THE SLENDER THREAD (Paramount, 1965) is a taut suspense drama filmed in black and white in pseudo-documentary style about the Seattle Crisis Clinic, a telephone service offering help to those on the brink of causing violence to themselves or others. The theme of communication, or lack of it, specifically on a personal level, is well explored by Stirling Silliphant's screenplay based on Shana Alexander's Life magazine article on the Seattle clinic.

Anne Bancroft plays Inga, a thirty-year-old working housewife who is attempting suicide for the second time. With only one hour left to live she calls the clinic, where a psychology student, played well by Sidney Poitier, has been left in charge. She tells him she has taken a bottle of barbiturates but she will not tell him where she is; he tries to keep her on the line until the call can be traced. Pollack uses a series of flashbacks to reveal to the audience how Inga came to the decision to end her life.

Her husband of twelve years, a fisherman by trade, has found out that their only son is not his. Though she tries to explain to him that she was 'only eighteen," he cannot find it in himself to forgive her. She first attempts suicide by drowning, but is saved by a necking couple on the beach. Several attempts are made to pull the pieces of the marriage back together by doing the things a family does together--going to church, socializing with friends--but Mark, her husband, cannot forget and in his anger asks her if she thinks not getting caught in a lie is the same as telling the

truth.   Robert Redford would ask Cliff Robertson exactly the
same question in Pollack's spy thriller, THREE DAYS OF
THE CONDOR (Paramount, 1975).

Mary Savage in her autobiographical book, Addicted to
Suicide (Capra Press, 1975), explains one of her suicide attempts: "On the previous day, I had gone to see my medical
doctor....   I came away with the feeling that he didn't care....
I had seen my therapist ... I felt that he didn't care either...."
She went on: "All of this was unreasonable, of course, but
reason had nothing to do with it....   There are cases when
the ravages of terminal illness might make suicide a logical
and justifiable decision, but for most of us, the attempt to
take one's life is a message of quite another sort.   In my
case, it said: 'I am rotten and useless.   Nobody can love
me, nobody does love me, therefore I must die.'"

Inga is alone and she too feels that no one cares.
Her husband is off on his boat fishing, her son is growing
up and has his own friends, and her boss is out of town on
a skiing trip.   She has nothing to do and she feels "strange."
She walks into a hospital and asks to speak to one of the
doctors.   When he arrives he tells her that she must be admitted before he can help her.   Would she be able to leave
when she wanted?   That depends....

Where does a woman or a man go to just talk with
someone when he or she feels helpless and hopeless, alone
and scared?   In THE SLENDER THREAD it is quite clear
there is no place at all to go unless one wants to be treated
as a patient, not a person.

Pollack captures this sense of irony throughout the
film, especially in the contrast between communication on
civic and individual levels.   The advanced equipment of the
telephone company and the police department are shown--walls
and aisles of files, wires, machines working together in perfect harmony to find Inga.   Communication on a personal
level, however--between Inga and her husband or Inga and
the clinic's volunteer--is arduous and often ineffectual.   And
although contact is made between the student and Inga and
help does arrive in time to save her, her future is dubious.

Pollack filmed THE SLENDER THREAD on location in
Seattle.   The film opens with an aerial shot of the city.   "I
love aerial shots," Pollack once said.   "I like seeing a place
from far away, seeing the world in which the characters are

going to play out their drama.   It gives a broader significance
to what's going on."

    Two of Pollack's most memorable aerial photography
shots (a technique he continues to use in films like BOBBY
DEERFIELD [Columbia, 1977] although he has stated that they
are "faddish" and that he is self-conscious about using them)
appear in his second film, THIS PROPERTY IS CONDEMNED
(Paramount, 1966).   The first comes in the prologue of the
film when Mary Badham is seen balancing herself on a railroad tie as the camera pulls back to an aerial view of the
town.   Although not as impressive to the viewer as the later
shot of Natalie Wood in the train window, it was technically
a more difficult shot.   "We had to land a helicopter on a
flatcar which we made.   It was no bigger than a table," Pollack explained.   "We had to hold the skids down.   The blades
of the helicopter were blowing Badham's hair so we had to
start the blades turning in flat pitch--parallel to the ground--
so they made no wind.   Then we had to push the flatcar
away, which gives the start of the dolly, and then get far
enough away that the wind wouldn't blow her.   When the helicopter lifted off the flatcar we had to push the car half a
mile down the track to get out of the way of the shot."

    The later shot of Natalie Wood in the train begins
with a close-up of Wood through a train window.   Slowly the
camera pulls back and then up and over the train and then it
appears as if the picture spins around in the frame.   To accomplish this effect the helicopter had to gain enough speed
so that it could roll over on its side.   It took a full day to
film the beginning of the shot because it was so difficult to
get the helicopter close enough to the train for a close-up;
the blades overlapped the train car top.

    THIS PROPERTY IS CONDEMNED was suggested by
Tennessee Williams' one-act play of the same name.   Williams'
play focused on an adolescent boy and girl discussing the
girl's dead sister, Alva.   Fred Coe, Edith Sommer, and
Francis Ford Coppola, the director of THE GODFATHER
(Paramount, 1972), utilized Williams' play for the opening
and closing scenes in their screenplay collaboration.   The
meat of the film is Alva's story told in a flashback through
her younger sister's eyes.   Natalie Wood plays Alva.

    Pollack's films are often set in a past era but "the
point of view deals with the present," he says.   "I am interested in the relevance of the past to the present, and, of

course, the future." THIS PROPERTY's setting was the decaying South, Dodson, Mississippi during the Depression.
Basically, the story reconstructs Alva's attempt to escape
from Dodson and from her mother, who is greedy and seeks
to make use of Alva's promiscuous behavior to aid her own
escape from Dodson. The mother's plans are threatened by
Owen--Robert Redford in his first role in a Pollack project--
who falls in love with Alva after he arrives in Dodson to
handle the railroad's retrenchment. Owen leaves Dodson,
feeling duped, when he hears Alva's mother discussing her
plans to move to Memphis with Alva.

While drunk, Alva proposes marriage to her mother's
boy friend, played by Charles Bronson, who actually loves
Alva. She is attempting to prove to her mother that no one
really cares about her and that the boys of the town really
come to the boardinghouse to see Alva. Alva leaves her new
husband in the middle of their wedding night after taking his
money and the marriage certificate and heads for New Orleans
in search of Owen. They find each other and are portrayed
in touching, romantic scenes as being very deeply in love.
Owen proposes marriage but Alva balks. Her mother arrives
and threatens to expose her. Alva becomes frightened and
runs out of the apartment into the rainy night. We never see
her again but we are told by her younger sister that she died
of a lung infection, just like in the movies.

Pollack felt that Alva was basically a whore despite
all this talk about "gentlemen callers" by her younger sister.
A key scene was cut by the producer, John Houseman, whom
later Pollack would cast as the head of the C.I.A. in THREE
DAYS OF THE CONDOR, a part written especially for Houseman: after Alva runs out of the apartment we see her one
more time back in Dodson trying to pick up a traveling salesman. But Houseman insisted that it be cut because there
were too many endings. Pollack admits that he has a proclivity for multiple endings that drives people crazy.

THE SCALPHUNTERS (United Artists, 1968), an unconventional comedy Western with an original screenplay by
William Norton, his first, incorporated some new ideas into
a cliché-ridden genre. Pollack filmed on location in and
around Durango and Torreon, Mexico. He shot in continuity,
which he would also do in THEY SHOOT HORSES, DON'T
THEY? (Cinerama, 1969), an uncommon practice due to the
tremendous expense involved. It was Pollack's first Panavision film. His subsequent films, though usually intimate

stories about people, have also been shot in this medium.
He has been criticized for this practice, being called "Holly-
woodish" and "too grand." But for Pollack, "Panavision is
the only medium you can work in where you never lose the
sense of the environment.... In the tightest close-up you
spill off the edges of the face and you spill off to a sufficient
degree to know where you are." In other words, no cheating.

The setting in THE SCALPHUNTERS is a barren, dusty
Western landscape. Joe Bass, a trapper played by Burt Lancaster, knows much about the new land and he respects it.
He is thrown together with Ossie Davis, a runaway slave,
when his furs are taken by a hunting party of Kiowa Indians
and then by a gang of scalphunters. Davis is educated: "I
can read, write, and cipher," he tells Bass. Bass asks him
if all that "book-learning" can fill his stomach. He proceeds
to teach Davis about the things the land has to offer. However, there is a silent mutual contempt between the two men,
due in large measure to the difference in their skin color,
although it is never mentioned. Davis literally rolls into the
camp of the scalphunters, who are led by Telly Savalas. He
learns they are headed for Mexico, where slavery is illegal.
Davis decides to stay with them. He explains to Bass, when
Bass tries to get him to leave their camp, that a slave doesn't
pick his master, he goes to the highest bidder. Savalas bids
Mexico.

Bass attempts to get the furs back by himself by ar-
ranging catastrophes along the scalphunters' trail. Unsur-
passed in Western movies is a rock slide which Pollack filmed
on a small rocky ledge along which the wagons are traveling.
Davis sees the difficulties that Bass is having and tries to
persuade Savalas' mistress, played superbly by Shelley Winters, who believes in astrology and who smokes big stogies,
that Savalas will die if the furs are not left behind. She understands and agrees to help. In the next scene, after the
pack horse is supposedly left behind, we see Winters with a
huge black eye, courtesy of Savalas.

Davis was correct. The resolution of the film comes
when Bass puts locoweed in an isolated waterhole on the
scalphunters' trail. The horses go loco and the scalphunters,
frightened and discouraged, tell Savalas to give up. Four men
are already dead. Davis admits knowing the man who is causing all the trouble and offers to go and talk to him. Davis
and Bass have it out finally about Davis's servile attitude toward whites. Davis tells Bass he wouldn't last ten minutes

as a black man. They go down to talk to Savalas, but he is
hiding under a grave mound. He emerges and fights with
Bass. He ties up Bass and is about to scalp him when Davis
steps in and kills Savalas. Winters stands on the side-lines,
finding it hard to believe that all this could happen over some
lousy, smelly furs. Bass is lying on the ground, still tied
up, as Davis struts around enjoying his moment of glory.
Bass asks Davis to untie him but he won't; instead he tells
Bass someone ought to beat some sense into him. Davis is
ready to fight on Bass' level, not through civilized cunning
or artful dodging, but in fist to fist combat. They begin to
fight in the dirt. They roll into the waterhole and keep slugging.

     While they are at it, the Kiowas arrive and take the
furs and the wagons and Winters, who finally resigns herself
to the fact that she will never get to Mexico and enjoy the
amenities of life a woman in her profession--prostitution--
deserves. With a gun in her hand and about to shoot a Kiowa,
she shrugs and says, "What the hell, they're only men. I'll
be the damnedest white squaw in the whole Kiowa nation."
Meanwhile Bass and Davis are exhausted and caked with mud,
their color indistinguishable. Bass offers Davis a drink.
Davis, remembering the first time he met Bass, when the
Kiowas originally took the furs, recalls that Bass then told
him that they could get the furs back because the Indians would
drink the whiskey that was also packed on the mule. He tells
Bass that the wagon the Kiowas took has two cases of whiskey
in it and that by nightfall there's going to be a bunch of drunken
Kiowas with a fine pack of furs. They ride off on Bass's
horse together. Bass has learned that he does need help in
getting the furs back, that he cannot make it alone. Davis
has already learned much from Bass and still has a lot to
learn about the strange new land, but more importantly he
has learned that as long as he believes he is a slave, he
will be. They are friends with each other and with the land;
they need be friends because, after all, they're only men.

     David Rayfiel, whom Pollack met while working in
television in 1962, has done all the final rewrites on Pollack's
films, although he has only been credited on CASTLE KEEP
(Columbia, 1969) and THREE DAYS OF THE CONDOR. Rayfiel's collaboration with Daniel Taradash on the screenplay
for CASTLE KEEP was based on William Eastlake's novel
of the same title. It was the first time Pollack used a novel
as the basis for one of his films. Subsequently all his films
but one--THE YAKUZA (Warner's, 1975), which was an original screenplay--have been adapted from novels.

Upon release, CASTLE KEEP was considered by most
to be too talky. "Part of the reason it's so talky," explained
Pollack, "is that both David Rayfiel and I had such reverence
for the novel. It's a great work and we were so in love with
it. That's one of the great tragedies of the motion pictures.
You spend all this money buying a great book and the best of
it never gets into the picture. Rayfiel and I would come
across passages which were absolutely glorious pieces of
writing. Then we kept putting more and more in."

Pollack went to Novi Sad, Yugoslavia in early 1968 to
begin location shooting. The film was set in the Ardennes
during the winter of 1944, around the time of the Battle of
the Bulge. A castle was built in Kamenitza Park, 230 feet
long, 164 feet wide, with a main tower 115 feet high. Heavy
snowfall and sub-zero weather conditions brought outdoor
shooting to a halt in February; and by March the snow had
almost completely disappeared. The crew brought in marble

Sydney Pollack on location in Yugoslavia directing CASTLE
KEEP (Columbia, 1969). Photo courtesy of Eddie Brandt's
Saturday Matinee.

dust to simulate the now missing snow but the Yugoslavian
government forbade its use because they said it was ruining
their park.   The crew often had to work with faulty equipment because it was impossible to get parts and supplies
easily without it becoming a "political situation."   In April,
while filming the final battle scenes in which only the draw-
bridge was to be set on fire, the entire castle burned to the
ground.   Pollack kept the cameras rolling during the confla-
gration; the fire necessitated the use of a studio for the filming of the remaining interior shots.

     Despite all these problems, coupled with a poor box-
office reception, the film was a fair critical success.   It is
Pollack's favorite film: "The central question which is raised
is whether it is worth saving man, or the best that man can
do.   Now the answer in the material is that it's man.   Sooner
or later you have to take a stand, no matter what is destroyed;
otherwise you have Nazi Germany.   It doesn't matter what
has to go.   What matters is that man survives....   It's a
very unrealized film, but there are still many things about
it that I really like."

     The film closely followed Eastlake's satiric, surreal-
istic war novel.   The story is about eight wounded American
soldiers who happen across a castle in the Ardennes.   They
are headed by one-eyed Major Falconer, played by Burt Lancaster, who believes the Germans plan a counter-offensive
attack and so occupies the castle as a delaying tactic.   Falconer was a rancher before the war and one is reminded of
the invincible hero of old Western movies when he single-
handedly wipes out a German patrol or when he tries to rally
the retreating wounded and the deserters while sitting atop a
white horse!   The castle is owned by the Comte de Maldorais
(Jean-Pierre Aumont), who believes that his castle and the
art works housed within it must be spared from destruction.
He is impotent and wishes an heir for the castle, so he does
not object when Falconer sleeps with his young, beautiful wife/
niece, Astrid Heeren in her first screen appearance.   Patrick
O'Neal plays Captain Beckman, a former art historian who
is sympathetic to both views: Falconer's, the side of man,
and the Count's, the side of art.   The rest of the men, an
Indian, an aspiring black novelist, an almost minister, an
ex-cowboy who lavishes his love for horses on a Volkswagen,
and a piano player who drinks too much, seem uninspired by
either cause and pass most of their time at the local brothel,
The Red Queen, in St. Croix, a small town near the castle.
Peter Falk is entertaining in his role as Sergeant Rossi, a

baker before the war, who seeks out the local baker's wife--
her husband is "gone"--and who spends his happiest moments
of the war warming both the ovens and the baker's wife.

When the Germans arrive, Falconer's men rally to the
cause and even enlist the whores of The Red Queen to help in
the fight, but before they can reach the castle they are killed
in the formal rose gardens. The Count is killed by the Germans when he attempts to betray the Americans, offering the
Germans access to the castle via an underground tunnel, in
an effort to save the fortress. Soon only Beckman, Falconer,
Al Freeman, Jr., playing the black would-be novelist, and
the Countess are still alive. Falconer, who cannot see beauty
in art, finally sees beauty in a woman, the Countess, and he
has Freeman take her away from the castle even though she
wants to stay behind with him, having fallen in love with him.
The Germans move in. The wanton destruction of man and
art continues. Pollack was trying to say "that neither side
was right and there has to be another way ... a better way."

The soldiers themselves appear an anachronism in a
tenth-century castle and their actions and dialogue also add
to the dream-like quality of CASTLE KEEP. The ex-cowboy's
Volkswagen is pushed into the moat by his buddies and they
shoot at it with their guns when it refuses to sink. The ex-
cowboy arrives and drives the car out of the moat. The
whores at The Red Queen pose in grotesque body contortions
while music-box melodies tinkle and red lights flash in the
background. Peter Falk keeps asking if anyone heard a bird
scream. "It's like something I've never heard before. Like
a bird ... a woman ... a world coming to an end." Gar-
goyle heads flash on the screen. One is reminded of Nietzsche's
Zarathustra who, when visited by the soothsayer, hears the
cry of the higher man, "... then the cry resounded again,
and longer and more anxious than before; also much closer
now."

Pollack is fascinated with the technical side of filmmaking and in working with Eastlake's surrealistic novel he
was given an opportunity for experimentation in film techniques. "I kept trying to find visual ways to reinforce the
sense of surreal," Pollack once said. "I tried to visually
create a sense of imbalance." He dispensed with traditional
framing and lighting. When a close-up of an actor was being
shot, "where the left side of his face would be very close to
a lamp, we would key-light him from the right.... When you
look at it you don't know quite what's different, but you re-

spond on an unconscious level." Pollack also worked at creating a certain mood by rebalancing colors. The castle interiors were pushed toward a warm, rose color and the exteriors were done in cold tones. Henri Decae, the French
cinematographer, who has worked with Claude Chabrol and
François Truffaut, was the photography director. He would
also work with Pollack on BOBBY DEERFIELD (Columbia,
1977).

Pollack's pessimistic view of man's inability to cope
and find meaning in an impersonal world reaches its peak in
THEY SHOOT HORSES, DON'T THEY? (Cinerama, 1969). It
is his tour-de-force as a filmmaker at this early stage in his
career. The story was adapted from Horace McCoy's Hollywood novel, set at a dance marathon during the Depression
era, which had established McCoy in France as the first
American existentialist writer. Upon its publication, McCoy
was offered a job as a screenwriter in Hollywood; it lasted
for twenty years, during which time he had approximately 100
screenplays to his credit. McCoy also wrote one other Hollywood novel entitled I Should Have Stayed Home (Knopf, 1938),
but it was not until the 'fifties when Scalpel (Appleton, 1952),
his last book, was published, that he had a "bestseller."
McCoy considered himself a serious writer and spent his
entire writing career battling with publishers to disassociate
himself from the violent, sensational, hard-boiled writers of
the 'thirties with whom he was constantly linked.

Screenwriter James Poe, who had worked on the scripts
for AROUND THE WORLD IN 80 DAYS (United Artists, 1956),
CAT ON A HOT TIN ROOF (M-G-M, 1958), and George Roy
Hill's TOYS IN THE ATTIC (United Artists, 1963), wanted to
try his hand at directing. The film rights to McCoy's novel
had originally been bought in 1949 for $3,000. Among others,
Charlie Chaplin had considered bringing it to the screen but
They Shoot was deemed too "down-beat" for American filmgoers. In 1966 Poe bought the rights for $50,000 and pro-
ceeded to write the screenplay while seeking a producer. Poe
settled on Robert Chartoff and Irwin Winkler and was given a
budget of $850,000 and an extremely short shooting schedule.
Poe did not want any stars in the film except for Lionel
Stander in the role of Rocky, the marathon's emcee (a character Poe changed drastically from the novel).

Soon, however, the picture was out of Poe's hands.
ABC Pictures Corporation wanted to cast Jane Fonda as
Gloria, an undiscovered actress turned cynical and bitter by

the pain and hurt she has suffered in life. Fonda, who had
been consistently cast in sex kitten roles prior to this time,
was now in France and pregnant, which would mean a delay
in filming. Poe resisted until they offered him, in exchange
for accepting Fonda, a longer shooting schedule. Martin
Baum, the new president of ABC Pictures, who had previously been a movie agent, began casting his ex-clients in
the film--Gig Young, Red Buttons, Susannah York. Poe fought
vociferously but finally acquiesced; however, he was soon
cancelled as the film's director because it was becoming an
important, big-budget affair. Sydney Pollack was assigned to
the picture.

"... They Shoot Horses, Don't They? is a splendid
novel to begin with, and in essential form and content a very
'cinematic' one," Pollack wrote in his Foreword to the screenplay which was issued with McCoy's original story in paperback form in 1969. "It demanded to be treated with great
care and attention to Horace McCoy's intents and methods.
Which is not to say that a literal, line-by-line transcription
was called for--a novel is not a film script and will not serve
as one. So, for the delicate job of translating--rather than
transcribing--from the one medium to the other, I went to
Robert E. Thompson, a man who both loved and understood
the novel. He wrote the final screenplay in about six
weeks...." (The emphasis is Pollack's.)

Robert E. Thompson and James Poe were both given
credit for the screenplay although Poe's treatment was essentially changed with the exception of the additional characters he had developed: the Harlowesque actress played by
Susannah York, the aging sailor played by Red Buttons, and
Rocky, the emcee, played by Gig Young. Poe had intended
THEY SHOOT to be a melodrama. In his screenplay the
Robert character, a well-intentioned, but dumb, aspiring
actor, played by Michael Sarrazin, who assists Gloria in her
suicide, and Alice, the Harlowesque untalented actress, who
suffers a breakdown later in the film, do fornicate in a storage room, and Gloria (in Poe's script she was running away
from a pimp), in an effort to get back at Robert, who is
Gloria's dance partner, steals Alice's sequinned dress.

In Pollack's and Thompson's version Alice and Robert
are in the storage room but there is no privacy and very
little time. Robert appears nervous and preoccupied. Gloria
sees them coming out of the room and, believing that they
have had intercourse, although they have not, goes to Rocky's

office and offers her sexual services to him but will not allow
him to touch her. Gloria resigns herself, at this point in the
film, to being a loser and to the view that Robert is really
no different from anyone else. Gloria's inevitable and final
defeat is obvious and logical, an expression of existential
philosophy. It is Rocky who steals Alice's dress and ration-
alizes to Robert that he did it for the "good of the show....
You think they're [the audience] laying out two-bits a throw
just to watch you poke your head up into the sunlight? Or
Alice look like she just stepped out of a beauty parlor? They
don't care whether you win! ... They want to see a little
misery out there so they can feel better maybe. They're
entitled to that."

    In McCoy's book the marathon is aborted by the police
when a shooting occurs while it is in progress. (There is
also a good deal of pressure exerted on the promoters by the
Mothers' League of Good Morals.) In the film--it is the only
major difference between the two--Gloria and Robert are asked
by Rocky to get married during the marathon because, as he
explains to Gloria, even if she and Robert win they would not
receive the full amount of the advertised prize money. The
winners must pay for the losers; the winning couple's expenses
will be deducted--food, shoes, laundry bills, and so on. Rocky
states, "Naturally, you don't win, you don't pay. I'm not out
to cheat nobody." Gloria laughs and then returns to the rest
area to pack her bags; at that point the final mishap occurs
and she decides to get off "this merry-go-round"--a silk
stocking that was bought with money she had saved by not
riding streetcars for a month is ripped accidentally by Robert.
She goes out onto the pier with Robert and attempts suicide.
When she cannot bring herself to do it, she asks Robert to
help. Robert shoots her. As Robert is taken away by the
police, the marathon continues and Rocky's voice is heard,
"... While the clock of fate ticks away. While the Dance of
Destiny continues. While the marathon goes on and on and
on and on. How long can they last? !"

    "McCoy was writing about people who go 'round and
'round putting one foot in front of the other," Pollack wrote
about THEY SHOOT, "waiting for a pot of gold at the end of
a rainbow; they continue because the prospects of reality in
the outside world are just too tough. I think that's the reason he didn't have a winner in the marathon: that would have
been antithetical to his concept, which was what we have since
learned to call existential and absurdist.... It seemed that
the shooting and the ending of the marathon left questions

open as to what might have become of Gloria if the dance had
played itself out. Would she still have committed suicide?
Even if she had won? And so, retaining McCoy's concept of
'no winners,' we tried to bring the characters to his conclusion without using the shooting."

By 1933 dance marathons had been outlawed in many
states for being cruel and inhuman. They had started as a
fad in the 'twenties and became a racket in the 'thirties and
did not completely disappear until the 'forties. Pollack read
books and newspapers about the period and talked to people
about marathons, including some who had actually participated
in them. By the time he came to film THEY SHOOT he had
a "good feel" for the atmosphere of a marathon.

The entire film, except for the opening flashback of
Robert's boyhood experience, when his grandfather puts a
horse out of its misery after a fall, and the trial sequences
which were filmed as flashforwards, takes place in the Pacific Ballroom dance hall situated by the ocean. (In McCoy's
novel, time present is the trial and the marathon is a flashback.) Because every scene takes place on the dance floor
or in the male or female rest areas, which are overcrowded,
the atmosphere of claustrophobia is overwhelming to the
viewer. "To emphasize their feeling of being trapped, I had
all the exit signs made in red, about ten times larger than
normal," Pollack explained. "In most of the shots you can
see the sign even when it's out of focus. But behind the
characters there was always that little arrow which said
somewhere there was still a little promise--a way out."

Particularly effective are the derby race sequences--
the crowd pleasers--in which the marathon contestants, dressed
in track uniforms, race around the dance floor for ten minutes. The last three couples are eliminated. The actors and
actresses actually ran nine minutes in the first derby. (Pollack shot in continuity in order to capture the deterioration
and fatigue of the marathon dancers in the dance sequences.)
It is hard for the viewer to breathe while watching these
races. In the second derby Red Buttons, who is temporarily
Gloria's partner, has a heart attack. Pollack used slow motion photography ingeniously in this sequence. The contestants
are seen stumbling and staggering in slow motion--they are
too exhausted to run--while "California, Here I Come" plays
in slow speed on the sound track. Buttons' face, tired and
haggard, is shown in close-up, and just as he has the attack
the action jolts into normal speed. Gloria hauls him across
the finish line and he dies.

Upon release THEY SHOOT was criticized for being too "heavy-handed." Pollack was nominated for the Best Director Oscar and Gig Young received the Oscar for Best Supporting Actor for his portrayal of Rocky. Many reviewers felt that he was an exploitative, one-dimensional character and the true villain of the marathon. Pollack rallied to his defense: "When we place blame for our failures, we must look in the right place. Young was not to blame for the dance marathons; they were the result of social attitudes, and not just the feelings of those characters watching and exploiting the dancers. What interested me most in the movie were those forces within the value structure of our society that keep everyone trying to succeed despite the devastating odds against them. What made those people in the dance marathons keep trying to make it? In both HORSES and JEREMIAH JOHNSON the heroes are also the victims. Everyone who sees HORSES is right there at the marathon cheering on the dancers. That's why the audience is so uncomfortable. They came to watch people suffer in the movie just like the audience came in the 'thirties to see people suffer in the marathon."

JEREMIAH JOHNSON (Warner's, 1972), filmed on location in Utah, was produced by Sanford Productions, a company formed in 1971 by Pollack and director Mark Rydell. THE COWBOYS (Warner's, 1972), directed by Rydell, SCARECROW (Warner's, 1973), and NIGHT MOVES (Warner's, 1975) were also produced by Sanford Productions before the company was disbanded due to financial difficulties.

"Liver-eating" Johnson--the moniker for the real John Johnson--so the legend goes, killed approximately 247 Crow Indians; he cut out and ate(!) the liver of each of his victims. Johnson began this bloody vendetta when he found his Flathead Indian wife, who was pregnant, slaughtered by a Crow hunting party. The legend about Johnson, who died in 1900, inspired two books: a non-fiction account based on interviews and letters about the life of mountain men and those who knew, or knew of, Johnson, entitled Crow Killer, The Saga of Liver-Eating Johnson (Indiana University Press, 1958), by Raymond Thorp and Robert Bunker, and Mountain Man (William Morrow, 1965), Vardis Fisher's last fiction work, which was named the outstanding Western novel of 1965 by the National Cowboy Hall of Fame. The National Cowboy Hall of Fame chose JEREMIAH JOHNSON as the Best Western Theatrical Motion Picture for 1972.

Pollack read both works after reading an original screenplay on the Johnson legend by John Milius. Pollack felt Fisher's character, called Sam Minard, was too "Paul Bunyanesque.... That's not the way I saw the picture. Mountain Man has some wonderful lyrical verbal passages.... But I still felt he [Fisher] missed for me in some very human areas.... I was more interested in the choices that a man makes, and how Jeremiah ends up victimized in a sense by his own choices." Edward Anhalt collaborated with Milius on the final script, adapted from both the Thorp/Bunker book and the Fisher book.

Pollack had considered casting Burt Lancaster in the role of Jeremiah Johnson, as the central character was called in the final screenplay, but he wanted to capture the aging process that occurs both physically and mentally in Jeremiah, and so cast Robert Redford instead. "That was one that was really close to me; it took place where I live [Utah]," Redford said about JOHNSON. "The reason Sydney was so good on it was that he understood how I felt. We went through a lot of anguish on that picture. It went on for months. We'd talk and talk and argue and we could never articulate what we wanted. Choices were made by both Sydney and myself that just weren't explainable. The crew didn't know what we were doing. It was just me wandering through the mountains and then suddenly it was put together and there it was."

Jeremiah seeks out a new way of life as a trapper and a mountain man in an effort to escape from the corruption of civilization. He is young and, although he has the accouterments necessary for this kind of self-sufficient existence, he is improficient in their use. He meets Bear Claw, an engaging character played brilliantly by Will Geer, who addresses Jeremiah as "pilgrim" while teaching him the art of survival in the mountains. Jeremiah learns quickly and is soon on his own, living the isolated life of a mountain man. He has several encounters with Indians. One of these leaves him with the responsibility of a traumatized boy whose family, except for the mother who has gone insane and is incapable of taking care of the boy, was butchered by the Indians. In another encounter he acquires a Flathead Indian wife who is named Swan. In time a love of sorts develops between Jeremiah and Swan; however, it is shortlived. When Jeremiah is asked to assist the Cavalry in rescuing some stranded settlers, he takes them through the Crows' sacred burial grounds to save time. Upon his return to the cabin he has

built for his new family, he finds Swan and the boy mercilessly slaughtered by a Crow hunting party. The one-man
war against the Crow nation begins when Jeremiah kills a
small band of Crows, although he soon finds himself the
hunted when the Crows seek revenge for the deaths of their
people.

Pollack was strongly criticized for romanticizing the
disillusioned drop-out who becomes as corrupt as the way of
life from which he wanted to escape. "Everyone reads into
the film what they want," Pollack said while explaining the
Johnson character and what he was trying to do in the film.
"Robert in HORSES is a forerunner of Jeremiah. He is innocent. He is good in the most simple and most primitive
sense, so much so, that he will kill. Johnson kills, and kills
and kills. People who kill are not all simplistic villains.
They are people like Jeremiah Johnson, who became a legen-
dary character. He is likeable. I like him myself. He does
terrible things, but I cannot hate him. He is a good man
who makes mistakes like any of us.

"... Jeremiah is a legend told in much larger-than-
life style. He is a man who achieved heroic stature and
ended up with nothing. He had a lonely and empty life. I
would have called the film THE BALLAD OF JEREMIAH JOHN-
SON, had it not been for THE BALLAD OF CABLE HOGUE
[Warner's, 1970, directed by Sam Peckinpah]. The story involves the emptiness of the legend.

"... I did not mean to give Jeremiah a Christ-like
image, although some have given him that interpretation. I
was striving for a sense of mysticism. There is a lot of
dialogue in the film with innuendo and mysticism. The other
mountain men survive because they do not get involved. Jeremiah's problem was his humaneness in an inhuman atmosphere. What destroyed Jeremiah was the set of values we
uphold. He could not escape them. Jeremiah tried to practice another set of values that he did not understand."

Ralph Brauer, in his article "Who Are Those Guys?
The Movie Western During the TV Era," contained in Focus
on the Western (Prentice-Hall, 1974), called JEREMIAH
JOHNSON the first ecological Western. "In the struggles of
the mountain man Jeremiah Johnson with the mountains, weather,
and Indians we see an image of ourselves and our own relations with the environment. ..." Brauer went on to say that
Johnson "as a tragic figure is one whose soul is disputed

over by two forces--the settlers and the Indians. The settlers symbolize progress, 'civilization,' taming the land as
opposed to the Indians' preference for living with the land."
Jeremiah's greatest mistake is his deliberate trespassing on
the burial grounds, which he knows is a violation of the Crow
Indians' belief in the balance of nature, in order to save the
immobilized wagon train, which he, as a white man, feels
responsible for. It is this unintentional, momentary, yet
fatal choosing of sides that causes Jeremiah's subsequent
grief and despair.

In order to portray the Indians' point of view accurately Pollack had a Flathead and a Crow Indian working as
advisors on every sequence in which an Indian appeared in
the film. Before a scene was shot the script was submitted
to the tribe for agreement on its authenticity: if it was not
historically accurate or if the Indians did not agree with what
was in a particular scene, it was dropped from the script.
The Indians spoke in their own language or in French (which
some tribes spoke at the time). Also, the Indian code of
honor was faithfully depicted: for example, when Jeremiah
corners a Crow Indian, the Indian sings the death chant which
had never before been portrayed in a film.

Pollack shot five different endings to JEREMIAH JOHN-
SON before he decided to use the most ambiguous one, the
one which would leave questions in the viewer's mind. Jeremiah meets Bear Claw again and there appears to be a par-
allel drawn between the two men, although it too is left ambiguous. In some of the most beautiful winter photography
in the film, Jeremiah and Bear Claw sit around a small
campfire, both dressed in animal skins. Little dialogue is
exchanged between the two men. Jeremiah hints that he may
go higher into the mountains. He seems to have come to an
awareness and understanding of the land--living with it--which
had always eluded him. Bear Claw and Jeremiah part company. As Jeremiah, older, isolated and weary, continues on
his journey, a Crow chief, off in the distance, raises his hand
in a salute which Jeremiah returns.

Pauline Kael stated in her harsh review of the film
that "when the Crows, recognizing Jeremiah's courage, end
their war against him, the chief gives him a peace sign,
Jeremiah signals him back, giving him the finger. In that
gesture, the moviemakers load him with guilt for what the
white Americans have done to the Indians, and, at the same
time, ask us to laugh at the gesture, identifying with his
realism."

Jeremiah does not give the rival Indian the "finger."
Pollack sent a letter and a film clip of the last scene to
Kael when he saw her review.   Her reply was: "When did
you switch the ending?"

Unfortunately, critics and others often misinterpret or
"see" things in a film that are not intended by the director
at all.   This can work in either a negative or a positive
fashion, as Pollack explained in his own case.   "I often get
credit for deep insights that are not even in my mind.   The
French critics are great on this.   They see a ray of sun in
the corner of a frame and think I am talking about the evolu-
tion of a new civilization.   At times, I am accused of ma-
liciously destroying some concept or person, when I certainly
did not intend that effect.

"Each person carries his own ideological framework,
hangups, cultural conditions and momentary concerns into a
darkened theatre and interprets the motion picture in accordance with his frame of mind at that moment.   That is a factor
over which we have no control.   If individuals feel boxed in
by society, they may view Jeremiah as a hero.   But that is
not what I intended him to be.   In fact, the audience is not
getting what I hoped for out of the film.   I wanted people to
see and understand the bizarreness of Jeremiah's motivation.
But the audience remembers things like the slapstick bear
sequence and a good many other wrong things.   The responsibility, however, is mine.   If I failed in my intentions, perhaps I did not make a very good film."

JEREMIAH JOHNSON is, however, an enduring and
timeless film that is often seen playing as the top-bill at
local theatres across the country.   For some the film carried an anti-war message, since Jeremiah is donned in soldier's pants early in the film; for others, like Brauer, it
was a reassessment of man's relationship with nature; and
for still others it sparked an interest in the man behind the
legend.

John Johnson was a man who had always been capable
of taking care of himself.   Around 1895 his health began to
fail him and friends were forced to help him out.   Johnson
constantly worried about being a burden and he certainly did
not like having to accept charity.   His friends, realizing this,
suggested that he might be happier at the Old Soldier's Home
in Los Angeles.   He went to California and was admitted on
21 December, 1899; he died exactly one month later.   He was

buried in the "San Juan Hill" section of the veterans' cemetery in West Los Angeles.   "If Johnson could never live in a
crowd, he was buried in one," wrote Thorp and Bunker in
Crow Killer.

The seventh grade students at the Lancaster, California
junior high school had taken an interest in Johnson.   They
took it upon themselves, with the help of their teacher Tri
Robinson, to make arrangements, 74 years after Johnson's
death, to bury him where he had wished to be buried, somewhere in the Northwest.   They arranged to have his remains
shipped to Wyoming.   Pollack and Redford were invited to the
re-burial ceremony.   Johnson now rests in Trailtown, a non-
commercial museum, one mile west of Cody, Wyoming.

Pollack read Arthur Laurents' novel, The Way We
Were, which was published by Harper & Row, in galley form
and was not only touched by the love story but also liked the
political atmosphere of the 'forties as a background to the
story.   "The 'thirties, 'forties, and 'fifties are very rich
periods from a cinematic point of view," says Pollack, whose
final decision to direct a film is largely influenced by setting
and period--along with, of course, the story.

Laurents was given sole screen credit as screenwriter
on THE WAY WE WERE (Columbia, 1974) although there were
some five other writers who would bring in revisions during
the shooting of the film produced by Ray Stark.   Stark and
Pollack had disagreements about several scenes in the middle
of THE WAY WE WERE which Stark felt should be cut, including background material on the Katie and Hubbell characters as well as the political ramifications of the era.   Pollack says that had he not been totally convinced that Stark
was right, the sequences would not have been eliminated.

Pollack wanted Robert Redford for the role of Hubbell,
the handsome All-American boy of limited ambitions to whom
things come easily except for commitment.   Redford turned
the project down twice because he felt the character was
"shallow and synthetic" and too one-dimensional.   "Sydney
said, 'Trust me, it can be good, and I think it's something
you ought to do.'"   Redford explained how he came to accept
the role: "One of the reasons Sydney wanted to do it was
that he identified with the character of an uncommitted man.
Finally, I just took the part on faith.   Together we totally
reworked the character of Hubbell."

Barbra Streisand, whom Laurents had in mind when
creating the Katie Morosky character, a young Jewish woman
with a social conscience, was cast in the part for which she
was nominated Best Actress by the Motion Picture Academy.
Pollack enjoyed working with her. However, he was determined to break her away from her usual performance à la
Streisand. "I wanted people to forget she's Streisand--which
they never did--and see her as Katie Morosky. She's a very
talented girl, but because she started as a performer she relies on performance devices, rather than on the reality of the
scene. She's capable of acting. I think she was very, very
good in THE WAY WE WERE."

The story deals basically with Katie's and Hubbell's
mismatched love for one another. They meet at Cornell University where Katie is a dedicated, and often over-zealous,
member of the American Communist League and Hubbell is
the school idol, participating in many sports events and in
extra-curricular activities like Carol Ann, the campus sweet-
heart, played by newcomer Lois Chiles. All of this is told
in flashback. Katie has ambivalent feelings towards Hubbell
while in school and it becomes even harder for her to cope
with them when he confides in her and shares his dream of
being a writer.

The film opens in New York approximately five years
after their graduation; Hubbell is a Navy man and Katie
works at a radio station and does volunteer work for causes
she believes in now. Katie and Hubbell meet accidentally and
fall physically in love. Problems develop though, because
however much Katie respects Hubbell's talent as a writer--
his first book has been published and Katie critiques it for
him while constantly prodding him to work on a second book
by doing things such as buying him a typewriter--she cannot
accept his way of life, which includes his phony college friend
J.J. (Bradford Dillman, whose character goes through significant changes in the course of the film) and Carol Ann, now
J.J.'s girl friend, who advise Hubbell to sell the movie
rights to his book and move to California.

Hubbell, for Katie, is another cause to fight for and
although ultimately it cannot work because of the different
types of people they are, it does for a short time and they
are married. Hubbell sells the film rights to his novel and
they move to Tinseltown with J.J. and Carol Ann, now J.J.'s
wife. Hubbell is forced to make compromises while adapting
his novel for the screen in order to keep his job as a screen-

writer, but in the process he loses any integrity as a writer
he may have had.   Katie is pregnant and becomes involved
with supporters of the Hollywood Ten who plan to go to Washington, D. C. , to protest the HUAC blacklistings as being un-
constitutional.   Despite Hubbell's objections, Katie goes to
D. C. and thus insures the demise of their relationship: Katie
cannot change her ways any more than Hubbell can his.   They
stay together until their daughter is born.   (The studio had
wanted a happy ending for the film, but Pollack would not go
along with it.)

     A recurring theme in Pollack's films is the idea that
people do not learn from nor understand their mistakes, and
so are destined to repeat them.   His protagonists travel in
circular patterns, often ending up where they began.   In THE
WAY WE WERE, Pollack was finally able to portray this idea
by giving the viewer one last glimpse of Katie and Hubbell
after they are divorced, when they meet again accidentally in
New York.   Katie is handing out "ban the bomb" literature
and Hubbell is now writing teleplays, obviously never to finish
his second novel.   Pollack had tried in THIS PROPERTY IS
CONDEMNED to show Alva back in her home town picking up
a salesman.   In JEREMIAH JOHNSON, for the original ending, Pollack shot a sequence in which Jeremiah was seen
frozen solid in exact duplication of the frozen man Johnson
had found when he first came to the mountains; but Pollack
dropped it because he felt it was "excessive, and nobody understood it. "   In THE WAY WE WERE one comes full circle
and there is a sense of closure to Hubbell's and Katie's relationship.

     THE WAY WE WERE is rather unusual in its treatment
of the Hollywood fantasy which has become a cliché in celluloid love stories: boy meets girl ... boy pursues girl ...
boy loses girl ... boy gets girl back.   The film reverses
the stereotyped sex roles--a hardworking girl can get the
good-looking All-American boy.   Especially interesting is
the point in the film when Hubbell calls the relationship off
because he feels Katie can't relax, pushes too hard, and takes
things that happen in the world too personally.   Katie, wanting Hubbell back, and unable to sleep, calls him and asks
him to come over to talk to her as a best friend would.   She
promises she will not touch him!   The Katie character is
portrayed as being highly motivated by sex, much more, in
fact, than Hubbell is.   It is Katie who is aggressive--a mas-
culine trait--throughout their entire relationship while Hubbell
remains passive--presumably a feminine trait.

The film was nominated for seven Oscars and won two:
Best Original Song, "The Way We Were" (sung by Streisand),
lyrics by Alan and Marilyn Bergman, music by Marvin Hamlisch; and Best Original Dramatic Score, also by Hamlisch.
THE WAY WE WERE had an excellent box office and it appears on the list of the fifty top grossing movies in America.
The critics felt it was "another on again, off again" love
story.   Redford felt that the critics "won't own up to their
emotions.   They feel that it's got to be off-center or bold
before they can accept it.   THE WAY WE WERE is about
two people who come together and why it goes wrong.   Intellectually you know they shouldn't be together, but on a gut
level you want them to make it because you like them and
because they like each other.   That's a fair emotion."

In the early 'sixties the samurai film began evolving
into what is now known as the yakuza film, a Japanese gangster film.   Prior to 1964 all sword films were period pieces
because in 1868 the Japanese government had banished the
samurai and his sword, so that by legal definition a man with
a sword was considered an outlaw.   The samurai film had
had one theme, giri-ninjo (duty-humanity), so for a samurai
duty was humanity, humanity was duty.   Giri-ninjo could not
be applied to a modern-day gangster: he was considered an
outlaw just by virtue of carrying a sword, and thereby violat-
ing his "duty" as a member of the state--in other words,
there could be no yakuza hero.   This was remedied by pro-
viding the yakuza film with two themes, giri and/or ninjo,
so that a gangster could have humanity without duty or vice
versa, thus making it possible for a criminal to be honorable.
(Yakuza, literally translated, means gambler or good-for-
nothing, but has come to mean gangster and is used in reference to the Japanese underworld.)

Paul Schrader, screenwriter for Pollack's contribution to the genre, THE YAKUZA (Warner's, 1974), wrote in
an article for Film Comment on yakuza films that: "The
Japanese gangster film aims for a higher purpose than its
Western counterparts; it seeks to codify a positive workable
morality.   In American terms, it is more like a Western
than a gangster film.   Like the Western, the yakuza-eiga
chooses timelessness over relevance, myth over realism; it
seeks not social commentary, but moral truth.   Although the
average yakuza film is technically inferior to an American or
European gangster film, it has achieved a nobility denied its
counterparts--a nobility normally reserved for the Western."

Robert Aldrich was originally slated to direct THE
YAKUZA but Warner's pulled him off the project because the
film's star, Robert Mitchum, refused to work with him. Pollack was offered the picture and was given Schrader's script
to read. "It was in very rough form," Pollack said. "However, I felt it contained a very powerful idea. I think I ultimately chose to do the project because of the last scene,
which is an ultimate connection and reconciliation of two people of absolutely opposite cultures--one Eastern and one West-

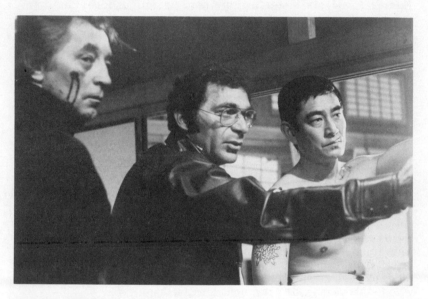

Sydney Pollack directing Robert Mitchum and Takakura Ken
in THE YAKUZA (Warner's, 1974).   Photo courtesy of Eddie
Brandt's Saturday Matinee.

ern. It was a kind of understanding, totally emotional and
nonverbal.   I kept thinking of the poem by Robert Frost:

> 'The woods are lovely, dark and deep,
> But I have promises to keep,
> And miles to go before I sleep....'

In Japan I suppose you would translate that as giri--duty,
honor, and obligation.   In my terms it was just tremendous
respect and the limits to which one will go to keep one's word."

Mitchum played Harry Kilmer, an ex-private eye, who, out of a sense of obligation to pay off a debt of friendship, accepts an assignment from George Tanner, an L. A. -based shipping magnate, played by Brian Keith, to rescue his kidnapped daughter from Japanese underworld figures whom Tanner is trying to swindle out of an arms shipment. Kilmer recruits a former member of the yakuza, Tanaka Ken (Takakura Ken, Japan's number one star, who has appeared in well over 200 films since 1956), who owes Kilmer a favor-- Kilmer saved his sister, with whom he fell in love, and her daughter from a life of destitution and prostitution during the occupation of Japan. The assignment forces Kilmer to face many things about himself and his past, his love for Tanaka Eiko (Kishi Keiko), which he hopes to rekindle, and his enmity with Eiko's brother, who is really her husband.

Pollack shot on location in Japan, which he felt was very advantageous for getting a feel for the land and its customs, and he even talked with members of the yakuza. "I had a Japanese crew and cameraman," Pollack said. "They were wonderful to work with. For the American scenes I used an American cameraman so you actually get a subtle difference in style. The way they do things in Japan is radically different from what we are accustomed to here. For one thing the cameraman in Japan operates the camera himself. For another, they don't have large lighting units like we have, so they light the way they paint, an area at a time. They might take a frame of film and start in the upper left-hand corner and just work their way across to the right and then go back to the left again. By the time you finish there will be thousands of very small units."

THE YAKUZA is permeated with a sense of claustrophobia, especially in the Japanese footage, as most of Pollack's films are, but the pace is much slower, remaining true to the traditional Japanese style. The sword work of the action sequences is balletic and beautifully staged. Pollack explained the differences in working with swords, compared to other kinds of action scenes in film: "They don't contain the staccato impact that Western fights contain. Gun shots and punches are very staccato; they're over in a second. There is no grace necessarily connected to it. But sword work is different. I had to learn a whole new way of shooting."

THE YAKUZA did not fare well at the box office nor among the critics, who felt it was another bloody and violent

Japanese Mafia/samurai entry. However, they seemed to
ignore the fact that Pollack was working in a relatively new
genre that has not even come of age in its native land--yakuza
films are making the slow transition from a "B" to an "A"
genre in Japan. Film critic and screenwriter, and now director, Paul Schrader put it aptly: "As greater demands are
made of it, the traditional yakuza-eiga film will respond by
either rising to maturity or slipping into self-parody."

Robert Redford was back for THREE DAYS OF THE
CONDOR (Paramount, 1975), a film based on James Grady's
Six Days of the Condor (W. W. Norton, 1974), an unimagina-
tive spy novel in which seven people working for the American
Literary Historical Society are killed when one of its members
stumbles upon the CIA's use of the book society to smuggle
morphine into the States. One man, code name Condor, escapes being eliminated when he is literally out to lunch. The
rest of the story focuses on Condor's adventures while elud-
ing the killers hired by the CIA, now after him.

Many changes, all for the better, were made in the
screenplay by Lorenzo Semple, Jr. , with an extensive rewrite
by David Rayfiel, who changed the drug smuggling plot to a
radical group within the CIA. When Pollack originally read
the story he thought it complete and "absolute nonsense. However, I liked it because it moved very fast. Besides the fact
that it was contemporary, there were a lot of things I had
never done. I thought it would be nice to go to work someday and not have to worry about what everything meant or
whether or not I was being a Fascist. I liked the idea of
being able to concentrate on making a sequence dazzling. In
the end, however, we worried about all the same problems
anyways."

The book society's headquarters was altered to New
York, where some location shooting was done rather than
Washington, D. C. , as in the novel. The major changes,
however, were in the conceptions of the characters: Joseph
Turner (Condor); Kathy, the girl Turner forces to harbor
him until he can figure out why the society's employees were
hit, so that he can save himself; and lastly Journet, a hired
killer. Condor, in Grady's novel, is a crude and often adolescent protagonist who belches loudly, sneezes profusely,
has harmless voyeur tendencies--he'd prefer to go without
his morning coffee rather than miss the bosomy girl's ascent
up the steps outside his office window--and is described at
his job in the following manner: "... [He] sat down, put his

Sydney Pollack discussing a scene with friend and star of
THREE DAYS OF THE CONDOR (Paramount, 1975), Robert
Redford.   Photo courtesy of Eddie Brandt's Saturday Matinee.

feet up on his desk, farted, and closed his eyes."   Obviously,
this character did not match the Redford persona.   In the
film Condor is an intelligent, happy, joking Redford, donned
in wire-rimmed glasses, who inadvertently acts as a catalyst
in the deaths of his co-workers.   The duties of the American
Literary Historical Society are to read and then feed into a
computer all espionage plots and codes and related acts which
appear in world literature.   Condor is puzzled by a mystery
book that didn't sell well, yet was translated into Dutch, Spanish, and Arabic languages.   He is advised by CIA Headquarters
in D. C. to drop the matter because, after researching Condor's suspicions, they have found nothing to be concerned
about.   Condor returns to the office and finds his co-workers
all shot to death, including Janice (Tina Chen), his girl friend,
who also works for the reading society.   Condor believes he
too will be killed and so sets out to find refuge somewhere.

Pollack and Rayfiel felt it was unrealistic for Kathy--

Wendy in Grady's novel--who is a pretty and intelligent girl
not to have a love interest in her life until Condor shows up,
as is the case in the book.   The character was changed to
a neurotic photographer whose boy friend is awaiting her arrival in Vermont--they had planned a skiing vacation--when
Condor kidnaps her.   The character was difficult to cast because it was so undefined.   They decided on Faye Dunaway,
who could deliver rather comic and sarcastic dialogue while
at the same time impressing upon the viewer her complex
emotional personality.   Pollack develops Kathy's neurosis
through the use of photographs she has taken of lonely scenes
of empty park benches and streets lined with bare trees, and
which she has hanging on the walls of her apartment.   The
apartment lacks warmth and brightness, as do her dull colored
clothes.   Her neurosis is also developed through her dialogue
--"I take a picture that isn't like me ... but it has to be.
I put them away."

        "I wanted to make a film about suspicion and how de-
structive suspicion really is," said Pollack, "because it's
the opposite of trust which is the basis of society and all relationships.   Eventually you have to trust somebody or you
can't go on living.   Initially Kathy is a suspicious girl.
Joseph Turner, played by Robert Redford, is just the opposite.   As the film progresses they shift roles.   This happens
during the short period of their relationship--about twenty-four
hours."   Pollack originally had Kathy and Condor travel together for a short time while being pursued, but he felt it
just didn't work right.   Instead, they separate at a railroad
station; Kathy goes back to her boy friend and Condor continues in his search for the truth.

        Condor finally discovers the truth: a radical group
within the CIA has tentative plans to invade the Middle East
for its oil.   Because Condor knows too much he must keep
on running or be killed, because with the information he has
on the CIA he could put them in a very embarrassing position.
The only person who respects and understands Condor's para-
noic situation is Journet, played by Max von Sydow, who in
the book is known as Maronick.   The character was changed
drastically for the film because Pollack felt that in the book
he was just "a horrible, horrible man--a pure mercenary who
kills strictly for money.   He was the kind of mustache-twirling
villain that just bores me.   So we began to construct a man
whose amorality was more solvent than the CIA morality.
The von Sydow character is an honest bad guy, which I prefer any day to a lying good guy.   Now I'm not saying it's

better to be a killer and admit that you're a killer than to be the CIA. What I am saying is that this man knows that economics determines who are the good guys and who are the bad guys, if there are any such things. Therefore he chooses to isolate himself from society and make his own morality. He relies only on his own excellence. There's no cause to believe in; no side to take. Today one country is right; tomorrow it's another."

Pollack has a penchant for using a lot of close-ups in his films, which may well be a carry-over from his early work in television. "Close-ups allow me to instill my own rhythm into a scene," says Pollack, whereas in a master shot he feels locked into whatever rhythm the actor gives him. Close-ups were used particularly well in THREE DAYS OF THE CONDOR, in the exciting fight sequence between Condor and a phony mailman which takes place in Kathy's apartment. The action was choreographed--Redford on the defensive and the mailman on the offensive--so that Redford would not come off as a superman. Close-ups of Redford, Dunaway, who distracts the mailman so that Condor can get his gun, and the mailman are interspersed with the fine action.

What makes THREE DAYS interesting is its unusual solution: the political issues are thrown at the American public. Condor goes to the New York Times with his story and then confronts Cliff Robertson, playing Mr. Higgins, the CIA's New York-based Deputy Director, who is basically a "yes" man, about the validity of the scheme to invade the Middle East. Higgins explains that it's a political game they play. The American consumer's wants and needs are extremely demanding and they don't really care how things like oil, gas, or food are acquired; so they play games. He tells Condor he's done a lot of damage. Condor walks away saying that he hopes he has done some damage.

THE OTHER LOVE (United Artists, 1947), directed by André de Toth, was adapted from German novelist Erich Maria Remarque's unpublished story, Beyond. The film's soapy love triangle plot featured Barbara Stanwyck playing a dying pianist on a rest cure in a Swiss sanitarium, David Niven as her physician who is madly in love with her, albeit silently, and Richard Conte, in his first on-screen romantic role, as a cruel-hearted race car driver/gigolo with whom Stanwyck has one last fling.

Remarque published a revised version of the story, dedicated to former actress Paulette Goddard, his wife at the time, in novel form under the title Heaven Has No Favorites (Harcourt, Brace & World, 1961). It was used as the basis for Pollack's most recent film, at the time of this writing, BOBBY DEERFIELD (Columbia, 1977). DEERFIELD was the first film in which Pollack took on the dual responsibility of producer/director; Alvin Sargent supplied the screenplay.

Heaven Has No Favorites had been kicking around Hollywood for a long time as a possible movie property; in fact, the Crest paperback edition published in April, 1962 announced at that time that Heaven was "soon to be a major motion picture." Paul Newman was once considered for the lead role and Catherine Deneuve for the role of Lillian. When Pollack came finally to film Remarque's story, Al Pacino, who had to learn to drive a car for the part, was cast in the lead; Lillian was played by Marthe Keller. Neither star, however, seemed up to portraying Pollack's conceptions of the characters and the story.

Remarque's novel and Pollack's film have very little in common other than the basic story-line: a race car driver falls in love with a young, beautiful, dying woman. In the novel, Remarque's character, Clerfayt, who escaped from a prison camp, a memory which frequently haunts him, lives from car race to car race. He meets Lillian, a woman half his age who has only weeks, possibly days, left to live, in the same sanitarium where Clerfayt's co-driver, who is also afflicted with tuberculosis, is staying. Clerfayt falls in love with Lillian, despite his snobby mistress's warnings and protestations, but ironically, he dies in an auto race shortly before Lillian dies from consumption. Death and fate are the two main themes of the book and the sanitarium setting and its patients play an important part in the story. (Remarque was no doubt influenced by Thomas Mann's masterpiece Der Zauberberg [S. Fischer Verlag, 1924], although Remarque's story is trite and pedestrian by comparison.)

In the film version Pollack wanted to focus on a younger man--called Bobby Deerfield--who is so completely cut off from his emotions that even when he experiences deep grief or pain, he cannot give in to these feelings. In contrast is Lillian, a woman who is open and straightforward; however, she too must hold back certain emotions in her own

way, because she is dying. Pollack wanted to show the
changes--the "resurrection"--which Bobby undergoes by being
exposed to a woman like Lillian and having a relationship with
her. Lillian dies in the film; Bobby does not. Bobby's mistress, Lydia, played by Anny Duperey, is hardly developed
as a character. The sanitarium and auto racing serve only
as a background to the story.

Pacino, who has proved himself capable of both dramatic and light comedy roles, did not appear to go through
any major or minor transformation in the course of the film,
and is indeed the same blasé character from beginning to end.
His singing and Mae West impersonations--antics from Bobby's
repressed childhood which Lillian brings out in him--are weak
and verging on pathetic, although obviously sincerely essayed
by Pacino. Keller's portrayal of Lillian, a dying woman supposedly blessed with wisdom and insight into the meaning of
life during her last days, is stiff and without depth. Perhaps
the fact that Keller and Pacino became romantically involved
with one another off-screen affected their performances.

Sargent's screenplay incorporated extraneous and often
confusing story elements along with some heavy dialogue reek-
ing with profound and deep meanings which were troublesome
for the average viewer, as the inadequate box office proved.
For instance, Bobby believes there is a concrete explanation
for an auto wreck which occurred during a recent race and
so he watches a film of the accident over and over again,
looking for a reflection of light which may have temporarily
blinded the driver or an object on or near the track which
may have caused the accident. Bobby remains obsessed with
this conviction throughout the entire film; however, nothing is
ever discovered. One is reminded of Michelangelo Antonioni's
first English film, BLOW-UP (M-G-M, 1967), in which many
questions are posed, but none answered, about a possible
murder which is supposedly photographed.

BOBBY DEERFIELD was shot on location throughout
Western Europe and its photography is stunning and memorable. The French loved the film but it was only the Al Pacino enthusiasts that drew what little audience there was into
American theatres. Pollack stated that on his other films he
could do research but on DEERFIELD he could not, because
he was telling a story about a man who changes. Apparently
American filmgoers weren't interested in that kind of story
combined capriciously with the LOVE STORY (Paramount,
1970) ingredient: the untimely death of a young woman.

Few directors have worked in such a wide variety of
genres as Sydney Pollack has in such a short span of time:
Westerns, melodrama, romance, gangster film, frontier mountain man film, spy thriller, and war film. But unlike many
of his contemporaries--John Frankenheimer, Robert Altman,
John Cassavetes, Sam Peckinpah, John Schlesinger--Pollack
has not enjoyed serious attention or a cult following. One is
in fact hard pressed to find a critical analysis on Pollack's
work or a retrospective of his films.

Yet Sydney Pollack is an artist with a creative imagination and a filmmaker of integrity. His main concerns have
been with man's search for meaning in an indifferent world
and the tenuousness and fragility of people and their relationships. Although his views on this continuous, life-long search
appear to be rather skeptical and pessimistic, Pollack has
consistently devoted himself to creating the best work of art
possible. He has proved his ability to extract from actors,
especially women, subtle and extraordinary performances so
as to reveal the conflicting and contradictory natures of his
characters, where other directors might only try to cash in
on the performer's box-office draw. Since he is more concerned with motives than actions, Pollack utilizes setting to
reflect or mirror the inner workings of his protagonists. He
has dealt with sensitive matters without moralizing or trying
to right a wrong or distorting the impact of his story. He
is a filmmaker with forceful ideas and an ever-growing and
maturing personal vision.

Robert Redford once said of Pollack: "Sydney is melancholy, but he's getting wiser about using that in his work.
He used to let moments go on too long; but now his experience
tells him when to cut things off. Basically he's a romantic.
I think that's one of his virtues. There aren't many men
around who can say honestly and openly, 'Isn't that a beautiful scene?'"

Sydney Pollack is such a man.

SYDNEY POLLACK

A Film Checklist by Vicki Piekarski

Director
_____

1.   THE SLENDER THREAD (1965). P: Paramount.

C: Anne Bancroft, Sidney Poitier, Telly Savalas, Steve Hill. 98m.

2. THIS PROPERTY IS CONDEMNED (1966). P: Paramount. C: Natalie Wood, Robert Redford, Charles Bronson. Color. 110m.

3. THE SCALPHUNTERS (1968). P: United Artists. C: Burt Lancaster, Ossie Davis, Shelley Winters, Telly Savalas. DeLuxe Color. Panavision. 102m.

4. CASTLE KEEP (1969). P: Columbia. C: Burt Lancaster, Patrick O'Neal, Jean-Pierre Aumont. Technicolor. Panavision. 106m.

√5. THEY SHOOT HORSES, DON'T THEY? (1969). P: Cinerama. C: Jane Fonda, Michael Sarrazin, Gig Young, Susannah York. DeLuxe Color. Panavision. 129m.

√6. JEREMIAH JOHNSON (1972). P: Warner's. C: Robert Redford, Will Geer, Stefan Gierasch. Color. Panavision. 108m.

√7. THE WAY WE WERE (1973). P: Columbia. C: Barbra Streisand, Robert Redford, Bradford Dillman. Color. Panavision. 117m.

8. THE YAKUZA (1974). P: Warner's. C: Robert Mitchum, Takakura Ken, Brian Keith. Technicolor. Panavision. 111m.

9. THREE DAYS OF THE CONDOR (1975). P: Paramount. C: Robert Redford, Faye Dunaway, Cliff Robertson. Technicolor. Panavision. 117m.

10. BOBBY DEERFIELD (1977). P: Columbia. C: Al Pacino, Marthe Keller, Anny Duperey. Metrocolor. Panavision. 124m.

Chapter 2

SAM FULLER

by David Wilson

I

Between 1944 and 1945, the 16th Regiment of the First Division of the United States Army fought its way from France into Nazi Germany. After the war, one of its members, an ex-newspaper reporter named Samuel Michael Fuller, decided to make a movie called THE BIG RED ONE. Until 1978, it was the most famous war movie never made. During the thirty years he waited, Fuller turned down the direction of THE DESERT RATS (20th-Fox, 1953), THE YOUNG LIONS (20th-Fox, 1958), THE LONGEST DAY (20th-Fox, 1962), and CROSS OF IRON (Avco-Embassy, 1976).

Above: Samuel Fuller. Photo courtesy of David Wilson.

In 1957, a trade paper said THE BIG RED ONE was
going to be produced at RKO, with John Wayne starring.   In
1958, a Warner Brothers release said its studio was going
to make it.   In 1959, a Columbia release claimed: "At 47,
Fuller has the richest years of life ahead for him, for he is
writing a novel, The Big Red One, based on the exploits of
his famed World War II Division, and following publication of
the book sometime late in 1960, he will realize his dream
since 1946--that of filming the greatest war movie ever made
--THE BIG RED ONE."

Again, in 1965, Fuller spoke about shooting THE BIG
RED ONE.   He said he wanted to make it in seven countries,
starring seven women, five men, and 15,000 soldiers.

In 1977, Peter Bogdanovich was watching some of the
most crucial moments in Fuller's career.   Bogdanovich was
producing his first picture, THE BIG RED ONE, and, finally,
Fuller was going to direct it.   Shooting was going to start in
June, 1978, with a three million dollar budget.   Lorimar Productions had agreed to bankroll the project; Lee Marvin,
Jeanne Moreau, Stephane Audran, and Christa Lang, Fuller's
wife, were named as the stars.

Bogdanovich puffed on a cigar in his living room near
the campus of the University of California.   He had picked
up the cigar habit from Fuller.   "I met Fuller when I first
came to Hollywood," he told me.   "It was in 1964 or early
1965, shortly after he became a popular director in Europe.
I just looked him up because I thought he was a good director.
I got there at two in the afternoon and left him at about two
in the morning.   He told me stories and we talked about the
pictures that we both wanted to make.

"He told me about THE BIG RED ONE.   I said, 'Jesus,
when are you going to make that?'   He said he didn't know.
Ten years later, in 1975, he was still trying to get something
else done.   I said, 'Jesus, Sam, stop fucking around with all
those lousy scripts!   Why don't you write that good one, the
one you really ought to do, THE BIG RED ONE?'   You see,
I don't really have any interest in producing.   I just wanted
to see that movie.   It seems to be the picture Sam was born
to make!"

II

In the late 'sixties liberalism became the least excus-

able offense in a motion picture. American audiences were
still prepared to make THE SOUND OF MUSIC (20th-Fox,
1964) or LOVE STORY (Paramount, 1970) a financial hit,
but "pure entertainment" was a phrase the critics held in
increasing disfavor. Robert Wise, who produced more hits
than most of his contemporaries, was never considered serious enough to possess any reputation at all. Eccentrics were
applauded as directors, were awarded the crowns of shock,
science fiction, and schlock film. Unlikely, low budget producers and directors like Roger Corman received unexpected
accolades. Corman, who had once directed ATTACK OF THE
CRAB MONSTERS (Allied Artists, 1957) and SORORITY GIRL
(American International, 1957), was distributing Ingmar Bergman's films in the U. S. Occasionally, American critics went
slumming on side streets way past the marquees of first run
theatres, down streets where they discovered new merits in
"B" films from the 'forties and 'fifties. One day, they came
across Sam Fuller, a director already admired by writers in
European film magazines like Movie and Cahiers du Cinéma.
Perhaps the American critics had seen Fuller's pictures late
at night on television, in the hours before dawn when almost
any picture appeared chaotic, and Fuller's pictures were the
most chaotic. If Fuller was anything, he was distinctive.
His pictures were energetic or they were as slow-moving as
documentaries. They looked honest. Fuller became a cult
director.

In 1976 and 1977, the 'fifties revival erupted with
malteds and bobby sox spilling across American television
screens. Fuller's movies, grimy and lined with fatigue, were
also products of the 'fifties which found favor. They capital-
ized on a mixture of nostalgia and admiration. Among the
cognoscenti, Fuller was considered a salty spokesman for
American filmmaking. In 1969, an interview with Fuller took
up nearly 70 pages in The Director's Event (Atheneum, 1970)
by Eric Sherman and Martin Rubin. In each of the three
years, 1969, 1970, and 1971, books titled Samuel Fuller were
released by English publishers. Movietone News released a
special Fuller issue in the summer of 1976. Fuller wrote two
articles for American Film; Film Comment took an unusual
step and allowed Fuller to rewrite an interview.

Clearly, Fuller generated a great deal of interest.
Amid such a wealth of details and plot synopses, it is almost
inevitable that a new entry in this crowded atmosphere must
spend some time in examining the perspectives of these com-
peting essays.

It appeared that not only critics but publishers were
attracted to Fuller. In almost every one of the interviews,
even in the three books, the bottom line was not the pictures
Fuller had made, but those he planned to make. Between
1965 and 1977, the period of Fuller's greatest critical attention, he completed only three motion pictures. Nearly one
dozen more features were planned at one time or another.
Their titles appeared in a stream of footnotes: CAINE II,
PEARL HARBOR, POWDER KEG, THE TOY SOLDIERS, THE
KID FROM SOHO, FLOWERS OF EVIL, BATTLE ROYAL,
BALZAC, and others. In 1966 Fuller wrote The Rifle, a
novel about the Vietnam war. The book was in its galleys
when his publisher decided to stop its fiction line. In 1972,
he had spent three weeks shooting RIATA, a "psychedelic
Western," when he was fired. In 1976, the sets had already
been built for ALAMO CHARLIE when the deal fell through.
While he waited, he wrote novels; 114 Piccadilly and Dead
Pigeon on Beethoven Street.

Would-be producers failed to come up with money.
That was the problem. "I had seven of those," Fuller said,
"one after another. You can be blackballed, you know, and
it doesn't have to be politics. You can be blackballed by
promises. Just remember that!"

It was Fuller's collection of unsold scripts and uncom-
pleted pictures which seemed to fascinate people. Writers
summed up their essays by listing the pictures Fuller had
not made. Even separate scenes were described, as Nicholas
Garnham did in Samuel Fuller (Secker and Warburg, 1971).

"[Fuller] described recently to a group of which I was
a member a forty-five-minute shot that he plans for his next
movie. The sequence follows an American patrol being pursued through the jungle by the Vietcong. The track will
stretch the distance it takes that patrol to go in forty minutes, and Fuller will then use two cameras and overlap them
at the beginning of each ten-minute magazine, changing from
one to the other just as you change from one projector to
another in the cinema, and, as he put it, 'I'll tell the actors
they must keep going; whatever happens they must keep up
with us, I'm not waiting for them.'"

In 1977, Fuller hadn't made an American film in more
than ten years. For perhaps the first time in his career,
his pictures were included in the curricula of university film
courses. THE BIG RED ONE seemed to put Fuller's reputa-

tion on the line. With Bogdanovich producing, it offered him
a saleable cast, a sympathetic producer, and his biggest budget. It had taken him so long to make THE BIG RED ONE,
he said, because he couldn't decide what to leave out and what
to put in. He had a lot of material.

"I've been working on the book a long time in my
head," he said, "and I've made many notes. I didn't know
what to use. In other words, let's say I've got forty or fifty
incidents and I only want to use one. I'd use one and I'd say,
'No, that's no good. I think I'll use another one.' I kept
stalling. It was terrible. What was good for me was to sit
down and write that script and, boy, did I hit the bone....
This one here is very close to me. After this, I'm finished
with it. It's all here, in two volumes, and the script is
finished."

Fuller and Bogdanovich disagreed in only one area of
the picture--color, or the lack of it.

Bogdanovich preferred a black and white film. "I just
don't think war pictures look real in color," he said. "I
think the blood looks silly.... I think A BRIDGE TOO FAR
[United Artists, 1977] could have been a better picture in
black and white. All those movie stars would have looked
more like real people. There's something about black and
white; it certainly helps the actor. Color is distracting, it
has to be very carefully handled. You can do it, but it seems
to me, if you're doing a war picture, particularly a World
War II picture, it should be black and white. I don't understand the reason for color, unless it's somebody's idea of
what is commercial--or what isn't."

Fuller wanted to use color. He wanted to start the
picture in black and white. He wanted to go into color.
Then he wanted to go back to black and white.

"Lee Marvin, my soldier, is looking for a dead American, when he feels the earth quake," Fuller said. "This
horse comes charging towards him. It stomps him, and he
rolls, and it stomps his rifle, splintering the stock. Then
he sees his nightmare. He sees a big cross, Christ on a
cross, on a twenty-foot mound, with a big crown of thorns.
English, French, and German telephone wires make up the
thorns. Gnats and beetles crawl in and out of the goddamned
eyes, right through the nostrils, out the damn mouth. Marvin
hangs to the cross for support. He has no rifle, only a

trenchknife, and the horse runs up the mound after him.
Every time the horse slams at him, Marvin hides behind the
beam.   Christ starts to sway, the feet move, the ankles, the
support--'Whang, whang, whang.' The telephone wires start
going this way, then that way, and the ants start going crazy.
Finally, Marvin slams the blade into the cushion of the horse's
hoof two or three times and the horse takes off.   Marvin
doesn't know what the hell is going on.

"He makes his way back to the American lines where
his captain is having a drink:

" 'Did you ever see a crazy horse?'

"The captain says no, so Marvin takes out a cap and
cuts off three inches of red piping.   The captain asks him
what the hell he's doing.

" 'I'm making a patch.'   He holds up the red stripe.
'We're the First Division, Number One, what the hell?   I
had to kill a goddamned Hun to get this son of a bitch.'

" 'Where did you kill him?'

" 'Over by Christ on a cross!'

" 'When?'

" 'Three hours ago, or whatever the hell it was!'

" 'Did he say anything?'

" 'Yeah, he gave me the whole line of bullshit.   The
war's over!'

" 'Finish your drink.'   When he finishes the drink, the
captain says: 'The war's over.   It's been over for four
hours.'   The captain feels sorry for Marvin.   He says, 'You
didn't know it was over?'

"Marvin says, 'He did.'

"And as he says, 'He did,' we cut to that little red
stripe, and bam!   The screen begins to open with that red,
and the red begins to form the patch, whooo, bigger, bigger,
bigger, big, you see a million lights, you're in the deck of
a ship, and it's the beginning of the North Africa campaign!"

III

It is easy enough to start an argument with a group of
film scholars, but it might be easiest and most divisive if you
mention Fuller's name. It's like a flip of a coin; his initials
can get you the loan of a print or a punch in the nose. In
Europe, his abilities have long been admired. In the U.S.,
the reverse has most often been true. Between 1965 and 1978,
Fuller was unable to finish a picture for an American producer. He worked in Mexico, he worked in Germany, he
started several pictures, and he appeared as an actor, but
he didn't direct an American feature for thirteen years.

In a 1972 issue of Esquire, Peter Bogdanovich, even
then one of Fuller's greatest supporters, wrote, "Sam Fuller
is probably the most explosive talent ever to blast his way
through Poverty Row. Eccentric, iconoclastic, and in the
tradition of tabloid journalism, his pictures all bear the same
vibrant individualistic stamp.... Often extreme, his vision
of the world is reflected in broad, expressionistic strokes,
and belongs entirely to the movies; he has brought his feisty,
uncompromising zest for pictures into every frame he has
ever shot."

Fuller repaid the compliment a year later by casting
Stephane Audran as a Lesbian named Dr. Bogdanovich in
DEAD PIGEON ON BEETHOVEN STREET (Emerson, 1973).

In March, 1977, Fuller was an arresting figure, small,
bursting with energy, and 65 years old. His face was as ex-
pressive as a two-inch headline printed in red ink. Like
Bogdanovich, he believed THE BIG RED ONE could be his
masterpiece. Fuller spoke by stretching his hands and his
vowels; he was hanging on words to accentuate them. He
looked as if he'd like--if he wasn't sitting in his own office--
to spit on the floor. While he spoke he smoked cigars by
rolling a flame back and forth below the tobacco. He was
also a doting father, interrupting his conversation to ask his
wife a question about their two-year-old daughter, Samantha.
After his interview, he was going to make popcorn for the
first time in his life. He was going to dance across his
kitchen floor to avoid the flying grease and corn kernels,
holding his daughter up to see the exploding corn while Christa
measured out large helpings of butter into paper cups filled
with popcorn. There was something about Christa's voice
that made her an ideal heroine for her husband. Fuller
would also pick up a drink. Popcorn and beer.

It was easy to imagine him in his first profession, as
a newsboy, a short, fast talker on the streets of Boston and
New York.   He used to collect suicide notes.   Today he plays
his audience with the swift, chopped notes of a late-night,
last-edition headline.   He raises his arms, then dips them
to emphasize an image.   He is like a reporter with a big
scoop, a wild, surrealistic scoop.   Fuller likes to talk about
his plans for the next few months.

"What I want to do," he continued, "is to show the
people who the G.I.s killed.   You get to know them quickly,
you get to know everybody as they are killed.   I want people
to really feel it.   Oh, yes, yes, yes!   That's a human being
who dies.   I don't care if he's a bastard or a saint, he's a
human being!

"I'll give you a rough example.   I have a man who
will kill.   He's killed a lot of people.   He'll grenade, and
he'll shoot in the dark, but he won't kill if he sees a man's
face.   He's just got that one hang-up.

"He sees a man, and all he has to do is to lower his
rifle muzzle from one-sixteenth of an inch to one thirty-second
of an inch, and he's going to get the man right smack in the
face.   He tries to keep the gun down but he can't do it.   He
shoots two or three times but he misses.   The fellow next to
him asks, 'What the hell are you shooting at?   I don't see
anything!'

"Then the first man guides him, he aims, and as he
squeezes the trigger--I go right to the Frenchman in his
sights.   He's pissed off that the invasion took place.   He'd
been promised that he could return to Oran and see his new
baby.   He's telephoned his wife, and the baby, his first, is
nine and a half pounds.

"Now all this time the bullet is moving right towards
him and he doesn't know it.   The trajectory was given to a
man by another man who couldn't shoot him.   The Frenchman
had everything planned, and the men were going to throw a
party for him.   They had all pitched in.   They were even
going to get dancing girls.   Then the bullet hits him.

"Nine and a half pounds is the weight of an M-1 without a bayonet.   It wasn't a ten-pound rifle or an eight-pound
rifle, it was a nine and a half pound rifle.   That makes it
even-steven--so the guy gets killed."

Fuller had recently returned from Europe where he scouted locations and visited Wim Wenders, the West German director. Fuller watched the rushes of Wenders' new film in which Fuller was cast as an American gangster. Two more American directors, Dennis Hopper and Nicholas Ray, were also in the cast of THE AMERICAN FRIEND.

That morning, William Wellman, Jr. had called to see if Fuller could find a part for him in THE BIG RED ONE. Probably he couldn't, because the cast was small. The leads were an American sergeant, a German, and four young Americans. Fuller wanted Bogdanovich to play a character based on Fuller's wartime career.

How does Fuller prepare his actors for a battle film? "I work my ass off," he said. "We rehearse for a week. They carry packs, they gripe, they grouch, they bitch, they get dirty. I have them take their uniforms home so they can sleep in them. They look wrinkled and dirty; there's no smellovision, but the flavor is of urine."

He leaned back into his chair, an elder, big-city spokesman, one of the last of the hard-boiled intellectuals, a prehistoric "B" director. In many ways, he is an anachronism. Just maybe, if James M. Cain had written about a movie director, he would have looked like Fuller. Certainly he would talk like him. Fuller's fans, American and European, are probably at least as attracted to his personality as they are to his motion pictures, perhaps more so. The titles of pictures like UNDERWORLD, U.S.A. (Columbia, 1961), FORTY GUNS (20th-Fox, 1957), PICKUP ON SOUTH STREET (20th-Fox, 1953), SHOCK CORRIDOR (Allied Artists, 1963), and THE NAKED KISS (Allied Artists, 1964) describe them well; they are as seamy as their titles. The titles are almost always written in black and white or blood red, like the illustrations on the covers of old paperbacks, covers which often promised more sex and violence than the text delivered. Fuller's titles are like the datelines on a news story; they give times, dates, locations, and quotes. The films are like schematic diagrams. Often they lack a dimension of depth. There is a flatness in his scenes, a two-dimensional feeling heightened by the use of expressionist camera angles.

In 1977, Fuller's screenplays surrounded him in his study. He wrote them on cheap yellow paper at an old manual typewriter. Then he edited them and made clean copies on the same typewriter. Fuller wanted to direct, he said,

"because I didn't want any other banana heads to spoil what
I'd written." He was a screenwriter until 1949, when a "B"
Western producer named Robert Lippert gave him a chance to
direct. When the picture was released, reviewers called it
a "class" Western, Lippert's first.

Fuller spoke in the short, blustering announcements
of tabloid headlines. "I learned early," he said, "that it's
not the headline that counts, but how loud you shout it." Fuller's personality sounds like a headline.

No American has ever been more clearly an auteur
than Fuller. Between 1957 and 1964, he wrote, produced,
and directed nine films. He wrote the scripts for each of
the other ten films he directed between 1948 and 1977. He
moved sets and designed his own ad campaigns. In 1965, the
New York Times said, "On the average, Fuller spends ten
days and $200,000 making a picture." His pictures are fine
examples of Yankee ingenuity. He made them with bad acting
and twenty-five-man army divisions. Usually he shot on a
set because he couldn't afford a location.

Fuller likes to let his imagination go wild. His pictures also reveal a second impulse, one which leads Fuller
toward a harsh, uncinematic realism. The rigors of his
actors before a battle scene are just one example of this attention to detail. Fuller could have summed up this second
direction; indeed, he would like to sum up this direction in
one word--grit.

Two themes, one extravagant, the other naturalistic,
are more often than not at war in Fuller's pictures. A meld,
rather than an alloy, of styles, it is a quick-tempered mix
blended to the tastes of many European film critics. The
pictures are always dramatic, seldom realistic.

Nicholas Garnham, in Samuel Fuller (Viking, 1971),
took up the European's case for Fuller in a defense which is
too flimsy to account for three books on Fuller, let alone a
dozen major essays in film magazines.

"As far as American critics are concerned," Garnham
wrote, "there is a further cause of blockage where their own
cinema is concerned. This coalesces round the issues of
superficial realism. We accept, I think, that the central tradition of cinema is realist, that the recording of what is in
front of the camera has an important role to play. But we

should not make of this an exclusive requirement.... Talking
to Americans about American movies, one continually comes
up against this difficulty: they will dismiss a film because
they don't feel the sociological background is right. 'People
don't talk, dress, act like that' is levelled as a dismissive
accusation.

"What relevance has all this to a critique of Fuller?
He has, I think, been misjudged by British and above all
American critics because he does not satisfy, nor does he
intend to satisfy, the superficial desire for realism."

In most of Fuller's pictures, his tone is inconsistent,
making it easier to condemn his work than praise it. Manny
Farber, who named FIXED BAYONETS one of the top three
pictures of 1951 in Movies (Stonehill, 1971), was the critic
to capture most ably the haphazard mix of good and bad in
Fuller's work. "He has made nineteen no-flab, low or middle
budget films since 1949," Farber wrote in 1969, "any one of
which could be described as 'simple minded corny stuff ...
but colorful....' Fuller's scripts are grotesque jobs that
might have been written by the bus driver on The Honeymoon-
ers: 'Ok, I'll give you five minutes to clear out. If you're
not out, we're going to burn the place down.'

"The low budget appears to economize the mind of a
director," Farber added, "forcing him into a nice balance
between language and what is seen. Given more money and
reputation actors, Sam Fuller's episodic, spastically slow and
fast films would probably dissolve into mouthy arrogance where
characters would be constantly defining and apologizing for the
class separatism that obsesses Fuller."

In 1977 Fuller was still an extravagant paradox. He
was honored as much as a representative of a genre as he
was as a stylistic reference point. All of his pictures had
the same low-budget appearance. Often he appeared to favor
unknowns over box-office stars. His characters were bar
girls, American dogfaces, and cheap hoods. His stories were
like pulp novels. His largest constituency was in Europe.

"Fuller is the greatest unknown film director in the
world," the Italian director Bernardo Bertolucci said in 1977
in the magazine American Film. "His films are like the
black man's music--pure rhythm and violence and erotic suggestion. They are living things, living things. They live.
They cannot die. Fuller is like a god to me."

Fuller is also a romantic. His taste runs toward ex-
tremes. He is nostalgic over his memories of the early
twentieth-century newspaper business and his conversation is
filled with paeans to Gene Fowler and the New York Graphic.
He also remembers many incidents with the directors of the
French, English, and German New Wave. In his pictures,
Fuller is as self-conscious as a European director. His first
pictures were about Jesse James and the American West.
Now he is talking about making a world-wide mystery, with
top European film directors like François Truffaut and Bertolucci playing detectives.

Fuller is honored at film festivals and in the films
made by other directors. Peter Bogdanovich borrowed a
scene from PICKUP ON SOUTH STREET for WHAT'S UP
DOC? (Warner's, 1972). Jean-Luc Godard took a scene from
FORTY GUNS and used it in BREATHLESS (French, 1959).
In FORTY GUNS, the scene was jarring; it was tricky. "I
don't mind using tricky things," Fuller said, "if it can help
sell a character."

Fuller goes through the motions of realism, but the
world framed by his pictures is anything but realistic. He
wastes no time on romance between men and women. They
fall in love very quickly, often inexplicably. His transitions
are abrupt. Occasionally he uses an odd angle or a new lens,
or a special effect to show a character's distorted point of
view. Sometimes he edits his pictures like a propaganda
poster, as if he were plunging a dagger again and again into
his audience, shouting, "Do you get my point?"

His pictures are constructed like comic books, with
insane characters and paranoid dream sequences. They are
thickly plotted. His camera relishes deep, furtive close-ups
of eyes. Often his characters live in shadows.

Fuller's dialogue is narrative; often it has so many
twists and turns that it's difficult to describe one of his pictures without including a synopsis. His characters meet,
they travel together, they may even make love, but they rarely
change, unless they die. Fuller's pictures, especially his
war films, are like sensitivity training sessions on a road
to some remote Canterbury. Each man is on a stage, offering the story of his life for his companions' amusement. They
are all on journeys. It's hard to think of a Fuller character
who is not also an obsessively restless traveler.

Fuller's sense of justice is literal. In SHARK (Heritage, 1969), Burt Reynolds lives moment to moment in the Sudan. He finishes the picture as he opens it, as a hitchhiker waiting for a ride. Reynolds does not change, and Fuller's sense of balance has not been upset. In SHOCK CORRIDOR, when a reporter named Johnny Barratt captures a murderer, he must also replace him in an asylum. The pictures are governed by this surrealistic conservation of energy.

In RUN OF THE ARROW (Universal, 1956), a man is shot and wounded. The rest of the picture takes place in the time that it takes that same bullet to hit the man a second time and kill him. The bullet is both the catalyst and the curtain in RUN OF THE ARROW. Once it finds its mark, the picture is over, the balance recovered. Fuller delights in this odd balance of time, life, and object.

Fuller's office smells like old paper. He is surrounded by books and he pulls out manuscripts, pictures, and motion picture reels. Above a file cabinet, he keeps his novel, The Big Red One. Near the door, he has films of his locations. He held up two nearly identical photographs. "I want to show you something," he said. "I made a picture called SHOCK CORRIDOR. Do you know the story? A newspaperman is going to crack a murder in a nut house so he gets himself admitted as an insane person. He solves the crime and ends up a catatonic. That's the story. Here's the French poster for SHOCK CORRIDOR, and here's an ad for ONE FLEW OVER THE CUCKOO'S NEST (United Artists, 1975). Aren't they close? I think that's very interesting!"

In 1977, Fuller shared more with Peter Bogdanovich than a one-picture contract. Like Bogdanovich, Fuller was a movie fan who paid his favorite directors, men like John Ford, Howard Hawks, and Herbert Brenon, the same kinds of tributes Bogdanovich has accorded Hawks and Ford. An interview with Fuller is likely to include anecdotes about Ford, William Wellman, and Raoul Walsh.

Fuller talked about other movies, ones he had seen while growing up in Worcester, Massachusetts. "When I was a boy," he said, "my mother would take me to a theatre every Saturday. It cost you a nickle to see Jack Hoxie, Buck Jones, George Walsh, Tim McCoy, Ken Maynard, William S. Hart, and Tom Mix, who was my favorite cowboy. One time Buck

Jones had a personal appearance near our home and he had
Silver, his horse, with him. He said, 'Come on up and touch
Silver' and all the kids lined up. Terrible things were happening, Buck Jones probably didn't want to be there, but there
he was, with all the kids. There was a dream there that
should have never been spoiled for me.

"I love the West," he said. "I'll go to see any Western that has some kind of flavor to it. I mean, if you made
a Western, I'd like to go see it. The war pictures are too
easy. It's just a question of what I want to use. I even used
a little touch of war in I SHOT JESSE JAMES (Screen Guild,
1949). I had Bob Ford come out of a saloon, and he's shot
at, several times, in the night. He shoots back, and a voice
says, 'Don't shoot, I'm out of bullets,' and a little boy comes
out. That's the old story of the enemy, when he says, 'Don't
shoot! Don't shoot! No bullets!' I wanted to use that, because that's the easiest time to give up.

"When I made a Western, I really wanted to make
something that I would have liked to have seen myself. I
think--what would I have liked to have seen when I was a
kid?"

Fuller has appeared in several motion pictures. He
played a director in Dennis Hopper's strange, disjointed 1970
picture, THE LAST MOVIE, in BRIGITTE ET BRIGITTE,
directed by Luc Moullet in 1966, and Jean-Luc Godard's
1965 film, PIERROT LE FOU. Godard asked him, "What is
film?"

"The film is like a battleground," Fuller said. "Love,
hate, action, violence, death. In one word--emotion."

Everybody, Fuller said, wants to get into the movies.

                                    IV

Fuller's first and longest love was the newspaper business. "Page One and the screen," he wrote in the inaugural
issue of American Film, "are bedmates." Newspaper headlines and reporters appear in almost every one of his pictures;
they are as common as busts of Beethoven.

Born in Worcester, Massachusetts, on 12 August, 1911,
he was a newspaper boy in Boston, peddling the Worcester

Samuel Fuller on the set during the filming of THE LAST
MOVIE (Universal, 1971).   Photo courtesy of David Wilson
and Samuel Fuller.

Telegram, Boston Post, and Boston American.   His father
died when he was twelve.   When his mother moved to New
York, he became a delivery boy for the photographers on
the New York Evening Journal, a paper which had five or
six different front page editions every day.   After each shot,
he took the photographic plates back to the office.   He left
the Journal to join a scandal sheet, the Evening Graphic,
where he took a position as head copy-boy.   He also began
to write stories; he had decided that he wanted to be a crime
reporter.

     "I loved it," he said.   "I loved the whole idea of
newspapers.   It made me feel like a Merlin, a magician,
because I knew something before the rest of the city knew
it.   I loved to go to the composing room.   My dream was
to be a reporter, then an editor.   I saw a story written, then

it was shot down to composing, then brought up in a galley,
where a man checked and double-checked it and they took the
goddamned galley back to composing.   Then they brought up
a proof.   I watched the presses run, until they came up with
a wet paper. . . .   All I had to do was rub my hand against it,
and the whole thing smeared.   That's how fresh that cheap
ink was."

    Over fifty years later, Fuller's excitement reappeared
when he talked about his first press card.   "It was gold," he
said.   "You could go anywhere that a cop or fireman could
go.   Lineups, everything!"

    Fuller was fifteen when the elevator at the Graphic
went out of order.   He cornered his editor in the stairwell
and threatened to quit the paper if he wasn't given a newsbeat.
The editor walked him back upstairs and into his office.   He
took out his own press card, scratched his name out, and
handed it to Fuller.

    "Now get your ass out of here," he said.

    "I ran down," Fuller said, "and I took a subway up
to Times Square, at 47th Street, off Broadway.   It was my
new precinct, a hot, very hot precinct.   The tenderloin.   I
walked down the street and I thought, 'Nobody knows I've got
a police card on me.'   I was looking for something, and
nothing happened.   A very disappointing day."   On one of his
first assignments, he covered an up-state suicide pact with
reporter Rhea Gore, John Huston's mother.   The pair broke
a sheriff's seal and spilled wine over the floor.   In black and
white, the wine looked like blood.

    After leaving the Graphic, Fuller traveled to California
where he sold articles to the Chronicle in San Francisco and
was hired as a police reporter by the San Diego Sun.   "I
covered police, but really, I could cover anything," he said.
"Somebody would be up, charged with something, and I'd follow through or go through a relative to get what we call now,
the RASHOMON flavor.   We did that for years.   We'd get two
or three different versions, and then we'd find out that there
was a ten-year-old kid around the corner who really saw the
whole thing.   I kept working on that until I got a call to do
a yarn for Republic."

    En route between San Francisco and San Diego, Fuller
visited Hollywood, where he met Herbert Brenon, a hard-

drinking, fast-driving Irish film director.   Brenon gave Fuller
his first cigar.   He took Fuller out in his roadster and tried
to talk him out of the newspaper business.   Gene Fowler also
tried to talk him into writing for pictures.   Their best argument was the size of Fowler's paycheck.   Fuller spent the
next fifteen years writing and ghostwriting screenplays.

One day the International News Service sent Fuller to
Hollywood Boulevard and Vine Street, where a girl was threatening to jump off a blimp.   It was a publicity stunt, but while
he was out on the story, Fuller met an acquaintance who was
a dance director with the Paramount stage show.   He told
Fuller he'd give him one thousand dollars for a good story
idea.   Fuller told him about an aquatic show in Fort Worth,
Texas, and the dance director said he'd use the idea.   Fuller
followed him home and picked up the $1,000.

He returned to San Francisco to cover a general strike.
Between assignments, he had begun to write short stories and
novels.   His first novel, Burn, Baby, Burn was written in
1935.   Test Tube Baby and Make Up and Kiss were published
in 1936.   In 1977, Fuller was surprised to find that the UCLA
library would not allow the books outside its building.   "Those
were terrible books," Fuller said, "and I don't know how
many I wrote under other names, too!   Very fast, and very
indifferent.   Cheap little exploitation books.   I was working
on a paper and this was extra money on the side."

He sold his first script, HATS OFF (Grand National,
1936), to the director Boris Petroff, in 1936.   His second
screenplay, IT HAPPENED IN HOLLYWOOD (Columbia, 1936),
was taken from a story by Myles Connoly.   A sentimental
story about a Hollywood cowboy on the skids, it starred
Richard Dix and was directed by Harry Lachman.

"I had a dinner in it with the Hollywood doubles,"
Fuller said.   "Dix breaks into his own home, he gets the
doubles together, and this kid thinks he's meeting all the
real stars: Eddie Cantor, W. C. Fields, Charlie Chaplin,
Mae West, Marlene Dietrich, and Victor McLaglen.   Dix has
lost his home, all he's got is his horse, and he becomes a
barker on a bus.   Then the gangster pictures come in, like
PUBLIC ENEMY [Warner's, 1931], at Warner's, and they
send for him.   He's supposed to hold up a bank in this picture.   They rehearse it, and when they say action, he can't
do it.   He's a Western star, a hero, and he can't be a crook.
When he needs money, he breaks into his house, he gets his

Colt . 45, and he goes back to the same bank where they re-
hearsed the scene, a real bank, and he remembers what the
director told him.   He's about to hold up the bank when two
gunmen come in, kill the clerks, and take the money.   Dix
is so shocked that he thinks he's back in a movie again.   He
takes aim, right on Hollywood Boulevard, and wham--he gets
one of them.   He's a real hero, and now he gets a job."
Fuller preferred the picture's original title, ONCE A HERO.

FEDERAL MAN-HUNT (Republic, 1939), ADVENTURE
IN SAHARA (Columbia, 1938), and GANGS OF NEW YORK
(Republic, 1938) were produced from Fuller's stories in 1938:
Fuller scripted the latter picture, a project Nathanael West
also worked on.   In 1940, BOWERY BOY (Republic, 1941) was
produced from a Fuller story.   CONFIRM OR DENY (20th-
Fox, 1941), directed by Archie Mayo and Fritz Lang, was
written by Fuller with a friend, Henry Wales.   Wales had
been a newspaper man on the Chicago Tribune.

"I told Wales I had a story," Fuller said.   "England
is in the war, they've been bombed, but the U.S. hasn't entered.   Everybody is living underground, in caves beneath the
cement sidewalks.   A bomb hits the Associated Press office,
where they've taken over an old wine cellar.   The bomb is
unexploded, but it is still alive.   They can't get out, and
nobody can get in.   I couldn't write it because I was working
on The Dark Page [Duell, Sloan, and Pearce, 1944].   Fritz
Lang started to direct it, but something happened, and he
didn't finish the picture.

"I wrote it, hopefully, with Clark Gable in mind.   I
had two things in there that I thought they ruined when they
made the picture.   The man is trapped and he can't get a
word out to dig him up.   There's a bomb in there going tick
... tick ... tick, right in the city room of the Associated
Press.   It's a big bomb, and it says, 'Hitler Is Coming.'
So he has to send a message to all Allied countries, around
the world, to reach the hotel manager fifteen feet away.   I
thought it was a pretty good trick.

"In the ending, when they dig him out, he gets the
teletype machine working and he sends his story out.   He
thinks that the invasion of England is on, that Hitler is coming.   He writes this story and he gets blown up with it.
They didn't have anything like that in the picture.   Instead,
he lives."

In 1942 Fuller entered the U.S. Army and was shipped
to Europe. He planned to rewrite The Dark Page when he
returned. He served with the Sixteenth Company of the First
U.S. Infantry Division, The Big Red One. In Sicily, he won
the Bronze Star, at Normandy he won the Silver Star. In
Germany, Fuller took shelter under a piano which had once
been Beethoven's. In 1973, he returned to the dwelling to
film DEAD PIGEON ON BEETHOVEN STREET.

In the meantime, The Dark Page was published; his
mother had sold his first draft. Fuller's hero, Carl Chapman, is a man who deserts his wife, changes his name, becomes editor of the New York Comet and remarries. When
Chapman's first wife reappears, he kills her, then uses the
crime to boost his paper's circulation. His publisher promises
him a $20,000 bonus when the Comet reaches a million paid
readers.

Actually, Fuller uses two heroes in his book, Chapman
and Lance McCleary, Chapman's top reporter. "What he
doesn't know," Chapman says, "I do; what he can't do, I
can. Together we're one." They also work as a team,
Lance unwittingly helping Chapman cover up the traces of
his murder. McCleary finds two men who can identify the
killer and Chapman kills both of them.

Fuller employed a shifting point of view in the novel.
His first chapter was written in the third person; the second,
third, and fourth chapters were written in the first person,
from Chapman's point of view. During the last, climactic
pages of The Dark Page, Fuller switched his narrator with
almost every paragraph. In The Dark Page, the device works;
Fuller was not always able to accomplish the same effect when
he used the device in pictures. He wanted to possess the
freedom of third person point of view, but he also couldn't
resist the intimacy of a first person narrator. The long
speeches of Fuller's motion picture characters, their dream
sequences, and the shifting camera angles were all employed
in an attempt to recapture the weave of points of view manip-
ulated throughout The Dark Page.

The central problem shared by many of Fuller's characters, including Chapman, McCleary, and Richard Dix in
IT HAPPENED IN HOLLYWOOD, is an inability to act. "Why
am I stuck to the floor?" Fuller wrote. "I've got to move.
It's too late--it's too late!" The lines resonated all the way
from The Dark Page to THE BIG RED ONE, in 1977.

The Book Critics of America selected The Dark Page
as the outstanding psychological novel of 1944. Howard Hawks
bought it for fifteen thousand dollars, then sold it to Columbia,
where it was made as SCANDAL SHEET in 1952, starring
Broderick Crawford and John Derek. Fuller was still in
Europe when the film sale was made. He had $1,000 wired
to him and he used it to stage a party at his rest camp near
the Belgian border.

POWER OF THE PRESS (Columbia, 1943) and GANGS
OF THE WATERFRONT (Republic, 1945), a remake of GANGS
OF NEW YORK, were produced from Fuller's stories. In
1948, SHOCKPROOF (Columbia, 1949) was directed by Douglas Sirk from a Fuller story and screenplay.

Later in 1948, Robert Lippert gave Fuller his first
opportunity to direct when he offered him a contract for a
quick, cheap picture. The head of Lippert Productions was
trying to turn out twenty-five independent pictures every year.
"I gave Fuller a chance," he said, "but I wouldn't have done
it if the story cost was fabulous, or if I was paying a star
$1,000 an hour for standing around." Fuller obliged Lippert,
writing and shooting I SHOT JESSE JAMES in ten days for a
$5,000 salary. Lippert gave Fuller Lippert's largest produc-
tion budget to that date, $118,000, and he completed the film
on 24 November, 1948.

In 1977, Fuller said he wanted to make another film
about Jesse James. "He was an evil squirt," Fuller said,
"a female impersonator at the age of fifteen. His first hold
up was on a hospital train. He gunned all the soldiers down,
all of them invalids. I'd show him doing that even before the
titles. And I'd never get backing on the project unless I financed it myself. If I did, I'd go right down the river.
There's ten million Westerns on T.V. They're a glut on the
market.

"You see, you've got to have a legend. Jesse James
has already replaced Robin Hood in this country. Our country
isn't old enough to have myths, but we've got a chance for a
legend. The legend of Jesse James will outlive almost every
other legend we have. I'd still like to make the picture,
knowing it will flop, knowing people will say, 'That son of a
bitch, he's against the goddamn West!' But I love the West.
That's the point."

Despite it's title, I SHOT JESSE JAMES wasn't Fuller's

picture about James; in fact, the film has little to do with
James, his assassin, Bob Ford, or with the complexities of
historical fact. Fuller said he wasn't concerned with Jesse,
the victim, but that he wanted to show a family man. Ford
is a composite of assassins, a man who also resembles
Gippo Nolan, the slow-thinking traitor who was featured in
John Ford's THE INFORMER (RKO, 1936).

"I wanted to do a series of assassin stories," Fuller
said. "First I wanted to do Cassius. He was pretty much
of the ringleader in the Caesar killing. I was interested in
the hesitancy of the actual assassination. 'Why me?' 'Why
not you?' 'Why not her?' 'Somebody's got to do it!' 'I'm
late for dinner.' 'I've got a date.' 'I don't feel very well.'
And they all begin to cop out. That's what I'm interested in,
an assassin's story, not who is going to be assassinated. I
don't give a damn about Caesar or Heaser or Heasar. They
don't mean anything to me. I'm talking about you and me.
We plan, plan, plan. Then, when it comes time for us to
do it, we hesitate."

Lippert refused to finance a picture set in Rome, so
Fuller gave him a list with the names of four or five more
assassins, including the assassins of Presidents McKinley and
Garfield. They settled upon Bob Ford, and Fuller began
shooting his script on the old sets at Republic Studios.

I SHOT JESSE JAMES follows the legend of James
already firmly established by Henry King in JESSE JAMES
(20th-Fox, 1940). In Fuller's picture both of his romantic
leads, Preston Foster and Barbara Britton, are featured above
Jesse (Reed Hadley) and Ford (John Ireland). Fuller had seen
Ireland in RED RIVER (United Artists, 1948) and he felt he
had accomplished a coup in signing him.

I SHOT JESSE JAMES begins with a hold-up; a teller
at a bank presses an alarm and Bob Ford, a member of the
James gang, is shot during the gang's escape. Jesse risks
his life to rescue Ford, sharing a slim piece of Oriental
wisdom with the gunman as they ride away: "You know what
they say," he says, "when you save a man's life, you assume
his responsibility."

Like Nolan in THE INFORMER, Ford betrays his friend
for a reward. Unlike Nolan, however, it's not so much the
money that triggers his gun, but an ironic desire for anonymity. Cynthy Waters, his show-girl mistress, thinks he should
give up crime and buy a farm.

Fuller introduces John Kelley (Preston Foster), then packs both him and Ford off to Colorado, where they hope to make their fortunes by discovering gold. Foster is like a boy from Western Union who trudges in from the snow every fifteen minutes with a telegram carrying the plot. Ford has less to do with the linear plot development. Ford's story is episodic; in each of his appearances, the guilt he feels over Jesse's death grows. His woman leaves him, strangers hate him, but he refuses to hide out; he will never change his name.

Ford meets a troubador in a bar. He'll sing a song "everybody likes" if Ford will buy him a beer. Ford springs for the drink, and the balladeer sings "The Ballad of Jesse James," and of "that dirty little coward, who shot Mr. Howard, and laid poor Jesse in his grave."

The singer stops after his first verse: "Don't you like my song?"

"I'm Bob Ford," Ireland says. "Sing it!"

Fuller's camera is subjective, and here its focus shifts from Ford to this anonymous, apprehensive singer. The transition is disruptive in its abruptness. Instead of advancing the story of Bob Ford, it nearly stops it.

Even earlier scenes before Jesse's death are filled with a heavily stated irony. Jesse hands Ford a loaded gun while he's taking a bath and asks, "What are you waiting for? There's my back." Ford picks up a sponge and starts to scrub.

After the murder, Ford makes a grisly deal with Ms. Waters' manager; the self-conscious gunman is going into show business. "I'm going to be a performer," he says. "A special added attraction. Every night, I'm going to show folks how I shot Jesse."

There is a sense of urgency in the frantic texture of I SHOT JESSE JAMES, as if Fuller was unsure whether or not he would ever have a second chance to direct. There is little in the technical repertory of his later films which did not arise from either The Dark Page or I SHOT JESSE JAMES. His themes, his weak heroes, and his moralistic dialogue are equally persistent.

Reviewers, perhaps those who had not seen Henry

King's JESSE JAMES, called Fuller's picture the most sympathetic portrayal of James ever filmed. "He may have been
one of the most cold-blooded desperadoes of the old West,"
one wrote, "but, apparently, Jesse James was also a staunch,
home-loving family man who took good care 'of the wife and
kiddies." The Hollywood Reporter called it "a class Western,
brilliantly acted, soundly directed, with a thoughtful screenplay." Variety announced that Lloyd T. Dinsford, the eighty-
eight-year-old censor in Memphis, Tennessee, relaxed his
decree banning any picture featuring Jesse James to allow I
SHOT JESSE JAMES in his city's theatres. It became Lippert's biggest money-maker.

After he completed I SHOT JESSE JAMES, Fuller said
he would like to write and direct one picture every year and
spend the rest of his time writing novels. He was able to
keep up the pace, writing, directing, and often producing his
pictures, for almost fifteen years.

The budget for THE BARON OF ARIZONA (Lippert,
1950), a second Lippert project, topped that for Fuller's first
entry. It opened with a gala press preview featuring a stage
show, costing a total of $10,000. Despite the preview, it
was greeted with less enthusiasm than the JESSE JAMES
project. The Hollywood Reporter claimed THE BARON OF
ARIZONA lacked action; Vincent Price and Ellen Drew, it
said, were miscast in the leading roles.

After its release, Fuller said he was disappointed with
THE BARON OF ARIZONA. Lippert had interfered with his
editing. After the preview, Lippert announced that a bulky,
unnecessary prologue to the picture would be eliminated; it
was not, however. John Griff (Reed Hadley), the first governor of Arizona, continues to offer a toast to the absent
Baron. He continues to pass a box of Havana cigars around
his room before beginning his story.

Unlike I SHOT JESSE JAMES, THE BARON OF ARI-
ZONA demands precedence over its separate scenes as its
audience is lured into the unfolding of a man's forgery. It
seems that people are always interested in con-men; it's an
axiom proven equally well by THE BARON OF ARIZONA and
by the bulky advances given to gunmen and criminals for
their paperback memoirs.

The film's time frame is extended across twenty years.
In the first stages of his fantastic, painstaking swindle James
Reavis (Vincent Price) falsifies gravestones and land deeds to

support a bogus Spanish land grant encompassing the entire
Arizona territory.   He names an orphaned girl the last Baroness of Arizona and journeys to Spain, where he enters a
monastery for a three-year stay to forge a new land grant in
the order's archives.   In the monastery, Griff's backstage
narration lessens; the story begins to move under its own
power.   After he is nearly lynched, Reavis is packed away
to spend six years in prison.

Nicholas Garnham finds the picture "uncharacteristically
dull."   Certainly, it lacks the grand, awkward gestures which
earned Fuller his cult audiences.   Despite this, the picture
works better than an examination of its separate episodes
might indicate.   In one of them Reavis confesses to his forgery, because, he says, "I fell in love with my wife."

In this setting, it's worthwhile to examine two lines
in Myron Meisel's essay on Joseph H. Lewis in Kings of the
Bs (Dutton, 1974).   Meisel sees a brand of emotional tough-
ness in Fuller's pictures which is not always there.   "Perhaps the loveliest of Lewis' neglected works, A LADY WITH-
OUT A PASSPORT (1950), might have been an ideal Samuel
Fuller project," he wrote.   "No Fuller character would suddenly pull up short and write out his resignation, giving as
his reason the simple declaration: 'I am in love.'"

On a lesser, almost comic level of auteurism, this
is the first project where one of Fuller's clearest touches,
his character's fondness for cigars, is visible.   After THE
BARON OF ARIZONA, Fuller's pictures contain almost enough
cigar and cigarette smoke to require a warning from the
Surgeon General of the United States.   Nearly everyone, male
and female, smokes.   Usually, they smoke cigars.   Griff
calls Reavis a "cheap, ten cent cigar wrapped in a Havana
leaf."   In his next pictures, Fuller created a character so
amoral that he lets a man go to his death so that he can get
his hands on the box of cigars the man was carrying.

Neither of Fuller's first two features holds up well
under repeated viewings.   In THE BARON OF ARIZONA,
Price and his Baroness fall in love as fast as Foster and
Britton in I SHOT JESSE JAMES; neither match is particularly plausible.   In each instance, Fuller appears unwilling
to study the intricacies of a man/woman relationship; it can
be a goal or it may be a causal agent, but it is something
to be gotten out of the way as quickly as possible.   The
women fall into two groups--the innocent (though she may be

a showgirl, stripper, or whore) and the older, experienced woman, ready to listen, to give advice to the men around her. The second is typified in later pictures; first, by Moe (Thelma Ritter) in PICKUP ON SOUTH STREET, then by Sandy (Beatrice Kay) in UNDERWORLD, U.S.A. In almost all Fuller's pictures, women are scarce. In THE STEEL HELMET (Lippert, 1951) and FIXED BAYONETS (20th-Fox, 1951) there is not a single woman in either cast.

After their disagreement on editing, Fuller left Lippert to write REARGUARD for Warner Brothers, directed by Dave Butler and released as THE COMMAND in 1953. Fuller returned to Lippert when he signed a deal giving him his first producing credit. Under their agreement, Lippert did not see or read the script for THE STEEL HELMET until the picture was released. Years later, Lippert, who went on to produce more than 300 films, including THE FLY (20th-Fox, 1958), said, "I'm interested in profit, not credit. If a film will bring more without my name on it, my name goes off."

THE STEEL HELMET looked like a low-budget mock-up of what Fuller said he wanted to accomplish in THE BIG RED ONE. The picture was not about war, a noun, he indicated, but about war, a verb, an abstract butcher.

"War is monotonous," he said. "You pee, and you eat, and you look at your weapon, and you march, and you kill, and you eat, and you pee, and you look at your weapon, and you march and you kill. You pull back and while you pull back you kill. You move forward, you kill, and it's dark. Then you might go out on a night patrol. You sleep, and you get up, and it goes on day, after day, after day. It's not really a nightmare, it's not even a group of robots. It's just a wheel. It keeps going around and around." The last title in THE STEEL HELMET is "There is no end to this story."

The picture is slow-moving, almost boring, but it ignites before the story is completed. It may be impossible for Fuller to study the boredom of combat without allowing his picture to succumb to that boredom. Nevertheless, reviews were positive. Variety called Fuller "a complete realist telling it in the grim terms of combat.... Each of the characters comes to life in well-stated writing that smartly avoids the soapbox in dealing with such subjects as Communists, Nisei, Negro, and conscientious objectors...."

The Hollywood Reporter said, "The customary way to appraise outstanding, moderate budget efforts in the independent field is to call them 'sleepers.' THE STEEL HELMET ... is no sleeper. Plainly, it was designed to be sound, intelligent, exciting, and thoughtful screen drama--and it emerges as every one of those things.... The grim pageant of belly warfare is carried out with few compromises."

THE STEEL HELMET, a runaway hit that cleared two million dollars, became a controversial box-office surprise. The excitement was generated by a scene where Gene Evans, as Zack, a helmeted World War II infantry veteran, shoots an unarmed Korean prisoner. "To me," Fuller told Martin Rubin, in The Director's Event, "this was not a shocker. But it was to the press. Tremendous shocker. A lot of editorials. Big full-page interviews asking, 'WOULD YOU SHOOT THIS MAN?' You see, I think it's a little stupid, when you're in war, to hold your fire just because a man puts his hands up. Five minutes before that, he was shooting at you. He runs out of ammunition; he can put his hands up. I mean, there's certainly no law. If there's a law in war, then we're really completely nuts. Now, we're only ninety-nine percent nuts. But if there's a law ... how can there be a law in an illegal act? ... The idea that we have laws and Geneva Conventions and rules and regulations is a cover-up for a lot of stupid things." Though Fuller received cooperation from the Defense Department and he used 150 feet of the Army's film footage for his battle scenes, the department objected to the murder scene and THE STEEL HELMET was not given its seal of approval.

In Iran, THE STEEL HELMET was banned when Communist demonstrations followed its release. In Rome, a theatre owner sent Fuller a bill after Communists pulled the seats out of his theatre during a screening of the film. "You can't please everybody," Fuller said. "I thought I had a pretty good story in THE STEEL HELMET, and I told it, the best I could then, and if people wanted to say, politically, it's this or that, I pay no attention to them, I really don't. They have nothing else to say so they say that.

"I was very fortunate that at least filmmakers--French, English, and Italian--they understood my pictures. I'm talking about men like Jean-Luc Godard. He's so much on the leftie side that if anything, he would smell fascism. On the contrary, he loved my pictures."

The photography and lighting for THE STEEL HELMET
carries the mood of early television. It was shot in ten days
on one sparse set, earning Fuller a reputation for resource-
fulness. For one prop, he painted a tank of cardboard and
supported it with a wooden frame. He shot his action scenes
in half a day when he rented Griffith Park for $125 and used
twenty-five university students as extras.

In the opening shots, Gene Evans, his hands tied behind his back with shoelaces, crawls across a stark Korean
battlefield covered with American bodies. There's a bullet
hole in his helmet and a scar across his forehead where the
bullet grazed him. Evans is the only unlikely survivor left
from his patrol. A Korean boy who rescues him quotes a
familiar Buddhist dictum: "Your heart is in my hands," he
says. "When I save your life, your heart is in my hands...."

After Evans has found another patrol and captured a
North Korean prisoner, the Korean P.O.W. tries to bait the
Americans. He tells Robert Hutton, a black medic, "I can't
understand you. You can't eat with them unless there's a
war." Why, the prisoner asks, do blacks have to sit in the
back of a bus?

"Maybe in fifty years," Hutton says, "I'll sit in the
middle, and someday, in the front. There's some things you
just can't rush."

Next, the prisoner approaches Richard Loo, a Nisei
veteran who handles the patrol's bazooka: "You've got the
same kind of eyes as me," he says.

The tone of THE STEEL HELMET leaps from the anachronistic to the prescient. Much of it, like the dialogue
given Hutton, Loo, and Steve Brodie, looks and sounds like
leftovers from World War II. There was also a look towards
the future, however, towards America's battlefields of the
'sixties and 'seventies, when the oppressive Asian geography
and customs rose to attack American soldiers who felt they
no longer knew what they were fighting for. The men in
Evans' new patrol fight for Korean independence, but none of
them can recognize the South Korean National Anthem. Twenty
years of American involvement in Asia could be summed up
in two scenes, a mixture of awe and destruction. In the first
scene, Driscoll's men take off their helmets in front of a
massive figure of Buddha. In the second, the Americans

leave; the temple is destroyed.   Only the Buddha remains
whole.

There is little romance or heroism in Fuller's vision
of war.   There are no winners in THE STEEL HELMET.
The picture is morally ambivalent; it is almost impossible to
cheer the Americans.   The Communist guerrillas dress as
women; they kill their prisoners and hide behind religious
shrines; but the Americans, too, shoot prisoners.   They are
no better, and no worse, than their opponents.   They are
just tired, bored soldiers.

THE STEEL HELMET made Gene Evans a star.   Before the picture, he had worked as a bouncer, a department
store Santa Claus, and a gas station attendant who slept on
a cot in a washroom.   One year after THE STEEL HELMET,
Evans was making $1,500 a week at Warner Brothers.

"I'd been working a day here and a day there," he
told Hedda Hopper, in 1952, "playing old prospectors and as-
sorted bums.   I had a long red beard and I looked wild, I
guess.   My agent Ernie Ohman read of a story, STEEL HEL-
MET, a fellow name of Sammy Fuller was making, and thought
I'd be good for the part of Sgt. Zack.   So I knocked off from
whatever I was doing--I think I was painting signs just then--
and we went over to his office and found about twenty fellows
sitting around waiting.

"I was nervous and as time went on and on I finally
went over to his receptionist and said, 'Either he sees me
right now or not at all.'   She said, 'But you're not next!'
I nodded and walked right in through the door while she gasped
and tried to stop me.   I came into a room where a lot of men
were sitting around interviewing people.   'I'm next,' I told
them.   I'd been waiting for eleven years and some of those
fellows outside had only been sitting there for an hour or two.

"A little guy with a big cigar sitting behind the desk
looked me over coolly and said, 'What have you got in mind
to play?"

On 11 July 1951, The Hollywood Reporter announced
that THE STEEL HELMET had made its first million dollars.
With the hit under his belt, Fuller signed a seven-year contract at Twentieth Century-Fox as a writer-director.   His
first idea was RED SQUARE, a semi-documentary about twenty-
four hours in the life of one of the guards at Lenin's tomb.

Fuller wanted to get behind the Iron Curtain with actors and
a camera crew. Production head Darryl Zanuck eyed Lippert's receipts and vetoed the idea. He asked Fuller to make
another Korean war picture. The Los Angeles Times called
the result, FIXED BAYONETS, a virtual repeat of THE STEEL
HELMET. That was exactly what Zanuck wanted.

Fuller signed three of his actors from THE STEEL
HELMET, Evans, Richard Monahan, and Neyle Morrow, and
moved his action to the snow-topped mountains of North Korea.
His set cost $143,000, almost $40,000 more than the budget
for THE STEEL HELMET. Evans was still the rugged, World
War II veteran, a member of The Big Red One, who had fought
from Tunisia to Czechoslovakia. His platoon is filled with
Fuller's customary six characters. One man is a Cherokee
Indian, another an Italian, a third a rich playboy. One of
them wants to open up a bowling alley when he gets back home.
All of them are more talkative than the members of THE
STEEL HELMET patrol.

Fuller shot FIXED BAYONETS on the Will Rogers
Memorial sound stage. Before he finished filming, he had
used 18 snow machines and 700 tons of ice to create snow,
and he had shot off 3,000 explosions. The temperature on
the set was kept at 35 degrees.

Captain Raymond Harvey, the picture's technical ad-
visor, said, "Every time I walk onto this set I have to pinch
myself to make certain I'm not imagining things." The real-
life Sergeant Zack, the opposite, according to Fuller, of the
Zack in THE STEEL HELMET, spent his honeymoon visiting
the FIXED BAYONETS set. Fuller's company barber and two
other members of his World War II platoon were also in the
picture. James Dean had a small part; Fuller gave him the
last line of dialogue.

The publicity department painted Fuller as an eccentric
primitive: "He sports a ski cap that he sometimes wears
backwards, a tan sport coat that falls almost to his knees,
black boots, jodhpurs, dark glasses, and a cane.

" 'Some people think I carry this for effect,' he says,
nodding to the cane, 'but I need it. I wrenched a ligament
showing some actors how to fire a bazooka.'

"Fuller keeps a .45 in a holster, strapped to his waist.
When he wants his actors to start a scene for FIXED BAYO-
NETS, he fires the .45.

" 'I don't like to shout,' he says, shouting, 'and I want
them ready to go.   When they hear a shot, I get a reaction.
I like reactions.'"

Another release counted nineteen casualties on Fuller's
set, a number accounting for "more injuries than were ever
brought in from the fire scenes for IN OLD CHICAGO [20th-
Fox, 1938], the simoon for SUEZ [20th-Fox, 1938], or the
cattle stampede for THE BIG TRAIL [Fox, 1930].   Gene Evans
suffered a burned hand.   Others had smashed kneecaps, broken
legs, and bayoneted feet."   When the picture was finished,
Twentieth Century-Fox sent the actors Purple Hearts.

"The gun was used for cueing," Fuller said.   "I had
the unfortunate experience where the walky talkies didn't work.
Nobody heard me so I'd shoot a gun--one shot, two shots, or
three, for signals.   Everything worked perfectly.   The gun is
the best cue for action.   There's no argument that you didn't
hear it, and it gets you in the mood.

"And I have never had a casualty.   One stunt man hurt
his leg jumping over a log after I told him to be careful.   Since
he was limping, instead of taking him off the payroll, which is
the normal thing, I said, 'Let's use him as a casualty.'   The
other stunt men said, 'Hey!   What the heck!   He's not working,
and he's getting paid.   We want to be casualties.'   The publicity
man thought it was a funny story.

"After the set was built," Fuller went on, "I mapped
out the action.   I wrote the script to fit the set, just as
though I were commanding a platoon in Korea and I found
myself in this mountain pass, and I had the job of figuring
out how I could hold off the Reds for eighteen hours."

Though Lucien Ballard's photography remains black,
white, and claustrophobic, FIXED BAYONETS is a much more
fluid, accessible picture than THE STEEL HELMET.   In
FIXED BAYONETS, Fuller is concerned with the ability to command men--of what it takes to lead a platoon of infantry soldiers.
You've got to have guts to lead," Evans says, "and it takes
brains to be a leader."   Corporal Denno (Richard Basehart),
fourth in the line of command, is a pack of neuroses who can't
stomach leadership.   He can't even shoot at the Koreans.

"I can take an order," he says, "I can't give one.
Some men are afraid of heights, other men are afraid of
water, and some men are afraid of being responsible for

other guys. That's me. I don't want to carry that load. I'll
do my job; I just don't want to lead, that's all. "

Denno's fear leads him to perform a desperate act,
courageous, and nearly suicidal, when he carries a dying man
through a mine field. By the time he reaches safety, the man
is dead.

George Jessel emceed a première held at Graumann's
Chinese Theatre on 5 December, 1951. A parade of military
units and a thirty-piece Army band joined the nightly Santa
Claus parade down Hollywood Boulevard. Jessel's remarks
were broadcast live over the Armed Forces Radio Service.

In 1952, Fuller's fifth picture, PARK ROW (United
Artists, 1952), also premièred at Graumann's. Once again,
Gene Evans starred. Fuller had dreamt of making a newspaper picture for some time. He produced the picture, mort-
gaging his house to raise money. A low-budget production,
it was also a flop. In 1969, Fuller said, "That picture still
hasn't paid for itself. "

"Zanuck liked the idea, " Fuller added, "and he wanted
me to have a big name actor in it, and he said, 'We'll change
the title and give you color. We made a very big picture
here called IN OLD CHICAGO and we can call this one IN
OLD NEW YORK. ' He wanted to make a musical with Gregory Peck, Susan Hayward, Dan Dailey, and Mitzi Gaynor.
A big color extravaganza. I can see his point. You have a
big musical number with a woman dressed as the Statue of
Liberty, singing 'I haven't got a leg to stand on, ' while they're
trying to get a pedestal for the statue. "

It's difficult to imagine Fuller directing a musical.
His version of Park Row, like those of the American West
and the Korean War, is a strict, male domain. Charity
Hackett (Mary Welch), Evans' rival publisher, acts more like
a love-struck teenager than a hard-nosed publisher.

It was not until PICKUP ON SOUTH STREET, a picture
where Fuller learned to pick pockets, that he became known
for violent movie-making. While he prepared it, he was briefly
slated to direct TWENTY THOUSAND LEAGUES UNDER THE
SEA (Buena Vista, 1954) at the Disney studios. Until it fell
through, the Disney assignment was as unlikely as a musical
version of PARK ROW.

PICKUP ON SOUTH STREET was set in New York but was shot in Los Angeles in twenty days. Newsweek called it a "slapdash of sex and sadism." The Saturday Review said, "lurid is probably the best word for it." The New Yorker called it "shoddy."

Samuel Fuller directing a scene from PICKUP ON SOUTH STREET (20th-Fox, 1953). Photo courtesy of David Wilson and Samuel Fuller.

According to Time, "PICKUP ON SOUTH STREET is a ninety-minute muscle-flexing exercise in violence. A pickpocket slaps a former roadhouse entertainer in the teeth, knocks her out with a right to the jaw, and revives her by pouring a bottle of beer in her face. The B-girl retaliates by conking him over the head with another beer bottle. A Communist spy beats up and shoots the girl, hits a cop over the head with a pistol, and kills an eccentric old necktie peddler. The pickpocket knocks out the spy by smashing his

head against a wall, slugs it out with him on a subway platform and on the tracks in front of an oncoming train."

Despite the negative reviews, PICKUP, completed on
16 October 1952, remains one of Fuller's best pictures.
The violence, which overwhelmed 1952 reviewers, is no longer
a shocking distraction. PICKUP ON SOUTH STREET was the
only Hollywood film to receive an award at the 1953 Venice
Film Festival. When it was released in France, it was dubbed
with new dialogue, changing Fuller's cold-war dialogue about
Red spying to a plot about drug smuggling.

According to Fuller, "The only reason I put Communism in--well, naturally, he's going to steal something out of
a purse. If it has microfilm, it's got to have information.
All right? So it becomes a reactionary picture. Everybody
said, 'Oh, my, this is a political picture, an editorial on
film.' I don't care about that. Listen, if I wanted to make
a picture about a young fella who loves to eat glass ashtrays,
it wouldn't surprise me if people said that's me, that I like
to eat glass ashtrays, and that's why I made it. I'm just
trying to show the stupidity of that critical approach."

Though Fuller's crime pictures are often placed within
the tradition of film noir, it is most probably because of elements of shading and setting, results of the lighting and camera movements. In Film Comment, the screenwriter Paul
Schrader wrote that film noir is "not defined ... by conventions of setting and conflict, but rather by the more subtle
qualities of tone and mood." Schrader named PICKUP ON
SOUTH STREET as a transitional film. Waterfront scenes
in front of Widmark's shack, he maintained, were in the noir
tradition, but the subway fight places Fuller within the crime
school of picture making in the middle and late 'fifties.

After PICKUP ON SOUTH STREET, the American Legion gave Fuller a plaque for his "fight against Communism."
The plot of spies and American subversives must have pleased
the paranoid group. Fuller received a screenplay credit when
PICKUP was remade in 1968 as THE CAPE TOWN AFFAIR.

HELL AND HIGH WATER (20th-Fox, 1954) must have
also pleased the American Legion. Fuller changed into a
Navy cap during the eighty-one-day shooting schedule. It was
a second cold war epic about a devious Soviet plot against the
U.S. It featured both of Fuller's noncommittal patriots, Richard Widmark and Gene Evans, as well as the newcomers Bella

Darvi and Victor Francen. It reunited Fuller with Johnson, the man in the publicity department who had scored the injuries in FIXED BAYONETS.

Miss Darvi, Johnson wrote in a release, was the sixth victim of injuries on Fuller's "jinx submarine" set at the studios.

"She received a slight concussion, lacerated tongue and scalp, when knocked to the deck by Richard Widmark.

"Miss Darvi, a survivor of World War II Nazi concentration camps, was treated on the set and returned afterwards.

" 'On this set, I've taken the worst physical beating of my life,' she said. 'In Hollywood, though, the food is better than in the Nazi camps.'

"Other victims: Actor Gene Evans, split a lip and cracked teeth, jumping through a hatch; David Wayne, sprained knee; Tommy Walker, cut eyebrow; Cameron Mitchell, cut cheek in a fight scene, and Widmark, cut on the palm of one hand leaping from a ladder." Later, according to a release, Darvi bit Widmark and the actor required a tetanus shot. Richard Loo and Neyle Morrow were uninjured members of the cast.

"Director Samuel Fuller has set out to prove that Twentieth Century-Fox' panoramic Cinemascope is also the most intimate of mediums," Johnson wrote. "For producer Raymond Klune's HELL AND HIGH WATER, he's taking the scopeful Technicolor camera into a cave, onto a life raft, down the sub's hatch, up its periscope and will feature close-ups of Bella Darvi's right eye, Richard Widmark's mouth, and Cameron Mitchell's tattooed chest." Joe MacDonald juggled the camera throughout this rigorous tour.

When the picture was released, the robust camera movements were noted, the potentials of Cinemascope applauded, but neither a close-up of Darvi's eye nor one of Cameron Mitchell's chest impressed the critics.

Time magazine called HELL AND HIGH WATER "a 'B' picture in Cinemascope. And worse luck, it is as long (103 minutes) as it is broad."

Bosley Crowther, the senior reviewer for the New York Times, called it "a monolith of the absurd."

HOUSE OF BAMBOO (20th-Fox, 1955), Fuller's first
picture made on location, was also the first American film
shot in Japan. Producers and directors who followed Fuller
into that country had to explain to the bewildered Japanese
that not all American directors wore helmets and shot revolv-
ers while they worked. After its release, Tokyo's largest
evening newspaper claimed that HOUSE OF BAMBOO "offen-
sively misrepresents Japan and Japanese."

Though the Japanese objections may have been valid,
they were hardly relevant to a story which really had very
little to do with their country. The leading characters were
all Caucasians, and the Japanese characters were no more
nor less typical of the Japanese than the Americans in THE
STEEL HELMET and FIXED BAYONETS were typical of
Americans.

"After the war," Fuller said, "I tried to sell Metro
a story about a group of men who were in the same platoon,
and when the war is over, they form a combination of criminals. They take Fort Knox, using the same military man-
euver with which they knocked out a pillbox on Omaha Beach.
The studio didn't buy it. So when I was asked to do BAM-
BOO, I figured I'd use that situation."

Robert Ryan plays the boss of the crime organization.
Robert Stack is an undercover agent from California who in-
filtrates the group. Like Jesse James' rescue of Ford in I
SHOT JESSE JAMES, Ryan saves Stack during a heist. Instead of suspecting Stack as a double agent, Ryan kills Cameron Mitchell. Ryan is killed during a chase in an amusement
park after he shoots into a crowd of women and children.

Again, MacDonald received praise for his photography.
The story, Saturday Review said, was "routine cops and robbers." Fuller cast himself as a Japanese policeman.

RUN OF THE ARROW, the first picture to be released
under Fuller's Globe Enterprises imprint, was produced by
R. K. O. in 1957 and released by Universal. It starred Rod
Steiger, Ralph Meeker, Jay C. Flippen, Charles Bronson,
Olive Carey, Neyle Morrow, and Colonel Tim McCoy. Joseph
Biroc worked as director of photography. Gene Fowler, Jr.,
was the film editor.

The original title for the picture, THE LAST BULLET,
was scrapped when Fuller decided it made his picture sound
too much like a typical 1957 Western. Despite this, the

bullet, the last shot fired during the Civil War, remains a
character as important as the helmet worn by Gene Evans in
THE STEEL HELMET.

Steiger and Meeker, appearing as Confederate and
Union soldiers, must be the most slovenly men on either side.
Steiger shoots Meeker, he steals his cigar butt, and hauls him
into a Confederate camp. The war is over and Meeker is the
last casualty. The bullet is pried from his body, inscribed,
and primed to shoot again. Steiger wears it like a pendant
around his neck.

Fuller shot RUN OF THE ARROW at a fort he built
twenty miles outside the city of St. George, Utah, in the
desert where Raoul Walsh was shooting THE KING AND FOUR
QUEENS (United Artists, 1957), with Clark Gable. The directors divided the desert into two to keep out of one another's
set ups. In the last scenes of RUN OF THE ARROW, the fort
is set afire by 150 Indians recruited from the Arizona Navajo
reservation.

The story is a marriage of realism and pulp. Steiger
is dirty and fat; a makeshift operating table is covered with
gore. Fuller tries to underline his dramatic scenes by adding eight or ten eavesdropping extras.

RUN OF THE ARROW showed the Indians in a sympathetic light. Fuller said he merely wanted to show that the
Indian's society was similar to white society. The scenes of
the battle and the renegades were standard fare, but the idyllic scenes in the Indian village were closer to a new kind of
Western pioneered by Delmer Daves in BROKEN ARROW (20th-
Fox, 1950). RUN OF THE ARROW allowed its Indians to win
their battle against the whites. Reviewers praised its photography, music, and story; it is the best of Fuller's Westerns.
His discussions about religion and national identity are easily
worked into the narrative. They never become as obtrusive
as they were, at times, in THE STEEL HELMET. Here,
also, a song is included. A banjo player in a wagon is driven
along a country road. Despite the pretensions of its closing
title (The End of This Story Can Only Be Written by You),
RUN OF THE ARROW contains a lyricism that seldom reappears in the blunter, compacted films which followed it. It
would take Fuller five more pictures, until UNDERWORLD,
U.S.A., before he would produce another major work.

Fuller saw his first issue of Cahiers du Cinéma when

Victor Francen sent him a copy with an article on his pictures.   The writer suggested that Fuller might have a foot
fetish.   Fuller stopped at a hospital supplies store on Sunset
Boulevard where a large model of a foot was used in the
store's advertising display.   He bought the foot and sent it to
the Cahiers critic.   "That was an interesting magazine," Fuller said.   "They thought everything was a fetish.   They loved
to write about things like that."

        Following RUN OF THE ARROW, Fuller returned to
finish his last two pictures with Twentieth Century-Fox.   The
first was CHINA GATE (20th-Fox, 1957), which was shot at
the Pathé lot, on the set William Wellman had built for THE
STORY OF G.I. JOE (United Artists, 1945).   CHINA GATE
was a scoop, showing mercenaries in French Indochina almost
a dozen years before John Wayne appeared in THE GREEN
BERETS (Warner's, 1968), the best known and most popular
picture from the Vietnam War.   Like the earlier Fox pictures,
CHINA GATE is steadfastly anti-Commie.   Indochina is en-
visioned as a pivotal battlefield in the war between Communism and the Western world.   Brainwashing is only one of the
threats with which Fuller's characters are concerned, and
"Better dead than Red" is their sentiment.   According to Fuller, he had an opportunity to make CHINA GATE in color,
but he chose black and white, a decision he later regretted.

        FORTY GUNS (20th-Fox, 1957), Fuller's last Western,
completed his contractual obligations to Twentieth Century-Fox.
The incidents in FORTY GUNS are almost as excessive as
those in CHINA GATE; his metaphors boil over with a cyclone
engineered by the special effects pro Bill Abbott.   "Sometimes," The Hollywood Reporter began its review, "it seems
Samuel Fuller goes about creating movies by thinking up striking scenes and then working out a plot to string them together."

        "On the level of plot," Phil Hardy concluded in Samuel
Fuller (Praeger, 1970), "the film becomes almost incomprehensible."

        FORTY GUNS, like THE MAVERICK QUEEN (Republic,
1946), starred Barbara Stanwyck and Barry Sullivan as an
attractive, rough-hewn romantic team.   In each of the pictures, Stanwyck shines above the dingy surroundings of her
"B" picture co-stars and scripts.   She won FORTY GUNS'
best notices for her efforts.

        Unlike Rod Steiger and Ralph Meeker in RUN OF THE

ARROW, the Westerners in this sexy 1957 release are obsessively clean.   The Bunnell brothers, who seem to be loosely
patterned after the Earps, spend almost a third of their time
in one or another tub at the community baths.   There is a
singing cowboy in this Western, and a title tune, "Woman
With a Whip."

Sullivan and Stanwyck, an impressive horsewoman
dressed in black, are characterized as irresistible forces.
Stanwyck leads her forty hired gunmen past a wagon which
carries Griff Bonnell (Sullivan) and his two brothers, Wes
and Chico (Gene Barry, Robert Dix), into town.   The wind
from the forty-one horses kicks up so much dust that the
Bonnells hit the tubs for their first bath as soon as they
reach town.

FORTY GUNS is filled with an impressive number of
details and plot twists.   Many of them are sudden.   The
camera flips from a third person viewpoint to the very fuzzy
point of view of a blind sheriff.   It hangs from a boom above
the Bonnell's wagon, then falls below it; it pans up and across
the back of the wagon.

Griff Bonnell, a U.S. Marshal, who says he never
misses, shoots Stanwyck when her murderous brother tries
to use her as a shield.   She lives, and in the last moments
of FORTY GUNS, joins him when he leaves the town on his
buckboard.

"I couldn't use my original ending," Fuller said.   "The
ending I originally shot was a powerful ending.   I had Sullivan
facing the killer, and Sullivan kills Stanwyck.   Then he kills
the boy and walks away.   That was the end.

"It's a rough ending.   I've seen so many pictures,
from HIGH NOON [United Artist, 1952] back, where the heavy
grabs the girl and holds her in front of him, putting the hero
in a hell of an embarrassing situation.   Always, at the last
minute, she pushes him away, and the hero kills him.   I
didn't like that in any Western.   It doesn't make sense.
That's why I wanted Sullivan not only to shoot Stanwyck, but
to kill her."

VERBOTEN (Columbia, 1958), Fuller's twelfth picture,
was a 1958 release set in Germany.   VERBOTEN was a hit
with Munich audiences, but was banned in Israel, where a
censor said: "Its contents are liable to hurt the feelings of

the public." Fuller's Globe Enterprises owned 75% of the picture, which was also the last film made by RKO Pictures. By the time it was completed, RKO had given up its distribution network and Columbia handled the domestic release; M-G-M distributed VERBOTEN overseas.

Fuller mixed newsreel footage with sequences shot in Hollywood to tell the story of the German "werewolves," delinquents who had been members of the Hitler Youth organization before the Allied Occupation. James Best played a soldier who served in the First Infantry Division. Fuller indulged in at least one of his passions in VERBOTEN when he added Beethoven and Wagner to the score by Harry Sukman.

THE CRIMSON KIMONA (Columbia, 1959), Fuller's first Columbia production, may be his most confusing picture. According to The Hollywood Reporter, with a tongue not at all in cheek, "Artistically, its total is not quite equal to the sum of its parts.... Fuller, with his many talents, has not yet learned to pre-edit his script on paper with the skill of Otto Preminger. Some of the points get lost...."

Variety said: "Fuller has some brilliant picture-making touches in THE CRIMSON KIMONA, and some counterbalancing moments of extreme naiveté." The detective story reminded the Los Angeles Mirror of the Dragnet TV series produced by Jack Webb.

On the other hand, THE CRIMSON KIMONA also became one of Fuller's most highly praised pictures. "In the crewcuts that abound in Little Tokyo," Phil Hardy wrote in Samuel Fuller, "the Japanese nun, the white women making Japanese dolls and the white policeman playing Kendo, Fuller gives visual evidence of the complex cultural mixture that is evolving. The communities are growing together of their own accord--with beneficial results, Fuller suggests, for Los Angeles and the whole of America.... Only Fuller could see a new striptease act as an example of crosscultural pollination."

Yet, Fuller's grasp is too wide in THE CRIMSON KIMONA: he attempts to tell two stories in a space that could cramp one. He has two deaths, two or three love affairs, an attempted murder, and several fist fights. There isn't enough room for the subtleties which Hardy projects into it. Again, it appears to be a case where one of Fuller's admirers has attempted to elevate his quirky, matter-of-fact filmmaking into coherent, ideological polemics.

In February, 1959, while he prepared his next picture, UNDERWORLD, U.S.A., Fuller said: "We're making better films today than at any other period in history. Twenty years from today, we'll all be talking about today as 'the good old days.'"

Fuller was forced to rewrite the script for UNDER-WORLD after the Chief of the MPAA Production Code said the first draft would be ineligible for the Code's Seal of Approval. The original script detailed the alleged methods used by gangland czars in recruiting prostitutes and it included a blow by blow description of narcotics traffic. The revised picture was released with a Columbia Pictures trailer where Fuller explained his reasons for writing the story, how he dug up and documented the facts, and how he wrote the script. The filmed interview was followed by scenes from UNDER-WORLD, U.S.A.

Variety called the picture "a slick gangster melodrama made to order for filmgoers who prefer their screen fare explosive and uncomplicated."

Fuller's instincts lean towards the scoop. If his perceptions are not as insightful as those of other newsmen (or writers, or directors), at least he was there first. He was proud that CHINA GATE included some of the first notices of Ho Chi Minh; that THE STEEL HELMET and FIXED BAYONETS were the first pictures set during the Korean War; that in 1957, RUN OF THE ARROW was truly a revolutionary Western. In 1977, Fuller claimed that THE BIG RED ONE would show elements of World War II which have never before been filmed. Being first, however, has not always meant the deepest or most accurate reportage. It also sets the perceptions into a fixed point in time, however accurate they may be at that moment.

An overly intellectual approach to Fuller's pictures conceals their pleasures. Their best moments occur not, as the Europeans might claim, in their analysis of American culture, but in the stylistic oddities he uses to underscore his themes. The search should not be for the subtle point in Fuller's work, but for the broadest, wildest, most exaggerated metaphor. That is where Fuller's greatest talent appears to lie.

After UNDERWORLD, U.S.A., Fuller made MERRILL'S MARAUDERS (Warner's, 1962), starring Jeff Chandler, Ty

Hardin, Peter Brown, and Claude Akins. Fuller said he
made the picture with the "discards" from THE BIG RED
ONE. The story is set during World War II, but the setting
is still in Asia; this time, the enemies are the Japanese in
Burma. The events in the picture are organized around a
march to Myitkyina, in Northern Burma. It was not as
tightly constructed as Fuller's previous battle films, nor was
it released to the same information-starved audiences. The
soldiers are still as ragged as those in THE STEEL HELMET,
the battles are even more lethal. Fuller directed the close,
man-to-man fighting with the experience he acquired in Germany during World War II.

The chief asset of MERRILL'S MARAUDERS is the
photography staged by William Clothier. A night battle,
where the actors are silhouetted against a backdrop of explosions, is its most memorable scene.

After MERRILL'S MARAUDERS, Fuller's deals began
to fall apart. He filled part of his time by directing an episode of the television series The Virginian for producer
Charles Marquis Warren. When Warren became executive
producer of Iron Horse, a series starring Dale Robertson,
Fuller directed five episodes. He declined the offer when
he was asked to become the series' regular director.

Fuller's critical recognition arrived around the time
that SHOCK CORRIDOR (1963) and THE NAKED KISS (1965)
were released by Allied Artists, a company which released
many low-budget prison and crime pictures during the 'fifties
and 'sixties. In 1959, Jean-Luc Godard had dedicated BREATH-
LESS to Monogram Pictures, an Allied Artists subsidiary.

SHOCK CORRIDOR is Fuller's most offbeat picture.
He'd planned on making a picture set in a mental institution
ever since he wrote a story titled Lunatic in 1946. Douglas
Sirk directed SHOCKPROOF from a Fuller story in 1948, and
Fuller planned on setting a battle inside a mental institution
in THE BIG RED ONE. In Sam Fuller (1969), the book produced by the Edinburgh Film Festival, Thomas Elsaesser
calls SHOCK CORRIDOR "Fuller's testament film ... his own
comment on his previous work."

Another opinion appeared in Film Quarterly: "In one
of the most preposterous and tasteless films of all time, a
newspaper reporter who desperately wants to win a Pulitzer
Prize has himself incarcerated in a mental institution, in the

Samuel Fuller shooting gun for a cue to action on SHOCK
CORRIDOR (Allied Artists, 1963).   Photo courtesy of David
Wilson and Samuel Fuller.

guise of a sexual deviate, with the intention of solving a murder committed there.... I am reasonably sure that we will
soon find Fuller's latest effort hailed by the Cahier/Movie
crowd, as 'Fuller's testament' or 'A Masterpiece--sympto-
matic of our age.' The film is, in fact, a cheap, nasty,
lurid melodrama with artistic pretensions, viz., hallucinatory
color shots of the Orient and Africa cut into the monochrome
print, a sententious quote from Euripides, and forced reminders of social responsibilities."

The wild, disturbing elements from SHOCK CORRIDOR
continued through THE NAKED KISS, which featured pederasty
and murder, with Constance Towers as a bald-headed prostitute who beats her pimp, then beats her well-to-do fiancé to
death with a telephone receiver. The picture was well described by the kind of shorthand that Variety uses to sum up
motion pictures: "Good Sam Fuller programmer about a
prostie trying the straight route.... Hooker angle and sex
perversion plot windup are handled with care alternating with
handicapped children 'good works' theme."

True to Fuller's code of conduct, the hooker goes
back to prostitution at the end of this picture.

Fuller's next picture was released two years later,
in 1967. The American-Mexican production which became
SHARK had been through many production changes before
Fuller began to work on it. Several writers, including Ken
Hughes and John Kingsbridge, were reported to be working
on a project that in 1966 was scheduled as TWIST OF THE
KNIFE, starring Dan Duryea, George Montgomery, and Curt
Jurgens. Byron Haskin was going to direct it. Fuller com-
pletely rewrote and recast the picture for Burt Reynolds,
Barry Sullivan, Arthur Kennedy, and Silvia Pinal before he
shot it in Mexico.

After a stunt man was injured during a fight against
a tiger shark the picture was dedicated to its stunt men. The
fight, and the success of Jaws (Doubleday, 1974), by Peter
Benchley, persuaded Fuller's American producer to change
the name of the picture from CAINE to SHARK. The picture
only received minor box-office attention until it was re-released
as MANEATER in 1975, and the picture cleared two million.
The newspaper advertisements for MANEATER claimed that
a man was actually killed during the shark fight. After the
re-release, Skip Steloff, one of the producers, called it "one
of the worst movies ever made."

CAINE was to be the first in a four-picture deal Fuller made with the production company, Heritage/Calderon. After the shooting, the picture was recut against Fuller's wishes. He asked that his name be removed from the credits. His script for a sequel, CAINE'S MEN, was never made and the director and production company parted on unfriendly terms.

The creaking, sunken treasure plot is enlivened by Fuller's treatment. Burt Reynolds plays Caine, a gunrunner in the Sudanese Desert. He escapes a patrol by tossing a stick of dynamite in front of a police jeep. Moments later, his car hits a rock and his brakes go out. He leaps from the truck before it rolls down a cliff and blows up. Reynolds is alone in a suddenly still and quiet desert. He stops a car and rides into a town where the only taxi has to be pushed. The razor in his hotel room is eighty-two years old.

Fuller had recently married Christa Lang. "The picture was a honeymoon," he said. "They said, 'Come on down to Mexico and do the goddamned thing,' and I did it. I wrote the story at the producer's home, every day, every night. I broke my ass on it.

"To give you an example of why I got angry with the editing, there's the scene where I have Reynolds in the truck. You didn't see the scene I shot. He jumps out, he tumbles down a very big hill and into the camera. Then he gets up, he looks around, and the truck is still going. It comes off the top of a mountain and explodes. That took a lot of time to rehearse. What I shot was one shot, one take. We had two trucks--everything had to be cued. I caught it just in time as it fell off the road. Do you see the difference? They had a lot of little cuts in it.

"Then there was the surgery of the kid on a barroom counter. I had one shot of the people watching the operation to show that they were in the room and I told the rest of the operation through the fans. A fan began to creak, then finally, it stopped. That was the boy's heart. Then it started to move, and to move and move. When they recut it they kept going back to the people. It may be unimportant to you, but it was important to me. That's why I spent so much time on that damn fan. I kept working on it, an hour or an hour and a half, to get that damn fan going the right way.

"There were other things. I staged a fight between Burt and three stunt men so it would take four seconds on

the screen. The first second is when he's confronted by them.
In the second second, he hits the first man, jumps the second,
and hits the third man. That's four seconds, and the fight is
over. Whew! Well, I had two cameras there, and they kept
intercutting them because they wanted to lengthen it."

Despite Fuller's disavowal, SHARK is easily identified
by his trademarks. When a diver is killed by a shark, Silvia
Pinal, one of his employers, gives the boy's mother some
money. The woman gives Pinal a crafty look; she wets her
thumb and begins to count the money.

Reynolds, like Widmark in PICKUP ON SOUTH STREET,
is an energetic con man; he is prone to fights and leaps into
boxes of vegetables. "Don't steal anything when anybody's
looking," he tells a boy. "Don't try to con a con artist."
"The last time a lady bought me a drink," he tells Pinal,
"she was no lady."

The rest of the characters in SHARK are equally un-
savory; they smoke thick cigars, they have bulging eyes and
bulging bellies. Pinal's hair is nearly white and she has dark
circles of make-up under each eye; Reynolds knocks her out
twice. In a barroom, Fuller pans from corrupt sheriff to
drunken doctor to the head of the city's rackets, as if they
were all suspects in an old stage melodrama. "I'm no informer," the doctor says, "I'm a physician. I'm a diagnos-
tician."

It was not until 1973, six years later, that Fuller completed another feature. DEAD PIGEON ON BEETHOVEN
STREET, a West German film produced in the English language, is surrounded by an atmosphere of déjà vu. We have
seen it before; its pacing almost parallels that of THE CRIM-
SON KIMONA. This time, the picture substitutes self-conscious humor for self-conscious polemics, and this time international statesmen are played as broadly as the villains in
UNDERWORLD, U.S.A. The move to a German production
was fortuitous. In the U.S., the mindless action of American-
International productions had taken over the low-budget category of filmmaking. Fuller's stories of crime, Communism,
and prostitutes had been overtaken by Hell's Angels, surfers,
and drugs. His brand of crime and Westerns were found on
television, but they only occasionally appeared in features.

Fuller was sixty-two years old when he made DEAD
PIGEON, and he had, it appears, learned to laugh over the

Samuel Fuller filming footage in 16mm on the set of DEAD
PIGEON ON BEETHOVEN STREET (Emerson, 1974).   Photo
courtesy of David Wilson and Samuel Fuller.

Fuller legacy as it was described in books and magazines.
He did his best to make it a "Fuller" picture.
Fuller, his
editors, his photographers, and many members of the rest
of his crew were pictured in the opening and closing credits;
many of them were dressed as the participants in a rowdy
parade. Fuller even played a part. He sat in a large office
chair, his body hidden, but an arm and a cigar poking out
from a cloud of cigar smoke.

V

        Christa was out on a drive with the baby. It was a
week before Christmas, 1977, and Samuel Fuller was hoping
for snow. There were only two sounds in his office; one was
his voice and the other was the snap from a match in his
hand.

        "I've got a lot of yarns," he said, "a lot of yarns.
I write. It's the only hobby I have. I love to top myself.
In other words, I love to give you a situation you can't get
out of, and then get you out of it."

        Fuller held out a notebook and a page typed with lists
of uniforms and rifles. A cigar between his lips, an infantry
helmet perched on a rifle beside his chair, he looked like an
Army Quartermaster in civies. The lists were for THE BIG
RED ONE.

        "It's my fault for the delay," he said. "I'm entirely
to blame. I stalled and stalled and stalled until I started to
fool around with the idea for the book. I wrote thirty or
forty pages, then I got into a picture, then another picture,
and it went on year after year. I knew I'd eventually finish
it.

        "THE BIG RED ONE won't be a typical war movie.
There won't be ten thousand tanks and five thousand planes
in it, with thousands of men charging after a hero. What Lee
Marvin and his squad will do has never been shown. This
story is about death and it's death done with a lot of humor.
In war, if you don't have that humor, you go crazy. You go
absolutely insane.

        "War is impossible to describe, as impossible to de-
scribe as it is to describe death. Saying that war is hell is
like jumping from a thirty-story building and saying it's dan-

96 The Contemporary Director

gerous. You can't make a real war picture because the audience can get up and buy popcorn at any time during the battle. They're never hurt. I feel strongly about this even though it sounds absurd. If we could have weapons behind the screen, and if, when the picture starts, once in a while, someone in the audience was hit, that would give the audience a feeling for the tension of a war. Naturally, you're not going to get anybody to come to the second performance.

"The closest we can get to a real war picture is to tell the small world of a squad, of Lee Marvin and four young men and three years of war. This is fictional life, based on factual death. That's the whole theme."

Fuller was not to officially begin production until June, 1978, but he planned to shoot his first scenes near Los Angeles within the next three or four weeks, as soon as snow appeared. He wanted to take advantage of the snow for a brief shot with Lee Marvin, Germans, and a tank. He was going to shoot the rest of the picture in Israel and Yugoslavia. While he was waiting, he was also working on a new script, a comedy.

"I've got a plan," he said. "I've got several scripts that I can't direct. I'd like to direct them, but I can't. I'm not going to be around that long. I have three that I want to shoot, and three or four that I'd like to unload. It will be interesting to see what other directors do with these scripts."

In October, when Peter Bogdanovich started to prepare his own picture in Singapore, Gene Corman replaced him as producer on THE BIG RED ONE. Corman was now in Yugoslavia where he was finalizing the agreements for shooting.

"I found a place in Tel-Aviv," Fuller said, "where I'm going to shoot a sequence for right after the invasion of Germany. You see, I'm shooting, in Israel, a sequence about the invasion of Nazi-land. The Israelis can't believe it.

"Six or seven months ago," he said, "I went to North Africa. It's all changed since the war. In Italy, I couldn't find what I wanted and at Omaha Beach, there's a momument and a cemetery. I'm going to film in Israel, where there are wonderful, desolate arid areas around the Dead Sea and the Jordanian border, without aerials or telephone poles. In Israel, the roads leading to desolate areas are perfect. That's number one. Number two, the flavor is right.

"It's almost physically impossible to get where I'd
really like to shoot. Even though we were there during the
war, you've got to remember that a lot of that equipment
never came back. This is not a war, only a motion picture."

Fuller tried to explain his work: "I've seen wonderful
pictures recently, comedies and dramas with nice boys and
nice girls and their problems. That's fine, but I can't get
into that kind of picture. I tried, but I want something that's
exciting. Why do we always have to have a nice boy, and the
heavy has to be a bad boy. I don't understand that, I never
will. It's not exciting to me if the man says to the girl,
'Look, I'll meet you in the corner drugstore at five o'clock.'
I wouldn't write that ... not unless I knew ... when the girl
walks into the corner drugstore, she's going to have her head
blown off.

"I think everything has worked out great for me. Forget whether I've made one or ten or twenty pictures. Now
that this big hump is over, the writing of THE BIG RED ONE,
I've got so many damn stories I want to tell. I'm just starting."

SAM FULLER

A Film Checklist by Vicki Piekarski

Director

1.   I SHOT JESSE JAMES (1949). P: Screen Guild. C:
      John Ireland, Preston Foster, Barbara Britton. 81m.

2.   THE BARON OF ARIZONA (1950). P: Lippert. C:
      Vincent Price, Ellen Drew, Beulah Bondi. 93m.

3.   THE STEEL HELMET (1950). P: Lippert. C: Gene
      Evans, Robert Hutton, Richard Loo. 84m.

4.   FIXED BAYONETS (1951). P: Twentieth Century-Fox.
      C: Richard Basehart, Gene Evans, Michael O'Shea.
      92m.

5.   PARK ROW (1952). P: United Artists. C: Gene
      Evans, Mary Welch, Bela Kovacs. 83m.

6.   PICKUP ON SOUTH STREET (1953). P: Twentieth
     Century-Fox. C: Richard Widmark, Jean Peters,
     Thelma Ritter. 80m.

7.   HELL AND HIGH WATER (1953). P: Twentieth Cen-
     tury-Fox. C: Richard Widmark, Bella Darvi, Victor
     Francen. Technicolor. 103m.

8.   HOUSE OF BAMBOO (1955). P: Twentieth Century-
     Fox. C: Robert Ryan, Robert Stack, Shirley Yama-
     guchi. Technicolor. 102m.

9.   RUN OF THE ARROW (1956). P: RKO-Universal.
     C: Rod Steiger, Sarita Montiel, Brian Keith. Tech-
     nicolor. 85m.

10. CHINA GATE (1957). P: Twentieth Century-Fox. C:
     Gene Barry, Angie Dickinson, Nat "King" Cole. 97m.

11. FORTY GUNS (1957). P: Twentieth Century-Fox.
     C: Barbara Stanwyck, Barry Sullivan, Dean Jagger.
     80m.

12. VERBOTEN! (1958). P: Columbia. C: James Best,
     Susan Cummings, Tom Pittman. 94m.

13. THE CRIMSON KIMONA (1959). P: Columbia. C:
     James Shigeta, Glenn Corbett, Victoria Shaw. 82m.

14. UNDERWORLD, U.S.A. (1961). P: Columbia. C:
     Cliff Robertson, Beatrice Kay, Larry Gates. 99m.

✓15. MERRILL'S MARAUDERS (1962). P: Warner's. C:
     Jeff Chandler, Ty Hardin, Peter Brown. Technicolor.
     98m.

16. SHOCK CORRIDOR (1963). P: Allied Artists. C:
     Peter Breck, Constance Towers, Gene Evans. 101m.

17. THE NAKED KISS (1964). P: Allied Artists. C:
     Constance Towers, Anthony Eisley, Michael Dante. 93m.

✓18. SHARK (1971). P: Excelsior. C: Burt Reynolds,
     Barry Sullivan, Arthur Kennedy. Color. 92m.

19. DEAD PIGEON ON BEETHOVEN STREET (1974). P:
     Emerson. C: Glenn Corbett, Christa Lang, Sieghardt
     Rupp. Eastmancolor. 102m.

Chapter 3

SAM PECKINPAH

by Jon Tuska

I

There was a time, after the trouble on MAJOR DUN-
DEE (Columbia, 1965), that Sam Peckinpah took to imparting
his directions to players or technical crew in a soft, almost
ominous voice. Working on CONVOY for United Artists' release, on location outside Albuquerque, New Mexico, Peckinpah took up whispering, so breathlessly at times as to be in-
audible. He had revised his diet to the extent that he now
drank beer for breakfast. While CONVOY was in production,
Avco-Embassy released CROSS OF IRON to American and
Canadian theatres, pursuing a policy of saturation bookings
to get it a maximum number of playoffs in the shortest possible time. It inspired the same critical vituperation accorded
all Peckinpah films since THE GETAWAY (National-General,
1972).

Something has happened to Sam Peckinpah. To quote
Billy the Kid's comment about Pat Garrett, "He's not the
same man any more." I was thinking that already when I sat
in a hotel room in the ancient part of Rome in May, 1976,
waiting for the international operator to call me back. Sam
wasn't in Rome; he was in Portoroz, Yugoslavia, filming the
location work for CROSS OF IRON. Sam's Czech secretary,
Katie Haber, who has been with him since STRAW DOGS (Cinerama, 1971), was staying, along with the cast and crew for
CROSS OF IRON, at the Metropol Hotel in Portoroz. But not
Sam; he was staying at a villa a short distance outside the
seaside resort town on the Adriatic. The picture was being
financed by Wolf Hartwig, the former porno king of Munich.
I had placed my call to Katie because, unlike Sam, she is
always easy to find, but on the Continent you can wait up to
four hours just to get a connection.

Sam Peckinpah.   Photo courtesy of Sam Peckinpah.

I had been visiting with Sam, on and off, ever since
he was in Durango, Mexico, filming PAT GARRETT AND
BILLY THE KID (M-G-M, 1973) which, in his original director's cut, is about as close as he is ever likely to come to
a definitive statement of his view of the human condition.
Hermann Hesse wrote in 1917 in his Prologue to Demian:
"We are permitted to understand each other; but we can only
interpret ourselves." [Wir können einander verstehen; aber
deuten kann jeder nur sich selbst.] Peckinpah hasn't given
an interview in his life. Instead, he interprets himself verbally while passing through various stages of insobriety. When
Max Evans, a long-time crony of Peckinpah's, wrote Sam
Peckinpah: Master of Violence (University of South Dakota,
1972), about his adventures with Sam on the making of THE
BALLAD OF CABLE HOGUE (Warner's, 1970), I was hopeful
that at last someone would interpret Sam other than Sam. It
proved a disappointment. I mentioned it to Sam and he said,
"What did you expect? Evans was a chickenshit. He didn't
dare tell the truth about that picture because he was afraid
of his wife."

As the sun set in Rome and the street below grew
noisier in the dusk, I recalled a prior visit with Sam on the
M-G-M lot in Culver City, California. He had completed
shooting on THE KILLER ELITE (United Artists, 1975), which
he felt was "a piece of shit," and was suing M-G-M for a
million dollars for having butchered PAT GARRETT AND
BILLY THE KID. I might have missed him entirely had he
not just been released from jail after slugging a Continental
Airlines employee while drunkenly attempting to board a plane
bound for Hawaii. Sam was sitting in one of the screening
rooms in the basement of the Irving Thalberg building when
I arrived at the lot, screening CABARET (Allied Artists,
1972) in an effort to find a suitable music track for the "piece
of shit." I had told him over the telephone that I intended to
attempt the impossible and was bringing my secretary, Vicki
Piekarski, along for the purposes of recording an "intelligent"
interview. Sam chuckled and said he would try to remember
all the Polish jokes he ever knew.

"Hello, Jon," Sam called out of the darkness as we
entered. "Sit down. Have you seen this picture?"

"No."

Vicki sat down next to me. Katie nudged us from behind.

"Want a drink?" she asked.

"What are you drinking?" Vicki inquired.

"Vodka and quinine water."

"Try it," Sam urged. "It tastes like monkey piss."

Katie handed us each a paper cup filled to the brim.

"Sorry," she said, "but there's no ice."

"How do you like it?" Sam asked. "Katie puts salt in it. That does something."

"It's not Scotch," I said.

"Monkey piss's better," Sam assured me.

When the lights came up, Sam saluted me with his cup.

"Want another?" Katie asked.

"Of course he'll have another," Sam said gruffly.

We had another, and another, and another. Sam is seldom away from some contingent of his coterie and it was no different now. A screenwriter and his wife were sitting on Sam's far side. Sam engaged them in a game of imaginary poker and lost a dollar.

"I ask myself why the fuck I make movies," Sam said to me, "and then I look at television and I know why."

He grinned. The lines in his face were deeper. His hair was sparser, iron-gray and natted. I had heard his face described as a battlefield, but if it was, the losses were far exceeding the wins by this time. He was dressed in white jeans, a plain shirt open at the neck, and a white jean jacket. His mirrored sunglasses dangled from an elastic cord around his neck.

"Why the fuck do you want to interview me?" Sam asked morosely. "I sent you copies of all the interviews I've ever given. Use them. I never say anything new."

"Maybe that's why."

"Want to see rushes from KILLER ELITE?"

I shrugged. As we walked out of the screening room, up the steps and outside into the afternoon sunlight, Sam fell in beside me. We lagged behind the others, with Katie in the lead.

"You've bought yourself a divorce," Sam said.

He had once met my ex-wife. He paused to relieve himself on the wall of a sound stage. He finished and zippered his jeans.

"I've bought myself five of them," he said, holding up a hand with five fingers outstretched.

"That's not in any of your interviews."

We resumed walking.

"There's a big difference between pussy and a good woman," he said.

"I've heard that from you before."

"What's wrong with it?"

"Sam, you're drunk."

"I haven't been sober in twenty years."

"Could it be that twenty years of drinking is affecting the way you make pictures?"

"Could be. My doctor told me I had to quit drinking when I started BRING ME THE HEAD OF ALFREDO GARCIA [United Artists, 1974]."

"So?"

"I quit. I started smoking marijuana. I didn't know what I was even doing any more. So ... I've gone back to drinking."

We stepped into the editing room.

"This is my editor, Garth Craven," Sam said, introducing me to a young, modish Englishman standing near a movieola. I had read in several film journals about the expertise with which Peckinpah always edits his films. If Sam edits at all, he does it while he's shooting. "This son-of-a-bitch has cut my pictures since GARRETT. How you coming?"

"I'm on the second reel," Craven said.

There was a case of Scotch set in a corner. Everyone was sitting around on easy chairs that had once been props, except for Vicki; she was perched on a high editor's stool.

"Let's have a drink, Jon," Sam suggested. "Katie, get some ice."

Sam poured Scotch into a paper cup for each of us, filling it to the top so we had to drink it down to make room for the ice. He looked at Vicki. She shook her head.

"One of us is going to have to stay sober if anyone is going to get this interview," she retorted.

"Hey," Sam said, trying to focus on her short, fluffy white-blonde hair and bronzed skin, "you ever been in pictures?" He collapsed into an easy chair in front of the stool on which she was perched, grinning foolishly.

"Yeah, I know," she told him, "I'd be perfect if you ever get a part for a girl with small breasts."

Sam frowned, grabbed her arm, and began chewing on it.

"Sit down here beside me," he said to me as he let go of Vicki's arm. He rubbed his cut and bruised knuckles. He had pleaded guilty to the charge of battery and had been released on probation with a two hundred dollar fine. "If I had it to do over," he observed, "I'd have hit him harder."

"That's just playacting," I said. But Sam, I knew, did upon occasion hit people, usually friends.

"Garth!" Sam shouted. "Start those fucking rushes."

The movieola began to turn film. We watched scenes shot from several different camera angles. Sam had the whiskey bottle beside him. He refilled our paper cups.

"You see what's up there?" he asked, staring gloomily at the small screen. "Every fucking thing I am is up there. There isn't anything else."

"Maybe there should be."

We watched another scene.

"Here," Sam demanded, "give me your cup." He poured more whiskey into his cup and then mixed the contents of the two cups together, as if he were preparing a Bromo-Seltzer. He handed back my cup.

"There," he said, "now we're friends, real friends."

He grabbed onto my hand and held me fixed with his eyes.

"I mean that."

"Listen, Sam, what about the interview?"

"Fuck the interview. What about me? Drink up."

"I haven't eaten all day."

"Then for sure drink up. You'll feel better."

I drank up. Sam let go shaking my hand. The reel ended.

"Put on another reel, God damn it."

"I have to go check on the cat," Katie said, getting up. Sam caught her around the hips and began caressing her backside. She leaned over and kissed him. Then he let her go.

"Do you like cats, Jon?" he asked.

"No."

"I don't like 'em either, but I'm getting to like this cat. Katie and I will be sleeping and this cat will jump on my shoulder and bury his face under my arm."

The next reel started and we watched rushes. James

Caan was blowing up a building. The scene had about it the
intensity Sam can always get, but somehow, even in rough
cut, the picture lacked life; it was the way Garrett's wife had
described him when they argued before he left her to hunt for
the Kid: it was dead inside.   Sam pulled out a couple of
crumpled cigarettes and handed one to me.   I lit them both.

"We've got to smoke a joint after this," he said.

"You can forget the interview," I said.   "I've forgotten
all the questions I wanted to ask."

"Good, then we can have a joint."

"I'm too sick now.   I can't mix liquors when I'm
drinking."

"Do you want to see another reel, Sam?" Garth asked.

"No, we've seen enough."   Sam turned to me.   "I
liked John Ford.   Did you ever meet him?"

"Yes."

"I never did, but I watch his pictures over and over."

I recalled, as he said it, that he had also disrupted
the testimonials to Ford the night Ford was to receive the
Medal of Freedom.   He rose from his seat and announced to
all the luminaries present that they should edit their remarks
to a two-reeler and get on with the show. He was very nearly
thrown out.

"I wish I didn't have to catch a fucking plane for Ma-
drid tomorrow," Sam said, clutching again at my hand.   "They
want me to make a picture in Europe.   Friends?"

"Friends," I said.

"The joint?"

"No, home."

"I only wish I knew where I was going to be.   Since
my home burned down, I don't have any place to live any
more."

"You sound like a Peckinpah character."

"You'll be back?"

"Yes, I'll be back."

"When?"

"I don't know."

I got unsteadily to my feet.   Vicki slid off the stool.
Sam shook my hand some more.

"Christ, I'm tired," he said, letting go and dropping
back into the easy chair.

Now, in Rome, it had been dark for two hours.   Sam
had helped me when I wrote The Filming of the West (Doubleday, 1976) and he had a copy of it.   "Tuska can say that he
believes Sam Peckinpah is the most important director of
Westerns to emerge since World War II," The Hollywood Reporter had commented in its review of the book, "but he reports truths which do less to document his conviction than
they do to demonstrate damaging abuses of that talent."   I
didn't want Sam to feel I had betrayed him.   I had discarded
all hopes of conducting an interview; now I would be satisfied
with simply drawing a portrait of him.   The telephone rang.
I picked up the receiver and got Katie right away.

"Where are you?" she asked.

"In Rome.   I will be there day after tomorrow."

"Good.   Sam won't be shooting.   I'll tell him you've
arrived ... almost.   He'll be glad to see you."

The connection was fading, so I quit while I was ahead.

II

Like most film directors, Peckinpah detests intellec-
tualizing about his films, quite probably because, as he says,
what's there is on the screen.   Yet it may well be possible
to elucidate what Peckinpah's films have meant to him without
at the same time treating them as some abstract social commentary existing in a vacuum.

In Peckinpah's best work there is such a primitive
force and disturbing emotional quality as to be unforgettable.

I have to question much of his rationalization for frequently
evoking violence and blood-letting, but there is no denying
that he is right in believing we must not live by half-truths;
and before he is criticized too harshly, perhaps it would be
well to remember the drawings of flowers, birds, and crude
houses done by thousands of small children on the walls at
Dachau while they waited unknowingly to be herded into the
collective gas chambers.   Men have done terrible things to
each other and the reasons for it cannot best be solved by
removing all visible reminders from the media.

Sam's father, David Peckinpah, summed it up to him
one day and Sam had Steve Judd repeat it in RIDE THE HIGH
COUNTRY (M-G-M, 1962): "All I want is to enter my house
justified."   This idea has kept him going.   Sam's ancestors
came from the Frisian Islands, off the coast of the Netherlands, and settled in Madeira County in the San Joaquin Valley
in nineteenth-century California.   Sam was born on 21 February 1925.   Peckinpah Mountain in Madeira County was
named after Sam's paternal grandfather and his maternal
grandfather was a Superior Court Judge.   Sam's father, also
born on the "mountain," practiced law in Fresno, where Sam
was born, and in his turn became a Superior Court Judge.
Sam's brother, Denver, is currently a Superior Court Judge
in Fresno County.   As a youth, Sam proved unruly and, as
a disciplinary measure, was sent to San Rafael Military Academy.   He entered the U. S. Marine Corps upon his graduation
and was sent to China, although the war was virtually over
and he saw no action.   When he was discharged after his
four-year hitch, his family urged him to pursue the law.   Sam
was confused and uncertain; he went for a time to Mexico and
then, upon his return, enrolled at Fresno State College.   He
met Marie (they married that same year, 1949); she was a
drama major.   After accompanying her to one of her classes
in stage direction, Peckinpah had found his vocation.

Sam was early attracted to Tennessee Williams' plays
and adapted The Glass Menagerie to one hour as a student
production.   Graduating from Fresno State, he enrolled at the
University of Southern California and earned a master's degree in drama.   His first job out of school was with the
Huntington Park Theatre, near Los Angeles, where he produced and directed nearly all the theatre's stage productions
for two and a half years.   After a summer of stock work,
accompanied by Marie, in Albuquerque, New Mexico, Peckinpah went to work with the stage crew at KLAC-TV in Los
Angeles.

Peckinpah was very intent on getting into the direction of motion pictures and, while still with KLAC, tried his hand at making short, experimental films. In his spare time he took to writing scripts, but he found writing, necessarily a solitary occupation, at odds with his gregarious temperament and, at times, even painful. He sought employment as a dialogue director, working in this capacity on films like GREAT DAY IN THE MORNING (RKO, 1956), until he came to the attention of veteran director Don Siegel, who hired Sam to do a rewrite of Siegel's script for INVASION OF THE BODY SNATCHERS (Allied Artists, 1956). Sam wrote in three parts for himself in the film, but he looked so different in those days as to appear unrecognizable to modern audiences. In 1955, Peckinpah was hired to write a total of twelve scripts for television's Gunsmoke, then a half-hour series, ten of which were adaptations of previous episodes from when the show had been on radio. The two original scripts were both rejected by the show's producer, Charles Marquis Warren.

For the next three years, Sam worked steadily writing scripts for a number of television Westerns, including Broken Arrow and Tales of Wells Fargo. Finally, in 1958, he rewrote one of his original Gunsmoke scripts and managed to interest Four Star Productions in using it as the basis for a new series to be titled The Rifleman. Dick Powell produced the pilot for this series and ran it as an episode for his network series, Zane Grey Theatre. Peckinpah's basic concept for the series was that a sharpshooter and his young son would encounter various adventures, each of which would in some way contribute to the boy's growing awareness of the world and his own values. Dick Powell, one of the "good guys" according to Sam, gave him his first chance to direct by assigning him several installments in the series once it was purchased by the network.

Powell then proposed to Peckinpah that he try conceiving a new half-hour pilot, which he could direct, to be included in the Zane Grey Theatre anthology for the 1960 season and Sam came up with the notion for The Westerner. Dave Levy of NBC liked Peckinpah's previous work and, primarily through his influence, the network bought this new pilot and Dick Powell Productions scheduled thirteen episodes. Sam was the producer for the series, in addition to writing and directing some of the episodes himself. Many of Sam's entries stressed comic and hyperbolic elements and perhaps the most carefully drawn Peckinpah character was series star Brian Keith's dog, Brown. It wasn't really Keith's dog; Keith would insist that

Brown was "nobody's dog"; but the two of them traveled together and watched out for each other.

After the initial complement of thirteen shows, The
Westerner was cancelled due to the controversial nature of
the material, but it did manage to win a nomination from the
Screen Producer's Guild as the "Best Filmed TV Series."
Brian Keith, who was slated to star in THE DEADLY COM-
PANIONS (Pathé-American, 1961), was instrumental in getting
Peckinpah signed to direct it.   Maureen O'Hara was Keith's
co-star and her brother, Charles B. Fitzsimmons, was the
picture's producer.   Fitzsimmons prevented Sam from tam-
pering very much with the script, and even the ending, which
Peckinpah substituted, was deleted and the original ending in-
serted again.   Yet, while Sam disowns the picture as "un-
workable," as well he might considering how intolerably slow-
moving and tedious it is to watch, he was able to inject into
it his own bleak perspectives of the Western terrain.

Sam's favorite Western author is Ernest Haycox, and
it is perhaps no coincidence that Sam's most successful theatrical Western, THE WILD BUNCH (Warner's, 1969), should
take for its title the title of one of Haycox's more effective
novels.   Haycox differed essentially from Zane Grey in that
he created a milieu of antipathetic circumstances which forced
his characters, confronted both by the barren wastes of the
West and the hostile elements rampant in them, to develop,
begrudgingly at first, and then thankfully, permanent loyalties
and a mutual interdependence.   Andre de Toth had been able
to capture something of this in MAN IN THE SADDLE (Columbia, 1951), a memorable entry in the long-running series
of Randolph Scott Westerns in the 'fifties and early 'sixties
which de Toth adapted from Haycox's novel of the same title,
and John Ford had based STAGECOACH (United Artists, 1939)
on one of Haycox's short stories.   Maureen O'Hara got a
chance to expose her naked body in a bathing sequence in
THE DEADLY COMPANIONS but Fitzsimmons audited all her
scenes, so Sam concentrated on the fragmenting friendship
among Brian Keith, Steve Cochrane, and Chill Wills, insti-
gated by Cochrane's lust for O'Hara.   Women, this early,
were viewed by Sam as a distraction, a danger, an object
for sexual heats, but only occasionally as beings with inner
resources.   Sam's marriage to Marie, after three children,
was falling apart, Sam felt, because of Marie's obsession
with material possessions and prosperity.   In the ambivalent
love affair between Keith and O'Hara, Sam diligently preserved
the last vestiges of his crumbling belief in the possible per-
manence of love relationships.

Peckinpah then went back to work for Dick Powell, directing an entry for the Dick Powell Theatre, as well as scripting an episode for the TV series, Pony Express, and directing "Mon Petit Chow" for a CBS installment in the Route 66 series. Peckinpah also co-scripted, co-produced, and directed "The Losers" for television, with Lee Marvin, Keenan Wynn, and Rosemary Clooney, which Powell felt might potentially be expanded into a network series.

It was on the basis of this experience and THE DEADLY COMPANIONS that Metro-Goldwyn-Mayer contracted Peckinpah to direct RIDE THE HIGH COUNTRY, a routine budget Western which was to star Joel McCrea, a has-been from many "A" Westerns, and Randolph Scott, whose series in collaboration with Harry Joe Brown, produced variously for Warner's and Columbia, had finally ended. Both McCrea and Scott were extremely wealthy men, largely because of investments in real estate. At lunch one day with Sam and Richard Lyons, producer on the picture, a coin was tossed and Scott was surprised to learn that the object of chance had been who was to receive top billing and that he had won.

When a child, Sam had been taught passages from the Bible by rote by his father. In this film, he first came to cast character actor R. G. Armstrong as a religious fanatic, and it is a characterization that has run as a thread through all of Sam's Westerns, whether Armstrong is playing the character or not. Sam's marriage, with Marie's fourth pregnancy, had become concentrated torment for him. He contributed to the screenplay and attempted to put into Edgar Buchanan's mouth, as Judge Tolliver, his own frustration: "People change ... the glory of a good marriage doesn't come in the beginning ... it comes later on ... it's hard work." The plot gives McCrea and Scott, outdated and anachronized by social change, no place in the emergent new world. Only loyalty, personal loyalty to an ideal, means anything, and a sense of honor: they can make a bad man good, as McCrea by dying can do for Randolph Scott.

With the birth of Matthew, his fourth child and his first son, Marie sued Sam for divorce in 1962. It meant a lot to him personally that RIDE THE HIGH COUNTRY was voted the "Best American Film" of 1962 by Newsweek Magazine, although M-G-M thought little of it and released it as the bottom part of a summer bill; as much as it meant that it was listed among the "Ten Best" by Time Magazine, beat out Fellini's $8\frac{1}{2}$ for the "Grand Prix" at the Belgian Film

Festival, and was awarded the "Diosa del Plato" for "Best
Direction" by the Mexican film critics. But Sam Peckinpah's
personal life, all that he had worked for, and believed in,
was in shambles.

Director Sidney Lumet brought Mary McCarthy's novel,
The Group (Harcourt, Brace, 1963), to the screen for United
Artists' release in 1966. In the novel Polly, one of the female characters who is having a love affair with a Stalinist
publisher separated from his wife, Esther, tells him at one
point: " 'You're going to go back to Esther. You think you're
not, but you are.' He was struck. 'Why do you say that?'
Polly waved a hand. '... You've never really left her. To
leave her, you'd have to change your life. And you can't.
It's all built in to you, like built-in furniture.' "

I will not say that Marie was unfaithful, because I do
not know, but in RIDE THE HIGH COUNTRY Sam does have
R. G. Armstrong kneel before his dead wife's grave stone
which bears the inscription: "Wherefore O Harlot, I will
judge thee as women that break wedlock and shed blood are
judged...." Sam undertook to alter completely the life-style
he had known. He sought reconciliations with Marie until
1969, but his life-style became more and more nomadic. He
tried living in houses, then shacks, then in trailers, then on
studio lots, and finally nowhere. He rejected material possessions. Money became meaningless to him. Dick Powell
died, and Four Star Productions died shortly thereafter. Producer Jerry Bresler hired Sam to direct MAJOR DUNDEE,
but as soon as production had started Bresler shaved the
shooting schedule from 72 days to 60 and the budget by a
million dollars--primarily because cost-conscious Columbia
Pictures was financing and releasing. Sam ignored Bresler's
dictates, and went on location to Mexico to film.

Sam had been drinking more and more over the years,
and it had intensified. "There's a big difference between
pussy and a good woman," Sam came to chant like an insidious Greek chorus in countless interviews. "You can triple
your distance with a good woman." Now he was alone, so
he took to living with whores. He came to feel they were
more honest than other women; married women fucked for
what they could get, and you never knew how much they wanted;
a whore set her price in the beginning.

Sam wanted to hold his production schedule on DUNDEE
at 72 days. He got constant flack from Columbia. He became

angry, because he knew he was getting a good picture; more
than that, an epic picture.   Charlton Heston and Richard Harris were the stars, Heston a Yankee, Harris a Confederate,
with the plot joining them in an uneasy alliance against the
war-like Apaches.   Heston said he was willing to return his
salary for the picture to Columbia, and did so, if Sam could
just continue production.   Columbia sent a field man to Mexico to close down the set.   Sam stripped his clothes off at
the airport and sent him packing.   Bresler and Columbia
waited until he had finished, and then, systematically, in the
editing process, cut from the finished film the thirty-five
pages of script that Peckinpah had been ordered to excise.
The film was released, and proved a commercial and critical
disaster.   Bresler had his revenge.   Sam Peckinpah was finished in Hollywood.   DUNDEE had featured James Coburn,
L. Q. Jones, Slim Pickens and R. G. Armstrong in its cast
--what would later become the Peckinpah "stock company" in
Westerns.   But right now Sam couldn't find a job, not anywhere.

He tried a reconciliation with Marie.   It didn't work.
"I love outsiders," Sam once said to me, "because unless you
conform, give in completely, you're going to be alone in this
world.   But by giving in, you lose your independence as a
human being."   Sam was alone.   He loved his children and,
frequently, Marie let him visit them.   Sam blamed DUNDEE
for the ruin of his marriage and his fortunes.   He tried writing scripts under five different pseudonyms.   He tried to
adapt James A. Michener's Caravans (Random House, 1963)
and contributed to a script for an M-G-M film to be titled
READY FOR THE TIGER.   He borrowed money.   Everything
he attempted "turned to shit."   He was miserable.   He worked
on the screenplay for THE GLORY GUYS (United Artists, 1966)
and Paramount hired him to script VILLA RIDES (Paramount,
1968), which was to star Yul Brynner; the actor didn't like
Peckinpah's script and had it changed during production.   Sam
applied for a job at the University of California at Los Angeles and managed to obtain a position lecturing in television
production.

Finally, Daniel Melnick, of Talent Associates, contacted Peckinpah to adapt and direct an ABC-TV network pres-
entation of Katherine Anne Porter's only well-plotted short
novel, Noon Wine.   Peckinpah, in his script, added several
scenes and sent them to Miss Porter for her approval.   She
was enthusiastic.   A long-time correspondent of mine, Katherine Anne later confessed in a letter to me that she loved

Peckinpah's version of her story better than her own.   She
felt he understood her characters with an unfailing insight.
Sam cast Jason Robards in the lead, with Olivia de Havilland
as his wife, and Ben Johnson and L. Q. Jones in support.

During the period of his "exile," Sam had worked for
four days on THE CINCINNATI KID (M-G-M, 1965) before
producer Martin Ransohoff, who would soon be responsible
for introducing Roman Polanski to his second wife, Sharon
Tate, fired Peckinpah on trumped-up charges that Sam wanted
to introduce vulgarity into the film via a nude scene; the truth
is that Ransohoff and Peckinpah could not agree on the direction the story was to take.   Sam had had a similar experience
in 1961 when he had worked on the screenplay for ONE-EYED
JACKS (Paramount, 1961), which was very much Marlon Brando's picture, and Sam had disagreed with Brando about Brando's desire to make Billy the Kid a hero.   ONE-EYED JACKS
marked Sam's interest in Billy the Kid's life and his desire
to treat it realistically on the screen.

The teleplay of Noon Wine won critical acclaim across
the country and the Screen Director's Guild voted Sam one of
the ten best television directors for the 1966-67 season.   The
vote won Sam an opportunity to direct a segment for Bob
Hope's Chrysler Theatre and the position at UCLA, but he
was indigent and in despair until he established a liaison with
Phil Feldman, an independent producer who had offices at
what was then known as the Warner Bros.-Seven Arts lot in
Burbank, California.   Feldman had produced YOU'RE A BIG
BOY NOW (Warner's, 1967), directed by Francis Ford Coppola, a director Peckinpah adamantly can't stand despite Coppola's later success directing THE GODFATHER (Paramount,
1972).   Feldman wanted Sam to direct THE WILD BUNCH,
based on a story by Walon Green.   Sam liked the property
because it gave him a suitable chance to vent the pent-up
frustration and violence he had experienced since DUNDEE
and because he could incorporate into it his pervasive suspicion of the Establishment, which forced men who wanted
freedom into ostracism and finally self-annihilation.   There
were no bad guys or good guys in THE WILD BUNCH, only
men destined by fate to extirpate their oppressions and manifest their over-riding greed by playing out against each other
an ineluctable dance of death.   Men were corrupted by the
System and, regardless of the odds, a man owed it to himself to stand with his companions.

Exteriors were filmed on location in Mexico and, while

shooting, Sam met Mexican actress Begonia Palacios, who
became his second, third, and fourth wife. Sam cast former
Mexican director Emilio Fernandez as Malpache, leader of a
Mexican revolutionary band. Since Mexican law required that
a Mexican be named as "stand-by" director, Sam selected
Fernandez. Fernandez and Sam struck up an immediate
friendship and, one night, when they were discussing an aspect of the screenplay and Sam was supposed to be at a dinner Begonia had prepared and she telephoned him because he
was late, Sam told her that a pimple on Emilio Fernandez'
ass, at that moment, was one helluva lot more important than
his future life with any fucking fiancée. It was in this spirit
that they conducted their engagement.

Critics, after THE WILD BUNCH's successful commercial release, claimed that Sam had introduced violence for its
own sake into the cinematic Western. This was nonsense,
most assuredly. The DOLLAR pictures produced by Sergio
Leone in Italy and scores of others had already begun the
trend. What Sam did achieve was to make a poetry of violence, to show the anguished features it wears in men who
are weary of having to live by its dictates and who no longer
know how to contend with its demands. The public and the
critics, however, ignored this, and made Sam Peckinpah's
name synonymous with an almost fascistic celebration of
screen brutishness. Sam wanted to keep working, after so
many years of unemployment, so he accepted the moniker,
and even came, after a time, to promote himself by means
of it and make it a crusade.

What Peckinpah and Fernandez were discussing the
night Sam was late for Begonia's dinner party was the notion
that a venemous scorpion could be killed by an army of ants.
The critics have made a lot of this image, which Sam put at
the very beginning of the picture. Rich Sassone, writing in
Filmmakers Newsletter in an article called "The Ballad of
Sam Peckinpah," says: "And if in our fear of facing up to
a few violently sick people we keep selling our freedom to
society for protection, who will protect us when that society
itself becomes sick? The scorpion has a poisonous sting;
but the collective violence of the ant army is infinitely more
deadly."

The sales executives at Warner Brothers were under-
standably apprehensive about what the public reaction would
be to THE WILD BUNCH. Phil Feldman suggested a number
of cuts in the picture which Sam, at the time, found perfectly

reasonable. A lot was made of the 3,624 editorial cuts of
film which went into composing the release version, and
sometimes, when critics remark on this, they do so almost
as if these were "deletions" from the film, rather than merely
an assembly of footage. The eight and a half minutes that
Warner's cut from the film were an effort to restrain the
violence when it was too vivid. Sam would eventually say
that THE WILD BUNCH was mutilated, but ninety-eight per
cent of it was left intact as he shot it.

Lucien Ballard, who had been with Sam on RIDE THE
HIGH COUNTRY, was with him for WILD BUNCH and stayed
with him for his next film, THE BALLAD OF CABLE HOGUE.
What Ballard, one of the most lyrical cinematographers in
Hollywood, missed in the BUNCH's final cut was a scene that
had to go simply because of running time--as it was, WILD
BUNCH ran 152 minutes. "We had some great stuff in the
desert that was cut out," Ballard recalled. "There was a
sandstorm where we could hardly see anything--when we cut
we had to shout to the actors to find their way back. At the
end we had a long dolly shot as they leave the desert. It had
rained, and you could see their tracks.... Sam and I worked
very well together. I would go to and from work with him,
so we would have that extra time to talk to each other--that
kind of thing is very unusual, but I think something comes of
that close proximity."

William Holden, who was the leader of the bunch,
summed up their code this way: "When you side with a man,
you stay with him. And if you can't do that, you're like
some animal. You're finished." In THE WILD BUNCH, Peckinpah depicted society, perhaps American society in particular,
as dominated by men with a sharp, aggressive, avaricious
temperament. He defended the violence in the film on the
grounds that life itself is violent and that the audience could
achieve some sort of catharsis, a purging of the emotions,
through watching it depicted in overwhelmingly powerful images, carefully constructed to create a montage effect.

THE WILD BUNCH had a domestic American and Canadian gross of $5,224,621, which did not make for a windfall
profit but at least covered its basic cost. Neither Warner
Brothers nor Phil Feldman knew even that much when Sam
began work on THE BALLAD OF CABLE HOGUE (Warner's,
1970), and so the studio became increasingly concerned at the
delays due to inclement weather in the Valley of Fire in the
Nevada desert, where Sam chose to shoot the exteriors and

some of the interiors for HOGUE, before finishing up in
Phoenix, Arizona, at the Western movie town set which still
stands there since Wesley Ruggles first constructed it for
ARIZONA (Columbia, 1940).

HOGUE was the only picture up to that time which Sam
really wanted to make; it is a love story, perhaps one of the
most poignant in any Western.   Jason Robards was cast as
Hogue, and the character was in every way a surrogate for
Peckinpah himself.   Stella Stevens had posed in the nude two

Sam Peckinpah directing Stella Stevens and Jason Robards on
the set of THE BALLAD OF CABLE HOGUE (Warner's,
1973).   Photo courtesy of Eddie Brandt's Saturday Matinee.

or three times when Sam contacted her to play the whore in
the film who falls in love with Hogue.   When Stella arrived
at the Valley of Fire, Sam greeted her, "Welcome to a place
of love."   She had never been treated before the way Sam
treated her; she committed to him totally, and felt, while
watching rushes of what had been filmed, that it was the best
picture she had ever done.

Peckinpah had long regarded SHANE (Paramount, 1953) as his favorite Western. He wanted in HOGUE to revise the basic myth of the Western which SHANE had embodied. HOGUE dealt with Sam's views of what he had come to consider the most essential issues in life: friendship between men, a man's relationship with a woman, the importunity of vengeance, a man's need to survive physically and financially in the world, the importance of having someone believe in you, and, above all, a reconciliation of Peckinpah's always ambivalent attitude toward the God of the Bible. That's a lot to incorporate into any film and keep it commercially viable. There is comedy and pathos and tenderness and hopelessness, as Sam had known these in his life.

"Bankers have believed in me," Sam once remarked when we were talking quietly, "producers have, releasing companies, the people who work for me--and then you believe that the picture you've made is the very best you possibly could have made, and it doesn't gross. It's very hard, sometimes." All the firings and quittings and tumult on any Peckinpah picture stem from his total absorption in his concept of the final cut.

HOGUE depicted women as Sam feels men should accustom themselves to regarding them. Stella Stevens, as Hildy, loves Hogue, finds him satisfying in bed, will cook and care for him for a time, enjoys having him scrub her naked derrière when she bathes, but she is determined to fuck her way to wealth and that counts most with her. Hogue desires Hildy; in his way, he loves her. But he has Peckinpah's philosophy of dealing with women: "Get in, get it over with, and get out." His soul hungers after vengeance against the men who left him to die in the desert. Sam felt that the injustices life had brought to him had crippled his ability to love; selfishness and selfish aims set the tone of human relationships.

Hogue makes friends with David Warner, the British actor, playing a phony preacher who likes to seduce his female converts. Gene Evans, outraged at Warner for so "converting" his wife, chases Warner to Hogue's desert shack. Originally Sam filmed a pitched battle between Evans and Warner with Hogue as the mediator, but he didn't like the way it played, and so all that survives of it in the release print is that after Evans rides off from talking with Hogue, Hogue has a bandage on his hand which is not explained.

Hogue does have his vengeance and Hildy returns, having fucked herself into a fortune. "We've got nothin' but time, Hogue," she tells him. "Nothin' but time." Hogue has exactly enough time to die, run over by an automobile, because in Sam's view the machine has destroyed finally our hopes for freedom. This is Peckinpah's ironic humor; you always get a little more out of every situation than you bargained for, and the little more is never what you wanted. (On location Sam slept so much in Hogue's shack that he wanted to bring it back to Malibu beach so he could live in it.) "Take him, Lord," Warner says over Hogue's grave, "but, whatever you do, don't take him lightly."

The picture cost almost three million to make. Warner Brothers decided it was non-commercial, consigned it to quick 'obscurity, and blamed Sam for its $1,191,485 gross. Sam became more embittered. He became, in his words, a "good whore." He went "where he was kicked." He had three pictures to make before he got a second chance for a wholly personal statement in PAT GARRETT AND BILLY THE KID, but by then events and circumstances had changed the nature and character of the statement he wanted to make.

ABC Films, with Cinerama releasing theatrically, contracted Peckinpah for a brace of pictures, commencing with STRAW DOGS, which was filmed on location in England. Daniel Melnick, who had sponsored Peckinpah's direction of Noon Wine for television, was the producer on STRAW DOGS. Sam felt that the original novel on which the film was based, The Siege of Trencher's Farm, had nothing to offer except its final scene, the raid on the farm, and so had it completely reworked for the screenplay.

There was a dual theme in STRAW DOGS: the recognition, on the part of the picture's star, Dustin Hoffman, that his wife, played by Susan George, was not a good woman, but basically "pussy," and that every man harbors in his soul the capacity for a violent outburst leading to the slaughter of his fellow man. Feeling Hollywood had mistreated him, Sam thought for a while that he might want to live in England. He leased a flat for Marie and the children and had them join him. He also had Begonia come to England. And, with his two former wives there, Sam took up with Joie Gould, whom he married a year later in Juarez, Mexico, while on location filming THE GETAWAY.

Susan George, who in her way triggers the violence,

is sexually assaulted in STRAW DOGS. She is raped twice,
once vaginally, once anally, and Sam was quick to defend the
anal rape as something other than sodomy, which the dictionary defines loosely as "perverse intercourse." "In the picture," Sam said in his famous Playboy interview, "Amy [Susan
George] is taken by one guy she used to go with and then she's
taken from the rear by another guy she didn't want any part
of anywhere. The double rape is a little bit more than she
bargained for. Anyway, I guess Miss [Pauline] Kael and her
friends have anal complexes. Perfectly justified in this day
and age." The picture ends with Dustin Hoffman knowing he
must leave Amy, that he must find his way alone in the world
without looking to "pussy" for more than it can deliver, and
that violence is an intrinsic part of him, as it is part of
everyone.

Sam hired Katie Haber in England and she was with
him during much of the shooting. When the final scene was
being filmed, with Dustin Hoffman and David Warner, playing
the village half-wit, together in a car, to simulate fog, Sam
had several smudge pots lit along the roadside. A fire broke
out and the firefighters had to be summoned to put out the
blaze. When he tried the scene again, still with smudge pots,
but this time more judiciously placed, it was Hoffman who
came up with the last line in the picture, responding to David
Warner that he doesn't know the way home either. The lurch-
ing of the car as Hoffman says this was caused by Katie Haber
bouncing her derrière on the trunk.

STRAW DOGS grossed four times what it cost to make.
The same cannot be said of JUNIOR BONNER (Cinerama,
1972), which was intended to be more in the gentle mode of
CABLE HOGUE. Lucien Ballard was the cinematographer and
Steve McQueen the star, but neither McQueen nor Sam could
save the film from tedium. There was insufficient conflict
and the characters weren't strong enough to carry the weak
storyline. Upon release, the picture fell $400,000 beneath
its negative cost in world-wide revenues.

As much as he would have liked, with films like
HOGUE and BONNER, to shed the reputation he had earned
as the "master of violence," there was no disputing the fact
that, to date, Sam's most commercially successful films had
been his violent ones, whereas HOGUE, which was artistically
successful at least, and JUNIOR BONNER, which was not, had
both lost money. THE GETAWAY, Sam felt, should therefore
be both an essay in violence and a poignant love story. But

what kind of a love story? Here, at the very least, was a
script that could build a dual parallelism: Steve McQueen's
betrayal by a murderous, violent element who is on his trail
and hoping to kill him, interposed with a lurid depiction of
"pussy" played by well-endowed Sally Struthers (known then
primarily for her role on network television's All in the
Family), and with the "good woman," the woman who, working with McQueen and accepting his dominance, could triple
his distance and carry him through to safety when, by herself,
she would be lost and fumbling in the world. It was an effective combination and the film grossed nearly fifteen million
dollars, ranking it as the second largest grossing film in the
United States in 1973.

Critics complained that the Struthers episode detracted
somewhat from the central tension of the plot, but Sam probably delighted the most in showing Jack Dodson, Sally's husband, tied up in motel rooms, while Al Lettieri, a killer who
is after McQueen, ravishes Struthers, with Struthers relishing
every minute of it. Ali MacGraw, the "good woman," was,
by comparison, dull and colorless.

Sam was working out of an office on the Samuel Goldwyn
lot and living in a house trailer on Malibu beach with his son,
Matthew, supervising the editing of THE GETAWAY, when the
deal was set for him to direct PAT GARRETT AND BILLY
THE KID. Because the public was thoroughly familiar with
the life and legend of Billy the Kid (M-G-M, which was financing the production, had made the film itself twice previously), Peckinpah could do with the property what he had been
unable to do with any Western he had ever worked on; moreover, he had watched Arthur Penn's THE LEFT-HANDED GUN
(Warner's, 1958) three or four times. THE LEFT-HANDED
GUN had treated Billy as a Christ-like figure, a martyr, a
twisted sacrifice to the propitiation of the existing social order.
Concurrently, Sam could seize precisely this opportunity to
amend the gross inaccuracies of ONE-EYED JACKS and portray the Kid as a vicious murderer. On location in Durango,
Mexico, using Chupaderos, a former Pancho Villa fort re-
furbished by M-G-M to look like Fort Sumner, New Mexico,
Sam could tell the story of Billy the Kid's clash with Pat Garrett as if it were Greek tragedy, where everyone knew how
the story ended and the emphasis, therefore, could be placed
on why it had to end that way.

"I'll tell you this," Dub Taylor reflected over breakfast one morning at the Campo Mexican Court where the cast

and crew were staying, "after Sam gets through nobody will
ever make a pitchur about Billy the Kid again.   This is it!
They'll never touch Billy after this."

      Sam cast Kris Kristofferson as Billy and James Coburn
as Garrett.   He assigned Rudolph Wurlitzer to write the
screenplay, but in production threw out nearly everything
Wurlitzer had done.   He wanted the story told in tableaux,
like stations of the cross in a medieval passion play, each
scene bringing Billy nearer his death and Garrett nearer his
own self-crucifixion.   He opened the film in 1908 with Garrett
as an old man being shot down at the instigation of the same
forces that had once hired him to murder the Kid and the
Kid's gang, ostensibly in a dispute over the land which Chisum
had given Garrett in exchange for dispatching the Kid.   As
each bullet tears into Garrett's body, there is a flashback to
1881, showing a chicken's head being shot off at Fort Sumner,
where the Kid and his gang are engaged in some target practice.

      Although there is nothing so dull as rehashing the plot
line of a motion picture, in this instance it might be justified
since M-G-M so edited the film as to make it incomprehensible, and it is doubtful that it will ever be seen as Peckinpah
intended it.   As originally conceived, it quite probably is
among the small handful of memorable Hollywood Westerns
and Peckinpah's masterpiece.

      There is no optimistic spirit of the land in PAT GAR-
RETT AND BILLY THE KID, no new frontier, only a vast
wasteland, a desert punctuated by silvery, surrealistic lakes
and streams.   Much of the film is photographed in shadow,
dusk, hazy light, or nightfall.   There is a hopelessness in
the terrain, an agonized loneliness in the principals, a frus-
trated quest for identity, a bitter confrontation with futility,
and, moving through it all, desperately erupting, a sustaining
violence, a lewd intimacy with death.

      Garrett comes to Fort Sumner to tell Billy that Chisum
and the other ranchers in the Santa Fe ring, who had recently
hired the Kid to be sheriff of Lincoln County, have now hired
Garrett.   The Kid and Garrett have ridden together for years;
now Garrett wants the Kid out of the territory.

      "Why don't you kill him?" one of Billy's henchmen
asks the Kid once Garrett leaves.

Sam Peckinpah in Durango, Mexico, on the set of PAT GAR-
RETT AND BILLY THE KID (M-G-M, 1973) with James Coburn.   Photo courtesy of Eddie Brandt's Saturday Matinee.

"Why?" Billy returns, gulping whiskey, "he's my
friend."

Cut to Billy and two cronies in a shack surrounded by
Pat and a flock of deputies.   The two cronies are shot to
pieces, but Billy surrenders, holding out his empty arms
sacrificially.   The Kid is sentenced to hang.   He plays poker
in a room above the jail with Garrett and Matt Clark while a
scaffold is erected outside.   R. G. Armstrong is on the scene
as a religious fanatic who, righteously holding a shotgun to
Billy's heart, demands, "Repent, you son-of-a-bitch."   Garrett leaves to collect some taxes, but before he goes, he
places a gun in the outhouse so that the Kid can make good
his escape.   Billy shoots Clark and Armstrong and rides off.

When Garrett gets back to Lincoln, he hires Jack Elam
as his deputy to hunt for the Kid.   Before he takes to the
trail, Garrett stops briefly to see his Mexican wife; the par-
allel scene shows the Kid following after Rita Coolidge at Fort

Sumner while a group of children heckle him. Stopping at the
military governor's mansion, Garrett refuses an additional reward for the Kid's capture from two capitalist investors. Jason Robards, playing Governor Wallace, is sympathetic with
Garrett's dilemma. The Kid, in the meantime, attempts to
collect the twenty head of cattle Chisum still owes him from
when the Kid was sheriff. This move outrages Chisum and
he has John Beck, who will later lure Garrett to his own
death in ambush, assigned to ride with Garrett to insure that
Garrett will capture the Kid. "This country is gettin' old,"
Garrett tells Beck, "an' I aim to get old with it. The Kid
don't want it that way, an' maybe he's a better man for it."

This is Garrett's refrain. He said the same thing to
Slim Pickens, playing a deputy sheriff, when he wanted to enlist Pickens to join him in killing some of the Kid's gang.
Pickens was fatally shot in the process. Pickens was building
a boat behind the jailhouse and had hopes of using it to leave
the territory. Garrett kills more of the Kid's gang. The
Kid decides to go to Mexico to hide but when Chisum's men
kill his friend Paco and rape Paco's wife, Billy determines
to return to Fort Sumner and organize a showdown with Chisum.
Emilio Fernandez was cast as Paco, the necessary Mexican
director assigned to the unit, and he brought his eleven-year-
old wife with him to the set.

Garrett and Beck meet Chisum at Chisum's ranch and
Chisum makes Garrett the offer of property which the viewer
already knows will eventually lead to Garrett's death at Beck's
hands. Garrett accepts the offer and, after spending some
time with the Kid's whore and three other hookers, Garrett
rides out toward Fort Sumner. The Kid knows Garrett is
coming but he relaxes his vigilance to sleep with Rita. To
this function, and its attendant loss of freedom, even the
"good woman" has been consigned.

On his way to Pete Maxwell's shack where the Kid
and Rita are making love, Garrett happens upon Will, the
coffinmaker, played by Sam Peckinpah. Will is putting the
finishing touches on a coffin and claims that when he is finished with it, he will put his belongings in it and leave the
territory for good. "Finally figured it out, eh?" Will asks
Garrett, turning down a drink. "Well, go get him. You
don't even trust yourself any more, do you, Garrett?"

Garrett shoots the Kid, pistol-whips John Beck, and
the next morning rides off alone, a child following after him,

throwing stones. Cut to Garrett riding in his buggy in 1908,
an old man met on the trail by John Beck, and again the
viewer is taken through Garrett's assassination.

Kris Kristofferson was drinking two quarts of whiskey
a day, as he had for years, while playing the Kid. Sam, on
location, was "pissed off" because gossip columinist Rona
Barrett had said Sam had a drinking problem. Through every
scene of GARRETT, the drinking had been constant and intense, and Kristofferson, at least, preferred the real thing.
In this way the film itself became a descent into alcoholic
despair, in which life itself could be reduced to permanent
depression punctuated by sudden violence.

After the studio truncated GARRETT prior to release
(James Aubrey, then head of M-G-M, said audiences would
be unable to follow the director's cut Peckinpah turned in),
Sam negotiated a deal with United Artists to film BRING ME
THE HEAD OF ALFREDO GARCIA, insisting he could bring
the picture in for under a million dollars by employing non-
union Mexicans. The script was confused, the direction uncertain, and the picture as released was the object of industry boycotts. It grossed only $672,151 in the United States
and Canada, in contrast to the $2,754,218 gross GARRETT
had--but then GARRETT had cost $4,345,000 to make.

United Artists turned around and handed Peckinpah
THE KILLER ELITE. Sam commenced production by confessing to the picture's star, James Caan, "We're really up
against it with this one. But I'm broke and I need the money."
The San Francisco location was cold and foggy. A reporter
for the Sunday Group newspaper syndicate described Sam as
"depressed and blue. He looks gray, bent--a slouching death
wish. He reddens, coughs, spits away part of a hangover....
Peckinpah is fifty but looks--in the AM--an enfeebled twenty
years older." That reporter made the mistake of taking Sam
too lightly. Sam didn't like THE KILLER ELITE, no matter
what he tried to do with it, and he was dejected by what M-
G-M had done to GARRETT.

                                III

When I got back to London from the Continent, the
National Film Theatre was having another Sam Peckinpah
retrospective. Peckinpah has long been popular in the United
Kingdom and it came as little surprise, a year or so later,

that the British-based E. M. I. Films, in making its entrance into American-produced commercial films, should have chosen Sam to direct the first picture, CONVOY.

I had left the Hotel Metropol very early in the morning, driving back to the Yugoslav-Italian border. The dense foliage of the great trees along the road interlocked high up, cutting off any view of the sky, so the dawn was forced to creep as a silver haze between their massive trunks. Sam had called me from his villa shortly after we had arrived at the hotel and, when he heard Vicki had accompanied me, suggested lunch, sending a car for us. We met at an outdoor restaurant located on a cliff overlooking the sea. Sam was with Lucky, a native Serbian who was acting as his guide and interpreter. Dressed in blue jeans with a jean jacket, despite the location, Sam claimed he was just an old, broken-down cowboy. It was sunny, but Sam, for once, wasn't wearing sunglasses.

Vicki handed him the packet of mail Katie had given us at the hotel. Sam began tearing open envelopes. There was a letter from one of his daughters telling him how she was doing at school. She addressed him as "Dear Father."

"That's a nice letter," Sam said, putting it aside.

The next letter was from one of the many children he had adopted financially through a Big Brother program. The third letter was from his Los Angeles attorney, advising him that he was being sued for a quarter of a million dollars for having committed battery.

"How long are you over here?" I asked.

"I'm not over here, Jon. I'm in exile." He squinted his gray eyes at me. "Have some wine. It's good Yugoslavian white wine."

"Mr. Sam is right," Lucky assured us.

"See," Sam said, holding out a hand that trembled with a quiet palsy, "if you drink to a certain point in your life, you don't get the shakes any more." He grinned.

"You're looking better than you did in the States," Vicki said.

"Yeah," Sam replied, "but I got a little gut now."

He patted his midriff. We had lunch and Sam ordered
fish. He asked Lucky to keep the head and tail for the cat.

"You still have the cat?" I said.

"Yeah," Sam said, "only it's a different cat. I find
it good company. When we're done shooting here, Lucky,
who by trade's a sailor--he quit the merchant service to work
with us--is going to take me scuba diving all through the Adriatic. Then I would like to make a porn flick. I've always
wanted to make a porn flick."

We had cognac. After several rounds, Sam suggested
we go down to the seashore to the editing shack so we could
watch rushes. He had the car brought around. On the way
there we passed the garden patch Sam was using as the battlefield.

"James Coburn says this new picture is about the violence men commit on themselves," I said.

"That's right in part," Sam said. "This is Jim's
third picture with me. CROSS OF IRON is about a group of
German soldiers retreating from the Eastern front. They're
finished and they're running, but they don't stop fighting. Coburn is the leader. You can see what a job Wolf Hartwig is
doing financing this picture just by looking at that exterior.
You've got to meet him while you're here. I can't tell you
what it's been like: delays, halts in shooting, no rushes, no
film sometimes. Wolf says it's all due to trouble at the
border. I asked him if not paying the crew was because of
trouble at the border. He's a Prussian. He was on the
Eastern front and has lead in his butt, so you know what direction he was going."

Sam cackled. His contract with Wolf called for a
$400,000 salary and ten per cent of the gross revenues. The
technical crew was international, although predominantly British. The coffee was a day old, but we drank it anyway. Sam
sat on an editor's stool and had rushes run. There were battle scenes and battle scenes. Somehow there was more loving
care and feeling in these clips and splices of film than, upon
release, there was anywhere in the picture.

"Ach, excuse me," a man said, standing in the doorway. He was of medium height, wearing a red shirt and red
trousers with a white belt, and had a bullet-shaped head.

Sam Peckinpah demonstrates for German actor Vadim Glowna
(center), how he wants a scene played in CROSS OF IRON
(Avco-Embassy, 1977).   Photo courtesy of Eddie Brandt's
Saturday Matinee.

        "This," Sam said, punching me in the shoulder and
grinning, "is our producer, Wolf Hartwig."

        Sam introduced me as Hartwig goose-stepped into the
room.

        "Ja, I know you," he said accusingly.   "You're just
like Pauline Kael."

        "He's not like Pauline Kael, Wolf," Sam corrected
him.   "He only writes about pictures after they're made, and
he never reviews them."

        "Ach, ja, an historian.   I tell you I know him."

Wolf began pacing back and forth, his head pressed down against his chest, hands clenched behind him.

"Vell, I'm glad you're here. I don't vant you writing about dis picture unless I am included."

"Oh, he'll be sure to include you, Wolf, won't you?" Sam said, punching me again in the shoulder.

"Sure."

"Ja," Wolf said, standing and nodding his head.

"Hello, Sam," Veronique Vendell said from the doorway. She was dressed in a tight red sweater that clung to her ample breasts and matched her red stretch pants. She entered the room, smiling. In the picture her part was biting off Arthur Brauss' penis, which was among the sequences edited from the American release version in order to give CROSS OF IRON an "R" rating.

"This," Wolf introduced her to us, "iss my former secretary, then the star of my sex films, and now my vife."

She rubbed the flat of her hand against her mound of Venus and more teeth came into her smile.

"Hello," she said to everyone in the room.

"Vell, now to get back," Wolf said, resuming his pacing, "I know dat Sam has probably toldt you of the difficulties ve'ff been haffing on dis picture."

"No difficulties, Wolf," Sam said, "just minor things like running out of film, or not getting paid. Another of the crew just quit."

"Ja, qvidt! Vell, I tell you Sam, anybody who vants to can qvidt, budt not you. You can't qvidt. I own you, Sam, until you finish dis picture. You and I are like brudders, like dis." Wolf wound his arms around himself and gave himself a tight squeeze. "You are my property, Sam. I own you." Wolf paused suddenly in his pacing and glared at me. "Und vot do you tink of dis picture so far?"

"I haven't seen enough of it to tell."

"Ja, vell I vill tell you von ting, it had better be very gudt. Do you know vhy? Because I got die great Sam Peckinpah to direct it for me. It had better be gudt. Do you hear dat, Sam? It had better be gudt!" Wolf started pacing again. "Ve haff a story to tell here, die story of how die German soldier feldt vhen die var vas lost. Dere haff been no pictures sympathetic to the Germans in die last var. Vell, dis vill be a first. A first!" He stopped to stare at me. "I haff to go now, budt I vant you to put in vot I haff said, exactly die vay I haff said it. Understand? Exactly!"

"Don't worry, Wolf," Sam said, "he will."

Hartwig said Auf Wiederseh'n all around and shook my hand, and then Sam's.

"I luff dis man," he said, holding onto Sam's hand and looking at me. "He'd better make a gudt picture, dat's all I got to say."

"I'll make your fucking picture, Wolf," Sam said.

Once he was gone, and Veronique with him, Sam clapped me on the back, and recommended that we all go to the hotel for a drink. Again he sent for the car.

"I get this fucking Mercedes," Sam remarked as we came out of the editing shack, "but Wolf drives an American Cadillac. The streets are too narrow and there's a lot of places he can't go with it, but it's the only car he'll drive, just so everyone knows it's Wolf Hartwig driving through."

At the hotel bar, we were joined by most of the cast and crew who were congregating for dinner prior to ascending to the casino on the roof to gamble. Katie was among them and she came over to join us. Arthur Brauss, the Nazi party man assigned to the morale of Coburn's unit and whom Veronique does in, strolled up. Sam introduced him to Vicki.

"When are your bosoms going to grow?" he asked, leering and scratching his crotch. "Turn around and let me see your ass." Vicki turned around. "You've got a beautiful ass." He was scratching again. "I should apologize, but the uniforms Wolf got us to wear are full of crabs. We're all scratching."

"I'll bet it was the uniforms," Vicki quipped.

"Just one Polish joke," Sam said to Vicki. "Come on. I'm the only one here other than Katie who doesn't have trouble pronouncing your last name."

"Okay, but just one."

"Ah," Sam sighed with pleasure. "Do you know what a Polish air conditioner is like?"

"No," Vicki said.

"It's one Polack sitting on top of a high stool flapping his arms while four other Pollacks turn him around and around, each holding onto a leg of the stool."

Arthur slapped the bar, laughing. Vicki smiled.

"All right, Jon, now I have one for you," Sam said, turning to me. "Did I ever show you how to masturbate a dinosaur?"

"No."

"Okay," Sam shouted down the bar, "clear the way."

He held his hands together and formed a large circle with his arms. He then ran, holding his arms in this position, to the very end of the long barroom and disappeared out the door. In a moment he returned, still running and holding his arms in a circle. He stopped where we were standing, puffing.

"That's how!" he wheezed. He was grinning happily. "I thought you'd like it. Now let me have another of those Irish cigarettes you're smoking."

I gave him the box.

"Let me send you a carton when I get back to London," I said.

"You're on."

Sam ordered all of us triple whiskeys. He was dispensing with the polite drinking. For every drink we had, Sam had three.

"Did you guys finally get the interview finished?"
Katie asked.

"I don't give any fucking interviews any more," Sam
said.

"No, " I told her.

"My God," she said, "how long is it going to take?"

"Probably the next twenty-five years," I replied.

Sam tipped his head back and thought for a moment.

"Yup," he said then, picking up his drink, "that's
just about right. "

The more he drank, the angrier he became. Finally
he decided he wanted to work on the script. Katie said she
hadn't typed the new changes as yet, and Sam began cursing.
He wanted to make more changes right away. He said he
was very pissed off. He didn't get into the elevator as we
stood in front of it; Katie did, and she was crying.

I knew then it would be impossible for me to write
objectively about Sam Peckinpah, because while he stood there
talking to us, suddenly nobody could touch him. He was isolated and alone and glowering, and I had come to love him too
much, as sometimes men come to love each other no matter
how beaten up they have been by life; and because however
good or bad his pictures were, they were all he had, and
they were his life.

SAM PECKINPAH

A Film Checklist by Karl Thiede

Director

1.   THE DEADLY COMPANIONS (1961). P: Pathé-
        American. C: Maureen O'Hara, Brian Keith, Steve
        Cochran. Color. Cinemascope. 90m.

✓2.   RIDE THE HIGH COUNTRY (1962). P: Metro-Goldwyn-
       Mayer. C: Randolph Scott, Joel McCrea, Mariette
       Hartley. Color. Cinemascope. 94m.

✓3.   MAJOR DUNDEE (1965). P: Columbia. C: Charlton
       Heston, Richard Harris, Jim Hutton. Color. Cinema-
       scope. 124m.

4.   THE CINCINNATI KID (1965). P: Metro-Goldwyn-
       Mayer. D: Sam Peckinpah and Norman Jewison.
       C: Steve McQueen, Edward G. Robinson, Ann-Margret.
       Color. Cinemascope. 113m.

5.   THE WILD BUNCH (1969). P: Warner's. C: William
       Holden, Ernest Borgnine, Robert Ryan. Color. Cin-
       emascope. 152m.

6.   THE BALLAD OF CABLE HOGUE (1970); P: War-
       ner's. C: Jason Robards, Stella Stevens, David
       Warner. Color. 120m.

7.   STRAW DOGS (1971). P: Cinerama. C: Dustin Hoff-
       man, Susan George, Peter Vaughn. Color. 113m.

✓8.   JUNIOR BONNER (1972). P: Cinerama. C: Steve
       McQueen, Joe Don Baker, Ida Lupino. Color. 103m.

✓9.   THE GETAWAY (1972). P: National General. C:
       Steve McQueen, Ali MacGraw, Ben Johnson. Color.
       122m.

10.   PAT GARRETT AND BILLY THE KID (1973). P:
       Metro-Goldwyn-Mayer. C: James Coburn, Kris Kris-
       tofferson, Richard Jaeckel. Color. Cinemascope.
       106m.

11.   BRING ME THE HEAD OF ALFREDO GARCIA (1974).
       P: United Artists. C: Warren Oates, Isela Vega,
       Gig Young. Color. 112m.

12   KILLER ELITE (1975). P: United Artists. C: James
       Caan, Robert Duvall, Arthur Hill. DeLuxe Color.
       Panavision. 122m.

✓13.   CROSS OF IRON (1977). P: Avco-Embassy. C:
       James Coburn, Maximilian Schell, James Mason.
       Technicolor. 119m.

George Roy Hill. Photo courtesy of Eddie Brandt's Saturday
Matinee.

Chapter 4

GEORGE ROY HILL

by Jacoba Atlas

I

A classic Us/Them dichotomy exists today at Universal Studios, the company that has produced such disparate films as AIRPORT (Universal, 1970), AMERICAN GRAFFITI (Universal, 1973), JAWS (Universal, 1975), and BLUE COLLAR (Universal, 1978). The split is between the filmmakers--the directors, writers, and producers who consider themselves artists--and the executives who consider movies an industry and have brought in computers to prove that the company can predict scientifically what movies audiences will want to see. These executives work out of a building known throughout Hollywood as the Black Tower, a monolithic shaft-like edifice with walls of dark reflective glass that dominates Universal's San Fernando Valley lot. The artists work out of a new low building, hidden from view by trees and a monstrous parking lot. Space in that Producer's Building, as it's called, is at a premium. When Verna Fields, once an editor, now an executive, fought to keep her office in the Producer's Building rather than move to the Black Tower, the struggle was seen as Ms. Field's attempt to allign herself once and for all with the artists rather than with the executives who had promoted her.

There is no question that producer/director George Roy Hill, the only director to have two films in the top ten box-office grossers of all time--THE STING (Universal, 1973) and BUTCH CASSIDY AND THE SUNDANCE KID (20th-Fox, 1969)--would work out of the Producer's Building. He has a suite of offices, carefully decorated, sprinkled with beautifully framed posters from all his films, including those not made at Universal. The only evidence of Hill's free-wheeling, maverick personality is the careless manner in which scripts are

135

piled all over the office and the way the man dresses. When
I interviewed him in 1977, Hill, without a project on the drawing boards, was comfortably clad in decidedly unchic overalls,
the sort of clothes a Kansas farmer might wear to pitch hay.

Despite this simplicity of appearance, Hill's contract
with Universal makes him one of the richest, and most costly,
directors in Hollywood. He earns $750,000 per picture, up
front, plus a healthy percentage of the profits, and in a system where someone's earning power is equated with one's
professional ability, Hill is up there with the best of an industry pantheon that includes such whiz kids as Steven Spielberg, twenty years Hill's junior, another Universal contract
director who had to go to Columbia to get CLOSE ENCOUNT-
ERS OF THE THIRD KIND (Columbia, 1977) off the ground,
and George Lucas, whose STAR WARS (20th-Fox, 1977) was
turned down by Universal before Twentieth Century-Fox decided
to give this science fiction space Western a shot.

Hill has had no such problems getting his projects
okayed by the Universal brass. The director was personally
recruited to the studio by Lew Wasserman, chairman of the
MCA-Universal board and generally considered to be the most
powerful man in a powerhouse industry. Wasserman gave
Hill complete autonomy and that's what the director enjoys,
even when the studio does not understand what in the world
is attractive about a certain project--a stance they assumed
when Hill turned in SLAP SHOT (Universal, 1977).

Hill, who felt compelled to write a defense of SLAP
SHOT for The Los Angeles Times and who plays Johann Se-
bastian Bach on the piano for an hour every morning, was
born 20 December, 1922 at Minneapolis, Minnesota. He was
educated at Yale as a music major and went on to study for
a doctorate in music. While at Yale, he studied under contemporary composer Paul Hindemith. The Second World War
interrupted his studies and Hill enlisted in the U.S. Marines,
serving in the Pacific as a flying major. He re-entered the
service during the Korean conflict. Between military stints,
he attended Trinity College in Dublin, Ireland. It was while
at Trinity College that Hill switched his major to acting and
for a time joined Cyril Cusack's Abbey Players. He has
spent periods of time as a singer in Southern France, a
guard at New York City's Metropolitan Museum, a gardener
at the Church of St. John the Divine, and, after returning to
the United States from Ireland, he joined Margaret Webster's
Shakespeare company and for nine months was in The Cred-

itors, a play given at the Cherry Lane Theatre off Broadway.
After being called back into service by Korea, he re-emerged
and wrote a teleplay based on his experiences, titled "My
Brother's Keeper," which he sold to the Kraft Theatre. He
also had an acting role in the teleplay and was gratified when
it won Kraft's Best TV Play Award. There followed a year
of adapting scripts and original stories for the Kraft Theatre,
during which time Hill worked himself into the postion of an
assistant director and finally a director. He directed Billy
Budd, The Helen Morgan Story, and Child of Our Time for
television. He turned to producing and was acclaimed for
his television production of A Night to Remember.

Hill's first directorial effort on Broadway was Ketti
Fring's adaptation of Thomas Wolfe's novel, Look Homeward,
Angel, and it won a Pulitzer Prize for Hill. When he directed Tennessee Williams' PERIOD OF ADJUSTMENT, he
was brought to Hollywood to direct the motion picture version,
which M-G-M released in 1962. Although Hill's future rested
in Hollywood, it remains to his credit that he directed the
television Playhouse 90 production of "Judgment at Nurem-
burg," which, for those who saw it, was far superior to the
subsequent motion picture version (United Artists, 1961), directed by Stanley Kramer.

In PERIOD OF ADJUSTMENT, Jane Fonda played a
young bride trying to cope with the mystery of marriage.
Following that family feud came an adaptation of Lillian Hellman's stage play, TOYS IN THE ATTIC (United Artists, 1963).
It starred Dean Martin and Maureen Stapleton.

THE WORLD OF HENRY ORIENT (United Artists,
1964) was based on a screenplay by Nunnally and Nora Johnson. Nora, Nunnally Johnson's daughter, was a novelist in
her own right. "Henry Orient is really a little like Oscar
Levant," Hill remarked at the time, "and when I tell you
that Peter Sellers plays him you can just imagine how mad
it all is.... Henry's a pianist and a woman chaser but he
meets his Waterloo when he encounters two American teenagers." Merrie Spaeth and Tippi Walker, both non-profes-
sionals, were cast as the two teenagers. Together with
Jerome Hellman, an agent, and like Hill an ex-Marine, George
Roy Hill formed Pan Arts Productions. When THE WORLD
OF HENRY ORIENT was finished, Hellman put Tippi Walker
under contract. Although HENRY ORIENT did not do well at
the box office, the film has its fans, not the least of whom
is Hill himself.

After directing what were essentially three small films, Hill went ahead into the epic HAWAII (United Artists, 1966), a sprawling movie based on James A. Michener's even more sprawling novel. The location was grueling and even the assemblage of a fine cast, including Julie Andrews, Max von Sydow, and Richard Harris, couldn't keep the venture from sinking.

The Mirisch brothers, disputing with Hill over the kind of film they, as the producers, wanted in HAWAII, fired Hill a total of three times. Hill's next venture was in a lighter vein, again with Julie Andrews, the sprightly musical, THOROUGHLY MODERN MILLIE (Universal, 1967), which also featured James Fox and Mary Tyler Moore. It was bright and clever, the sort of film that would have delighted audiences in the 'thirties, but which seemed strangely out of place during the turbulent 'sixties. Its release in 1967 coincided with student strikes, anti-war demonstrations, and the emergence of rock as a way of life. In such an atmosphere, gold-digging flappers might seem an unlikely idea. "I left MILLIE," Hill was subsequently quoted, "during the editing because I wanted a fast, light, and stylish movie. Instead Universal decided to make a road show picture out of it and added twenty minutes of film. Instead of a mindless bit of fluff, they hurt it by making the picture serious." When reminded that MILLIE was, as of that time, the second largest money-maker in the studio's history, Hill laughed aloud. "Guess they were right, after all," he confessed.

Hill personally struck gold with his next picture, BUTCH CASSIDY AND THE SUNDANCE KID. From a screenplay by William Goldman, this comic Western borrowed heavily from "new wave" directors like François Truffaut and even from home-grown artists like Arthur Penn, and the film caught the imagination of the public; like a juggernaut, the Butch and Sundance craze seemed to know no end-point. Nominated for Academy Awards, making a superstar of Robert Redford, making Paul Newman a millionaire, firmly establishing Hill as a winning director, BUTCH CASSIDY AND THE SUNDANCE KID holds the record as the highest grossing Western in history.

Hill's next project wasn't an easy way out. He followed BUTCH with an adaptation of Kurt Vonnegut, Jr.'s SLAUGHTERHOUSE FIVE (Universal, 1972). Vonnegut's book was a wretchedly written, nearly illiterate anti-war fantasy about peace and love. To film it brought Hill for the first

George Roy Hill directing Julie Andrews and Max von Sydow
in HAWAII (United Artists, 1966).   Photo courtesy of Eddie
Brandt's Saturday Matinee.

time into pure fantasy, a form he would return to three years
later, with much more success, in THE GREAT WALDO PEP-
PER (Universal, 1975). SLAUGHTERHOUSE FIVE, with brilliant cinematography by Czech cameraman Miraslav Ondrachek
and tight editing by Dee Dee Allen, almost suceeded in spite
of its difficult subject matter. But the cult followers that delight in Vonnegut on the printed page, or at least used to,
were not interested, apparently, in seeing him up on the
screen. SLAUGHTERHOUSE FIVE scarcely made back its
negative cost.

In THE STING (Universal, 1973), Hill bounced back with
a vengeance. Taking a second script by writer David S. Ward,
Hill honed the story into a nostalgic romp about con men that
proved irresistible to the public. Hill also reunited the winning team of Redford and Newman, spliced in the atmospheric
rags of Scott Joplin (a suggestion from Hill's son), and sat
back while millions poured in at the box office. THE STING
was nominated for seven Academy Awards; it won as Best
Picture and Hill won the Oscar for Best Director.

Once again, Hill could do no wrong, and he responded
to this freedom by once more tackling a difficult film, THE
GREAT WALDO PEPPER. When the film was explained to
the Universal executives, it must have sounded like a winner
--Robert Redford playing a barnstorming hero who comes to
Hollywood during the silent era. But Hill had something else
in mind and fashioned a lyrical film, one that pines very
softly for a grace and romanticism that America passed by.
The film was a moderate success, thanks in no small measure to Redford's box-office appeal, but it seemed to bewilder
audiences who wanted a simple, straightforward movie about
heroes. Hill didn't give them that.

Hill's most recent film has been SLAP SHOT, filmed
in 1976 from a first script by Nancy Dowd. It was a foul-
mouthed journey through the world of ice hockey, seen through
the limited scope of a small town team. Its star was Paul
Newman. Critics, who were beginning to see Hill as a benign entertainer, were shocked at the language and the violence on screen. The film was banned completely in Man-
chester, England, ironically, perhaps, because that town has
the reputation of being one of the roughest in Great Britain.
Hill himself was pleased at their response. Shaking up the
powers that be holds a special pleasure for him.

Since SLAP SHOT, Hill has toyed with several projects,

George Roy Hill with Robert Redford during filming of THE
GREAT WALDO PEPPER (Universal, 1975).   Photo courtesy
of Eddie Brandt's Saturday Matinee.

but has come up with nothing concrete.   Robert Redford has
said of him: "The world is slow to realize that George Roy
Hill not only is a vastly talented storyteller on the screen--
but also cosmically cheap."   Universal v.p. Jennings Lang
might agree with the latter comment, but not the way Redford
meant it.   "If you find anyone for whom George Roy Hill ever
picked up a lunch tab," he once remarked, "you'll have a real
exclusive."   For Paul Newman, Hill "has such an uncanny
sense of story and character that there's a reason for everything the wily bastard does.   With the little con games, he

George Roy Hill directing Paul Newman in SLAP SHOT (Universal, 1977).   Photo courtesy of Eddie Brandt's Saturday Matinee.

was effectively getting Redford and me into the spirit of the picaresque guys we were playing in BUTCH CASSIDY, and--who knows?--he even may have had something like THE STING in mind for us, way back then in 1969.   That's his scholarly approach to things."

What follows is the second interview George Roy Hill has ever given.   The first was for The New York Times.   I have therefore felt it best to reproduce the interview verbatim.

II

JA: Tell me something about your background ... you attended Yale University....

GRH: I got out of Yale in 1942 and went directly into World
War II, as a Marine aviator. I served in the South Pacific
for eighteen months and then came back and worked as a reporter in Texas for a while. Then I went to Dublin to do
post-graduate work at Trinity College, and it was really in
Ireland that I became interested in theatre. I had actually
always been interested in the theatre to some degree, particularly Irish theatre--Yeats, Synge. I was doing a doctor's
thesis at Trinity on the use of music and musical forms in
Finnegans Wake and Ulysses, so I was really studying James
Joyce. But I got sidetracked and started acting in Cyril Cusack's company at the Gaiety Theatre and then went on to the
Abbey Theatre, one of the most celebrated theatres in Ireland.
My getting into the theatre was really from a standpoint of
academics. I was a music major in college, I studied under
Paul Hindemith for a while, but the interest in theatre was
always there. I never took it very seriously because I al-
ways thought my life's work would be something else.

JA: You were in Ireland, in Dublin, working in the theatre
when Yeats and Maude Gonne were still alive. Did you have
any contact with them?

GRH: No, I never met Yeats.... I know that Synge was
already dead and although O'Casey was still alive he was living in England. I had forgotten Yeats was alive. And I didn't
even know then that Maude Gonne was alive. My God, she
was something else....

JA: What happened after Ireland?

GRH: I was never interested in directing until I got back to
the States and was called into the service in the Marine corps
for the Korean War, flying jets at that time. So my academic
and acting career was cut short. During the war, I started
to write. By this time I was almost thirty and to my amazement I started to sell. I sold a half dozen TV plays to Kraft
and other live television shows at the time, so when I got out
of the war, I was offered a job as a writer on the Kraft television show. In those days TV ate up material, so I started
writing and re-writing full speed. I also got involved in the
production as an assistant on my own work. When an opening for a director came up, the producers asked me if I
wanted to do it. I said fine, I'll take a crack at it. It's
odd, but directing was never a consuming passion. Again,

I was over thirty when I started directing. The first play I
did on Broadway was some years later, Look Homeward, Angel, and then it was ten years more before I did a film. That
was PERIOD OF ADJUSTMENT in 1962. I've been directing
ever since and have been interested in it, but it wasn't something I planned. If anyone had told me in college I would have
been a film director, I would have laughed. I didn't even
know what a film director was.

JA: How did you see your life going originally?

GRH: I come from a newspaper-oriented family, so I thought
I would go into the newspaper business as the rest of my family did. Otherwise, I suppose, teaching. I always thought it
was a good idea to teach until I actually started teaching. I
did a couple of sessions at Yale and I didn't like it at all.
I was very impatient with the kids. This was in the 'sixties,
late 'sixties, around 1968, and it was a very self-indulgent
time. They didn't want to actually do anything. I wanted to
get them on their feet and take them through the nuts and bolts
of directing, but all they wanted was to discuss some Italian
director's greatest films, and since I usually hadn't seen the
film, or if I had seen it, hadn't understood it, it was hard
for me to sit and listen to endless discussions about it. I
was never one for long discussions anyway. Even discussions
about my own films.

JA: Do you think because you're a writer, you're more
protective of a screenplay than other film directors might
be?

GRH: I don't know. I think both coming out of writing myself and having worked so long on Broadway where the word
is king, I respect words. On the stage ... it's interesting
... if you think back to great moments you remember, usually it's a vivid gesture, not a phrase; the words often escape you. But basically you have one visual image for the
whole evening on the stage, and you use technical things to
divert people. For instance, in terms of lighting you can
cut from one end of the stage to another to focus attention.
But you're limited. Words and the interplay of words is what
brings the drama about. So I learned that respect and I'm
probably more protective because of that. Also, though, I
do a great deal of improvisation, always within the context
of the words; or totally outside the context, so you're dealing
only with emotions. I have seldom, although I have done it,
let an actor go out and wing a scene. In SLAP SHOT, Andy

Duncan is terribly good at that, and often I would let him
say what he wanted, but that's very rare.

JA: You often work with the same actors. Why?

GRH: One is always comfortable with a stock company. You
know what you can get out of actors; you feel very comfortable.
It can be very exciting to work with new actors, but you don't
throw someone away just because you know their work and
know what you can expect.

JA: But can't that make you lazy as a director?

GRH: I suppose that could happen, but on the other hand I've
often worked with newcomers, or actors that have had very
little experience. Jane Fonda had done only one other film
when I used her in PERIOD OF ADJUSTMENT, and those two
little girls in THE WORLD OF HENRY ORIENT had never
seen a camera. Valerie Perrine had never seen a camera:
Michael Sacks was a total unknown when I used him in
SLAUGHTERHOUSE FIVE.

JA: What are the problems of integrating unknowns or non-
professionals with trained actors?

GRH: This is particularly evident in SLAP SHOT. Those
hockey players had never acted, but since they were playing
themselves it worked. They also had a lot of scenes with
Paul [Newman], but I have a theory, or not a theory but
something I've experienced: if an actor is natural and out-
going, gregarious and uninhibited and without any experience,
he'll be easy to deal with. And the great professionals, like
Bob [Redford] and Paul are easy to deal with. It's the people
who are in the middle, who have, let's say, quite a bit of
television experience, who are tricky. They are the most
insecure and therefore the most protective. They're unwilling to give unless they're sure. That's the area where you
run into trouble.

JA: How do you go about casting your movies?

GRH: In SLAP SHOT the script was written about a particular hockey team, so those characters all had real life counterparts. In some cases we had to cast professional actors
who could skate well because they had to carry more of the
drama, more substance of a scene. It's a question of balancing. The three boys in the supporting roles never had to

carry a scene; they just had to look right on the ice and since
they are hockey players it was fine. They were playing themselves in their own ambience, so we were coming to them,
rather than their being on a set. That might have been inhibiting to them. Also you have a feeling for actors. You
get to feel what's going to go well. I spent several evenings
out in bars with those guys before hiring them, seeing how
they function. You can make mistakes, but I've been very
lucky. With Valerie Perrine, that was another type of casting. She came in and read for me. I couldn't believe she
had never acted before. That happens. Someone walks in
and you can see right off they have talent. I think I'm very
open to new talent. In SLAP SHOT certainly most of the supporting roles were new talent. Also a new writer.

         I usually do movies that are written directly for the
screen. That wasn't true with my early films, but the rest
of them, with the exception of SLAUGHTERHOUSE FIVE, have
all been originals. I like that because it's good to work without preconceptions on how it's supposed to go. I want to ignore the auteur theory like the plague, but I think you get
something more satisfactory with something that's been created directly for the screen. Even if the source material is
as good as Gone with the Wind. It always fascinates me that
with directors who are using other people's material they still
get called auteurs. I don't think a director is an auteur unless he has a writing credit.

         It all becomes so unseemly, people scrounging for
credit, grasping and crawling. They're like a married couple
screaming at each other trying to take credit for a successful
marriage. Very distasteful. I don't know why people get into
that. What difference does it make? No one can remember
who built the cathedral at Chartres, but it stands and it's
great and that's the satisfaction. You can't tell who did what;
it's all interaction. Like Gilbert and Sullivan ... who deserves the credit? Neither of them did a damn thing independently. All those dreary operas. They were second rate
without each other. Recently there was this big controversy
in the press, started by David Rintels of the Writers' Guild,
about who deserved the credit on the Frank Capra films,
Capra or his screenwriter Robert Riskin. It was embarrassing. Rintels saying Riskin was better than Capra, and then
Capra was saying Riskin never did anything without him. It
was all so tacky. In fact, the two of them working together
were better than anything any one of them ever did separately.
That's nothing to be ashamed of. . . .

I don't know why it is, but movies belong to lots of
people. A director cannot be an auteur unless he writes,
directs, edits, and never listens to his actors or his wife:
then I guess he can say he did it all himself. If he wants
to.

JA: Are you surprised at the enormous success your films
have had financially?

GRH: I don't know. My favorite film, well my two favorites
are THE WORLD OF HENRY ORIENT and SLAUGHTER-
HOUSE FIVE.   ORIENT was not a successful film financially.
SLAUGHTERHOUSE FIVE did all right for the studio, but
just barely. We didn't lose on it, but we didn't gain. Those
two are unsuccessful films, yet they're my favorites. Whether
it's because of that loving the ugly child syndrome, I don't
know; maybe there's some of that. ORIENT has a great following, but it was not successful. I don't think you gauge
yourself in terms of feeling for a film because it's a financial
success or not. I have had an extraordinary run of successful films, but you don't think about that.

JA: How did SLAP SHOT do?

GRH: Better than I expected, because I knew the language
[four-letter words in profusion] would alienate some people.
The fact that it did so well is a surprise.

JA: What attracted you to SLAP SHOT?

GRH: I had done a lot of fantasy films, and I wanted to do
something that was realistic, and not in period. It seemed
to me, because I was doing a modern film, I had to use
modern language. Universal was very disturbed about the
language; it's a very PG-oriented studio. Then we got terrible reviews here in LA. The critics called it an ultraviolent film ... the same people who praise the films of
Peckinpah condemned SLAP SHOT. I don't know why, but
we got unanimously bad reviews here. Not only bad reviews,
but people went out of their way to say bad things. The papers ran negative letters for weeks. Arthur Knight [reviewer
for the trade paper, The Hollywood Reporter] said I should
have my mouth washed out with soap. He said Paul and I
did it because we felt guilty about the success of THE STING
and BUTCH CASSIDY. That was nonsense. I don't know,
but SLAP SHOT did something to this town. I shook them up.
I had no intention of doing that, but people were deeply angry

about the film. [Charles] Champlin [critic for The Los Angeles Times] was furious--and he never gets furious. He
was livid. Kevin Thomas wrote the first bad review for the
film in the Times. He called it ultraviolent and then some
weeks later Chuck came back and wrote another bad review
of the film. He said it shouldn't be released. It didn't hurt
us at the box office, but then I don't know what reviews do
anyway.

JA: They seem to make a difference with marginal foreign
releases.

GRH: Yes, that's true, but major American films aren't
hurt by reviews. We got a lot of letters condemning us for
making a movie with that kind of language, but curiously,
eighty per cent of the people who wrote hadn't seen the film.
They got their opinions from the newspapers.

JA: What was Universal's reaction?

GRH: They didn't ask for changes, although they blanched
when they saw the film. Actually they were loath to make
it in the first place. They liked the film a great deal more
than they liked the script. The script actually changed considerably since the first version of it. Nancy [Dowd] came
down to Jamestown and re-wrote all the time. But Universal
had great doubts about it. I think they were relieved when
they saw the final film, but they were still afraid of the language. However, to give them full credit, there was not even
a suggestion that I change a single word. I heard later there
was some clutching of hearts, but there was no direct oppo-
sition to me. They let me know they were worried, but that
was the extent of it.

JA: Then you're happy working at Universal?

GRH: Yes. I have autonomy, an independent wing. The
last five out of six films were made here. I'm comfortable.
It's not a studio that encourages young directors to be experimental, but I think that's changing. I have one more picture
on my contract here.

JA: What happened with your Entebbe project? You announced it in the trades, only to find a dozen other filmmakers also working on that idea. Did you actually think you'd
make your movie?

GRH: Yes. I had no idea until I announced the project that

some sort of race was taking place.   When that happened, the
studio agreed to drop the idea.   I didn't want to participate
in a race.   That's not movie making.

JA: Do you think you can go back to it in the future, look
at Entebbe as history?

GRH: No.   Everyone will say Entebbe's been done.   It's
an old project.   Everyone knows the story, the ending.   It's
too bad.

JA: How far along had you developed Entebbe when it was
dropped?

GRH: Just the beginning.   I went to Israel and had a fascinating time.   I don't know, another project might come of it.
I've always been somewhat of a Bible reader and, of course,
the moment I got over there I got interested in the historical
aspects.   I always wanted to do a story from Samuel I and II.
The story of David.   I fooled with that for a while, but it's
really just my own interest.   Since I've been in college I've
read the Bible.   But I guess I'm far more interested in it
from an academic point of view than from the view of a movie
maker.   Israel's a very compelling, fascinating place.

JA: Is the David project something you've nursed in the
back of your head?

GRH: Yes, definitely.   But doing a Bible story is so dangerous.   You're courting disaster, doing that period, or any
period in the Bible.   With a costume drama set in the desert,
there's language, behavior, all sorts of problems.   You get
fascinated by the early aspects of the Bible, who wrote what,
who re-wrote whom.   I love it; it's all fine; it's a great puzzle to me.   You start looking at the style of the writing, and
the language, and then what happened when the "editors" got
together to put the Bible down in writing.   But is that going
to be exciting in Omaha?   I've always been a little shy about
my enthusiasm.

JA: But isn't what you've just described a great mystery?

GRH: Yes, of course, I've looked at doing a film in that
way, look for the secret syndrome.   The novelty of discovery.
Trying to discover who David was is fascinating.   He did
many contradictory things.   For instance, he ran a protection
racket, and was really not very likeable at times.   Then
there's Saul, and it's so damn moving you forget everything

else.   It's very exciting.   Whenever I'm between projects I
go back to the Bible.   But who knows?

JA: How difficult is it for you not to be making a movie?

GRH: Very.   I chew walls.   I'm very difficult to live with.
But it's also hard to say yes to a project.   The idea of com-
miting yourself to a year and a half of something--the project
has to sustain you.   That's what you look for, not whether it
will be successful or not--all that doesn't occur to me.   I
have to wonder whether it will sustain me, whether it has
enough depth and enjoyment to it.   That's the measuring stick.
A lot of good things I like, but I don't think they'll hold up
over the long run.   It's different from when a director would
make three or four films a year, to ten television shows.
When I was doing that I could pluck blindly because I knew
that in a few short days I'd move on to something else.   But
now that the autonomy of directors has enlarged, it also means
we must spend more time with our material.   You start at its
inception, and go through post-production.   That never used
to be the case.   When I was working in television, I'd do one
show and have a dozen others on my desk to pick from.

JA: Do you ever get nostalgic for those days?

GRH: I get nostalgic for the working system we had on television.   Where you came into your office and the story department had three scripts for you to choose from, and you
read them over a two-day period and then picked.   I'd like
this one, and prepare another for two shows later on.   You'd
be working, so you'd never pay any attention to the reviews,
because the show was on the air and only your ego mattered.
Besides, by that time you were on to your next project.   So
from that point of view it was more enjoyable.   There's too
much riding on a damn movie.   Not just money, but too much
time invested.   You lose a year and a half.   Some directors
take three or four years.   How do you sustain interest?   What
other art work, if you call movies art, and I guess sometimes
it is--what other form, except the Sistine ceiling, takes that
length of time?   Beethoven didn't take four years to write the
Ninth Symphony.

JA: Must it take so long?

GRH: Part of it developed over the director's being anxious
for power.   In order to exercise power you have to exercise
the responsibility that goes with it.   It's time-consuming.   If

you finally get "final cut" on a picture, then you have to be there every minute if you're conscientious, and see it to the end. You have to determine that it's the best possible cut there is. If somebody else has "final cut," well, that gives you four months less. But if you want to go for power, then you have to go for responsibility.

JA: Does your energy ever fail on a film?

GRH: No, I've been awfully tired on a film, particularly being on ice skates all the time with SLAP SHOT. But I get a good night's sleep, and I don't socialize at all during the course of a film. And also, the adrenalin is high. You get really exhausted right after the film is over, right before the editing period. Then I turn my paunch to the sun and rest.

JA: You often pick films that are difficult to do logistically.

GRH: That's true. SLAP SHOT was impossible. WALDO was hard, but THE STING was a snap. We were able to shoot that mostly in the studio, where it's only a five-day week. But on location it's a six-day week and that's exhausting. WALDO was very hard, although I love flying. I used my airplane in the film. I sometimes go barnstorming in Nova Scotia. WALDO didn't do as well as I thought it would. It was successful, but not as much as I thought. It took a while to settle. It was a film I maybe tried to get too much into. But I'm very superstitious. I'll be happy if all my films earn over fifteen million dollars. I don't want to tempt the gods.

GEORGE ROY HILL

A Film Checklist by Vicki Piekarski

Director

1.   PERIOD OF ADJUSTMENT (1962).   P: Metro-Goldwyn-Mayer.   C: Jim Hutton, Tony Franciosa, Jane Fonda. 112m.

2.   TOYS IN THE ATTIC (1963).   P: United Artists.

C: Dean Martin, Geraldine Page, Yvette Mimieux.
Panavision. 90m.

3.   THE WORLD OF HENRY ORIENT (1964). P: United
      Artists. C: Peter Sellers, Paula Prentiss, Tippi
      Walker. DeLuxe Color. Panavision. 106m.

4.   HAWAII (1966). P: United Artists. C: Julie An-
      drews, Max von Sydow, Richard Harris. DeLuxe
      Color. Panavision. 189m.

5.   THOROUGHLY MODERN MILLIE (1967). P: Universal.
      C: Julie Andrews, Mary Tyler Moore, Carol Channing.
      Technicolor. 138m.

✓6.   BUTCH CASSIDY AND THE SUNDANCE KID (1969).
      P: Twentieth Century-Fox. C: Paul Newman, Rob-
      ert Redford, Katharine Ross. DeLuxe Color. Pana-
      vision. 110m.

7.   SLAUGHTERHOUSE FIVE (1972). P: Universal. C:
      Michael Sacks, Ron Leibman, Eugene Roche. Tech-
      nicolor. 104m.

✓8.   THE STING (1973). P: Universal. C: Paul Newman,
      Robert Redford, Robert Shaw. Technicolor. 129m.

✓9.   THE GREAT WALDO PEPPER (1975). P: Universal.
      C: Robert Redford, Bo Svenson, Bo Brundin. Tech-
      nicolor. 108m.

10.   SLAP SHOT (1977). P: Universal. C: Paul Newman,
      Strother Martin, Michael Ontkean. Color. 123m.

Chapter 5

ROBERT ALTMAN

by David Wilson

I

Robert Altman has spent twenty years trying to film
the Greatest Show on Earth. He has come close to succeed-
ing in the task at least five times.

Always, however, something has eluded him, some
small bit of information that has been unexplained or misun-
derstood, some reason why he has had to repeat his theme
in a new movie. Altman has an eagle-eye for American myths.
He has studied the effects of those myths with equal vigor.
Does our culture produce people who are more capable of
feeling, more capable of caring? Altman's films say it does
not, though he could add that we are a resilient, an optimistic, people. Altman could prove this resiliency by his own
career.

James Dean was the subject of Altman's second picture, THE JAMES DEAN STORY (Warner's, 1957). Dean
was twenty-four years old when he died in a 1955 car crash.
While Dean was climbing his brief ladder of success, Altman
was working at the Calvin Film Company in Kansas City.
There, Altman learned his trade. He produced, directed,
wrote, and edited his short subjects, he dressed his sets and
even sold his films. While he was working for Calvin, he
tried to break into the feature film market during trips to the
West Coast.

Two years after Dean's death, Altman arrived in Los
Angeles to co-produce and co-direct THE JAMES DEAN STORY
with George W. George. It took the pair one year to finish
the project. Though it was not a commercial success, the
documentary hit professional paydirt. George, as he had

153

Robert Altman.   Photo courtesy of Eddie Brandt's Saturday
Matinee.

wished, became a play producer in New York, and Alfred
Hitchcock asked Altman to direct episodes for his television
series. Altman accepted the offer. The two episodes he
shot led to almost ten years of writing and directing in television.

Twenty years after THE JAMES DEAN STORY, Altman
suddenly became the top director in Hollywood when he made
NASHVILLE, in 1975. Its scale and subject made it his most
accessible picture since M*A*S*H, the hit he directed in 1969.
NASHVILLE was also one of the fastest moving, most vital
pictures of his career.

I was in Los Angeles for the fifth time in two weeks,
asking someone on the phone if they knew of an agent for a
well-trained dog. I was writing a story titled "How To Make
It in Hollywood." In other words, "How Do You Become a
Movie Star?" ... "Who Should I Know?" ... "Does Talent
Count?" I figured a dog had a better chance.

I borrowed a tape recorder and interviewed two col-
umnists from The Hollywood Reporter. I called the Chamber
of Commerce to learn how to get my name placed on a star
in the Hollywood Boulevard sidewalk. That wasn't enough.
I called the Chinese Theatre on Hollywood Boulevard to learn
how to get my feet in and out of their wet cement. I walked
over to Dino De Laurentiis' opulent, oval reception room to
speak to a secretary about getting a part in KING KONG (Paramount, 1976) or BUFFALO BILL AND THE INDIANS (United
Artists, 1976), both in production at the time. She looked
me over and said I was too short for KONG, and Bob Altman
had already finished shooting BUFFALO BILL. She said she
had seen only one other person come in to an audition without an agent, and even then, he had a file stuffed with 8 x
10 glossies. I had nothing, but she said she'd get me an ap-
pointment. So much for that article.

A second magazine asked me for a piece on Ragtime
(Random House, 1974), the best-selling book by E. L. Doctorow which De Laurentiis had bought and scheduled for Altman. I called Lion's Gate, Altman's production company,
where an agent suggested I watch them film Altman's first
producing effort, WELCOME TO L.A. (United Artists, 1977).
In that way, I could talk to the cast, the director, Alan Rudolph, and later, I could interview Altman.

I was hungry, the call was over, and my editor was

out.   I decided there must be a restaurant within walking distance and I headed East on Wilshire Boulevard.   On the first
block I passed a travel agency and a furniture store.   After
two, three, four, and then five blocks, I still couldn't buy a
meal.   Finally, I saw a restaurant two blocks away.   It must
have been one of the last drive-ins in Beverly Hills.   I walked
inside, past two or three cars and a pair of car-hops dressed
in bobby sox.   I sat down and grabbed a menu.   Outside, two
policemen held back a small, lunchhour crowd.   Two motion
picture cameras and a reflector were set up inside a parking
space.   Behind the counter, a cashier was arguing with the
cook.   "They're holding them wrong," she said.   "They should
be holding the trays like this."   She reached down to her side,
with her arm at a forty-five-degree angle.

"My car may be in the picture," the cook said.   "I
wonder if I can charge them for rent?"

A waitress rushed past with a tray covered with dirty
plates and half-eaten omelettes.   "They've been here since
this morning."   She moved in front of me and winked.   "It's
a movie.   For T. V.   The story of James Dean!"

A week later, the agent picked me up outside the offices of the Los Angeles Free Press and we drove to the location, a narrow street above a rented house in Echo Park.
We walked towards the home and a girl from the middle-class
neighborhood gave us a note for Keith Carradine.   "From my
older sister," she said.   Outside, among the eucalyptus,
Geraldine Chaplin held an attaché case, Lauren Hutton held
a camera, and Carradine and Rudolph took turns hanging over
the side of a Valley Checker cab.   The director was in well-
worn jeans.   When Rudolph was satisfied with the performance,
the crew moved to a swimming pool for a short shot with
Sissy Spacek.   Then they broke for lunch.   Many of the leading characters were there that day.   Harvey Keitel was there
to make an off-screen telephone call.   The actress Christina
Raines, who wasn't in the picture, was there to watch her
boy friend Keith.

Almost two years earlier, Richard Baskin had been
working on his songs when he received a call from Gwen
Welles, an actress friend of his sister.   She had the script
for NASHVILLE and Robert Altman had recruited her to find
some songs to go along with it.   Baskin became excited over
the project and he approached the director with several songs.
He ended up collaborating on songs with many of the twenty-

four principal characters in NASHVILLE. One day during the
shooting, Rudolph was walking past Baskin's room when he
heard Baskin singing. Rudolph told Baskin he could make a
movie out of them. Altman agreed to produce the picture
and he brought in United Artists to back it. Now it was
called WELCOME TO L. A.

Altman stayed away from the set. He told one interviewer, "The only time I've been there was this morning,
when I woke up, because they were shooting in my house."

At the location, things were moving fast. It looked
as though it could be the last day of shooting, and before the
night was through, Rudolph would be shouting for a beer,
grinning, "I want to get un-straight!" After lunch, the crew
moved inside, where Carradine, a wire microphone taped to
his back, played one of Baskin's songs at the piano. Sissy
Spacek and Tom Thompson, Rudolph's assistant director, were
giggling while they read the ads in a sex magazine. The crew
set up for a scene at the piano, then for another scene at the
front door. Carradine juggled oranges while he waited for a
nude scene with Geraldine Chaplin.

"Bob is like a tremendous furnace that will burn forever," Rudolph said. He had dark eyes, a darker beard, and
shoulder-length hair. "Robert Altman can take ideas and reproduce energy out of them. He's an amazing person. Even
if you disagree with his choices, or misunderstand them, you
can see their logic.

"I hadn't worked as an assistant director for a year,
and on one Friday, I got a call to work on THE POSEIDON
ADVENTURE [20th-Fox, 1972]. Then Tommy Thompson, Altman's assistant director, called me to work on THE LONG
GOODBYE [United Artists, 1973]. I didn't know who Altman
was, so I told him I'd call him on Monday. That weekend,
I saw McCABE AND MRS. MILLER [Warner's, 1971] and I
was amazed. I decided to work with Bob. He was everything
he's cracked up to be--and more. He's the most economic
filmmaker that I know of. He works in a simple, deceptive
way, and he influences other people to contribute within his
framework. He's on such a selective level that you don't approach him with anything but your very best ideas, and you
don't even realize that the selection process is going on. I've
seen some of Bob's early shorts, even one for the Kansas
City Athletics, about how to play baseball, and it has some
touches that are amazing.

"After NASHVILLE, and after I finished the scripts for BUFFALO BILL and BREAKFAST OF CHAMPIONS, Bob said, 'You're ready. I'll protect you and I'll run interference for you. Just find something that you want to do.'

"Basically, WELCOME TO L.A. is about the people we've chosen to look at while we film a movie. It's not a travelogue or a documentary. We're looking at people and the Los Angeles influence. It's the breeding ground of all freedom of choice. The film really has no plot obligations per se. I think that's one of the main Altman influences. He's taught me that in the four years I've worked with him.

"The worst thing that could happen with this picture is if it comes out and it's an Altman movie with my name on it."

I'd never heard of Sissy Spacek but I remembered her from a T.V. movie. Her next picture, after WELCOME TO L.A., was CARRIE (United Artists, 1976), which would place her picture on the covers of half a dozen national magazines. In her dressing room, she spoke with a lithe Texas accent. She curled around her chair and described both CARRIE and WELCOME TO L.A. I asked her what she was doing in the company of Carradine, Sally Kellerman, Geraldine Chaplin, John Considine, and the rest of the cast, all of them familiar faces from Robert Altman's productions. "You're not one of Altman's people, are you?"

"I am now!" she said, and she seemed pleased by her answer. "I really feel like I'm part of the group, and I hope I'll work in some of these other pictures coming up. I hope so. I think that as they go along, they pick up people, anybody they're happy with, and they add them to the list. I'm ready to be their slave!"

"Why?"

"You have freedom! I'm improvising my dialogue, within the framework of the script, and it's fun. They know it's my first time working like this, so they made an extra effort for me. Alan explained this script to me, and I was still confused. I was used to hearing specifics. The picture is about people's inner relationships and about how few real people there are living in Los Angeles. People are different when they're with different people, and they're different when they're alone. That's really true. I remember when I first

started to date, when I moved to New York. I guess I went
out with about eight or ten guys regularly, and with their
groups of friends. With each one of those guys, I was a
little different, depending upon which slot needed to be filled
in what group. It's like, there were the crazies, and the ...
y'know what I mean? I was a little different Sissy with each
group. "

Spacek described how she broke into acting, and she
said, "It's terrible. If you want to be a lawyer or a doctor,
there's things you can study, and then you're certified. In
acting, it's crazy. Every time I'm in a film, I know it might
be my last. "

Keith Carradine didn't mind talking about Altman, Rudolph, or their pictures. In fact, he enjoyed it. He was
amused while I struggled to keep a thread of continuity going
in our interview, despite irregular, ten- or fifteen-minute in-
terruptions for his scenes. He walked over to where I was
watching the set and said, "I'm at your service!"

"Oh? ... what's it like working as a member of the
Altman players? You're one of the oldest hands. "

"Ha. I guess that's true. It's terrific. Otherwise,
I wouldn't be here. I love working. Altman's approach to
a scene is very loose. It's just a very free atmosphere,
and it's the same with Alan Rudolph. You can make changes
in the dialogue and script, and you're allowed to bring much
more of yourself to a part than in a more restricted atmosphere, where the screenwriter's words are the most precious
commodity. You can improvise to see what might work the
best.

"See, I don't think the audience needs things explained
to them. They're more intelligent than that. They can see
things and figure them out for themselves. I think that it's
more fun for an audience when they can do that. "

"Who are the directors with whom you'd like to work?"

"I refuse to answer that question. I'm too sick of
being asked it. There's a lot of good directors and I'd like
to work with anyone who I can sit in a room with and communicate, if I think they can make a good picture. "

"Many of your films have been made in a non-linear

style.   Is that the direction that you're most interested
in?"

"I wouldn't say that's true.   THIEVES LIKE US [United
Artists, 1974] had a very linear structure.   It's probably Altman's most linear film.   It was almost a direct translation
from the novel.   I had a very small part in McCABE AND
MRS. MILLER, and I suppose that wasn't very linear.   It
was an atmospheric film.   NASHVILLE, of course, had many
stories.

"Just because Bob seems to be the only one I work for
doesn't mean he's the only director I want to work for.   Actually, I've worked for a lot of other people.   I've done television, and I've done three films in Europe.   The first two
pictures were nothing to brag about, but the third was directed
by Jeanne Moreau.   I wanted to see what it was like working
in Europe, and those pictures were all very linear.   I'm glad
I did them, but one of them, an Italian comedy, was the worst
film I've ever been in.   It was playing in L.A. for a week,
and if it had been here any longer, I would have been disappointed."

"What's the best way to break into acting?"

"There's no way, you just have to be good, that's all.
If you're good, people will know it in an audition!"

"What about your family?   Has it been a help or a
hinderance?"

"It's been both.   It's been a help, but in some ways
... I'm very often called upon to answer for my family's
eccentricities, and I don't think that's fair at all!"

                                    II

          I wasn't sure what to expect.   When Playboy called
Altman "a maverick who constantly confounds Hollywood," it
was more austere than many of its newsrack competitors.

          In 1970, The Los Angeles Times called Altman "a
squeaky clean hippie-esque fellow of bear-like proportions."
In 1977, the Times said he resembled a "prairie Buddah."

          In 1971, on location for McCABE AND MRS. MILLER,

Aljean Harmetz for the New York Times described Altman:
"At 46, Robert Altman is Hollywood's newest 26-year-old
genius. The extra twenty years are simply the time he had
to spend, chained and toothless, in the anterooms of power,
waiting for Hollywood to catch up with him." The writer went
on to liken Altman to a character actor, a giant hawk, the
devil, Santa Claus, and ended up observing that Altman in
Vancouver reminded her of Alan Hale, Sr. in THE ADVEN-
TURES OF ROBIN HOOD (Warner's, 1938). Altman had made
a million dollars and lost two million. He had fathered four
children with three wives. He watched roller derby games
on T. V. , drank, doped, argued, skipped breakfast, brandished
an American Express card, and shrugged off sleep. He wrote
new scenes for McCABE AND MRS. MILLER every day. He
acted on hunches. Altman. Altman. The name rings in a
reader's ear. He sounds like a wizard.

It had rained in the morning, but the skies were clear
by the time I sidestepped the shallow pools of water covering
the streets and entered Altman's office ten minutes early.
The first thing I noticed inside was a pinball machine. I
wanted to play a game, but Altman was also there, waiting,
reading his interview in an issue of Film Quarterly. There
was a fire in his fireplace; the air was relaxed and drowsy.
His walls were draped with the props from BUFFALO BILL
AND THE INDIANS.

I thought of the metaphors. Was Altman devilish,
Christmas-like, or otherwise cherubic? None of those ad-
jectives seemed to fit. I remembered that he'd been married
to his third wife, Kathryn, for seventeen years, and I remembered a quote from her: "He's driven me crazy, but he's
never bored me!"

Altman was just a man, though he was one who looked
much younger than his years would ever admit. He possessed
an aura of physical strength. He didn't offer me a drink or
a smoke. We shook hands, and he looked so comfortable, I
told him not to get out of his couch. Instead, I settled in
beside him. While we spoke, he took a call from a friend.
Though NASHVILLE had received five Oscar nominations, including one for Best Direction, it had been declared ineligible
for awards in editing, costume design, and art direction. The
Academy of Motion Pictures had decided that the soundtrack
was ineligible. Altman appeared outraged, but he was also
resigned over the foolishness of the Academy regulations. At
any rate, he didn't look surprised. Alan Rudolph walked in,

but when he saw his producer in an interview, he started out, towards the pinball machine. "Oh," he said, "I've forgotten the letter."

Altman looked it over. "That's not a letter," he said, "that's an order!"

Ten minutes later, Altman received a second phone call, a warning that bootleg copies of the soundtrack for IMAGES (Columbia, 1972) were selling in a Westwood record shop. He gave his secretary two or three bills and sent her down to buy up the discs. She asked him if he thought they'd have any 45's. Then Harvey Keitel walked through the front door.

"Robbie De Niro got nice reviews in TAXI DRIVER [Columbia, 1976] in both trades," Altman said, "and so did you!"

"Yeah, I read Pauline Kael's review," Keitel said.

"How was Pauline's?"

"She gave it a rave and she mentioned a lot more about me than anybody else has yet. She loved the movie, and she singled me out. It looks like a big hit. So far, they're going four for four!"

"I think it sounds good. I'd like to see it."

Altman had to fly to New York for a screening of BUFFALO BILL on 17 February. Perhaps he'd be able to see TAXI DRIVER during the same trip. Keitel joined Rudolph at the pinball machine.

I tried to ask Altman another question, but it came out as a statement: "You watch the press pretty carefully."

"Yes. I think it's interesting. I take it seriously, but I don't care much for the gossip kind of reviewers. You know, someone makes a film, and you're anxious to see what the first reaction will be. They're films, they're not just movies."

"Whom do you like?"

"Anybody who makes some kind of picture that's good. I don't see too many films. I've spent every day of my life

working on one or two or three films. At night, when I'm
not doing that, I don't feel like sitting down and looking at a
movie. "

    "I was on the set for WELCOME TO L. A.   Everybody
there seemed to regard you with a great deal of affection. "

    "That's because I wasn't there!"

    "How do you like your new role as a producer?"

    "It's terrible.   It's really not any fun.   As a producer,
you are the enemy.   The producer isn't part of the action,
you can't be a part.   I've been working on RAGTIME and
some other things.   It's such a community when you're working on a film ... and the producer really isn't part of that.
There's just nothing for me to do beyond watching the budget,
but I'm going to produce a film for Bob Newton, and if Alan
Rudolph comes up with another project...."

    "He's using a lot of your actors. "

    "Yes, but they're not principals.   I've used a lot of
actors from one picture to another, but it's not what you'd
call a stock company.   You get to know somebody, and you
learn how they work.   It's just easier to work with somebody
you know.   It's a question of people's talents. "

    "How did you come up with the· RAGTIME assignment?"

    "Dino De Laurentiis bought it after the manuscript had
been turned down by the majors and he showed it to me.   I
like the writer and the way it was written--the style.   Now
E. L. Doctorow and I are developing his earlier book, The
Book of Daniel [Random House, 1971].   He's also writing the
script for RAGTIME.   He didn't want to write the screenplay,
so I was going to have Joan Tewkesbury write it.   Then we
met, Doctorow and I, and we became friends.   I convinced
him to write the screenplay, but it wasn't part of the deal
for the screen rights.   We haven't started on The Book of
Daniel yet, but I suspect that we'll write it together and produce it together.   We're writing RAGTIME together.   He's
doing most of the preliminary writing, then we talk.   RAG-
TIME is varying the way that any translation is going to vary
from one medium to another.   Doctorow is writing scenes
that aren't in the book.   He's writing a 'blueprint' for a film. "

"Do you feel differently working with a big best-seller?"

"I feel a little more comfortable, but I don't know how confining it's going to be. I know I've got an audience, I don't have to worry about finding one. Or, it had better have an audience, because it's going to cost a lot of money to make it. I think we're going to have to build sets on back lots. None of it exists any more."

"Are you working on any original screenplays?"

"No, not right now. We're doing a screenplay now, NORTH DOUGLAS FORTY, by John Burks, and we've got BREAKFAST OF CHAMPIONS, which Alan Rudolph did the screenplay for. The next thing we'll do, unless something comes up, will probably be the start of THE BOOK OF DANIEL."

"Have you ever thought of returning to film anything for television?"

"No. I wouldn't know how to do it. We're trying to think of new television concepts as an outlet for our films. We're editing NASHVILLE for television now, and when it goes on, it'll be an expansion of the picture, rather than a dilution. It will be about two two-hour films which will go on during two consecutive nights. The same thing will happen with BUFFALO BILL. RAGTIME might possibly end up being ten hours over five nights. The theatrical version will probably be two hours, two or three hours, but it will probably be broken down into two films. We're trying to accommodate the television audience by showing them more. You can do that on television, while you can't do that in a theatre. BUFFALO BILL could comfortably fit into three hours. We certainly won't have to cut the pictures down for T.V."

"Is it hard to set that up with the networks?"

"Well no, not really. I mean, it makes more sense to the television buyers, and to the networks, to buy something that just isn't old hat, but to buy something that is, in a way, new. They'll be buying two movies rather than one, so it makes economic sense to everybody concerned."

"You include a lot of shots of T.V. cameras and equipment in NASHVILLE...."

"That's only because that is what would be there.   In
NASHVILLE, those events would have been covered by television.   We covered them covering it. "

"And in CALIFORNIA SPLIT [Columbia, 1974] you had
characters watching T. V. "

"Well, people watch television.   When they're bored,
they just switch it on. "

"One more question.   How do you get started in the
picture business today?"

"It's difficult, very difficult.   I think television certainly seems to be the most logical way to go right now.   Television and documentary films.   Anything where you can get
people to pay attention. "

"What about working as an assistant director?"

"Acting as an assistant is good, but it depends upon
who you're working for.   It worked for Alan Rudolph!"

I looked at the pinball machine on the way out.   A
piece of paper filled with numbers was taped to one corner
of the glass, and each of the highest scores was followed by
Altman's initials.

Altman had made twelve features before NASHVILLE.
His style was indirect, his points oblique, and his characters
were usually dominated by fictions disguised as facts; often,
they were living out the consequences of someone else's lies.
Their masks as outlaws, con-men, promoters or astronauts
fell only occasionally, but they prompted Altman's most powerful moments.   In flamboyant, satiric films like NASHVILLE,
Altman attempted to deal with dozens of characters.   In his
smaller, more graceful pictures, IMAGES, McCABE AND
MRS. MILLER, and THIEVES LIKE US, Altman's tone was
gentler.

Whatever the scope of his motion pictures, Altman's
characters, his most crucial elements, remained very nearly
the same in every film.   They drifted across his sets like
character actors from a Warner Bros. stage.   It's paradox-
ical, but one of America's most distinctive directors also appears to be it's most democratic director.   Altman shares

the auteur's reins with his cast. He shuffles his characters
and performers, adding new settings, screenwriters, or photographers. Miraculously, his pictures manage to exceed expectations. Altman is not quite ready to be typecast.

Many of his pictures have the rough-edged appearance
of exposés, and the vision is accordingly cynical. The self-
conscious director deals in ailing legends; he juggles his camera around the conventions of Western, war, and detective
films. He is a reactive filmmaker, one playing with the expected events in these genres. He cuts against the grain,
diluting the expected exposition, punching up the odd, tangen-
tial elements in screenplays.

The scenarios are likely to be fantastic or futuristic.
Seven years after BREWSTER McCLOUD (M-G-M, 1970) was
released, the first man learned to fly under his own muscle
power. Not long after COUNTDOWN (Warner's, 1968), a man
actually walked on the moon. Jimmy Carter, a Presidential
candidate with speeches as simplistic as those of Altman's
fictional candidate, Hal Phillip Walker, was elected while
NASHVILLE was still playing in Southern theatres.

Time and characterization are plastic substances in
Altman's pictures, and his approach is much closer to sculpture than literature. He edits his pictures like a T. V. addict
spinning his television dial, his voice whispers beneath the
soundtrack, "You know, of course ... that this is only a
movie!" The comment is a bitter, double-edged sword; it
is almost a pun.

Altman sets up a carnival-like atmosphere during his
shooting; he gives his actors an uncommon degree of freedom,
and he photographs the results. Much of the content is structured after the film is in the can, and the audience is an in-
tegral part of his calculations. "In NASHVILLE," Altman
said, "the theatre audience is also the audience at the Grand
Ole Opry. The film is about that kind of world. I'm always
aware that the people watching my films are in fact watching
a film, and I don't try to disguise that fact. The audience
is furnishing an impact; they meet us halfway. They're going
to add something of their own experience. If they're just sitting there looking at it, it's going to be pretty dull."

Altman fits the standards for directorial stardom as
few of his contemporaries do, and he is expected to field
philosophic questions considered far out of the range of his

more mercenary peers. Since 1970, his career has received
almost as much of the same cultish attention as has James
Dean's posthumous legend. Altman had good reasons to be
tired of reporters who liked to ask him if he really did drink
on the job ... and, if he didn't mind, "How much?" Altman
is a candid man, but many critics still try to insist that his
motives and decisions are mysterious. At times, in the past,
he has appeared to be afraid that the passions in his pictures
are too baldly stated. In a prologue to BREWSTER McCLOUD,
a character asks the audience not to take the picture too seriously.

      "You've got to let a film develop on it's own," Altman
said. "At some point, it takes up life and tells you it has to
go in this direction or that one. Good actors and directors
can take that and go with it."

      Despite his iconoclastic reputation, Altman is one of
the few people working in Hollywood who perpetuate the pre-
corporate myths of the business. Sitting with him in his office, it was possible to believe there was a 50-50 chance he
might pick his next new star from the U. C. L. A. students
passing outside his window. People who work at his Lion's
Gate production company move up, and they move up quickly,
into the creative ranks. Four years after their first meeting,
Altman was producing Alan Rudolph's first film.

      Altman found himself in a position where he had to
discover new stars because he refused to create vehicles for
old stars. More than once, he had trouble with the Hollywood
unions for his willingness to go with a hunch and a low budget.
"If you do what they demand," he once said, "you have to use
actors instead of Indians, stuntmen instead of cowboys, and
extras instead of ... people." If Altman played by the Guilds'
rules, he might have been out of business within a year. His
companions were also renegades. The first time Vilmos
Zsigmond, the Hungarian cinematographer who filmed McCABE
AND MRS. MILLER, IMAGES, and THE LONG GOODBYE, got
into trouble with his union was when he personally operated a
camera on DELIVERANCE (Warner's, 1972). Leon Erickson,
Altman's art director, never returned to his film union after
his first visit, when he was refused membership. Altman
filmed BUFFALO BILL AND THE INDIANS in Canada, he
claimed, because there filmmakers don't have the same kinds
of pressures from unions. M*A*S*H was the last time Altman
used a member of the Screen Extras' Guild. In 1976, when
he announced THE EXTRA, a film to star Lily Tomlin as a

militant Hollywood extra, picketers from the Screen Extras'
Guild were marching outside his office.

Altman is a semi-retired gambler who is still fond of
taking chances.   He discovered the actress Shelley Duvall at
a party shortly before he started shooting BREWSTER Mc-
CLOUD.   The opportunity to use a license plate "DUV 222"
must have helped her cinch her contract for the avian picture.
In the first half of the 'seventies, Duvall became the actress
most closely identified with Altman.   After BREWSTER Mc-
CLOUD, she appeared in five more of his features.

Other members of Altman's acting team have been
Keith Carradine, Elliott Gould, Rene Auberjonois, Michael
Murphy, and John Schuck.   Each of them has appeared in at
least four of his pictures.   Murphy's amoral character was
the most familiar member of his group.   His smooth tongue
and good looks added up to Altman's caricature of a modern
Mephistopheles.   In McCABE AND MRS. MILLER, Murphy
was a negotiator for a frontier crime syndicate.   In NASH-
VILLE, he was an advance man for a popular, but nearly
anonymous, political candidate.

"I rely upon these people," Altman said.   "I know
what they can do and I'm lucky they want to work with
me again."

Altman's employees are usually enchanted with him; he
thrives on their attention and energy.   He surrounds himself
with a familiar crew, fashioning a concept which binds his
employees as closely to him as others are bound to a political
candidate.   The results have marked him as one of the most
productive American directors of the 'seventies.   Between
1967 and 1977 he has directed thirteen motion pictures and
produced two more, for Alan Rudolph and Robert Benton.   By
the summer of 1977, Altman was in Lake Bluff, Illinois, working on his sixteenth film, and his fifteenth picture, 3 WOMEN
(20th-Fox, 1977), was about to enter a general release.

After his first hit, in 1970, Altman said he was lucky
to have failed in the past.   "I learned to be comfortable with
it," he said.   "I also learned the hardest thing, to know the
difference between what I want and what I don't want.   I was
really lucky with the long gestation period, with failure.   If
I had had a hit, a major success, fifteen years ago, or even
five years ago, it would have destroyed me."

III

Altman was born on 20 February, 1925, in Kansas
City, Missouri. His education was undistinguished. In high
school, he drew cartoons behind the backs of his Jesuit teach-
ers. He also went to see movies. Later, he worked in one
of the city's meat packing plants. After he dropped out of a
junior college and the University of Missouri, Altman joined
the Air Force. During World War II, he piloted a B-24
bomber through forty-five missions over Borneo. "I organized an officers' club," he said, "so I could get to the liquor
the quickest." After the war, Altman tried writing novels
and plays in New York, but he returned to Kansas City and
the Calvin Company where he produced industrial films. Several times, he quit Calvin and moved to Hollywood, and several times he returned. During one trip to the Coast, Altman
met George W. George. Together, they wrote two screenplays. One of them was filmed in 1948 as BODYGUARD, directed by Richard Fleischer; the other was unproduced. Then
Altman returned to Kansas City.

In 1955, having quit Calvin for the last time, Altman
directed his first picture, THE DELINQUENTS (United Artists,
1957), in Kansas City. It starred an eccentric, ex-college
football player, Tom Laughlin. In Kings of the Bs (Dutton,
1975), Todd McCarthy had better than 20-20 hindsight when
he found that Altman was "unobtrusively laying the groundwork
for a vast number of the teen problem (or problem teen) pictures that were to follow.

"The youth exploitation field was untested and unchar-
actered," McCarthy wrote. "If he wanted to, Altman could
lay claim to having invented, in one picture, many of the
conventions of this subgenre." United Artists released the
picture, but it did little to further Altman's career. He remained in Kansas City. Twenty years later, Altman appears
almost embarrassed when THE DELINQUENTS is mentioned.

Altman told McCarthy, "Tommy Laughlin was just an
unbelievable pain in the ass. Unbelievable. He's a talented
guy, but he's insane. Total egomaniac. . . . I found that this
Laughlin kid was doing all the things that he'd heard about
James Dean doing, like he'd run around the block when he
was supposed to be exhausted and he'd say, 'OK, I'll sit there
on the fireplug, and when you hear my whistle, you start rolling your cameras.' Otherwise, he wouldn't do it."

"THE DELINQUENTS is a sordid and depressing 'study' of what is commonly called juvenile delinquency," The Hollywood Reporter said in its review of the picture, "although depravity would be a more accurate designation in this case."

The Los Angeles Times-News said, "Teen-agers go wrong and once again their parents are to blame."

Twenty years after THE DELINQUENTS, Laughlin became wealthy when he produced, wrote, and directed his own motion picture, BILLY JACK (Warner's, 1971). In the spring of 1974, Laughlin appeared, bearded and overweight, with a print of BILLY JACK at the University of California, Irvine. "Without question," he said, "BILLY JACK is the most popular film of all time. It has had the greatest impact on the youth of America that any film has ever had. More people have seen the film five times or more than any other film in history." Laughlin distributed BILLY JACK himself, four-walling theatres while his ads saturated television with testimonials from a cross-section of American adolescents. They usually claimed to have seen BILLY JACK five, ten, fifteen or twenty times. At the University, Laughlin was open to questions. "There's going to be somebody," he said, "who is going to ask me if I did my own karate in BILLY JACK ... I did!"

Then Laughlin launched into a far-reaching discussion on one of his favorite topics, the vices of American film critics. Pauline Kael, The New Yorker's film reviewer, was a target, and one of her favorite directors, Robert Altman, was another. "In the first picture I worked on," Laughlin said, without actually naming THE DELINQUENTS, "I had to practically direct the whole thing myself. The director was drunk half the time.

"Now," Laughlin added, "he's one of the favorites of the New York critics!"

In 1957, Altman directed THE JAMES DEAN STORY. He and George W. George had remained friends after BODY-GUARD, and George had become a competent screenwriter, teaming with George Slavin on fifteen screenplays. He wanted to become a producer. "What could I do?" he said. "Nobody was going to let me produce." Then George thought of filming a biography of James Dean. "Out of need," he said, "comes fulfillment." He called Altman, and though Altman was initially reluctant, he agreed to try to make the picture.

Each of them put up $12,500.   Neither of them knew anything
about James Dean.

The pair flew to Fairmont, Indiana, to conduct interviews in Dean's home town.   Later, they interviewed his fra-
ternity brothers, hired three different detective agencies to
help their research, and looked through 8,000 still photographs
of Dean.   Stewart Stern, who wrote REBEL WITHOUT A
CAUSE (Warner's, 1955), wrote the narrative for the picture
and Martin Gabel read it.   NBC offered Altman and George
$300,000 for a single showing of the film on television.   In-
stead, the two producers offered it to Warner Bros. in exchange for the rights to Warner's Dean footage, which included
a screen test for EAST OF EDEN (Warner's, 1955).   Warner's
also added a theme song, "Let Me Be Loved."   Despite a majority of favorable reviews, Newsweek called THE JAMES DEAN
STORY "just about the ultimate in an attempt to cash in on
personal tragedy."   It filled the lower half of a double bill
with THE BLACK SCORPION (Warner's, 1957).

"We had so many Dean look-alikes come to us for
jobs," Altman told Films and Filming, "that we figured out
a scheme of hiring them all as ushers for the première.   We
had people come to us with secret things to sell--an old shoe
or a dirty shirt.   You never saw so many freaks.   As for
that rumor about Dean not being dead, just too scarred to continue his career, well, he banged himself up so badly he died,
that's all.   That boy is well and truly dead!"

After THE JAMES DEAN STORY, Altman directed two
episodes for Alfred Hitchcock Presents, but he refused the
third script offered to him.   He moved to The Whirlibirds
series, where two episodes were scheduled every week.   "In
the end," Altman said, "I got so fast that I could do them in
two days flat.   I used to take terrible chances just to challenge the boredom of it all.   I remember one scene where
we had two guys walking through a thick wood.   It was a
static scene.   Anyway, I remember seeing a mock telephone
booth in the back of the prop truck, so I said, 'Get that booth
and put it among those trees."   So we did the scene--along
come the two guys, they come to the booth, one says, 'You
got a dime?' the other says 'No!'   The two guys walk on.
There was no line of dialogue about what was a phone doing
in the middle of a forest.   We never explained a thing.   And
when the producer saw the rushes--nothing.   I doubt if he
noticed anything out of the ordinary.

"I learned guerrilla warfare while I was doing television. I was actually doing what the French critics praise
the early American directors for. I was making films under
a system and trying to sneak my own personal messages
through all that veneer. I set out to make one of the Millionaire segments really erotic, but so that the top brass would
miss every nuance. And I did it. I got it by all of them
because those people can't see. In television, I learned to
say things without saying them."

Altman amassed nearly 200 television credits on shows
like Combat, Maverick, The Kraft Theatre, and Bonanza, and
he directed pilots for The Gallant Men and The Long Hot Summer. Dan Blocker, the big, good-natured star of Bonanza,
became one of Altman's close friends. When Blocker died
after he was cast as Roger Wade in THE LONG GOODBYE,
Altman dedicated the picture to him.

In 1963, Altman quit studio television to work on his
own projects. His first company, Westwood Films, shot
commercials, including ads for Chevrolet and Ford. He also
developed several T. V. pilots, and two screenplays, THE
BELLS OF HELL GO STING-A-LING, for Gregory Peck and
the Mirisch Brothers, and ME AND THE ARCH KOOK PETU-
LIA, filmed as PETULIA (Warner's, 1968) by Richard Lester,
with Julie Christie.

In 1967, Altman directed MOONSHOT for Warner Bros. -
Seven Arts, based on The Pilgrim Project (McGraw-Hill,
1964) by Hank Searls, a book which Altman had unsuccessfully
tried to option three years earlier. MOONSHOT became
COUNTDOWN, starring James Caan and Robert Duvall as a
pair of astronauts during the first U. S. lunar landing. Shortly
after Altman finished filming, Jack Warner fired him because
the COUNTDOWN dialogue overlapped. Altman was unhappy
with the way Warner had the picture edited. It became the
last picture where Altman was unable to release his final cut.

Besides the experiments with sound that led to Altman's
dismissal, there are several other effects which mark COUNT-
DOWN as one of his projects. The camera work has the appearance of cinema verité and the dialogue appears to be
spontaneous. Part of the picture was shot at the NASA Space
Center near Houston. Before the space shot begins, one astronaut tells his companion a lascivious anecdote. The audience can only hear the last line of the story: "You go down
there," he says, "and the first thing you notice, she's got a

little niche for your toothbrush...." As early in his career
as COUNTDOWN, some of Altman's best moments were hidden
in these marginal, throw-away gestures.

COUNTDOWN is also effective where Altman used art-
ifacts to build up his characters. Caan's son wears a toy
squeaky mouse around his neck, because, he says, his mother
won't buy him a real mouse. Instead of carrying a snapshot
of his son into orbit, Caan takes the mouse with him. Later,
while he is en route to the moon, Caan's wife reaches out,
with a delicate motion, to trace the path of her husband's
heartbeat on a medical chart.

Altman's preoccupation with communications is another
element visible in COUNTDOWN. When Caan's radio, his
only link to earth, fails, the astronaut can only hear the be-
ginnings and ends of sentences. On earth, a battalion of newsmen count the seconds before his supply of oxygen will be exhausted.

At its best, COUNTDOWN gave the audience a sense
of Caan's claustrophobia and isolation. When Caan finally
walks on the moon, blinking in the glare of sunlight reflected
from earth, the feeling he has is not of expanse and gratitude,
nor of a "giant step for mankind," but of loneliness on an inhospitable orb. Caan is a man alone, unable to communicate
with earth or the moon.

After COUNTDOWN, Altman directed THAT COLD DAY
IN THE PARK (Commonwealth United, 1969), starring Sandy
Dennis, Michael Burns, and John Garfield, Jr. It was the
first, but certainly not the last time that Altman decided to
film a picture in Canada.

Altman bought the novel, which was written by Richard
Miles and set in Paris, but the first draft of Gillian Free-
man's screenplay moved the plot to London. Finally, Cana-
dian hospitality convinced Altman and his two producers, Don
Factor and Leon Mirell, to make the final shift. Post-pro-
duction was completed in Hollywood. Over half the crew mem-
bers were hard-working Canadians who wanted to make THAT
COLD DAY IN THE PARK a showcase for future productions.
The picture became Canada's official entry at the 1969 Cannes
Film Festival.

Sandy Dennis received excellent notices for her part,
as a spinster obsessed with Michael Burns, though her career

was already well in eclipse before the picture was released.
According to Dennis, a short time before shooting started,
"It's almost impossible to say what my character is. I feel
strongly that she's quite insane. However, she is able to
deal with insanity. "

Michael Murphy, in his third production with Altman,
after parts in a T. V. pilot and COUNTDOWN, appeared in a
cameo role as a pimp. A week later, he reported to War-
ners-Seven Arts for his part as a priest in Elia Kazan's picture, THE ARRANGEMENT (Warner's, 1969).

The Hollywood Reporter called Altman's erotically
charged film "Three-fifths low suds detergent, one-fifth underground press, and a bit too much more than one-fifth Masters
and Johnson. "

Altman accepted M*A*S*H, his next project, after fifteen other directors had turned it down. "I read it and didn't
like it," he said. "But I saw in it the opportunity to do
something I had been working on for about five years, a
World War II farce. It had the same basic philosophy. I
had a meeting with Ingo Preminger, the producer, in my
office, and I told him what I felt about it. I told him I felt
it would have to be very loose, very rambling. Anything that
looked like construction had to come out. I talked for a long
time and I said, 'If you agree with me, I'd like to make the
picture with you. ' He said, 'I agree. ' He backed me 100
per cent, right down the line, and that's really how it got
done. "

M*A*S*H (20th-Fox, 1970) became Altman's biggest
commercial hit, making more than forty million dollars. It
also won the International Grand Prix award at the 1970 Cannes Film Festival. In March, 1970, it was banned from service installations by the United States Army and Air Force Motion Picture Service. One month later, the ban was lifted.

M*A*S*H and CATCH-22 (Paramount, 1970), the latter
directed by Mike Nichols, were released within a few months
of one another, but M*A*S*H was out first, giving it an opportunity to capitalize upon the publicity of its competitor. It
came in at $500,000 under budget; it was shot with fog filters
in forty-two days, and it took Altman three and a half months
to edit it to the reactions of his preview audiences. M*A*S*H
made Altman's reputation, but CATCH-22 died at the box office,
nearly ruining Nichols' career in Hollywood.

A revisionist history of the Korean War, M*A*S*H
was set between the boundaries of a wacky war spoof and an
anti-war statement.   The only gun in the picture is used by
a timekeeper in a football game.   M*A*S*H is short for Mo-
bile Army Surgical Hospital; the installation is three miles
away from the Korean front.   It begins soon after Elliott Gould
arrives in camp as a new chest surgeon.   His tentmates, two
more recently arrived physicians, try to shock him by loung-
ing on their cots drinking martinis.   "What's a martini without olives?"   Gould asks, as he produces a jar of ripe green
olives.   The trio, Gould, Donald Sutherland, and Tom Skerritt,
becomes a cynical, occasionally slapstick Three Musketeers,
cracking jokes and bones with equal fervor.   Their foils, the
priests and COs of the unit, whatever their rank, are ineffectual bureaucrats.   Everywhere, authority is mocked.   At times,
M*A*S*H appeared to lose its anti-war conscience, to shift
into the "war is hell, (but, oh what fun)" approach of a picture like THE WACKIEST SHIP IN THE ARMY (Columbia,
1960).   Andrew Sarris was one critic who was unimpressed by
the film's intermittent "Beetle Bailey mechanics," but The
Hollywood Reporter called it the best American comedy since
SOME LIKE IT HOT (United Artists, 1959).

The three leads set their full imaginations to work improvising schemes against those members of the surgical unit
who take themselves seriously.   Often, it appears, their complex plots are battles against reason itself.   A single officer
who takes the war seriously poses a threat to the protective
insanity of the other medics.   A crucial difference between
M*A*S*H and other war comedies is that Altman's heroes are
in no way military representatives.   They act like an anti-
war Fifth column, and Altman's lapses into military nostalgia
are few.

Head Nurse "Hotlips," played by Sally Kellerman, and
the Major, played by Robert Duvall, are a pair of hypocrites,
one praying to God, the other to the myth of military efficiency.   Gould and Sutherland broadcast their lovemaking when
they sneak a microphone under the Major's bed.   Before the
last reel of M*A*S*H is finished, both Kellerman and Duvall
are stripped of dignity; Duvall is wrapped in a straitjacket;
Kellerman is garbed as a silly, mini-skirted cheerleader.

Kellerman's speaking part started with nine lines in
Ring Lardner, Jr.'s script, but during shooting it grew until
she was billed immediately behind Sutherland, Skerritt, and
Gould.   Another major part, the voice of the unit's public

address speaker, wasn't in Lardner's script at all. Altman
used it to announce camp movies, including, before the fade-
out, "M*A*S*H, snatching laughs and love between amputations
and penicillin. " The system also reported the theft of ampheta-
mines. Lardner, who had originally taken the project to
Preminger, was unamused when he received M*A*S*H's only
Academy Award for his discarded screenplay.

M*A*S*H was a good service comedy, but it was one
containing a bitterness that was unknown before the late 'sixties. The picture's best known set-up was it's recreation of
The Last Supper, but the metaphor, however adroit, was
forced. Though every element was played for maximum laughs,
M*A*S*H was still about a dope-smoking, disillusioned army.
At times, the laughs were desperate, crossing the boundaries
of anachronism with jokes set ten years too early, directed
more towards the Vietnam War than Korea. "The American
Medical Association," one announcement from the P.A. warns,
"has just declared marijuana to be a dangerous drug."

The last major sequence in M*A*S*H is taken up by
an overlong football game reminiscent of the Marx Brothers'
sport in HORSE FEATHERS (Paramount, 1932). Between the
game on the field and the thousands of dollars in bets placed
by each of two rival army units, the war was almost forgotten.
Perhaps the North Koreans also had a piece of the action.
At the close of M*A*S*H, "Spearchucker" Jones, the hospital's
quarterback and neurosurgeon, leads his team to victory, the
war begins to wind down, and the men, albeit reluctantly, are
sent home.

BREWSTER McCLOUD (M-G-M, 1970) was the first
film in which Altman's Lion's Gate company was involved.
A dozen years after THE DELINQUENTS, it still has many
of the trademarks of a youth film. Altman moved away from
his substantial television credits to ally himself with the
counter-culture and with films produced by younger directors
like Hal Ashby and Martin Scorsese. Though Vice President
Spiro Agnew was one of the most admired men in the U.S.
at the time, Altman used a newspaper headlining Agnew's
bombastic remarks to line a bird cage. Sally Kellerman took
a brief, titillating bath in a Houston fountain, and two or three
episodes involving marijuana were at least as extraneous as
they were amusing. The film even included an extended car
chase. Though it was quickly dated, BREWSTER McCLOUD
remains Altman's favorite picture.

Robert Altman on stilts during filming of BREWSTER McCLOUD
(M-G-M, 1970).   Photo courtesy of Eddie Brandt's Saturday
Matinee.

        Margaret Hamilton, the Wicked Witch from THE WIZ-
ARD OF OZ (M-G-M, 1939), was cast as an eccentric woman
who sings the National Anthem before sporting events at the
Houston Astrodome.   The opening titles barely begin to unwind

before she shouts, in an unmistakeable screech, "You're out of tune, you're out of tune." When the Hamilton character is murdered, the camera pans to her feet and a newscaster refers to her "red rhinestone" slippers. At the close of BREWSTER McCLOUD, its actors are introduced as the rest of the OZ cast, including Dorothy, the Scarecrow, the Tin Woodman, and the Cowardly Lion. The conclusion was reminiscent of Federico Fellini's motion picture $8\frac{1}{2}$ (Italian, 1963). Even before the credits begin in BREWSTER McCLOUD, when the M-G-M lion starts to growl, this self-conscious trickery begins. Rene Auberjonois' voice overlaps the lion, saying, "I forgot the first line."

The references to the motion picture business continued beyond the introductions and postscript. A movie poster covered a door in a police lab and another character had a one-sheet poster for M*A*S*H in her living room.

BREWSTER McCLOUD starred Bud Cort, an inexperienced actor who had a small part in M*A*S*H. He also starred in HAROLD AND MAUDE (Paramount, 1971), Hal Ashby's counter-cultural film, a picture very similar to BREWSTER McCLOUD. Cort's baby-faced, innocent, and semi-conscious characterizations must have appealed to a young, 1970 audience, but his appeal was short-lived. By 1976, after directing SHAMPOO (Columbia, 1974), THE LAST DETAIL (Columbia, 1974), and BOUND FOR GLORY (United Artists, 1976), Ashby was ranked with Altman as one of America's top directors, but Cort had disappeared.

As with his later pictures, Altman framed BREWSTER McCLOUD by manipulating his titles and credits. When Altman smoothed out his style with the later pictures, THE LONG GOODBYE, CALIFORNIA SPLIT, and NASHVILLE, this device became no longer a joking reference to his medium, but a vital piece of the film's structure. As he chose to liberate the films from plot conventions, these framing devices became more and more important. Altman began to use them like old-fashioned titles, to set the time, place, and boundaries of his subject matter with a minimum of exposition.

BREWSTER McCLOUD maintains a tenuous hold upon a linear narrative, though the episodes themselves do not always work. A crew member on the picture recalled that, at one point, it took them ten minutes to find a copy of the script. Altman appeared to be enchanted with his supporting troupe and with bits of characterization which had little to do with Cort's Brewster. Six of the leading actors had also appeared in M*A*S*H.

Part of Altman's deal for shooting inside the Astrodome was an agreement that he would also hold the première for the picture there. Twenty-four thousand people showed up to see it on a screen fifteen stories high. According to Larry Cohen, a reviewer for Show, "Watching it in the Astrodome was like being locked out of your car at the drive-in with your ear pressed against the no-draft window, straining to hear the speaker inside. "

After BREWSTER McCLOUD, Altman's style became more evident in McCABE AND MRS. MILLER (Warner's, 1971). The leap in style between the two pictures is like that between a Mack Sennett and an Ernst Lubitsch film. Unlike the first, the second picture already bore the marks of a mature filmmaker. Altman had whittled his plot to a third of BREWSTER McCLOUD's convoluted length. By the time he began shooting, he had learned to suggest his themes instead of trying to bludgeon his audiences with them. For the first time, Altman really expected his audiences to bring their own expectations to a movie theatre. As in BREWSTER McCLOUD, music was important in McCABE AND MRS. MILLER. In the first, John Phillips, the founder of the pop group The Mamas and the Papas, was one of Altman's co-producers. He wrote and sang several songs. In McCABE AND MRS. MILLER, Altman used Leonard Cohen's moody ballads.

"Music is like a prop," Altman said. "It's something that helps reinforce the period in the arena we're dealing with. "

McCABE AND MRS. MILLER was shot in sequence in the Vancouver wilderness, where the cast and production crew lived in shacks and tents. The working title was THE PRES-BYTERIAN CHURCH WAGER and it was taken from McCabe (Macmillan, 1959) by Edmund Naughton. Naughton wrote the novel while he was working on the copy desk of the Paris Tribune in France. First, Elliott Gould was slated for Mc-Cabe, with Pat Quinn and Marianne McAndrew, but by the time it reached the screen, Warren Beatty was the man who shared top billing with Julie Christie. Beatty found it difficult to work within Altman's improvisational, open-ended system.

In McCABE AND MRS. MILLER, almost every one of the 125 male citizens of Presbyterian Church help to build

two city landmarks, a church and a whore house. McCabe
is a gambler who carries a Swedish gun and refuses to drink
his double whiskeys until he drops a raw egg in his glass.
His is the only gun in town, and rumor says that he may have
shot and killed Bill Roundtree, a gunman who is running for
Governor of Wyoming. Really, McCabe has never shot anybody. Really, he's a shabby, vulnerable con-man with one
idea. He's going to build a whore house.

A scene of McCabe being cheated in a bargain for
whores is intercut with a scene of men pulling a cross atop
the church's steeple. Slowly, McCabe's house becomes a
warm meeting place; the church, like its grim guardian, a
frowning preacher, remains empty.

"McCABE AND MRS. MILLER will have all the traditional elements of the classic Western," Altman told a reporter in Vancouver. "Warren Beatty plays the loner, the
roving gambler who brings order to a lawless town through
the strength of his personality. Christie is the comforting
woman who loves him. There's a gambling casino, a whore
house, a shoot-out, and all the other elements you'd expect,
but in this film we try to show the way it really happened....
McCabe is no fool who stands up and shoots it out with a
hired gunman. He shoots the gunman in the back. The gunman he shoots is called 'the Kid' and he is a kid--only fourteen. And Mrs. Miller is an honest to goodness whore.

"The Western is like an ancient ballad," he went on.
"We take advantage of the fact that audiences know the standard plots. We tell the story behind the ballad."

McCABE AND MRS. MILLER was the first among Altman's films which could boast a star-studded marquee. With
his screenwriter Brian McKay, Altman wrote several scenes
which he felt could help sell the project, but which he never
intended to film.

Altman shot his picture through a fog filter, creating
a translucent, dream-like atmosphere. The entire town was
rigged for rain, rain which turned to snow before the end of
shooting. Altman shot enough footage to make more than one
picture. He said the finished product could conceivably be
any one of several films, and when it was released, critics
called it everything from a frontier morality play to a plea
for free enterprise.

While the gentle-natured McCabe is a bewildered mumbler, Mrs. Miller is an industrious Capitalist. The Cockney woman arrives in Presbyterian Church and demands a partnership. "I'm a whore," she tells McCabe, "and I know an awful lot about whore houses." She promises McCabe that he can at least double his money if he agrees to take her in and split the income. He agrees, reluctantly, so she sends for new girls and sets their prices, a dollar fifty for each of the girls, except Mrs. Miller. It costs five dollars to spend a night with Mrs. Miller. Even McCabe gets no discount. When two men representing a large, corrupt mining company attempt to buy the brothel, McCabe refuses to sell. His intransigence makes him a target for three company-hired killers.

Before McCabe's inevitable shoot-out, Altman added additional layers of characterization and sub-plot. Shelley Duvall was cast as a mail-order bride, delivered to Bert Remson. When Remson dies in a scuffle defending her honor, Duvall finds herself with Mrs. Miller and the rest of her girls. Christie tells her to think of something else while she's working, to try counting the roses on the wallpaper. Keith Carradine rides into town, a young cowboy wealthy and randy enough to camp out in the brothel. "They weren't kidding about this place," he says. "Well! Who wants to be next?"

McCABE AND MRS. MILLER is Altman's most curious love story. McCabe resents paying five dollars each time he sleeps with Mrs. Miller. Not only does he love her, he figures, but he is also her partner, well-deserving of her attentions. Even the knowledge that their income is shared seems to give him little relief. Without the threat of the gunfight, Altman's eighth feature could have evolved into an elegant domestic comedy. "If you could just be sweet one time without money around," McCabe drawls. "I never was a percentage man. I suppose a whore is the only sort of woman I'd know!"

Though there were brief elements of the slapstick humor from M*A*S*H and BREWSTER McCLOUD, McCABE AND MRS. MILLER was controlled and passionate. The mood was set by Cohen's score and Vilmos Zsigmond's photography. Zsigmond's work has a lush, but grainy and realistic appearance. "We pre-fogged the film," Altman said, "to get a little antique effect to it." In McCABE AND MRS. MILLER and in his next two pictures, Altman used Zsigmond wisely, and

Zsigmond became one of the best young cameramen to surface
in the 'seventies. Much of Altman's success, and much of
what has been described as his photographic technique, rested
with Zsigmond. The last scene in McCABE AND MRS. MIL-
LER, where McCabe bleeds and freezes in the snow while the
rest of the townspeople fight to stop a church fire, is rarely
matched in the rest of Altman's work.

Altman wrote the story for IMAGES in 1968, when he
was living on a beach in Santa Barbara. It was scheduled
for production in Canada in late 1969, starring Sandy Dennis,
but was not filmed until 1972. In IMAGES (Columbia, 1972),
the director's self-conscious concerns appeared within a new
setting. Before he settled on Ireland, Altman scouted European locations from Sweden to Spain. In Ireland, four members of the crew ran their cars off the mountain roads during
the forty-two-day shooting schedule, and Altman's own car
was stolen. IMAGES was sent to the 1973 Cannes Film Festival as the first Irish entry ever made.

IMAGES has no blaring loudspeakers or movie posters;
its setting is not as exotic as those of BREWSTER McCLOUD
or McCABE AND MRS. MILLER. The comparisons between
Altman and European directors became most obvious in IM-
AGES. The distinctions between objective and subjective narration were blurred into abstraction. The plot ran in one direction, then it turned and cut back against itself, like a river
hitting a dam. IMAGES borrowed the pace of a mystery, but
its narrator is untrustworthy.

Two of the actors in IMAGES, Rene Auberjonais and
Hugh Millais, were fresh from parts in McCABE AND MRS.
MILLER. Susannah York, who rewrote part of her role, received the Best Actress award at the Cannes Film Festival
in 1973. During pre-production, Altman said he was taking
out all the words that made sense and was replacing them with
words which made no sense. The remark was undoubtedly
facetious, but it also illustrated the confusion of York's character.

The conflict between real and imagined events begins
early. When Miss York answers a telephone, the voice on
the line is unfamiliar. It changes to that of someone else in
mid-conversation. "Cathryn," it purrs, "do you know where
your husband is tonight?" When Auberjonois, York's husband,
arrives, she begins to imagine that he is another man.

The narrative is ordered around Cathryn's distorted perceptions. She is a worthy heroine, one fighting against her own guilt-ridden schizophrenia. "You are dead," she tells a man who haunts her, "but you have been dead for three years. You can't be here. I won't let this happen." Finally, in an admirable effort of will, Cathryn decides to destroy the phantoms.

Altman allowed IMAGES to become all but completely divorced from continuity. Almost immediately he disrupts time. When Cathryn attacks two ghosts, both of them, Millais and Marcel Bozzuffi, bleed. Instead of conveniently disappearing, their bodies litter her floor. She tries to piece together a jigsaw puzzle but despairs. "I won't be able to finish this," she says. "There's too many pieces missing."

Shortly before she arrived on the set, Susannah York had completed a children's book about unicorns. Altman added the book to York's character; he made her a writer and allowed her to read the book during her descent into madness. When York finally completes her puzzle, the painting is of a unicorn.

The rain in McCABE AND MRS. MILLER gave it the soft sense of a reverie. In IMAGES, the atmosphere was heightened by the continual use of mirrors and prisms. Miss York was divided into three women by a mirror. Which, she might have asked, is the real one?

Finally, Cathryn confronts her demonic other self. The two meet on opposite sides of a car window on a mountain road. Cathryn speaks both parts while the phantom mouths her words and demands to be let inside. York backs her car away, then charges forward, knocking the double over a cliff, to the bottom of a mosscovered waterfall. When she returns home, the second woman remains, "It wasn't me you killed," she says, and the camera zooms to Auberjonois, bruised and dead, lying in a pool of water below the falls. In one frightening instant, the layers of fantasy are peeled away.

IV

"In Hollywood," Raymond Chandler wrote in The Long Goodbye (Houghton-Mifflin, 1954), "anything can happen, anything at all." Chandler was right, and many other writers, including Nathanael West and Aldous Huxley, have observed that same fact. The sense, often malignant, that anything can happen, to anyone, is one that infests Southern California.

I lived in Laguna Beach, an hour's drive from Los Angeles, and I was driving to Beverly Hills for a three-day Robert Altman festival. In L.A., Altman was certainly a star. Even Shelley Duvall and Michael Murphy were applauded when they made their entrances--on screen.

On the way to the Altman festival, I passed by two hundred billboards and a freeway accident. When I passed the wreck, a dwarf was getting out of the first car to check his damage.

I stopped at a bookstore across the street from the theatre and traded quips with an ex-Mouseketeer who wore an earring in one ear. He was looking for a book with his name in it. He told me that he was Marilyn Monroe's godchild, the youngest burlesque comedian in the country, and I believed him. He was with a shapely, blonde, bored woman three or four inches taller than he. He told me he was in a new picture with George Hamilton, but he said he couldn't tell me the title. He didn't get along with Hamilton but he'd do anything to work with Joey Heatherton. She was also in the picture.

I asked him to tell me the title.

He drew closer and whispered, "THE HAPPY HOOKER GOES TO WASHINGTON."

The three boulevards, Hollywood, Sunset, and Santa Monica, are like black holes in space, sucking the rest of the world into their grasp. We were on Santa Monica Boulevard. Within fifty miles of us there were giant tires, doughnuts, flying carpets, and replicas of the Taj Mahal and the Matterhorn. Forty miles away there was a drive-in church where the ex-Black Panther leader Eldridge Cleaver gave Christian lectures. Thirty miles away, there were walking, talking replicas of American Presidents, and sixty miles away there was an English ghostwriter helping our disgraced ex-President write his memoirs. Between the landmarks, there was enough neon to pave every street in Hollywood, to take us past the gawkers, the peddlers, the pimps, and the hustlers.

The first film on the festival program was THE LONG
GOODBYE (United Artists, 1973). When, in December, 1974,
Robert Altman was surrounded by film students at the American Film Institute mansion in Beverly Hills, they asked him
questions like, "Could you talk a little about why you wanted
to do THE LONG GOODBYE, how that came to you, and what
you intended to do with it?"

"I was in Ireland making IMAGES," Altman said, "and
I was living in England. Jerry Bick, who had the rights to
THIEVES LIKE US, had THE LONG GOODBYE set up. He
asked me to do it but I said no. I think Peter Bogdanovich
wanted to do it with Lee Marvin or Robert Mitchum. Jerry
came to my house and said, 'David Picker of United Artists
says that he'll go with Elliott Gould as Philip Marlowe. Do
you think that'll work?' I spent two hours convincing Jerry
that I thought Elliott Gould was the only person who could
play Philip Marlowe. I ended up talking myself into doing
THE LONG GOODBYE."

THE LONG GOODBYE received enthusiastic previews,
but when it opened in March, 1973, business was so bad that
United Artists pulled it out of circulation. After it received
favorable reviews, however, the film was re-released with a
new ad campaign.

Chandler managed to capture the smoggy texture of
Southern California like no one else. In The Long Goodbye,
a character's dialogue stretched into rhetoric: "In this lovely
white kitchen," Chandler wrote, "the average American housewife can't produce a meal fit to eat, and the lovely shining
bathroom is mostly a receptacle for deodorants, laxatives,
sleeping pills, and the products of the confidence racket called
the cosmetic industry. We make the finest packages in the
world, Mr. Marlowe. The stuff inside is mostly junk."

Robert Altman admitted that he read only one third of
Chandler's novel, so he must have missed those words in the
second half of the book. Chandler's detective was not Altman's, but Altman clearly shared the same cynical vision of
Southern California. A hypnotic fear drove both Chandler and
Altman; it fueled them with enough power for two different
projects, a novel and a film, with the same titles. It was
a fear that the values of Hollywood, its emotional and architectural texture, represent the future for the rest of the world.
"Hooray for Hollywood" is a theme as well as a song in THE
LONG GOODBYE. Despite water or gasoline shortages, Holly-

wood's seductive imagery floods the world. Nearly everywhere, it is regarded as a mecca of sun, fun, youth, and
sex. Altman's characters, like Chandler's, are desperately
flamboyant transients. They have reached the end of the
world and there are no fire escapes for any of them, neither
towards nor away from heaven.

    In THE LONG GOODBYE, Altman's exposition was as
brisk as it was brief. "I've gotta be the nicest neighbor,"
the lackadaisical Marlowe boasts, "I'm a private eye!" In
one scene, we meet Marlowe, learn his profession, and see
his home and a glimpse of his neighbors. When that is completed, Altman moves from Chandler's deft 1954 plotting, to
1973, a period inappropriate for old-fashioned heroics. Altman's Marlowe is a scruffy Elliott Gould. The setting is
still in Hollywood, but the odd epicenter of the story has
moved to Malibu. Altman used his own home as the set for
much of the picture.

    By 1973, Marlowe and his ethics were a sham. First,
he's awakened from a stupor by a hungry cat. Then he's
chased by dogs. He complains about the price of macaroni
at a supermarket. Then he's arrested. Altman turned Chandler's novel into a character study filled with grotesques. Marlowe was no longer a romantic figure who refused to talk to
the L.A. police out of a sense of justice and outrage; in Altman's picture, the impetus is confusion. Gould's Marlowe is
a man out of control, one riding with chance and steeled
against fear by the rhythm of his own wisecracks.

    Terry Lennox, the man who precipitates the action in
The Long Goodbye, has also changed. Chandler's Lennox
was a soulless war hero with a scarred face. Altman's Lennox was played by Jim Bouton, a professional baseball player
who wrote a bestselling exposé, Ball Four (World, 1970).
Bouton is a tanned, blond cipher, a smiling California hedon-
ist. The rest of Altman's casting followed the same ingenuous
pattern. Altman picked Mark Rydell, a film director, to play
Marty Augustine, a psychotic Jewish hood who smashes a coke
bottle against his mistress's face and threatens to emasculate
Marlowe. Rydell took the assignment in order to get a look
at Altman's way of working. His next picture, CINDERELLA
LIBERTY (20th-Fox, 1973), reflected the influence, and the
character he played in THE LONG GOODBYE, Augustine, received a screen credit.

    Sterling Hayden, an actor, explorer, and writer, played

the alcoholic novelist Roger Wade. "This is my last movie
role," he said. "I'm going out on this one. It will be the
only role I'm not ashamed of. I'm going to let it all out.
All of it. It's easy because the role of Roger Wade's so
close to myself. A man who drinks because he's afraid of
fear and failure, afraid he may be a coward."

Despite United Artists' reluctance, Nina van Pallandt,
best known as Clifford Irving's mistress, was cast as Mrs.
Wade. Henry Gibson, who had been a regular on the National
Broadcasting Company's faddish television series Laugh-In,
played a sinister quack doctor, Verringer.

The third set of newspaper ads for THE LONG GOOD-
BYE, those designed by Altman, featured a drawing of him
sitting in a director's chair in what looked like a page cut
from Mad magazine. "Hi!" he said. "I'm high-powered director Robert Altman and I'm here on location filming my
latest high-powered movie, THE LONG GOODBYE.

"Here's our star. Elliott Gould! Gould plays Philip
Marlowe, a hard-bitten, cynical private eye trying to solve
an incredible mystery!"

"With so many other actors around," the Gould drawing asked, "why did you pick me?"

"That's the mystery!"

"This is Nina van Pallandt, who portrays a femme fa-
tale involved in a deceptive plot of shadowy intrigue!"

"How do you want me to play it?"

"From memory!"

In his use of Johnny Mercer's song "Hooray for Hollywood," his off-beat casting, and a gate guard who does imi-
tations of Barbara Stanwyck and Walter Brennan, Altman continued his preoccupation with American entertainment. There
were also other self-conscious bits which Altman added to
THE LONG GOODBYE. Leigh Brackett, who co-wrote the
screenplay for THE BIG SLEEP (Warner's, 1946), taken from
a Chandler novel, also wrote the screenplay for THE LONG
GOODBYE. In the picture, when Augustine's mistress switches
on her car radio, when Marlowe visits a funeral in Mexico,
and when Marlowe hears the chimes at the Wades' home, they

all play "The Long Goodbye," Mercer's theme song. When
Marlowe is booked into the county jail, his picture is taken
with a twenty-five-cent photo machine, the same kind of ap-
paratus that is usually found in drugstores and carnival ar-
cades. After his fingerprints are taken, Marlowe is led to
an interrogation. He spreads the ink from his fingers under
his eyes like a professional football player and tells the cop
that he's "Getting into my make-up for the Notre Dame game."
Then he spreads the ink across his cheeks and sings "Swanee."

In a nightmarish hospital scene, Marlowe's roommate
is wrapped in bandages, like a mummy. For a moment, it
appears that the man is Marlowe. "You're going to be O.K.,"
he tells the bandages. "I've seen all your pictures too!"
Then the mummy hands him a harmonica as he starts for the
door. "I'm not Mr. Marlowe," the detective says, when a
nurse interrupts him, "--that's Mr. Marlowe over there."

There are many elements in THE LONG GOODBYE
that marked it as one of Altman's most successful pictures.
Zsigmond's photography was haunting, but never obtrusive.
The night scenes, including the scenes of Wade's death, were
breathtaking. The plot was less craftsmanlike, and the connections between Marlowe and the Wades, Terry Lennox, and
Marty Augustine were never really made clear. The characterizations and story construction were problems which earned
THE LONG GOODBYE the enmity of many Marlowe fans.
Critics also reacted strongly against the violent final scene
in Mexico, where Marlowe finally confronts and kills Lennox.

"Marlowe," Lennox says, "You're a born loser."

"Yeah," Marlowe replies, as he raises his gun, "I
even lost my cat."

"I was trying to do something in the spirit of Chandler," Altman said. "He used no story. You couldn't figure
out his plot. He used his plot as an excuse to put up about
a hundred little thumbnail essays. I tried to do pretty much
the same thing." Though he never finished The Long Goodbye, Altman did ask his cast to read Raymond Chandler Speaking (Houghton-Mifflin, 1962), a collection of Chandler's letters
and essays.

The unexpected violence at the close of THE LONG
GOODBYE was a means of signing off that also became a
trademark in Altman's pictures. M*A*S*H and COUNTDOWN

were the last pictures in which Altman finished with anything
approaching a conventional climax.   After COUNTDOWN, he
went far to avoid traditional plots.   His pictures became es-
say-like and, usually, they moved forward at a deceptively
slow pace.   The problem was simple: how do you end a picture that has contained no beginning or end?   In an Altman
film, an apocalypse becomes the solution.   The films end
with the lifespans of their heroes.   Brewster McCloud dies,
McCabe dies, Lennox dies, and Susannah York's husband dies
in IMAGES.   The trend continues through Altman's later efforts.   These death scenes are not just an easy, sensational-
ist way to finish a picture; in Altman's case they are really
one of the few ways he can manage to stop them.

Despite favorable reviews, THIEVES LIKE US (United
Artists, 1974), the second Lion's Gate-United Artists production, is a little-known picture.   It was a remake of Nicholas
Ray's 1948 production, THEY LIVE BY NIGHT, based on the
novel Thieves Like Us (Stokes, 1937) by Edward Anderson.
Altman asked each of his leading actors to read the book twice
before he began shooting in Mississippi.   His screenplay,
written with Joan Tewkesbury, took some of the dialogue
straight from the book, and the period authenticity was ex-
acting.   There was not one actor ranked as a star in the
cast, but members of Altman's regular casts, Keith Carradine, Shelley Duvall, John Schuck, and Bert Remson, performed ably in the ensemble effort.   Duvall's Keetchie was
the only survivor amongst the thieves.

In part, the audience for THIEVES LIKE US may have
been pre-empted by earlier mixtures of young love and blazing guns, like BADLANDS (Warner's, 1974), THE SUGARLAND
EXPRESS (Universal, 1974), and BONNIE AND CLYDE (Warner's, 1967), the last directed by Arthur Penn.   Wet, bleeding, or surrounded by gunfire, Faye Dunaway never stopped
looking like a fashion model in BONNIE AND CLYDE.   On
the other hand, no one began to talk about the dour THIEVES
LIKE US fashions after Altman's picture was released.   Unlike Warren Beatty's Clyde and his obtuse sexual thrills,
Keith Carradine stalked the banks in order to survive.   The
small audiences who made their way to THIEVES LIKE US
found a picture much closer to Fritz Lang's YOU ONLY LIVE
ONCE (United Artists, 1937) than Penn's violent hit.   Unlike
Beatty and Dunaway, Carradine and Duvall were not a pair of
glamorous, gun-toting robbers.   Both of them looked like awkward, Depression-born teenagers.   Embarrassment clung to
them like the dust on the window of one of their getaway cars.

THIEVES LIKE US begins when three unextraordinary
prisoners on a Southern chain-gang hi-jack a car and decide
to team up as bank robbers.   After collecting a good number
of news clippings from their robberies, the three split up.
T-Dub (Bert Remson) is killed, Chicamaw (Schuck) is captured, and Bowie (Carradine) settles in with Keetchie.   He
dreams of becoming a professional baseball pitcher.   The
robberies are easy, perfunctory gestures.   For the most
part, no one is hurt.   The camera, like Bowie, usually remains in the car.

Bowie can hardly communicate when he is not telling
a woebegotten joke.   His gun is more a plaything than a
weapon.   T-Dub is a jovial, mildly insane scoutmaster, a
bank robber, it appears, simply because he could never have
as much fun doing anything else.   His hands shake and his
eyes glaze before he enters a new bank.   "This will be my
thirty-third job," he says.

John Schuck's menacing performance as Chicamaw did
little to shake him from his regular roles as a big, dumb
buffoon.   In M*A*S*H he played a physically overendowed,
mentally undernourished dentist.   In BREWSTER McCLOUD,
he played Michael Murphy's dimwitted chauffeur.   When Schuck
landed a spot on a television situation comedy, he played a
robot policeman named Yoyo.

Despite the informal, unromantic bank robberies,
THIEVES LIKE US erupted with several beautifully constructed
episodes.   Bowie's death was one of them.   Duvall watches
it from a motel office while State Troopers pump bullets into
the couple's motel room.   The camera is on her, recording
her slow motion torment as she screams and smashes a coke
bottle against the wall.   The picture was shot in sequence and
the scene was shot one day before the picture was completed.
Duvall couldn't stop crying until an hour after she finished it.

The rough contrast between joking and nightmare also
appears during a car accident.   The action is swift; the
screams of an injured driver stand out against the ease of
the earlier sequences.

Several of Altman's most tender moments in any film
are those when Duvall smiles or blushes after listening to
Bowie's jokes: ("Do you know what the Mississippi state
animal is?   A squashed dog in the road!").   Altman was able
to make his most unattractive heroine expand to the outlines

of Shakespeare's Juliet. He dwells upon her eccentric, incongruous features, her too-big ears, and teeth, until her
audience is forced to admit that yes, he was right, she is
beautiful.

THIEVES LIKE US may have been Altman's least autobiographical picture. The men in the carefully devised period
piece were held at arm's length, more so than ever before.
None of them possessed even the semblance of authority or
control. Altman's next picture, CALIFORNIA SPLIT (Columbia, 1974), was probably Altman's most autobiographical picture, but the men in it are equally dishevelled. They devise
their lives around coinflips.

A modest financial success, CALIFORNIA SPLIT ranks
with THE LONG GOODBYE as Altman's most raucous picture.
Altman's trademarks are out in force--his overlapping dialogue,
the distended, self-conscious plotting, and the illusion of spontaneity. At one point, Elliott Gould, as exuberant as he was
downcast in THE LONG GOODBYE, joins in a coincidental
sing-along with the soundtrack.

Critics and audiences found it difficult to get a handle
on CALIFORNIA SPLIT, a gambling story. The exposition is
sketchy, though a second story arises more subtly from the
first. When the partners, Gould and George Segal, win, their
victory is hollow. Their pithy bankrolls are poor substitutes
for intangible needs like love and friendship.

Altman sets the frame for CALIFORNIA SPLIT when
he allows his camera to linger over a slide show on gambling
etiquette. Gould and Segal meet in a card game. Segal is a
career man on a binge after recently separating from his wife.
Gould, his accidental friend, plays an accomplished, obses-
sive gambler, pulling a bunco job on everybody he meets,
whether it's a robber or five basketball players in a park.
Late in the picture, he tries to bet a Milky Way bar at the
Reno crap tables. Together, Gould and Segal portray crea-
tures of the night, gambling anywhere and everywhere, including brightly lit casinos and card parlors filled with stubborn,
dropsied old women. Segal follows Gould; he is more than
willing to abandon his own life-style, but he will not allow
Gould to glimpse it. He remains an observer. Like the
audience, his presence mocks the manic Gould character.
Ultimately, Gould is the bitter partner.

"Charlie," Segal says, after their big gambling win,
"there was no special feeling."

Gould tries to joke, to make Segal laugh. For the
first time, he fails. "Don't mean a fucking thing," he says,
"does it?"

"We have to go home."

"Oh," Gould replies, suddenly grim, "where do you
live?"

CALIFORNIA SPLIT is a travelogue. A boxing scene
takes place at L.A.'s Olympic Auditorium, where Altman
puts on five bouts. Other scenes range from bottomless bars
to race tracks. Everywhere, a bet is Altman's impetus.
When Segal is hot, when he is winning at the crap table, the
gamblers around him are angry at any interruption. They
demand he roll his dice, then they clap him on the shoulders
when he wins. Gould's madness is relaxed and amusing.

Gould's roommates are two prostitutes played by Paula
Prentiss and Gwen Welles. Prentiss is addicted to T.V.;
Welles is like a little girl. She falls in love with every client
and is as thrilled as a Junior High cheerleader when Gould
hints at a real date. Bert Remson, who plays one of her
clients, wears a dress he bought in Omaha. Never before,
he says, has he had "the balls to wear it."

Altman's next picture was NASHVILLE (Paramount,
1975). It became his best-known feature. The picture is
set within the citadels of Southern image--recording studios,
the Grand Ole Opry; members of the audience run to the front
of the auditorium to grab snapshots of Altman's stars--Ronnie
Blakely, Henry Gibson, and Karen Black. Nashville is a
city stretching to fill its image.

NASHVILLE gave Altman his greatest financial return,
even greater than M*A*S*H, which was a great financial success, he said, for other people. United Artists had told Altman that they wanted to make a picture about Nashville even
before they released THE LONG GOODBYE. After CALIFOR-
NIA SPLIT, Altman couldn't find a major studio to bankroll
his project, so ABC financed it and Paramount distributed it.

Twenty-four characters meet in a massive freeway
jam-up in NASHVILLE. Before they meet again, five days
later, they are each followed on their paths through the country music capital.

NASHVILLE reserves its greatest scorn for a woman, a BBC reporter played by Geraldine Chaplin in her first role for Altman. She wanders through recording sessions and automobile graveyards, garbed in tape recorders, microphones, and quoting French. "I'm walking in a graveyard," she gushes at the recorder. "The dead here have no crosses, nor tombstones, nor wreaths to sing of their past glory, but lie--in rotting, decaying, rusty heaps."

"Opal wasn't really a journalist," Chaplin said. "And certainly not for the BBC. She was just lying. The BBC wouldn't hire anyone so dumb. And such a bad journalist. She never got anything. She was always talking all the time. I know a lot of people who talk like Opal, but none of them are journalists, and none of them are English. They're mostly French." In the final cut of NASHVILLE, however, Opal was never revealed as a fraud.

There were, apparently, many other scenes which were also taken out of the feature. Altman shot a great deal of film, rarely taking more than three takes of any one scene. By the time he finished, Altman had shot nearly seventy hours of film, including more than forty songs. His editor estimated that there were ten good scenes for every one that ended up in the final print. At one point, Altman considered releasing two films, with each of them covering twelve of the twenty-four characters. Pauline Kael saw one of the early cuts, and on the basis of what she had seen, she wrote a rave review for her New Yorker column. NASHVILLE opened to controversy.

Joan Tewkesbury, who wrote the screenplay for NASH-VILLE, had been associated with Altman since she worked as a script girl on McCABE AND MRS. MILLER. In THE LONG GOODBYE, Marlowe met a real estate agent named Miss Tewkesbury, and in THIEVES LIKE US, Tewkesbury appeared in the final scene with Shelley Duvall. To write the script for NASHVILLE, she flew to Nashville and spent five days there before she returned to L.A. and plotted her twenty-four characters on a wall. The original screenplay had nothing to do with politics. When the trials for the Watergate break-in began, Altman began to add characters, eight in all. Tewkesbury continued writing on the set all the way through the shooting schedule.

Much of the attention given NASHVILLE was centered upon its screenplay. Tewkesbury was written up in interna-

tional magazines in articles which concentrated on the collaborative origins of the script. "The shooting script," Altman
said, "is the thing that we decide to present to the guy who's

Robert Altman directing NASHVILLE (Paramount, 1975).
Photo courtesy of Eddie Brandt's Saturday Matinee.

going to put up the money." Almost no one, however, in
considering Altman or Tewkesbury, paused to remember that
contract directors like William Wellman and Howard Hawks
had worked closely with writers on their sets since the 'thirties. Hawks was also fond of overlapping dialogue.   Actors
like James Cagney were especially helpful to novice screenwriters who were still learning to write movie dialogue. Gary
Cooper's advice was equally stringent: "Whatever you do--
make me a hero." Despite Tewkesbury's success, it wasn't
the script that generated most of NASHVILLE's power, but
direction. NASHVILLE gets by on its performances.

Despite the immediate pleasures of watching a well-
crafted screenplay unfold, many NASHVILLE characters lacked
the depths and wholeness of those in the movies which preceded NASHVILLE. The characters are not only grotesque,
but they risk caricature. "If you take all those twenty-four
characters," Altman told Playboy, "you can break each one
down into an archetype. We carefully picked those archetypes
to represent a cross-section of the whole culture, heightened
by the country music scene." Bert Remson, Michael Murphy,
Henry Gibson, Keith Carradine, Barbara Baxley, Shelley Duvall, and Gwen Welles had all worked with Altman in earlier
pictures. Lily Tomlin's part was originally written for Louise
Fletcher, but Fletcher, who had come out of retirement for a
role in THIEVES LIKE US, didn't want to leave her children
for seven weeks of location work in NASHVILLE. Later, she
received an Oscar for her work in ONE FLEW OVER THE
CUCKOO'S NEST (United Artists, 1976), the picture she made
instead of NASHVILLE. Robert Duvall was to have played
the part taken by Henry Gibson, but he and Altman failed to
come to a financial agreement. Many of the other actors
took salary cuts in order to work on the film.

Many of the characters have brief, incomplete appearances. Elliott Gould and Julie Christie showed up in a party
scene. Karen Black's role was cut severely. In the finished
cut, she does little more than sing. Other characters, including the "Tricycle Man" played by Jeff Goldblum, and Duvall's "L.A. Joan" contributed little more than brief laughs.
Duvall was originally cast for a singing part, but according
to Tewkesbury, "Shelley can't sing, but she does have great
style. She can make $10 of junk clothing look magnificent.
Bob and I let her costume herself, centering the character
around the clothes."

Occasionally, the juxtaposition of characters becomes
too coincidental. Barbara Harris appears behind a curtain at
a men's smoker for no apparent reason. While Gwen Welles
does a hesitant striptease, Harris gnaws at a chicken leg.
The sudden appearances of Gould and Christie were equally
unlikely.

Despite some reservations about its accuracy, and
despite the inevitable backlash suffered by almost any film
with such a great hoopla raised before its release, NASH-
VILLE was recognized as a spectacular accomplishment.
Many critics wondered if Altman would ever be able to equal
it. Like the best of his earlier work, it had the stylistic

advantages of a collage. It was an intricate, complicated
juggling act. A contemporary picture, its characters were
recognizable despite their fragmentary development.

Among the elements which Altman tossed into the air
was the political platform of Hal Phillip Walker, a third party
Presidential candidate. The soundtrack for the Walker campaign was as prominent as the twenty-four main characters
on the album jacket for the NASHVILLE recording. Altman
kept a Hal Phillip Walker bumper sticker on his car during
the entire shooting schedule and "Walker for President" buttons were liberally available.

There were many effective scenes in NASHVILLE. In
one of them, Ronnie Blakeley has a breakdown on an Opry-
land stage. As Barbara Jean, the Queen of country music,
she appears as a woman pilloried by her fame, a Country/
Western Marilyn Monroe. Blakeley wrote the break-down
scene and she was running a high fever when it was shot.

In a Nashville bar, Keith Carradine sings the Academy
Award winning song, "I'm Easy," while the camera cuts between his bed partners, Chaplin, Duvall, and Christina Raines.
Chaplin giggles about their amorous adventures; Raines stares
at him vengefully. Duvall just stares while Carradine tries
to woo Lily Tomlin, a married woman sitting in the back of
the room. Robert Daqui, a drunken, sympathetic black, also
tries to pick Tomlin up; he brags that he only needs fifteen
minutes of sleep every night.

In the long last scene in NASHVILLE every element
comes together at a rally for Hal Phillip Walker. The stage
is surrounded by a large, rippling American flag. Most of
the characters are in the audience, the others are on the
stage when Barbara Jean is shot. Until this point, Barbara
Harris has been a tattered dreamer. She wants to grow large
under the alchemy of the entertainment industry. In the confusion, she is handed the microphone, and she leads five
thousand hungry extras in "It Don't Worry Me," a second persistent song in NASHVILLE, one rife with its own ambiguities.
The cycle of country music fame is ready to begin anew, it
appears, after the resurrection of Barbara Jean in Barbara
Harris.

Altman put on a real show to draw a large enough
crowd for his final scenes. One of the extras painted a picture of the twenty-four main characters and gave it to him.

When the crew returned to Beverly Hills, the painting was used for the ad campaign, and Dan Perri, who had done Altman's titles since CALIFORNIA SPLIT, used the painting for the brief record commercial he designed and directed for the opening credits.   Later, ABC Records used the painting for the cover of the actual NASHVILLE soundtrack.

After NASHVILLE's success, it surprised many when critics labeled BUFFALO BILL AND THE INDIANS (United Artists, 1976) a second-rate production. It starred Paul Newman, Burt Lancaster, Joel Grey, Harvey Keitel, and Geraldine Chaplin, and it took up where NASHVILLE left off, with a large American flag filling the screen.   Once again, America was seen as advertising, self-promotion, and theatrics.   In BUFFALO BILL, it was American history that was questioned. Is it all an elaborate hoax, recorded to the decrees of show business?   Perhaps.

Annie Oakley, the most attractive character in the picture, asks Buffalo Bill, "Sitting Bull wants to show people the truth.   You can't allow that just once?"

"No," Bill says, "I got a better sense of history than that. "

BUFFALO BILL AND THE INDIANS may have been partially set up for failure after the adulation of NASHVILLE, and surely there were critics who laid in wait, hoping Altman would slip.   Still, many of them covered their bets, adding a final line to their reviews, something like, "but even second-rate Altman is better than.... "   At Lion's Gate, where hopes were high for the picture, the notices must have stung.

During the filming at the Stoney Indian Reserve in Alberta, Canada, Joel McCrea, the star of William Wellman's BUFFALO BILL (20th-Fox, 1944), met Altman.   "I'm going to make BUFFALO BILL," Altman told him, "but I'm not making that BUFFALO BILL. "   Altman's Buffalo Bill, well-played by Paul Newman, is a fake.

Altman's picture was tinted like a daguerreotype.   According to a publicity handout, the film colors were inspired by the paintings of Frederic Remington.   Five-hundred-thousand dollars' worth of antiques were accumulated to help set the period, and a 5,000-seat arena was built for the Wild West Show.   Joel Grey's part, as Nate Salisbury, the show's producer, was partially based upon the florid publicity material

from the original show.   Salisbury plans, he says, to "Codyfy
the world."

BUFFALO BILL AND THE INDIANS was marginally
based upon Arthur Kopit's play Indians, but neither Altman
nor his scriptor, Alan Rudolph, took a look at the play before
the screenplay was completed.   Altman attempted, in the soliloquies of William F. Cody and Ned Buntline, to make his
own comments about fame.   "History," Buffalo Bill says,
"ought to take a lesson from us."   The man is entranced
with his legend.   Quite simply, the buffalo killer wants to
own history.   Sitting Bull, Buffalo Bill's new attraction, calls
history disrespect for the dead.

As with LITTLE BIG MAN (National General, 1970),
directed by Arthur Penn and starring Dustin Hoffman, the
events surrounding Custer's Last Stand are used to make Altman's case.   Both pictures were responses to the heroic
Custer portrayed by Errol Flynn in THEY DIED WITH THEIR
BOOTS ON (Warner's, 1942) directed by Raoul Walsh.   Altman's Buffalo Bill has Custer shot in the back, then scalped,
for the sake of what he calls "history business."

Cody manages to hire Sitting Bull, played by Frank
Kaquitts, for $40 a week to re-enact his battle with Custer.
"Welcome to Buffalo Bill's Wild West ..." he greets the chief,
"... me and my staff are the best at what we do, and what
we do is make the best seem better.   So when you hear what
we got planned for you, you'll wonder why you didn't get into
the business sooner!"

"The whole picture," Altman said during the scripting,
"is just a dialogue between Buffalo Bill and Sitting Bull set
in the Wild West Show."   Sitting Bull is a small Indian, un-
inflated by press agents or dime novelists; Cody is almost a
corporation.   He can't seem to understand why history has
chosen to record the Indians' victories and not his own fab-
rications.   His fame is hallucinatory.   At times, it threatens
to send him into madness.   He tries to emulate the quiet dignity
of the aged Indian leader, but fails, imprisoned by the webs
of his promoters.

Despite their obvious differences, Sitting Bull and Buffalo Bill have much in common.   Both of them sit on the edge
of legend, waiting only for death to be absorbed into myth.
Sitting Bull has his words funneled through the voice of an
interpreter.   The interpreter is bigger than the fragile looking

chief; for Cody's purposes, he is more of an Indian. After
Sitting Bull's death, the interpreter takes over his place in
the Wild West Show. Finally, Buffalo Bill has defeated Sitting Bull, even if it must be by proxy. Before his adoring
audiences, Bill pulls a headdress from the interpreter and
lifts it above his head like a war trophy.

BUFFALO BILL AND THE INDIANS was, perhaps, too
similar to NASHVILLE. It may also be that Altman's senti-
ments are too closely connected to the 'seventies to be able
to escape into the 1880s. His message is more closely allied with the manipulations of 1984 than the peccadillos of
Buffalo Bill's Wild West Show. Undoubtedly, Buffalo Bill can
be recognized as the forefather of our carefully packaged can-
didates, as diverse today as Sonny and Cher and Richard Nixon,
but to put the slogans of a twentieth-century P.R. whiz into
Cody's mouth may have been too heavy-handed. Altman may
have taken the same liberties in presenting BUFFALO BILL
AND THE INDIANS that he accuses Buffalo Bill of taking with
his Wild West Show. P.T. Barnum would be a more appropriate hero than Cody.

The rhythm of BUFFALO BILL AND THE INDIANS is
also much slower than that of NASHVILLE. The camera possesses far less fluidity in its movements and the characters
are usually shown in medium shots. The scale of a Wild
West rodeo makes it impossible for Altman to recreate the
intimacy of his earlier pictures. The style is rhetorical and
the politics anachronistic. Altman's cuts to his narrator,
Ned Buntline (Burt Lancaster), ripped by the flow of his story.

Only once, when Geraldine Chaplin takes her bows as
Annie Oakley, does the camera recapture its visual excitement. It occurs when Oakley attempts her first left-handed
shots in front of an audience. Chaplin had broken her shoulder
when she fell from a horse during shooting, so Altman let her
play Annie's part with her arm in a sling. As she makes her
first bull's-eyes, her excitement is almost sexual. "Faster,
faster," she shouts, between the shots, as Wild West cowboys
circle the arena, holding targets above their mounts. The
brief scene steals both Cody's and Altman's shows.

After the twenty-four characters in NASHVILLE, BUF-
FALO BILL AND THE INDIANS narrowed the number of the
cast without adding clarity. The characters played by Grey
and Harvey Keitel were too submerged in Newman's Buffalo
Bill to come truly alive themselves. If Altman was attempting

to recreate the success of his character sketches in NASH-
VILLE, the attempt was doomed. NASHVILLE, like M*A*S*H
and McCABE AND MRS. MILLER, grasped much of its strength
from its ability to play against stereotyped characters who
were already familiar to an audience. In BUFFALO BILL,
the satirical foils are less clear. They remain enigmatic,
unsympathetic figures, half-way between NASHVILLE and Mc-
CABE AND MRS. MILLER. Instead of creating a new image
of Buffalo Bill, Altman stranded his audience between the old
and new characteristics.

                                        V

        After Altman finished cutting BUFFALO BILL AND
THE INDIANS, but before it was released, Dino De Laurentiis
took him off the RAGTIME project and the 340-page screen-
play was junked. They had disagreed on the editing of BUF-
FALO BILL. "I lost a fortune on BUFFALO BILL AND THE
INDIANS," De Laurentiis said, in late 1976. "My money!
Make another picture with Bob Altman? You kid me?"

        "What had been particularly bizarre about the Altman/
De Laurentiis encounter," Andrew Sarris wrote in the Village
Voice, after the firing, "is that while Altman had been labor-
ing to patch up an avant-garde tapestry of Buffalo Bill's Wild
West Show, De Laurentiis has been hanging around the World
Trade Center with a rubber dummy of King Kong. How then
could the absurdist Altman have ever joined forces with the
ridiculous De Laurentiis?"

        When I returned to Lion's Gate in 1977, the pinball
machine was gone and Altman was in France. From France,
he was scheduled to fly to Chicago to shoot A WEDDING,
a forty-eight-character farce which had evolved from a remark he made to a reporter. It was co-written with John
Considine and was to star Geraldine Chaplin, Howard Duff,
Desi Arnez, Jr., Lillian Gish, Carol Burnett, and Nina van
Pallandt. It sounded like an unlikely cast, but an engaging
list for a cocktail party. Two of Altman's first casting
choices, Shelley Duvall and Sissy Spacek, had dropped off
his bandwagon. Before he left, Altman described the picture
to his co-workers as a two-hour M*A*S*H football game.

        After a year of work, Altman was off RAGTIME. An-
other deal with Warner Bros., for the YIG EPOXY, described
as M*A*S*H in a bomber parts factory, had also fallen through.

E. L. Doctorow had decided that he didn't want Altman to direct The Book of Daniel. Peter Falk, Lily Tomlin, Sterling Hayden, Clevon Little, Ruth Gordon, and Alice Cooper had been cast for BREAKFAST OF CHAMPIONS, but no one at Lion's Gate seemed to know what had happened with the project or whether or not Altman was still working on it. Later, I learned it had been shelved. The turn of events was unlikely. Had Altman been knocked out of the business in less than one year after the release of NASHVILLE?

Altman went home. Instead of searching for another large project or a property to option, he dreamt a story, then titled it 3 WOMEN (20th-Fox, 1977). He put together a quick deal with Twentieth Century-Fox over a thirty-page outline and a cast of Shelley Duvall, Sissy Spacek, and Janice Rule. Altman shot the picture in Palm Springs and finished it a week ahead of schedule. 3 WOMEN received excellent notices, glorying in Altman's instant come-back, but then it was pulled from release. Months later, it began to play at revival houses. WELCOME TO L. A. had also been released and Altman didn't want to hurt its potential by releasing his new picture too early. A second picture produced by Altman, directed by Robert Benton, THE LATE SHOW (Warner's, 1977), starring Lily Tomlin and Art Carney, had done well in reviews, but had died at the theatres.

At Lion's Gate, I was waiting for Dan Perri to return from a late lunch. Perri had an informal relationship with Altman, despite their adjacent offices. Perri free-lanced. He had recently prepared the titles for ALL THE PRESIDENT'S MEN (Warner's, 1975), TAXI DRIVER (Columbia, 1976), and STAR WARS (20th-Fox, 1977), and he planned, some day, to direct features himself. I wanted to ask Perri about the ad campaign for 3 WOMEN. The ads looked like a new approach to Altman's audience, establishing him as a "class act" in the tradition of European directors. The newspaper ads had been so delicate, so conscientiously styled, that they looked like wedding invitations, despite their newsprint. The design for the 3 WOMEN poster, by Altman and Perri, was dominated by three large photographs. In the center photograph, the most striking of the three, Sissy Spacek held a gun which bisected her face.

When Perri arrived we entered his office and sat beside a glass bookcase containing more than thirty film books. Perri had his own pinball machine. This time the initials "DP" commanded all the highest scores, as well as the lowest.

I asked if it was the same machine from Altman's office, but
Perri said it wasn't. "He took the machine home," he said.
"I guess he got tired of it. About a year ago I got everyone
on BUFFALO BILL AND THE INDIANS to chip in for a present. Then I bought it for him. He made a lot of money
with it, at one dollar a game." Perri liked to play his own
pinball machine he said, while he was on the telephone.

He handed me two small stickers emblazoned with the
figures of Buffalo Bill and Sitting Bull from BUFFALO BILL
AND THE INDIANS. "I designed them for our stationery,"
he said, "before the film began shooting. I wanted to give
it the feeling of a dime novel. Bob liked it so he had shirts
made with the design for the crew." Perri pointed to the
wall behind me: "That's the first poster I designed for BUF-
FALO BILL AND THE INDIANS." It had a photograph of Paul
Newman in rich, antique colors, giving it a Wild West flavor,
but also the flavor of one of the rock and roll posters from
the Fillmore West. Perri pointed out another poster on a
far wall: "That's the second. They went up at theatres before the picture arrived. By the time the picture reached a
general release, United Artists had cooled on BUFFALO BILL
and they made up their own poster.

"The photographs for the 3 WOMEN ads were photographed by Jean Pagliuso, a top New York fashion photographer. She's worked with Bob since CALIFORNIA SPLIT."
Again, Perri gestured towards his BUFFALO BILL posters.
"Those are her photographs, the same ones which were used
in the paperback script of BUFFALO BILL. In the past, Bob
has given prints of the photographs to members of the crew
and cast as gifts.

"She shoots dozens of rolls of film while she's on location, using the locations and the sets, but they aren't production stills, not really. Instead, she tries to capture the
feeling of the film, by drawing upon what Bob has already
completed. She works with the cast for her photographs, then
she prints them and hand-tints them.

"We didn't think of the audience," Perri went on.
"Those ads just seemed appropriate to the picture.

"I've gotten into experimenting with optics during my
work on titles, and now it's almost become a hobby. Bob
had an idea for the end of BUFFALO BILL AND THE INDIANS.
He was going to shoot the last scene, and optically, I was

going to freeze the audience while Newman continued in motion. The implication would be that Buffalo Bill lives on,
the show   the spirit...."

"His hucksterism lives on," I said. "And then, I
imagine the arena crumbles, the film dims, and the L.A.
skyline rises up, with telephone wires, sound stages, and
radio antennas!"

"Well," Perri said, "that's the implication, but Bob
changed his mind. It didn't look like it was going to work!"

I asked Perri which were his favorites among Altman's
features. He thought for a moment before answering, "Mc-
CABE AND MRS. MILLER ... THE LONG GOODBYE ... and
BREWSTER McCLOUD."

We had already spoken about BREWSTER McCLOUD.
I told him that I thought it was disjointed, rebellious, and
corny, but fun. It also looked like it had been fun to make.

"Yeah," he said, "yeah ... but that's Bob. That picture is Bob!"

I started for the door, remembering three moments
from Altman's movies, when Marlowe skipped down the street
in THE LONG GOODBYE and when Shelley Duvall decided to
start her life over again after Carradine's death in THIEVES
LIKE US. Robert Altman had lost four big projects in less
than four months. He'd have to start over again, too. I remembered Barbara Harris at the end of NASHVILLE, singing
over and over again, "It don't worry me, it don't worry me."
I thought of Altman. The man is an odd sort of prizefighter.
His best moves have always come after the count.

ROBERT ALTMAN

A Film Checklist by Vicki Piekarski

Director

1.   THE DELINQUENTS (1957). P: United Artists. C:
       Tom Laughlin, Peter Miller, Richard Bakalyn. 72m.

2.   THE JAMES DEAN STORY (1957). P: Warner's.
     D: George W. George, Robert Altman. Narrated by
     Martin Gabel. C: Marcus, Ortense, Markie Wins-
     low. 82m.

3.   NIGHTMARE IN CHICAGO (1967). P: Universal. C:
     Charles McGraw, Robert Ridgely, Ted Knight. Color.
     81m.

4.   COUNTDOWN (1968). P: Warner's. C: James
     Caan, Joanna Moore, Robert Duvall. Technicolor.
     Panavision. 101m.

5.   THAT COLD DAY IN THE PARK (1969). P: Com-
     monwealth United. C: Sandy Dennis, Michael Burns,
     Susanne Benton. Eastmancolor. 110m.

✓6. M*A*S*H (1970). P: Twentieth Century-Fox. C:
     Donald Sutherland, Elliott Gould, Tom Skerritt. De-
     Luxe Color. Panavision. 116m.

7   BREWSTER McCLOUD (1970). P: Metro-Goldwyn-
     Mayer. C: Bud Cort, Sally Kellerman, Michael Mur-
     phy. Metrocolor. Panavision. 105m.

✓8. McCABE AND MRS. MILLER (1971). P: Warner's.
     C: Warren Beatty, Julie Christie, Rene Auberjonois.
     Technicolor. Panavision. 121m.

9.   IMAGES (1972). P: Columbia. C: Susannah York,
     Rene Auberjonois, Marcel Bozzuffi. Technicolor.
     Panavision. 101m.

10. THE LONG GOODBYE (1973). P: United Artists.
     C: Elliott Gould, Nina van Pallandt, Sterling Hayden.
     Technicolor. Panavision. 111m.

11. THIEVES LIKE US (1974). P: United Artists. C:
     Keith Carradine, Shelley Duvall, John Schuck. Color.
     123m.

12. CALIFORNIA SPLIT (1974). P: Columbia. C: El-
     liott Gould, George Segal, Paula Prentiss. Metro-
     color. Panavision. 109m.

13. NASHVILLE (1975). P: Paramount. C: Keith Car-
     radine, David Arkin, Geraldine Chaplin. Color.
     Panavision. 161m.

14.   BUFFALO BILL AND THE INDIANS (1976).   P:
        United Artists.   C: Paul Newman, Burt Lancaster,
        Joel Grey. DeLuxe Color.   Panavision.   123m.

15.   3 WOMEN (1977).   P: Twentieth Century-Fox.   C:
        Sissy Spacek, Shelley Duvall, Janice Rule.   DeLuxe
        Color.   Panavision.   123m.

Chapter 6

DICK RICHARDS

by Jon Tuska

I

      Dick Richards was born in New York City on 9 July, 1930. Growing up in New York, he went to the movies frequently and enjoyed genre pictures, Westerns, adventure and detective films. He attended several Ivy League schools but discovered that his real interest lay in still photography. During the Korean conflict Richards served in the Army as a photo-journalist. After his return to civilian life, he embarked on a career as a commercial photographer. His photographs appeared in Life, Look, Vogue, Time, and Esquire, as well as in other places. He started photographing for commercial advertisers like Levy's and Volkswagen. From this

Above: Dick Richards and Sally Kellerman posing on the set of RAFFERTY AND THE GOLD DUST TWINS (Warner's, 1974). Photo courtesy of Eddie Brandt's Saturday Matinee.

it was an easy transition to filmed commercials for television.

Richards wanted to try his hand at a theatrical film. While researching a spot for the Heinz Company which would feature a cattle drive as a background, on location in the Southwest, Richards came across an old man in a rest home whose stories of his boyhood in the Old West, when combined with E. C. Abbott's We Pointed Them North (University of Oklahoma Press, 1955), became THE CULPEPPER CATTLE COMPANY (20th-Fox, 1972) upon release. Richards sketched out his ideas and took them to Gregory Prentiss, a student teacher at New York University, and asked him for help on it. Eric Bercovici, a veteran screenwriter, helped Richards polish it. When the script was finished, Richards gave it to agent Paul Helmick, who showed it to Elmo Williams, then head of production at Twentieth Century-Fox Film Corporation. Williams liked it and wanted to schedule it for production. "Fox is actually allowing me to do a dramatized documentary," Richards said at the time, "--no women, no romance--just a realistic look at what it was like in those not-so-good old days."

CULPEPPER was to be shot in Mexico for its exteriors. Richards set up a working formula he would follow in all of his subsequent films. "What I do," he said, "is, I visit all the existing sets, and I photograph them from different angles. Then I go away with the script for several weeks, go over it and break it down into shots. Using the photographs, I set up a kind of war-room, so that I can figure out all my camera angles and coverage. In this way, I have time on the set to work with my actors and to make changes if I feel I have to."

Richards had long been an admirer of John Ford and he wanted to assimilate the Ford "look" in CULPEPPER. He even went so far as to hire one of Ford's old cutters and with every scene he would ask the cutter how Ford would have done it.

"There was a whole feeling," Richards said, "in the Charles Russell paintings and the Remington paintings--soft, always late day and long shadows, an early morning feeling. I tried to match those feelings. I tried to marry all the feelings of the early John Ford, Remington, Russell, Hawks-- all the classics, all the people who had created the Western mystique."

Of course any Western centering its primary action around a trail drive and seeking to imitate a classic structure invites comparison with Howard Hawks' RED RIVER (United Artists, 1948). Hawks in making his film had in mind the basic plot of Mutiny on The Bounty (Little, Brown, 1932), and John Wayne as Tom Dunson achieved the proportions of the tyrannical Captain Bligh. The borrowing of this plot was due in part to Borden Chase, who wrote the book Blazing Guns on the Chisholm Trail (Curtis, 1946), on which the screenplay was based, and Chase received credit for his own work on the screenplay along with Charles Schnee. "It had everything going for it," Donald C. Willis wrote of RED RIVER in his book The Films of Howard Hawks (Scarecrow, 1975). "It's what you wish every movie could be and what very few are: exciting, funny, moving, beautiful, majestic. I think it's successful on all levels and in almost every area: the mythic level, the interpersonal level, mise-en-scène, acting, dialogue, detail, music, characterization, plot, theme, photography, setting, humor. And it's more than the sum of those parts."

In an interview with Jacques Rivette and François Truffaut for Cahiers du Cinéma, Howard Hawks said: "Quand j'ai fait RED RIVER, j'ai pensé que l'on pouvait faire un Western adulte, pour grandes personnes, et non pas un de ces quelconques 'cowboys'...." [When I made RED RIVER, I thought it might be possible to make an adult Western, for mature people, and not one of those about mediocre cowboys.] Hawks pursued his customary technique of weaving together a number of individual stories and interpersonal conflicts against the background of a cattle drive, and finally resolving them when John Wayne and Montgomery Clift confront each other for a climactic showdown at the end. The milieu as much as anything compelled these two central characters to assume an enlarged stature.

Richards went to the opposite extreme in making his cattle-drive Western. Not only were there no women and no romance, as there had been in all of Ford's and Hawks's Westerns, but there were no heroes in CULPEPPER and, in fact, no heroic deeds. "Our history and our being, I feel, really started with the opening of the West," Richards remarked, "and I felt that this culture should be told as it really was."

That there were no heroes and no heroic deeds--or that there shouldn't be--in a "modern" depiction of frontier times was scarcely original with Richards, but rather epigonal.

Dick Richards' effort at a "realistic" Western with Gary Grimes
(standing) and trail drovers from THE CULPEPPER CATTLE
COMPANY (20th-Fox, 1972).   Photo courtesy of Eddie Brandt's
Saturday Matinee.

Budd Boetticher, in his exceptional series of Randolph Scott
Westerns in the late 'fifties, introduced an innovation whereby
the villains were far more spectacular and interesting than the
isolated and introverted hero invariably cut off from the social order around him, a state of existential exclusiveness
which the villains envied and, at times, sought to emulate.
From this evolved the attempts to demythologize the treatment
of the Old West in the 'sixties and 'seventies. William Fraker,
the cinematographer turned director for MONTE WALSH (National General, 1970) starring Lee Marvin and Jack Palance
(both formerly heavies in Westerns), cast them as two obsolescent cowboys during the range depression of the 'nineties
and credited Western painter Charles B. Russell for the art

work on the titles. This notion of combining a story demyth-
ologizing the Old West with pictographic nostalgia reminiscent
of Remington and Russell was also evident in WILL PENNY
(Paramount, 1968), starring Charlton Heston as a quiet, self-
sufficient, aging wrangler desperately trying to eke out a
livelihood in a profession that was dying; the film had no
glamour. John Ford told Peter Bogdanovich that he liked
SHE WORE A YELLOW RIBBON (RKO, 1949) because he had
"tried to copy the Remington style there--you can't copy him
one hundred per cent--but at least I tried to get his color and
movement, and I think I succeeded partly." Apparently others
thought so as well, since SHE WORE A YELLOW RIBBON won
an Academy Award for Best Photography. In his effort to
capture the same pictorial quality in CULPEPPER, Richards
did not fall very far short of the mark and his Western is in
many ways quite striking visually. The effects with sunlight
bathe the entire production in a burnished glow and many of
the tracking shots are memorable. Richards' cattle drive
may be dustier and grimier than the one in RED RIVER (with
Richards using fewer steers), but that is consistent with his
basic intention in making the picture. CULPEPPER's shortcoming is its fragmentary plot.

The story-line concerns sixteen-year-old Gary Grimes,
who signs on with Billy "Green" Bush, playing Culpepper, to
learn how to be a cowboy. Grimes is involved in a stampede
perpetrated by rustlers, which results in the rustlers getting
shot down; a raid on the trail herders' cavvies by horse
thieves which results in the horse thieves getting shot down;
and an attack on a group of settlers which results in the at-
tackers getting shot down. After this last episode, Grimes
drops his gun belt and rides off toward home, having decided
not to become a cowboy.

Even here a few contrasts come to mind. In CAHILL,
U. S. MARSHAL (Warner's, 1973), Gary Grimes plays one of
lawman John Wayne's two screen sons, only this is a traditional Western with the dominating Wayne persona, and here
Wayne suggests that the only possible response of a true Westerner to Grimes' similarly foolish and cowardly antics in
CAHILL would be that he drop his pants instead of his gun
belt and receive a good licking. Although nominally directed
by Andrew V. McLaglen, CAHILL came the year after CUL-
PEPPER and it represents, certainly, Wayne's personal reaction to the Grimes character as depicted in Richards' documentary. Nor was such a reaction totally one-sided on
Wayne's part. The most obvious contrast with CULPEPPER

is THE COWBOYS (Warner's, 1972), directed by Mark Rydell, in which John Wayne recruits a group of youngsters to help him on a trail drive. When Bruce Dern and his gang of rustlers shoot and kill Wayne and run off with the herd, the youngsters rise to the occasion and through strategy and ruthlessness wipe out the cattle thieves and reclaim the herd, getting it to market safely.

Richards' intention was for there to be no heroes in CULPEPPER, but even critics who were sympathetic to this approach and who were willing to admit the visual beauty of the film came out sounding like the reviewer of the picture in Films and Filming: "And the ending? Well, I challenge anyone to sit through a five-minute blood bath which finishes as a heavenly choir leading into 'Amazing Grace' [sung on the soundtrack] and keep a straight face."

Philip French, a college professor who tried as a novelty to reduce all recent Westerns to manifestations of various political ideologies, managed to read into CULPEPPER a rather profound message when contrasting it with THE COWBOYS in his book Westerns (Viking, 1974). "Here we see a sixteen year old Texan," French wrote, "joining an arduous cattle drive out of a romantic desire to live the cowboy's life. He too becomes a man, but the film's authors--and to a lesser extent the boy himself--show real awareness of the kind of man he is becoming as he is initiated into the squalid pleasures, the self-seeking, the random violence around him. Without ever making it too explicit, Richards seems to be implying that the Culpepper Cattle Company is America--a business ploughing relentlessly on, totally amoral, fighting when it must, compromising when it can, a few deranged or misguided members galloping off from time to time to pursue 'idealistic' Vietnam-like missions on the side which neither adversary nor apparent beneficiary justifies."

This kind of political interpretation leaves me cold. For one thing, film analysts like French are too quick on the draw with analogies about what "represents" America. Jim Kitses, in his book Horizons West (Indiana University Press, 1970), said of Sam Peckinpah's THE WILD BUNCH (Warner's, 1969) that "the Wild Bunch is America." I imagine that both the Culpepper Cattle Company and the Wild Bunch might represent America, but, if so, they do so in the minds of critics who wish to editorialize on these conjectures, and were not intended to be such according to their respective directors.

What Richards really wanted to accomplish in CUL-
PEPPER--to make a Western with documentary realism--he
did accomplish. The picture won a gold medal from the
Spanish Film Institute for its photography. By remaining
cognizant of the limited income such films have at the box
office--MONTE WALSH grossing $2,300,000; WILL PENNY
grossing $1,314,130--Fox budgeted CULPEPPER at a little
over a million and was able to come out financially. Richards having spent so many years in advertising in an effort
to persuade the American television culture of the desirabil-
ity of all manner of products, CULPEPPER by contrast provided him an opportunity to shatter a glamorous myth and
reveal the life of the average cowboy to have been filthy,
violent, and without reward. He neglected story, as opposed
to the stress his models, Ford and Hawks, always placed upon
story, and therefore failed to engage the viewer emotionally
and intellectually as some other well-plotted and provocative
efforts have recently: Westerns such as, in ecological terms,
Sydney Pollack's JEREMIAH JOHNSON (Warner's, 1972), or
in economic terms, Robert Altman's McCABE AND MRS.
MILLER (Warner's, 1971), or in terms of an anti-corporation
Western, Sam Peckinpah's PAT GARRETT AND BILLY THE
KID (M-G-M, 1973). Richards belongs in that tradition which
has introduced dubiety and ambiguity into treating the American westward expansion, but he is hardly among those who
have excelled at it. Yet, even though the story disappoints
in CULPEPPER, there is some compensation in the haunting
poetry of the photography. CULPEPPER comes off best viewed
as a visual experience and, like Arthur Penn's later THE
MISSOURI BREAKS (United Artists, 1976), can be enjoyed
best on a pictorial level.

Richards' next cinematic enterprise, RAFFERTY AND
THE GOLD DUST TWINS (Warner's, 1974), was again both
generic and epigonal. Produced by Michael Gruskoff, who
had produced the ecological protest film, SILENT RUNNING
(Universal, 1972), and Arthur Linson, a rock manager and
music publisher, RAFFERTY was a formula road picture.
It came hard on SCARECROW (Warner's, 1973), directed by
Jerry Schaltzberg and starring Gene Hackman and Al Pacino
as a pair of itinerants. Richards himself summed up the plot
for his film this way: "RAFFERTY is about a fifteen-year-
old girl, played by Mackenzie Phillips, a thirty-five-year-old
would-be singer, played by Sally Kellerman, and a twenty-
year career veteran and former Korean War Marine played
by Alan Arkin. This guy doesn't know what to do with his
life; he's working as an instructor at the Motor Vehicle Bureau,

and the two women kidnap him because they want to go to
New Orleans and they've got no way of getting there.   The
girl [Phillips] pulls out a gun, puts it to his head, and says,
'We want to go to New Orleans'; and it's about their experiences together.   It becomes very funny."

Only, according to The Hollywood Reporter and other
trade reviews, RAFFERTY wasn't very funny and the Reporter
blamed Richards' direction, which it called "heavy-handed"
and incapable of evoking "most of the humor of the misad-
ventures in the script."   Perhaps, too, within a year the
mood of the country had changed; the feeling of indeterminate
loss, which had been so sustained as an undercurrent only
during the 'thirties and which recurred henceforth only in the
briefest flashes, as in Preston Sturges' SULLIVAN'S TRAVELS
(Paramount, 1941) with Joel McCrea and Veronica Lake, may
well have submerged in the lapse of time between the successful release of SCARECROW and RAFFERTY.   But just as
likely, one of the problems with RAFFERTY can be attributed
to a grave oversight on Richards' part--and one which he
sought to correct in FAREWELL, MY LOVELY (Avco-Embassy,
1975), where he gave Marlowe, the central male character,
a friend--actually two friends.   If not a love story, a road
picture, since it employs no series character and, unlike so
much American fiction, has no solitary protagonist, must at
least have one friendship, the way SCARECROW does between
Hackman and Pacino.   Sally Kellerman deserts Arkin before
RAFFERTY is over, completely destroying the "family romance" that most of the picture is spent building.   However
amusing Arkin's madcap drive across the grass outside the
orphanage at the end of the film, with Phillips in the car, it
is anticlimactic and somehow the viewer is left with the feeling that the adventures of this duo will not be as interesting
as when they were a trio.

Shot in and around Hollywood, then on location in Las
Vegas, Phoenix, and Tucson for five weeks, RAFFERTY depicted the outlandish threesome of Arkin, Kellerman, and
Phillips cheating others out of liquor, money, gasoline, and
food--the staples of the American way of life if kept in that
order--until they wind up, not in New Orleans, but in Kellerman's home town of Tucson.   Mackenzie Phillips is a fugitive
from an orphanage.   In her attempt to get money, she thinks
of trying prostitution but satisfies herself with petty larceny.
She is arrested and Kellerman runs off with a Country and
Western singer.   Arkin decides to follow Phillips to the orphanage and bail her out, although his motive in doing so is
far from clear.

"Casting," Richards has said, "has always been a hobby of mine and even when I was doing commercials, I was well-known for it. I think it's true, as a lot of people have said, that it's as much as ninety per cent of the movie." But casting alone is insufficient. Alan Arkin possesses a splendid capacity for both comedy and drama, but it was not utilized in RAFFERTY. Mackenzie Phillips is somewhat type-cast; in her personal life she surpasses in disorientation any of the alienated roles she has had (most recently having been found lying unconscious on Hollywood Boulevard from an over-dose of narcotics), yet in RAFFERTY her brittle characteri-zation needed Kellerman's softening presence to properly bal-ance it. Direction and script have to be in accord with cast-ing. In RAFFERTY, in my opinion, the script more than the direction constituted the let-down, and there was nothing the cast could do about that.

II

"I used to like this town," Raymond Chandler had his detective Philip Marlowe remark in The Little Sister (Houghton-Mifflin, 1949). "A long time ago. There were trees along Wilshire Boulevard. Beverly Hills was a country town. West-wood was bare hills and lots offering at eleven hundred dollars and no takers. Hollywood was a bunch of frame houses on the interurban line. Los Angeles was just a big dry sunny place with ugly homes and no style, but good-hearted and peaceful. It had the climate they just yap about now. People used to sleep out on porches. Little groups who thought they were intellectual used to call it the Athens of America. It wasn't that, but it wasn't a neon-lighted slum either." By the time Chandler finished writing about it, Los Angeles had become a "tired old whore."

"There were no reflectors marking traffic lanes at that time," Richards commented about the problem he had making his film version of Raymond Chandler's novel Farewell, My Lovely (Knopf, 1940), a period piece. "There were no red-painted curbs to restrict parking. Even the traffic lights and corner stop signs were of a different design. The fire hy-drants in 1941 were unlike those we use today. We had to rip out all the modern stuff so nothing would seem incongruous --and then we had to replace it when we were through. In fact, what appears in the movie to be a single continuing walk down a couple of blocks is, in actuality, a compendium of maybe ten to fifteen briefer shots, photographed at separate locations in order to avoid the intrusion of visuals that wouldn't fit the period."

Elliott Kastner and Jerry Bick, who had packaged THE LONG GOODBYE (United Artists, 1973), based on another Chandler novel, with Robert Altman directing, had had to take Elliott Gould with the deal to get financing. The improbability of Gould portraying Marlowe hadn't concerned Altman in the least; Altman had, in fact, talked himself into directing the picture while trying to convince Jerry Bick of Gould's "rightness" for the part. When GOODBYE grossed $959,000 at the box office, United Artists turned an unsympathetic shoulder on Kastner and Bick's proposal for a third make of Farewell, My Lovely. Kastner was finally able to get the British financier Sir Lew Grade and the British-based International Television Corporation to co-finance. Dick Richards was asked to direct. He would sign to do the picture provided Robert Mitchum was cast as Marlowe. Kastner got Mitchum for Richards.

When I talked to Dick Richards, he was in preproduction on MARCH OR DIE (Columbia, 1977); FAREWELL, MY LOVELY had been released and had proved both a critical and a commercial success. We were in the office suite Richards was occupying at the Samuel Goldwyn studio on Santa Monica Boulevard. Richards sat poised behind his desk, his blue-green eyes attentive.

"Robert Altman updated his treatment of Marlowe. Why didn't you?"

"I was given an updated script when I was offered the picture," he replied. "I turned it down. I thought it was sacrilegious to screw around with that book."

"What happened then?"

"It was the same producers as on THE LONG GOOD-BYE, Elliott Kastner and Jerry Bick. They told me to make any changes in the script I wanted to make. David Goodman and I rewrote the whole thing, making it a period piece."

David Zelag Goodman had received Academy Award nominations for his scripts for MONTE WALSH and LOVERS AND OTHER STRANGERS (ABC Films, 1970), and had written the screenplay for Sam Peckinpah's STRAW DOGS (Cinerama, 1971).

"I have to admit that the way you did it, it worked,"
I said. "When THE LONG GOODBYE was in preproduction,
I didn't think it was possible for it to be brought off as a
period piece."

"THE LONG GOODBYE is very late Chandler," Richards said. "FAREWELL, MY LOVELY is from Chandler's
early period. I think he wrote well in that period. His dialogue is sharper. Everything was better. I tried to stay
true to Chandler. The dialogue is what makes Chandler stick.
That I wanted to keep. There was a lot about the book that
was unbelievable. But not the dialogue."

"You changed the plot. You substituted a cat house
for the asylum Chandler used in the novel and a madam for
the psychic, Jules Amthor."

"I didn't like Amthor as a villain. That's one of the
things I found unbelievable in the novel. It played better, I
thought, the way we changed it. And we created a sub-plot.
We gave Marlowe a friend. In the novels, he has no one."

"In the novels," I said, "he can't trust anyone enough
to make him a friend."

"Well, that's where Bob Mitchum came in. He played
Marlowe like a man of his age. He's tired. Marlowe is
tough, smart, but fallible. He can say, almost at the end,
'Now, I get it.' It's nearly too late. But he knows how to
get information."

"How did Mitchum take to the role?"

"Oh, he liked the role. But he worried about how he
would be accepted, playing Marlowe. Bob Mitchum is a great
sardonic character. That's the way I wanted him to play
Marlowe. And, of course, he had always wanted to play
Marlowe. We talked over the role quite a bit. But we
agreed what kind of guy Marlowe was. We even improvised
on the set when something didn't sound right."

RKO Radio Pictures had originally purchased screen
rights to Farewell, My Lovely and had used it as the story
line for THE FALCON TAKES OVER (RKO, 1942), with George
Sanders in the starring role. The Falcon series had its own
successful formula for crime detection with a high comic tone,
and the only real flaw of TAKES OVER was Chandler's rather

convoluted plot. The characters belonged to Chandler's stark
view of Southern California and were out of place in New York
City being investigated by the debonair Sanders. The police,
represented by James Gleason and Edward Gargan, were buf-
foons compared to the brutal and secure men Chandler had
drawn.

Edward Dmytryk brought the novel to the screen as
the first film featuring Philip Marlowe by name as the detective, with Dick Powell in the role. Principally because of
Powell's reputation as a singer and dancer, the title of the
film was changed to MURDER, MY SWEET (RKO, 1944). It
is perhaps the best Marlowe film other than LADY IN THE
LAKE (M-G-M, 1947), which was directed by and starred
Robert Montgomery. Powell's flippant yet hard tone was appropriate, although he lacked the biting sarcasm Robert Montgomery later brought to his characterization.

"Did you look at MURDER, MY SWEET?" I asked
Richards.

"I looked at MURDER, MY SWEET and at the Falcon
picture. I wanted Los Angeles to be seedy in my film, the
way it had been when Chandler described it. We shot the
whole picture right here. I used the Queen Mary for the
gambling ship."

"Chandler based Bay City in the novel on Santa Monica.
Eddie Dmytryk told me they used to lock up Santa Monica at
night. Chandler drew his cops as corrupted men. You didn't."

"No. For me, the picture was about Marlowe. In
THE CULPEPPER CATTLE COMPANY, there were no heroes.
Marlowe is a hero. We debated for months on how to handle
the last scene, where Marlowe gives money to the widow. I
wasn't so concerned with corruption. There's plenty of that
in the picture. I wanted to stress Marlowe's honesty."

To play the cop who is sympathetic to Marlowe--one
might almost regard him as much of a friend as Jimmie
Archer is, playing Georgie, the newsstand proprietor who
helps Marlowe and even gives him a place to stay--Richards
cast John Ireland. It is Ireland who at the denouement decides for once to put duty before the pay-offs the force receives and to see the case through. Maybe that could have
happened in 1941. As for Marlowe's turning over the two-
grand fee paid him by the gangster Brunette, Newsweek com-

mented: "Having muttered 'What a world,' he gives his fee
to a fatherless son of one of the murder victims, a little boy
who happens to be black. By doing so, this Marlowe unwittingly commits the movie's final 'unspeakable' horror: he
turns Chandler's hard-boiled hero into a soft-boiled liberal."

In more than one way, Farewell, My Lovely was a
comic novel, a satire, the closest Chandler ever came to
imitating the hectic tradition of Nathanael West at his best;
that is, his most inanely relevant. In chapter eighteen, where
Marlowe meets Mrs. Grayle for the first time, there is hy-
perbole, the comic tone approaching the grotesque. The absurdity of the characters and the situation they find themselves
in is nowhere more evident and, if a reader is ever inclined
to laugh out loud, sitting alone in a room with nothing but a
book in front of him, this scene might provoke it. None of
the film versions brings it off. Richards' handling of the sequence is marred because of his shift of emphasis from the
ridiculously sensuous to the seriously, or at least tantalizingly,
erotic. If there is nothing more annoying to a woman than
the sexual pretensions of a man toward whom she isn't re-
motely attracted physically, there is for Chandler's hero nothing quite as idiotic as the sexual innuendos of a female who
is a murder suspect and, therefore, morally dubious.

"I saw what Bob Altman had done with THE LONG
GOODBYE," Richards concluded. "I was impressed to see
him try to do what he thought was something fresh with Chandler. I said to myself that I'd like to see if I could come up
with a style for Chandler."

The style Richards came up with went farther than
expert casting, including Mitchum. He retained the back-
telling technique which is the only way a screenplay can pre-
serve Chandler's caustically disrespectful and incisive descrip-
tions of people and places. There was something peculiar
about indoor light in the 'forties, and Richards managed to
recapture it, a moody, soft glow rather than the harsh illu-
mination to which we have since become accustomed. Mitchum's presence, so reminiscent of his work from the 'forties
in films like OUT OF THE PAST (RKO, 1947), a classic of
film noir as is MURDER, MY SWEET, stands almost as a
critique of the era. If it wasn't as bleak, desolate, misbe-
gotten, and corrupt as our own, it was nonetheless all of these
things to a lesser degree, and Mitchum makes certain that we
recognize it.

The historian Arnold Toynbee once said that a civilization can be judged by the way in which it treats its old people. Unlike Roman Polanski, who wanted a period feeling in CHINATOWN (Paramount, 1974) and so had to shoot over sixty-five per cent of the film on sound stages, Richards wanted even his interiors to be filmed on location in Los Angeles. He used close to forty actual locations, but it only served to make him all the more cognizant of America's lack of respect for old age--in his words, "architectural as well as human." When Richards remarked that he wanted Los Angeles to appear seedy, he didn't mean that Los Angeles today is less seedy than it once was, only that the seediness is different, today working from the inside out.

Another thing Richards overlooked in the Chandler novel, primarily because he was limited to the John Ireland character, was the reason why the police always brutalize Marlowe. Robert Altman caught it. The police are paid not to exercise their power, not to make arrests, to look the other way, and so they begin to hunt for opportunities to flex their muscles. Ultimately helpless citizens--petty criminals, traffic violators, private detectives--afford them these opportunities. Chandler said it over and over in his books: as long as the public is going to stand by and tolerate crooked politicians and big league mobsters, they cannot expect more from the police than to have law and order rammed forcibly down their throats and occasionally stop a bullet.

FAREWELL, MY LOVELY was filmed in thirty-seven days at a cost of $2,300,000, an interesting figure when contrasted with MURDER, MY SWEET, which required forty-four days and cost $450,000. Even while we talked, Richards had just returned from scouting locations for MARCH OR DIE and was this time entrusted with a $9,000,000 budget. David Zelag Goodman was again engaged to write the screenplay.

Yet, upon release, MARCH OR DIE proved another epigonal, generic film, devoid of any real story value. It dealt with the French Foreign Legion in Northern Africa and had an international cast headed by Gene Hackman, icy, and expressionless Catherine Deneuve, Max von Sydow, Ian Holm, and Terence Hill. The production was once more a joint venture between Sir Lew Grade and International Television Corporation, with Columbia Pictures releasing. Perhaps the most promising aspect of the film might have been the characters, but they turned out to be clichés. Gene Hackman plays an American major in the Legion who spends his time being bitter with dialogue like "There are no heroes in war, only survivors," and, to the Arabs, "Let the French bring you into the twentieth century." Catherine Deneuve is always perfectly coiffured and attired despite being thousands of miles distant from boutiques and beauty parlors, and is otherwise undistinguished. Ian Holm is a murderous but ostensibly noble--according to the murky screenplay--Arab chieftain. Max von Sydow portrays an inhuman, monomaniacal archeologist and Terence Hill is Marco the Gypsy, momentarily attracted to Deneuve's wooden personality and, following Hackman's death, the man destined to take Hackman's place leading the Legion.

Newsweek concluded its review: ".... Director Dick Richards wants both to glorify the swashbuckling glamour of the French Foreign Legion and to reveal the French, who are callously pillaging the Arabs' art treasures, as colonial rapists. From the start, the story is set on an ideological suicide march. Who, in fact, are the good guys and bad guys here? Richards, with an eye on the overseas market, plays it both ways--and plays it badly. You root for the movie to come to a swift end." Having set out to make MARCH OR DIE a formulary combination of GUNGA DIN (RKO, 1939) and FOUR FEATHERS (United Artists, 1939), Richards may have been thrown off by the fact that the colonial French embodied objectives different from those of the colonial British. What he came up with was a movie, not a film, so familiar in its cliché characters and situations as to be as predictable as its dialogue.

If there has been a notable shortcoming to this point in Richards' work as a contemporary filmmaker, it could well be his reliance on generic film ideas; he has had only one qualified success. Richards is a director of more than competent technical proficiency and so chances are quite good that, should he abandon the generic with all its clichés, references to old pictures, novelty variations on the obsolescent theme of good guys vs. bad guys for want of a truly cogent story, and the nostalgia attached to all of these, he might be able to take a bold, individualistic step forward on his own; if he does, his best films may still lie before him. One thing is certain. If he is to make better films, he will have to resolve that there is no escape from the necessity for a strong, compelling, integrating story line.

DICK RICHARDS

A Film Checklist by Vicki Piekarski

Director

✓1.   THE CULPEPPER CATTLE COMPANY (1972).   P:
       Twentieth Century-Fox. C: Gary Grimes, Billy "Green"
       Bush, Luke Askew. DeLuxe Color. 92m.

2.   RAFFERTY AND THE GOLD DUST TWINS (1974).   P:
       Warner's. C: Alan Arkin, Sally Kellerman, Macken-
       zie Phillips. Technicolor. Panavision. 91m.

3.   FAREWELL, MY LOVELY (1975).   P: Avco Embassy.
       C: Robert Mitchum, Charlotte Rampling, John Ireland.
       Fujicolor. 97m.

4.   MARCH OR DIE (1977).   P: Columbia.   C: Gene
       Hackman, Terence Hill, Max von Sydow.   Color.
       106m.

Hal Ashby.   Photo courtesy of Eddie Brandt's Saturday Matinee.

Chapter 7

HAL ASHBY

by Paul Frizler

I

When I interviewed Hal Ashby in 1978, his stringy white hair and scraggly white beard made him appear older than his 46 years. But after talking to him for a couple of hours, I felt that his infectious enthusiasm, continuous energy, and casual profanity suggested the spirit of a man about twenty years younger.

In his beachfront living room in Malibu Colony, an elite Southern California area, the wiry Ashby interrupted his narrative by answering a constant stream of phone calls from such friends as Peter Sellers and Mick Jagger. Occasionally Ashby would scan the waves that came menacingly near his sliding glass window. He didn't seem nervous, though any apprehension on his part would be understandable, considering the heavy winter storms of 1978 which brought threats of inundation to many of his wealthy neighbors, including rock superstar Linda Ronstadt.

In the 'seventies, Ashby went from being one of Hollywood's most successful editors to becoming a movie director. His directorial career began in 1970 and in one decade he has become one of Hollywood's top directors. All of his films, from his very first one, have been well received by either critics or the public, or both.

THE LANDLORD (United Artists, 1970) was an exceptionally impressive debut, gathering many laudatory reviews. Pauline Kael "loved much of it" and The New York Times called it "a wondrously wise, sad, and hilarious comedy." Ashby claims that many friends in the industry--perhaps forgetting CITIZEN KANE (RKO, 1941)--told him that it was the

223

best first directorial effort they'd ever seen. While few critics allowed their praise to become so extravagant, a number
of them commented on Ashby's assured and mature technique,
a big compliment for a first time director.

Others were amazed at Ashby's ability with actors.
Many of the performers in THE LANDLORD had never before
been so effective. An ability to coax superb performances
from actors was unexpected from a director who had spent
years in editing rooms.

With each subsequent film, Ashby's position became
more secure: HAROLD AND MAUDE (Paramount, 1971),
THE LAST DETAIL (Columbia, 1974), SHAMPOO (Columbia,
1975), BOUND FOR GLORY (United Artists, 1976), and COM-
ING HOME (United Artists, 1978).

After this record, his future projects are anticipated
with as much interest in the press as a new film by Francis
Ford Coppola or Steven Spielberg. Even though he hasn't yet
been embraced by all the serious critics--Andrew Sarris, for
example, has not yet found a consistent style in his work;
hence Ashby must not be an auteur--his work has received
positive critical analysis in film journals. Ashby's opinion
of himself is quite high; he has very few regrets about his
films. He is convinced that he has the sensitivity, the skill
and the talent to be an outstandingly successful director.

Ashby's self-confidence is truly remarkable and seemingly unshakeable. When, during our discussion, in playing
the devil's advocate, I would present a critical objection to
some aspect of one of his works, he would always be uncon-
vinced. For instance, in response to Pauline Kael's and
Vincent Canby's objection to the way Ashby, in the manner
of AMERICAN GRAFFITI (Universal, 1973), used the original
records of the late 'sixties as the score for COMING HOME,
Ashby said they were both wrong, and if he could do it over,
he would add more songs. "I wish," he said, totally convinced, "I could have made the film wall-to-wall music."

Ashby's strong adult ego seems an unlikely development after his insecure and troubled childhood. He was born
in Ogden, Utah in 1932 of parents whose marriage was shaky.
Ashby is reluctant to dwell on his unhappy childhood. His
parents were not Mormons in a community where virtually
everyone was a member of the Church of Latter Day Saints.
Their marriage fell apart in 1937. At the age of five, Ashby

was confused and deeply disturbed by his parents' divorce.
When he was twelve, his father killed himself, an event which
traumatized Hal and made him rather surly and difficult both
at home and at school.

Ashby hated school and became a high school dropout
in his senior year.   He drifted from job to job and from
woman to woman.   He was married and divorced twice by
the time he was 21.   In 1953 he hitchhiked to Los Angeles.
After he tried about fifty or sixty odd jobs--"You name it;
I did it"--he ended up as a Multilith operator at the old
Republic Pictures.

"One day, while running off ninety or so copies of
some now-forgotten old Western, I flashed on the idea of becoming a film director.   With the hope of achieving my directorial dream, I plied my Multilith trade and asked everyone for advice.

"'The best school for a director,' they told me, 'is
in the cutting room.'"

After much persistence he was accepted as an apprentice editor.   Luckily, his timing was right and the union was
in a position to allow him to join.   Ashby believes that using
editing as a path to directing was the right decision.   "When
film comes into a cutting room," he says, "it holds all the
work and efforts of everyone involved up to that point: the
staging, writing, acting, photography, sets, lighting, and
sound.   It is all there to be studied again and again and
again, until you really know why it's good, or why it isn't.
This doesn't tell you what is going on inside a director, or
how he manages to get it from head to film.   But it sure is
a good way to observe the results, and the knowledge gained
is invaluable."

Ashby's union kept him working for eight years as an
apprentice before he was eligible to begin cutting.   He gets
a pained expression on his normally benign face when he dis-
cusses the experience: "What you have to do as an apprentice, I can tell you, is horrendous!"   The long grind, he
feels, tends to cut down most of the talented cutters whose
creativity remains locked in them.   "It can become a full-
out struggle just to hang on during those eight long years.
Some good talent has gone down the tubes in the process."

During Ashby's eight-year ordeal, he went to work as

a fourth apprentice editor on THE BIG COUNTRY (United
Artists, 1958), a multi-million-dollar production directed by
William Wyler. The editing crew was headed by Robert
Swink, who eventually became Ashby's mentor. Bob Swink
trained him in everything from technical aspects to a philos-
ophy of film; he proved an excellent teacher.

"Once the film is in hand," Swink said, "forget about
the script, throw away all of the so-called rules, and don't
try to second guess the director. Just look at the film and
let it guide you. It will turn you on all by itself and you'll
have more ideas on ways to cut it than you would ever dream
possible." Swink also advised him to use his instincts and
to be persistent. "Don't be afraid of the film. You can cut
it together twenty-six different ways and, if none of those
works, you can always put it back into daily form, and start
over."

Swink and Ashby got along so well that Ashby "almost,
but not quite" forgot that he wanted to direct. Swink took
Ashby along with him on his next four films: THE DIARY
OF ANNE FRANK (20th-Fox, 1959), THE YOUNG DOCTORS
(United Artists, 1961), THE CHILDREN'S HOUR (United Artists, 1962), and THE BEST MAN (United Artists, 1964). It
was on the last picture that Swink gave him the opportunity
to cut a few sequences. "You know," Ashby recalls, "I used
to come in at three in the morning and cut until eight. I'd
get the room ready for Bob, who came in at eight-thirty or
nine, and work as his assistant until eleven, then go back in
the next morning at three. Those were long, hard hours."
Stuart Millar, producer of THE BEST MAN, relates that when
he saw his picture's banquet scene he recognized Ashby's
special cutting talents.

Finally, Ashby's eight-year ordeal ended when Swink
got him a job on THE GREATEST STORY EVER TOLD (United
Artists, 1965) as a fourth assistant editor. From there he
went on to THE LOVED ONE (M-G-M, 1964), where he jumped
all the way to chief editor. Ashby did the first cut on the
film and then, quite abruptly, director Tony Richardson left
to finish the editing in London, leaving Ashby behind. After
a period of depression and unemployment, he was introduced
by John Calley, who had produced THE LOVED ONE, to
Norman Jewison. The director was looking for an editor for
THE CINCINNATI KID (Universal, 1965). The Jewison/Ashby
team clicked, and they continued working together for THE
RUSSIANS ARE COMING, THE RUSSIANS ARE COMING (United

Artists, 1966), IN THE HEAT OF THE NIGHT (United Artists,
1967), and THE THOMAS CROWN AFFAIR (United Artists,
1968).

Ashby loved working with Jewison because Jewison
never stood over his shoulders in the cutting room. "He let
me select and cut his films as I felt it. It was an editor's
dream and, in the end, it brought me two Academy nominations, and one Oscar for IN THE HEAT OF THE NIGHT."
On his next picture, GAILY, GAILY (United Artists, 1969),
Jewison made Ashby associate producer, a position where he
was able to gain experience in pre-production and production.
He scouted locations and evaluated scripts when he was not
working as Jewison's editor. While Ashby had been editing
THE THOMAS CROWN AFFAIR Jewison had asked him, "What
do you want to do when you grow up?" Ashby had gone dumb
for a long moment, standing with a stupid grin; after an in-
terminable pause, he had blurted out: "I want to direct.
That's where it's at, isn't it?" Jewison had replied: "Right!
Let's find something for you." While they were shooting
GAILY, GAILY, Jewison read the script of THE LANDLORD,
which was to be his new directing assignment. Aware of
scheduling problems which he couldn't resolve, Jewison casually asked Ashby, "Why don't you direct LANDLORD?"
Ashby responded by jumping up and doing a dance around the
office. Jewison offered to produce THE LANDLORD and they
set out to persuade the Mirisch Brothers and United Artists
to invest $2,000,000 so an unknown could direct his first
movie. Ashby thought at the time that the studio bosses con-
sented to his directing because they thought that with Jewison
producing, "If Ashby falls on his ass, Jewison can take over
and we'll be covered."

II

Ashby launched into the demanding job of directing
THE LANDLORD (United Artists, 1970) by casting the film.
He quickly realized the awesome responsibility of making de-
cisions--final decisions. His major fear was that he would
be unable to communicate his thoughts to the actors. He felt
more secure in other areas: camera composition, placement
and coverage. Though he never doubted the abilities of his
actors, he was afraid he couldn't explain to them what he
wanted them to feel. Inevitably, after a week or two of rehearsals in New York, when the first day of shooting began,
Ashby was unable to breathe. Fear had made him sick. His

doctor diagnosed walking pneumonia and ordered him to bed.
Ashby said: "Hell, no!" and asked him to pump everything
he had into his arm, rear, or foot, as necessary.   Three
days of heavy medication and he recovered--with three days
of directing behind him.

Jewison, who was afraid of intimidating Ashby, stayed
away from the set for the first six weeks.   Ironically, when
he did finally come to New York and visited the set, his criticisms of Ashby were not those of a director but those of a
producer--he complained about the schedule and the budget.
Ashby interrupted him: "Norman, what the hell are you talking to me about?   You're the director."

Jewison looked at him for a second, laughed, and
said, "That's right!"   Those were his last words as a producer.

Other pressures still existed.   The Mirisch Company
criticized the photography: it was too dark; they couldn't see
the actors' eyes.   Ashby explained that he wanted the look of
the ghetto footage to contrast with that of the rich Long Island
estate with its cloudlike, white on white pastels.   The pressure stopped when the Mirisch brothers saw the later footage.
Their new complaint was that Ashby had fallen behind schedule.   Somehow, he convinced them to make a schedule which
would allow room for his tendency to shoot a tremendous
amount of footage.

Finally, the shooting was over and Ashby was thrilled
when he saw that much of his personality had come out in
THE LANDLORD.   He was also excited that he had great
rapport with all the actors, not only with Beau Bridges, who
was already a close friend, but also with new acquaintances:
Lee Grant, Pearl Bailey, Lou Gossett, and Diana Sands.

The many actors, both major and minor, were blessed
by a delightful script by William Gunn based on Kristin Hunter's novel (both writers happen to be black).   The script developed the characters in a rich, rounded, complicated manner
and avoided stereotypes.   Ashby's ability to direct actors in
this, his first time out, was remarkable.

Edgar Enders, the film's title character, played with
appealing sensitivity by blond, blue-eyed Beau Bridges, is a
rich white boy from Long Island who buys a tenement house
in the middle of the Brooklyn ghetto with the idea of refurb-

ishing it into a groovy townhouse pad. He plans, for example, to knock out all the floors up to the skylight and dangle a huge, spectacular psychedelic fixture from the ceiling. At 29, Enders is convinced that he needs to move away from home, particularly from his crazy mother, and establish his own piece of landed property before he's 30. He soon finds nothing but resistance. The blacks refuse to move. Worse still, they won't pay the rent. Presently he finds them using voodoo on him--the placement of magic eviction powder at his front door. His life is threatened: "One gunman's most unforgettable memory might be you!"

Bridges' performance is convincing. He manages to hold in suspension his compassionate side when he's attacking his family's selfishness, and his blithe, egotistical side when he casually shrugs off a married tenant who has just borne him his child. This duality is captured faultlessly by Bridges in a style which is impossible to reduce to a simple formula.

Diana Sands is haunting as the hapless, pregnant tenant. She is married to a brutish, violent, impotent husband (played with suitable paralytic rage by Lou Gossett) and has such a shattered ego that she attempts to strengthen herself by nostalgically remembering her one moment of glory: "I was Miss Sepia of 1957."

Another tenant is Professor Duboise, played by Melvin Stewart, who attempts to instill pride in the young blacks in his classes so that they can grow up with strong egos and a sense of their worth. He focuses instruction on the importance of their understanding that "black is beautiful." There is a marvelous scene where we see Enders watching the ritualized catechism of Duboise's class while he flashes back to himself as a tow-headed youth in a middle-class school.

The most delightful tenant is Marge, a black earthmother, played by Pearl Bailey, who attempts to educate Enders as to the disparate life-styles of ghetto blacks. Her honesty and street smarts make Enders more aware of the effete, sterile atmosphere of his family's life in a huge white mansion (one could almost call it a plantation), complete with colored servants who serve poolside drinks.

The family is portrayed with broad, satirical strokes, so close to the point of caricature that they clash in tone with the realistic portrayal of the ghetto residents. But Ashby does manage--though barely--to hold the discordant styles

together. The screwball Enders family ranges from the ab-
surd--Bob Klein as a boob who boasts, "My family's in na-
palm"--to the hilariously pathetic: Susan Anspach as a plastic
hippy who convinces herself that "our whole family are octo-
roons."

The most skillfully defined portrait in the Enders family is that of Lee Grant as Bridges' mother. Despite her
imbecility and blindness (such as trying to convince her son
of her lack of racial bias by reminding him, "Didn't we go
together to see GUESS WHO'S COMING TO DINNER?"), she
does somehow manage to remain sympathetic and real. This
feat is amazing when one realizes that her main concern, besides her continuous dance lessons, is the Spinal Meningitis
Spring Festival Charity Ball. There is one scene with tenant
Pearl Bailey that is absolutely dazzling. Lee Grant gets
smashed while being served a luncheon of soul food and she
becomes progressively more human. During the sloshiest
part of the scene she suddenly bursts out (while dressed in
a grotesque hat, eating ham hocks with her gloves on): "Shit,
I forgot my lucky number!"

Somewhere during the course of this film, Enders
meets a lovely black discotheque dancer who is light enough
to pass for white. Played strikingly by Marki Bev, the dancer
and Enders fall in love; this is the only aspect of Enders'
venture that ends happily. All of his other plans, both al-
truistic and opportunistic for the black tenement, come to
nothing and damage his naive but sincere faith in the American dream.

Structurally, the film skillfully juggles its satirical
thrust with dark insights into the realities of the urban racial scene. At times bordering on melodrama, at times approaching farce, the varying styles are remarkably controlled
by Ashby. One adept decision was to have Gordon Willis,
Ashby's cinematographer, underexpose all of the Brooklyn
ghetto scenes and overexpose all the scenes of the Long Island mansion. This underscores the contrast in the two
worlds. The ludicrousness of the Enders is as light and
frothy as their life style; the insanity and duplicities of the
tenement dwellers are dangerous and desperately corrosive.

This impressionistic photography, coupled with the
flashy editing, fragmented narrative, flashforwards, repeater
shots, and straight-to-the-camera soliloquies produce a style
that threatens to turn into surrealism--but Ashby made it all

work in a film that is both hilarious and haunting. Looking
back on his first effort recently on TV, Ashby wanted to go
back and re-edit the movie. In his characteristically funny
way, he says: "I saw about 108 things I wanted to do to THE
LANDLORD or maybe 208 things or maybe 808 things, I don't
know; but I called them [ABC] and I said, 'Hey, listen you
guys: give me three weeks and I'll give you a whole new
film.' And they said, 'Well, no.'"

Yet, despite its many good reviews, the film was not
a big success. Its main problem was that United Artists released five other movies on black themes the same month it
released THE LANDLORD; it just got lost in the shuffle. One
of these films (that immediately got buried) was LEO THE
LAST (United Artists, 1970); it had a plot astoundingly similar
to that of THE LANDLORD. The only one of the six to make
it big at the box office was COTTON COMES TO HARLEM
(United Artists, 1970), an easily exploitable sex and violence
entertainment that in its crude way United Artists knew exactly how to promote. THE LANDLORD, offering more sophisticated pleasures, did not get the advertising campaign
it deserved and did not do as well as it should have.

Before THE LANDLORD was even released, Robert
Evans at Paramount gave Ashby the script for HAROLD AND
MAUDE. The script seemed so funny that Ashby found himself laughing aloud. He was also afraid to direct the film
because he feared that it might be impossible to transfer
those laughs to the screen; the scenes which worked well on
paper would, he thought, when visually presented, appear
stupid. He decided to turn down the offer. After further
consideration, however, he decided to take up the challenge.
The script for HAROLD AND MAUDE was written by Colin
Higgins as his thesis for a Master's degree, prior to his
successes in SILVER STREAK (20th-Fox, 1976) and FOUL
PLAY (Paramount, 1978). Higgins was living in the guest
house of Eddy Lewis and when he fell behind in the rent he
gave his script to Lewis's wife as part payment. She read
it, thought it sensational, and in three days they had a deal.
Originally the deal was for Higgins to direct the film but when
Ashby spoke to Evans--in Higgins' presence--Evans said that
he was not going to let Higgins direct it. Ashby, still reluctant to do it, said, "Bob, I'm not going to direct the man's
film; let him direct it." Evans said no. He had given Higgins $7,000 to shoot tests, had looked at the tests and found
them stiff. Evans told Ashby that if he wouldn't direct it,
he would get someone else to do it. Ashby asked Higgins
his opinion. He said he'd love to have Ashby direct it.

Almost immediately, it seems to Ashby in his recol-
lection, he cast the parts, checked the locations and otherwise prepared the film. The principal cast: Ruth Gordon,
Bud Cort and Vivian Pickles proved a delight to work with.
Ruth Gordon, cast as a near octogenerian, told him she would
do anything he asked her except smoke cigarettes (she does,
however, smoke a joint from a hookah).

As they started shooting, a decision was made to have
Cat Stevens write the music for the film. He was very hot
at the time, his Tea For The Tillerman album just having been released. He wrote and recorded the title song and
the memorable tune that runs through the picture and becomes
the theme: "If you want to sing out, sing out, if you wanna
be free, be free...." Stevens was going to write a complete
score for the picture but became too busy, so Ashby asked
him if he could take the rest of the numbers for the film
from his other albums. Stevens was quite willing to do this.
Working on the score became one of Ashby's biggest thrills
during production.

When the editing was completed, Ashby showed the
film to executives at Paramount, and they were quite uncomfortable with it. Until the first public preview, Ashby was
despondent about the film's chances.

"I sat in the balcony," he recalled, "and at the scene
when Bud Cort, in one of his many suicide attempts, chopped
off what seemed to be his hand, a guy about three or four
rows in front of me went bananas and laughed so hard, he
fell out of his seat."

Ashby was amazed to see the whole audience responding raucously with laughter. Overwhelmed with his power to
elicit such an intense response from an audience, Ashby left
the theatre convinced the film would be an incredibly huge
success. It was therefore a major disappointment that the
Christmas release of HAROLD AND MAUDE was greeted
largely with hostility or indifference by the nation's major
film critics. Vincent Canby in the New York Times set the
tone for the country when, after the world première (Paramount released the film with very little fanfare) in New York,
he advised his readers to miss the film. The story of a love
affair between young Harold (Bud Cort) and elderly Maude
(Ruth Gordon) was, to him, distasteful. In fact, Canby seemed
to echo a priest in the film who was horrified by the thought
of Harold's firm young flesh merging with Maude's "sagging

breasts and flabby buttocks." Canby's critique was firm in
its denunciations, questioning only which scene was the worst
--the one in which Maude sings or the one in which Harold
sets himself afire by a swimming pool.

Most of the major reviewers followed Canby. Others
ignored the picture. Pauline Kael missed reviewing it during
the busy Christmas season (when Hollywood traditionally releases its major blockbusters). In some communities, however, the film received outstanding reviews--most particularly
by the university film reviewers of small college towns. The
film began to catch on. This led to a growing word-of-mouth
publicity which kept the film constantly in release and, ultimately, it became a favorite at the nation's big city repertory
cinemas. The prints became shabbier as the years went by,
but the audiences became bigger and more appreciative. Finally, in the spring of 1978, Specialty Films, a Seattle-based
firm responsible for resurrecting KING OF HEARTS (France,
1967), a box-office failure that became a financially successful cult film, made new 35 millimeter prints of HAROLD AND
MAUDE, and booked the film around the country. On its revival, critics called the film a "contemporary classic," "a
charming film," and "a work of art."

Higgins had written the script originally as a play and,
in that form, it has been performed continuously in France
for the last five years. It has also played in many other
countries in the world--except the United States. Higgins also
wrote a novel version which has been translated into over a
dozen languages, including a language text designed to instruct
Japanese students in the English language. In the United States
the film has broken longevity records at many places, including theatres in Minnesota, Massachusetts, and Wisconsin. To
the young, the film has become a film like KING OF HEARTS
and ROCKY HORROR PICTURE SHOW (20th-Fox, 1975). They
want to see it over and over again.

And the film deserves it. HAROLD AND MAUDE is a
magnificent film, perhaps Ashby's masterpiece, a marvelous
tribute to the human spirit, a spirit that can somehow survive
a repressive environment (Harold) or even a concentration
camp (Maude). Laced with hilarious black comedy, HAROLD
AND MAUDE balances a touching love story with trenchant
satire. From a phony suicide by hanging to Harold's near
suicide by car crash, the film never ceases to be original.
As Bud Cort plays the character, Harold is a morbid, pallid
young man who lives with his control-addict mother (played

with incredible finesse by Vivian Pickles).   Harold drives a
hearse and attends funerals for diversion.

In the course of the film, Ashby reveals many excellent directorial touches.   As just one example: after one of
Harold's suicide attempts, his mother gives him a cold, pierc-
ing look; he is looking into the camera at the audience, sharing his motives with us.   Their eyes meet and the look they
give each other saves pages of dialogue explaining their an-
tagonistic relationship.   In his second film Ashby directed
with an assurance that was impressive.   No doubt the film
will continue to grow in reputation until it is universally recognized as a classic.

After the initial box-office failure of HAROLD AND
MAUDE, Ashby found firming up a directing deal a bit more
difficult.   In 1973 he became involved in a project at M-G-M
during the studio's lemming-like days.   The star was to be
Jack Nicholson, and Ashby had the female lead cast when
various executives at the studio told him that they didn't want
her.   Ashby left the picture, feeling that if he couldn't cast
the film the way he wanted, someone else was going to direct
the film.   Jack Nicholson sympathetically walked off with
Ashby and presented Darryl Ponicsan's novel, The Last Detail (The Dial Press, 1970), to him as an alternative.

With a script by Robert Towne and with Lynn Stall-
master as casting director, Ashby went to work preparing
the movie.   He was unable to get any cooperation from the
U.S. Government to film necessary military exteriors, so
he went to Canada where the Government allowed him to use
a military base just outside of Toronto.   Most of the film
was shot there except for a bus station scene in Norfolk.

There was an immediate problem with the cast.   Ru-
pert Crosse, the actor who had been slated to play Mulhall,
the black sailor, was notified during pre-production that he ·
was dying from cancer (he died shortly after shooting began
and was replaced by Otis Young).   Crosse remained astoundingly cheerful during his ordeal and continued, every time
Ashby spoke to him, to tell jokes and laugh.   "I wanted to
say to him, 'You are dying; don't laugh!' But instead I
laughed with him.   When I worked on the film I was about
to direct, I decided that despite the dreadful situations facing
the central characters, I would often show them laughing."

The studio executives at Columbia did not laugh, how-

ever, when they saw the finished film. The producer, Gerald
Ames, recalled that some executives felt that the film was
junk and unworthy for the studio to release. A major concern of the hierarchy was the brutally coarse language of
Nicholson and the other stars. THE LAST DETAIL was probably the most foul-mouthed movie from a major studio at that
time; it was subsequently eclipsed by films such as SLAP
SHOT (Universal, 1977). The studio believed they would never
recoup part of their investment from a TV sale. Ashby had
his editor, Robert Jones, work on an expurgated version which
would be acceptable to American television. It took 200 cuts
and dubbing of different words over the original sound track.
When it was eventually shown on TV, the editing was so skillfully done that the film seemed to have lost little of its impact. Still, Columbia decided not to promote it and it might
not have been released at all had it not been for its success
at Cannes. Producer Ames took it to the May 1974 Film
Festival and it received the widest and largest enthusiasm of
the international critics.

THE LAST DETAIL's American release was met with
considerable praise by the nation's press. Critics who had
panned HAROLD AND MAUDE, only to watch it become an
underground classic, found much praise for the reality, humanity, comedy, and originality of THE LAST DETAIL. Richard Schickel said the film had "genuine distinction." Pauline
Kael felt the film to be a vast improvement over Ponicsan's
novel. She credited Robert Towne, who wrote the script,
with taking what was good in the novel, fine-tuning it, and
changing those aspects that he and Ashby didn't like.

The major change was in the ending. In the novel,
the two sailors, having brought their prisoner (who was sentenced to jail for eight years for stealing from a polio dona-
tion box) to the brig, get so emotionally involved that they go
AWOL, get busted, and one of them gets killed. Ashby thought
it a very powerful, dramatic ending, but implausible. Never
for a moment did he or Towne believe that these two lifers
would go AWOL because of the Navy's rotten policies. The
film's ending is much more honest and, ironically, more
moving than the one in the novel. Another change from the
novel was a new scene in a restaurant, very reminiscent of
a similar one in FIVE EASY PIECES (Columbia, 1970), the
famous one in which Nicholson has his confrontation with a
waitress. There is a similar argument over a cheeseburger
in this film, but Towne put it in the script, not Ashby, and
it is used effectively to point up the difference in character

between Buddusky (Jack Nicholson) and meek Meadows (Randy
Quaid). Even though it seems unoriginal, it works so well
in THE LAST DETAIL that it would have been a shame to
lose it.

During the course of the film there are some remarkable scenes and memorable moments. One, when Nicholson
becomes outraged at a redneck, racist bartender in Washington; another, when the three men are arguing about sleeping
arrangements in a hotel room; a third, when Meadows, before bolting, gives Muley (Otis Young) and "Badass" Buddusky
(Nicholson) the hand signals for good-bye. And perhaps the
most amusing: Nicholson tells a story--not in the original
novel--about a whore in Wilmington who had a glass eye.
For a dollar service charge, she'd take it out and wink off
her clients.

Nicholson's performance is sensitive and dynamic.
Alternating between a super-masculine braggart and an attentive friend, he manages to encompass a full range of emotions
within the given confines of his character--a dissipated Navy
lifer. Whether boasting of his reasons for being a sailor--
he likes the way Navy pants make his dick look--or solicit-
ously worrying about Meadows, he is always convincing. As
Mulhall, Otis Young is not so fortunate. His character is
more stable, quieter, and, compared to Nicholson, he seems
empty. Despite this, however, he is an excellent performer
and a perfect foil for the explosive Buddusky and the ingenuous Meadows. Randy Quaid's hapless klepto is an oversized
and underbrained scapegoat whose appealing innocence and
exasperating behavior are equally mixed.

The lesser roles are quite skillfully played, especially
Carol Kane as an ethereal whore. Michael Chapman's flat
photography seems appropriate to the tone of the film, though
sometimes the desolation of the streets places too much emphasis on the central action, as if there were no other world
out there but that of the central characters. More peripheral
composition would have eliminated a certain emptiness that
the film sometimes conveys. Perhaps Ashby did this inten-
tionally. It certainly has a different visual style from all the
other films he has directed.

The editing and use of opticals are particularly stunning. He often--surprisingly--uses old-fashioned, lingering
dissolves (e. g. , in the bus sequence). Especially effective
is his use of double exposure near the end of the film, when

he overlaps the men, breathing hard after the big chase, with a slow fade to Portsmouth Prison. The time lapse is almost as long as the dissolves in George Stevens' A PLACE IN THE SUN (Paramount, 1951). At other moments Ashby resorts to quick jump-cuts. He does this most strikingly in the hotel room sequence where he cuts from one actor to the same actor and it's clear that hours have elapsed. This violates a basic rule of editing which would require either cutting to a different actor or dollying out from some object in the room. Yet the effect works well. The look of the actors-- mainly the extent of their dissipation--, the changes in their relative positions, and the different conditions of the room, all clearly indicate to the audience the passage of time. The startling cuts result in creating a properly dislocative effect, very appropriate to the rhythms and tone of the scene. Ashby's editing background enhances his director's skills very markedly in THE LAST DETAIL.

Only one aspect of the film was widely criticized: the musical score. At first, Ashby had planned on only using eighteenth-century British band music. He soon rejected this idea because the available recordings were too short and so sad that they gave the film an excessively lugubrious tone. He ended up using a few of these recordings very sparingly. One, for example, was successfully used at the scene of the winter picnic when Nicholson is muttering his monologue. For the rest of the film, Johnny Mandel scored martial music. Generally, these antique military airs are too loud and obtrusive, overly insistent in a way that focuses too much emphasis on the irony of the film's anti-military attitudes played against these super-patriotic anthems.

This one weakness, however, does not severely damage an otherwise fine work. It is too bad that Columbia did not promote the film properly. Ashby blames the crisis in the studio's management which coincided with the film's release. Nonetheless, the film is often revived at repertory cinema houses where it usually receives large and enthusiastic audiences.

Soon after finishing THE LAST DETAIL, Ashby was signed by producers Saul Zaentsz and Michael Douglas to direct ONE FLEW OVER THE CUCKOO'S NEST. Disagreements over the screenplay led him to resign from the project. Ultimately, of course, Milos Forman took over and the film went on to become one of the most successful of all time. Ashby, however, immediately went to work on his next proj-

ect, which would turn into his first critical and box-office
smash--SHAMPOO.

It was Warren Beatty who asked Ashby to direct SHAM-
POO.   The star had been working on the idea of a film about
a hairdresser since BONNIE AND CLYDE (Warner's, 1967).
It was then titled HAIR (a change was made when the Broadway musical opened) and a couple of scripts had been written,
both by Beatty and Robert Towne.   When Ashby agreed to do
the film, he got together with Towne and Beatty in a penthouse
suite at the Beverly Wilshire Hotel where, working virtually
around the clock, they synthesized the previous scripts into
what finally became the screenplay for the film.   Towne did
most of the actual writing, discussing all the ideas, problems
and dialogue with Beatty.   When the two of them were finished
with a segment, they would present it to Ashby who would
critique it, occasionally suggesting changes.   Ashby claims
that the working sessions with Towne and Beatty were ideal.
He became extraordinarily impressed with Beatty's brains,
humor, and, most of all, his serious concern.   Ashby was
glad to be able to direct him in the part of George the hairdresser who gets turned on as much by blowdrying a girl's
hair as by having sex with her.

Beatty was ideal for the part, Ashby felt.   The only
problem was that he had to do a great deal of motorcycle
riding; and, even though he took some lessons, he never felt
comfortable riding.   He terrified the crew with some near
spills, and everyone became worried about him getting hurt
and causing shooting to come to a halt.

The locations were all in the Los Angeles area: The
Bistro, the canyons of Beverly, the house in which a wild
party takes place in Holmby Hills (where Ashby's set designer
added many details, such as the cabin, the hot springs, etc.).
But the most memorable sets are the varied and numerous
places where George carries on his ubiquitous couplings--beds,
bathrooms, sofas, floors, et al.

The plot, set within twenty-four hours of George's
life, is as convoluted as a French farce.   George, who works
in a fashionable Beverly Hills salon, is engaged to Jill (Goldie
Hawn), but he often services Felicia (Lee Grant), the aggressive wife of a rich lawyer, Lester (Jack Warden), from whom
George is trying to borrow enough money to open his own
salon.   Lester's mistress, Jackie (Julie Christie), who is
also Jill's best friend and a former girl friend of George's,

takes up again with George in between his styling appoint-
ments, thus making a double cuckold out of his would-be bene-
factor (actually triple when you consider that George also
knocks off Lester's daughter, played by Carrie Fisher, during
a brief lull in his frenetic fornication). If this makes the
plot seem almost incestuous, it is. It is one of those movies that make you believe that there are, in fact, only two
hundred people in the world, and that the rest are created
by mirrors.

The setting of the film is the time when the first
draft of the screenplay was written: election eve, 1968, when
American counter-culture would be appalled to see Nixon become their leader. The first film nostalgically to mime the
late 'sixties, SHAMPOO evoked the generation gap, mini-skirts,
the Beatles, strobe lights, Spiro Agnew's hypocritical holiness,
psychedelia, and the dizzying hysterical freedom of the begin-
nings of the sexual revolution. The performances of the players, who constantly dash in and out of bed, are breathtaking.
Beatty plays the aggressively heterosexual hairdresser, George,
at times cool and smooth, at other times frenzied and awkward. He manages to make both sides of his character seem
consistent, his natural delight in giving women pleasure leading inevitably to the intense situations which make him frantic.

Julie Christie's performance as a high-strung beauty
is unbelievably dynamic and sexy. She plays a basically ruthless bitch with amazing sympathy and intelligence. As the
hapless, hysterical Jill, Goldie Hawn is beguiling and soft,
although she can be bold and blunt, as when she tells George,
"Grow up! You never stop moving. You never go anywhere."

Lee Grant is a perfectly rapacious Felicia. Seemingly
a tyrant, she can be tender and vulnerable, her face register-
ing an inner desperation. Jack Warden as the shyster Lester
is exceptionally good, too. He is satirized as a buffoon who,
for business purposes, supports Nixon/Agnew--but who is
ready to try anything, even an outdoor orgy with flower children. It's an amazingly complex performance in a rich, var-
iegated role.

Ashby's skill with actors is especially evident in his
handling of Carrie Fisher as Felicia's and Lester's daughter.
Her low-key, well-paced acting is in direct contrast to the
foolish, overblown performance she later gave in STAR WARS
(20th-Fox, 1977). Ashby, who was so worried before THE
LANDLORD about his ability to communicate with actors, has

become an assured director who, when blessed with the fully
rounded characters in this script, can elicit consummate performances from actors who, with him, can work at the top
level of their abilities.   His skill in directing the film is
evident in other areas, as well.   From the opening scene of
a couple screwing in the dark (while the credits and Paul Simon's music serve as carnal counterpoint), to the final scene
of Beatty standing alone on a hill watching Julie Christie drive
out of his life, the movie is a succession of dazzling images
and brilliantly staged scenes.

One of the best-directed scenes introduces Julie Christie.   For a long time we do not see her face and when we
finally do, we are overwhelmed by its beauty.   The scenes
in the salon are done with a marvelous orchestration of overlapping dialogue.   They recall Robert Altman at his best or,
perhaps even more pointedly, Howard Hawks in films like
BRINGING UP BABY (RKO, 1938) and HIS GIRL FRIDAY (Columbia, 1940), farces which are also frantic in tone and pace.
As contrast to this would-be furious sex-play, and in order
to make everything else seem real, things occasionally happen
which shock us, as well as the actors, into realizing that bed-
room games, even in Beverly Hills, are occasionally interrupted by the devastating problems that are part of the human
condition.   The most effective of these scenes occurs when
George's boss Norman (played effeminately by Jay Robinson)
learns, at the salon, that his teenage son has just been killed
in a car crash.   Momentarily everyone is stunned, but soon
the various people are busy again with their random and randy
sex lives.

And sex is precisely what SHAMPOO is about.   A few
reviewers complained about the incessant sex theme and found
the film distasteful and unfunny.   But most critics were enchanted.   Everything about the film was praised, from the direction, script, and acting to the superb cinematography of
Laszlo Kovacs, the subtle, understated musical score of Paul
Simon, and the perfectly timed editing of Robert Jones.   For
once the public was in agreement with the critical consensus
and SHAMPOO was an enormous box office triumph.   At last
Ashby was in a position to get the kind of treatment that is
only reserved for those directors who produce big money-
makers.   As soon as the evidence of SHAMPOO's success
was apparent, United Artists gave Ashby the green light to
do a seven-million-dollar super-production based on the life
of Woody Guthrie--a film which was ultimately released as
BOUND FOR GLORY.

III

By the time Ashby got involved with the Woody Guthrie story, most of the problems in the project had been solved; but prior to his involvement, there was a great difficulty in persuading United Artists to invest the kind of money necessary to make the film. Producer Harold Leventhal bought the rights to Woody's autobiography in the mid-'sixties. After several screenplay drafts by various writers, none of which was successful in molding Woody's stream of consciousness into suitable dramatic shape, Robert F. Blumofe, former production chief of United Artists, came into the project in 1971. United Artists had already wasted four years and a lot of development money. Another script--also unsuccessful--was done, and United Artists, unhappy with the results thus far, pulled the plug. At that point Leventhal and Blumofe had to put up $25,000 of their own money for Robert Getchell (the writer of ALICE DOESN'T LIVE HERE ANY MORE [Warner's, 1974], directed by Martin Scorsese) to try another draft. All of the other writers had been contemporaries of Woody and the producers felt that a younger writer might be better able to handle the project. Most of the other scripts had covered too much of Woody's life. They tried to show Woody as a legend.

"We wanted to show him as a real person," Ashby relates, "who created great songs like 'This Land Is Your Land.'"

Getchell's script, which ultimately became the shooting script, centers on the four years when Guthrie bummed around the country between 1936 and 1940. This was the period of the Okie migration that John Steinbeck and John Ford had captured in the novel and film versions of THE GRAPES OF WRATH. When Ashby signed to do the film, he watched THE GRAPES OF WRATH (20th-Fox, 1939) with the producers.

"Wow," he said with characteristic enthusiasm, "that was a wonderful movie. I knew I had to do my best to keep our movie from looking too much like it."

Getchell's script managed to humanize Woody, keeping the film a biography, not a hagiography. Nonetheless, the script seemed to Ashby to lack mythic resonance. It was too intimate; Woody came off as a Depression-era drifter who floated around and occasionally sang. Ashby added some epic, sweeping scenes, and tried to convey more of the social back-

Hal Ashby and David Carradine during filming of BOUND FOR GLORY (United Artists, 1976). Photo courtesy of Eddie Brandt's Saturday Matinee.

ground by depicting Woody's feelings about the land. "The
locales were there," Ashby said, "they just weren't being
used. "

        Ashby and his actors often changed dialogue on the
set, so much so that the script sometimes came to be merely
a starting point for improvisation, a technique which Ashby,
out of necessity, would later refine in COMING HOME. Ashby's choice of David Carradine to play Woody was a daring
piece of casting.   Carradine had already built up a Hollywood
myth as a wild man with a reputation for being difficult.   His
career had been largely limited to the television series Kung
Fu and to Roger Corman's exploitation quickies.   In BOUND
FOR GLORY Ashby managed to elicit a performance from
Carradine that is hauntingly real; his Woody is a sensitive
artist who can be tender to the widow Pauline, callous to his
wife, and smugly startling to a pretentious couple who are
giving him a ride: "I found out," he says disarmingly, "the
more you eat, the more you shit. "

        Convincing United Artists that Carradine was right for
the part was a difficult task.   For one thing, everybody thought
he was too tall.   Ashby, however, who had seen him on stage
in The Royal Hunt of the Sun, thought he was sensational.
Only with a couple of successful screen tests were they able
to persuade United Artists that Carradine was the best choice.
Woody's wife and son were satisfied.   They both felt that "he
has Woody's vibes. "

        Leonard Roseman's score manages to capture the scope
and power of much of Woody's music, even though he occasionally resorts to overly lush arrangements.   The hundred
or so violins which swell up when Woody leaves for California
to "So Long, It's Been Good to Know You" seem inappropriate.
Yet most of the time the score is a joy.   Carradine's singing
does full justice to Woody's own style.   (When, at the very
end, Woody's own voice is heard singing, the effect is not at
all disturbing; in fact, it becomes very moving, especially
after hearing Woody proclaim, "I hate a song that makes you
think you're born to lose, songs that bring you down.   I fight
that kind of song.   I like songs that make you take pride in
yourself. ")

        Michael Haller's excellent production design, Haskell
Wexler's stunning cinematography, and Robert Jones' editing
all combine to produce a film with many memorable scenes.
The spectacular effect of the dust storm, with its muted effect

on the blighted setting, is impossible to forget. Ashby uses
a lot of lingering dissolves, particularly in the Texas sequences. Many vivid scenes stand out; for example, a man
playing music on a lone string stretched out on a hand-carved
stake of wood. And, only in a few places (the sequence in
the Airplane Cafe, for one) does the film seem reminiscent
of THE GRAPES OF WRATH. Interestingly, some of the
scenes, particularly those on the freight train, remind me of
William Wellman's WILD BOYS OF THE ROAD (Warner's,
1933).

     Ashby's staging and control seem masterful throughout
much of the film. The sequence when Woody, broke and hungry, asks the pastor of the Christian church for a job so that
he can earn a meal is pointedly bitter in Ashby's controlled
fashion. The pastor refuses him bread and gives him a ser-
mon instead. Another wonderful scene takes place when Woody
tells his lover, Pauline, "Yeah, I'm married." There are
many amusing scenes in California as Woody tries to make
it on a radio program while keeping up his agitation for union-
izing farm workers. Ashby manages to capture Woody's rest-
lessness--"I just can't sit still. I always feel I should be
off somewhere else." Woody's social concern for the masses
does not seem to affect his behavior to his family. His root-
less nature allows him to mistreat his own wife and kids while
going on the road to better the condition of the masses.

     If BOUND FOR GLORY failed to gain a big audience,
it was not because of its radical themes and the unsympathetic
personal life of Woody which it presented. It was because
Woody's life, despite careful writing, did not structure itself
dramatically. Although the nation's critics were divided on
the merits of the film, most praised the acting, direction,
and photography. But even for those critics who praised it,
the film did not really build; it somehow never peaked. And
so, although the film will probably break even by the time
of its TV release, BOUND FOR GLORY was not the tremendous success for which United Artists had hoped.

     COMING HOME represented a departure for Ashby in
filming, in that principal photography was begun without having
anything even close to a completed script. On BOUND FOR
GLORY, Ashby had already experimented with improvisation
and last-minute script changes. On this film, he was forced
into continuous improvisations and writing a day or two ahead
of shooting.

COMING HOME sprang from the collective foresight
of Jane Fonda and her long-time friend, Bruce Gilbert. Fonda
had felt a need for increasingly demanding roles, particularly
at that point in her career, the early 'seventies. THEY
SHOOT HORSES, DON'T THEY? (Cinerama, 1969), KLUTE
(Warner's, 1971), and A DOLL'S HOUSE (Paramount, 1973)
were behind her and she needed something substantial to fill
the void. Both Fonda and Gilbert, as a result of their association with the anti-war movement, had become interested
in the problems of Vietnam veterans. They were appalled to
realize that nearly everyone had overlooked the wounded survivors who had served their country by sacrificing parts of
their bodies. Confined to crutches and hospitals, these veterans were silent testimony to the senseless waste of the war.

Gilbert and Fonda moved ahead with the project, engaging the as yet untried scenarist Nancy Dowd (who later
won critical acclaim for her original screenplay of SLAP SHOT)
to work with them in bringing the story to life. They emerged
well over a year later with a long, unwieldy screenplay. "It
was 220 pages originally," says Gilbert, "which was far too
long. But it did prove to us that a screenplay was indeed
possible."

Waldo Salt, the noted screenwriter who had won an
Oscar for MIDNIGHT COWBOY (United Artists, 1969), was
approached to write the next draft. Salt agreed enthusiastically
to do the project and suggested Jerome Hellman as producer.
Hellman persuaded everyone to pick Ashby as director. Ashby
and Salt didn't like Nancy Dowd's script at all, and proceeded
to work fresh. Ashby is particularly incensed at Nancy Dowd's
screen credit. "Not a single word or idea," he maintains,
"from her script was usable." Unfortunately, just as production began, Waldo Salt had a major heart attack and Ashby
was left with a script that was promising but a long way from
being completed.

Ashby then hired his film editor, Robert Jones, in the
capacity of writer. And the two of them began filming in an
unusual manner--one that was possible only on the large budget
Ashby had to work with. Every third day or so, filming would
cease and the cast would do a series of improvisations on an
up-coming scene. Then Jones and Ashby would write a script
based on the most successful improvisations. This procedure
added an additional month and a half to principal photography.
(Considering the nine months on editing supervision, Ashby
spent over a year, full time, on this film.)

The actors helped tremendously in this grueling process. Jon Voight was originally cast as Jane Fonda's husband. During his preparation for the role, however, Voight felt a growing attraction toward the character of Luke Martin, the paraplegic veteran who has an affair with Fonda during her husband's absence. His commitment to the role grew, much to the delight of Hellman and Ashby.

"We knew," says Hellman, "that Jon would turn himself inside out in an effort to absorb the reality of the part." Voight's enthusiasm soon landed him the role. He did it justice. From blind rage to a poignant anti-war speech, his acting is genuinely affecting.

Bruce Dern succeeded Voight as Captain Hyde. The role was an extremely demanding one, requiring Dern to transform himself gradually from a gung-ho Stateside Marine to a disillusioned and disheartened veteran. He did quite well, considering that his part is the least convincing. It is especially difficult to believe that this man would commit suicide, no matter how upset he became. Some of his lines near the end of the film are preachy, reminiscent of Arthur Miller at his worst. To Jon Voight's "I am not the enemy," Dern lugubriously replies, "Maybe the enemy is the fucking war."

Ashby exercised his usual meticulous care in casting the supporting roles. Penelope Milford was well cast as Jane Fonda's close friend, the casual but troubled Vi Munson. Robert Carradine, youngest member of the famous acting family, was chosen for the featured role of Vi's disturbed brother, Bill, a promising young musician who returns devastated from the war. His performance is chilling.

In the central role of Sally Hyde, the ex-cheerleader whose consciousness rises as she turns from a bland, unquestioning Marine wife to the aware radical, Jane Fonda is superb. She is most remarkable in the early scenes when she plays so sharply against type. "People look at me, cheery Sally, the Captain's wife. Sometimes I think I'm becoming what they see." Her scenes with Jon Voight are particularly sensitive. The sex scene between her and Voight, when ironically she has her first orgasm, is one of the most moving and erotic scenes in the recent liberated cinema.

Other powerful scenes mark the picture. The opening improvisational scene at the VA hospital is powerful, an example of <u>cinéma verité</u> that plunges the viewer into the reality

of war's historic plunder of the soldier's body. And the final
scene, when Voight pleads with a high school class not to get
sucked into the recruiting hype, is overwhelmingly poignant--
even though Ashby mistakenly intercuts it with the worst part
of the movie: Bruce Dern's suicide.

After COMING HOME was finished shooting, Ashby decided to use rock music from 1967-1968 as his score. The
problems with obtaining clearances and lack of advance planning made this difficult. Nonetheless, a large number of rock
hits from 1967 can be heard as contrapuntal background to the
drama. From the Beatles' "Hey, Jude" to the Stones' "Out
of Time," songs are used to evoke the period. Sometimes
obtrusive ("Strawberry Fields Forever" is particularly distracting), generally effective (the Chambers Brothers' "Time"
is magnificently used to heighten the scene of Dern's return
from the FBI, disturbingly aware of his wife's infidelity), the
music has helped the popularity of the film. United Artists
chose not to exploit it in advertising the way Universal did
with the rock and roll in AMERICAN GRAFFITI.

COMING HOME did well critically and, after a slow
start, did well commercially--a surprising development in
view of its downbeat, taboo Vietnam theme.

Stung by critics who claim that he has no inner vision
of his own, Ashby is determined to prove that he is more than
an excellent craftsman, that he is also an instinctive filmmaker
with something to say. Ashby is particularly upset by critics
who claim that he is too eclectic, with no consistent style or
point of view of his own. Moira Walsh, for example, writing
in the periodical America, generalizes about Ashby's abilities.
She speculates that because of his editing background, "he is
apparently better at co-ordinating someone else's content than
supplying his own." Reading these reviews one would think
it is a natural assumption that an editor would invariably make
a limited director. The successful careers of such former
editors as Edward Dmytryk, Mark Robson, Alain Resnais,
Robert Wise, Lloyd Bacon, and David Lean suggest otherwise.

It is naive to believe that the style and abilities of a
director are predictable on the basis of his career prior to
entering the field. Writers turned directors (e. g. , Preston
Sturges, John Huston, Billy Wilder) are not solely involved in
script and dialogue; former cinematographers (e. g. , Nicolas
Roeg, Jack Cardiff, William Fraker), not only interested in
visuals; and former actors (e. g. , Henry King, Henry Hathaway,

Raoul Walsh), not exclusively concerned with performances. It is true, nevertheless, that often a director's background does affect his films. A director whose training was extensive in a particular field could certainly be expected to continue his interest in that field, even though he assumed the role of director. But many people who are talented in one area can also be talented in others. And some seem totally to lose interest in their prior specialty. Looking at the films they've directed, one can readily tell Herbert Ross's and Bob Fosse's backgrounds in dance, but Leni Riefenstal's is not so easily apparent (one might suspect her of having been an editor). John Cassavetes and David Butler, both actors, evolved into directors whose techniques couldn't have been more diametrically opposed. And former producers Stanley Kramer and Alan Pakula couldn't have turned into more antithetical directors in their styles. Vincente Minnelli's background in art direction does not totally explain his uncanny talent in successfully manipulating large numbers of people in extravagant musical numbers. And, while Richard Lester's background in TV commercials, Mitchell Leisen's in interior set design, Sidney Lanfield's as a jazz musician, Andre Cayette's as a lawyer, Peter Bogdanovich's as a film historian, and even Budd Boetticher's as a bullfighter can definitely be discerned in some of their work, it hardly explains the multi-faceted talent evident in their direction.

Hal Ashby's background as an editor is evident in much of his filmmaking, but it does not completely explain his comprehensive success. His ability with actors, his control of camera placement, his knack for comedy, and his exceptional visual style do not necessarily follow from the editor's craft. But his special interest in montage, continuity and timing are talents for which his long apprenticeship was valuable preparation.

Next to writing, stage directing, and acting, editing is the most common route to becoming a film director. Because of the Byzantine structure of the cutter's union (its requirement of eight years' apprenticeship before being allowed to cut a single film) and the difficulty of persuading producers to allow a good editor to switch from editing to directing, most would-be directors have opted to get into directing by way of another discipline. Creating successful screenplays used to be, and still is (e. g. , John Milius, Colin Higgins, Frank Pearson), a surer way to get an opportunity to direct. Screenwriters' concentration on plot, dialogue, themes, and character would seem to offer good training to a director who is blessed

with a perceptive eye and a personality that could obtain good
performances from actors. A director like Howard Hawks,
with his dual background in writing and editing, would seemingly have had the ideal training to become a great director.

These days, of course, directors (e. g. , George Lucas,
Francis Ford Coppola) often come out of film schools where
they have had training in all of the aspects of film production
and have spent a good deal of time studying the films of the
past.   Pauline Kael believes this is precisely what's wrong
with films today, as the new directors are too narrow and
specialized; all they know is filmmaking and film history.
She believes that film students should become broadly educated in a liberal field like philosophy.

Ashby impresses one as a cultured, sensitive man who,
without formal schooling, has learned what he needs to perform the divergent tasks of directing.   He may not have a
consistent vision and his style may shift radically, depending
on the subject he is working on.   But there are certain themes
and motifs which seem--even after only six films--to be apparent.   His films invariably deal with the classic theme of
the Bildungsroman--the education of a young person.   The
naive landlord, the neurotic Harold, young Woody, ingenuous
seaman Meadows, complacent Sally Hyde, all go through a
process of learning.   Even George in SHAMPOO seems to
learn something at the end--even if it's only the emptiness of
his life.   When asked about his persistence in dealing with this
theme, Ashby shrugged his shoulders and said: "I guess everybody's always growing up." It's interesting to note that the
films he's inclined toward for future projects have this theme
as their central problem.   Perhaps even the auteurists like
Andrew Sarris will eventually come to embrace Hal Ashby.

HAL ASHBY

A Film Checklist by Vicki Piekarski

Director

1.   THE LANDLORD (1970).   P: United Artists.   C:
        Beau Bridges, Pearl Bailey, Diana Sands.   DeLuxe
        Color.   113m.

2.   HAROLD AND MAUDE (1971). P: Paramount. C:
      Ruth Gordon, Bud Cort, Vivian Pickles. Technicolor.
      90m.

3.   THE LAST DETAIL (1973). P: Columbia. C: Jack
      Nicholson, Otis Young, Randy Quaid. Metrocolor.
      105m.

4.   SHAMPOO (1975). P: Columbia. C: Warren Beatty,
      Julie Christie, Goldie Hawn. Technicolor. 109m.

√5.   BOUND FOR GLORY (1976). P: United Artists. C:
      David Carradine, Ronny Cox, Melinda Dillon. DeLuxe
      Color. 147m.

√6.   COMING HOME (1978). P: United Artists. C: Jane
      Fonda, Jon Voight, Bruce Dern. Color. 127m.

Chapter 8

PETER BOGDANOVICH

by David Wilson

I

"Every picture," Peter Bogdanovich once said, "is a learning experience. There's no such thing as making a picture without learning something. I don't think it's possible."

Until 1964, Bogdanovich had been an off-Broadway director who wrote about movies so he could get into theatres for free. When his production of Once in a Lifetime failed he decided he wanted to move to California and start directing motion pictures. He said he wanted to make fifty films. "The greatest thing in the world is to make pictures," he said at the time. "I don't understand how anyone can do anything else!"

Bogdanovich has produced the best journal of his work himself, it would appear, in his remarks and in the many autobiographical columns he has written for magazines like Esquire and New York. They indicate an unprecedented degree of directorial self-consciousness. Rarely has a film-maker been so elaborately defined by his own self-perceptions.

Perhaps there is yet one mystery which remains in Bogdanovich's life. 1977 was the year he decided not to make a picture. He was going to take a break. It was a surprising decision from a thirty-eight-year-old director who had measured twenty years of his life by the motion pictures he had either made or seen. Seven years before this break, Bogdanovich had been the hottest director in Hollywood.

In 1970 he had been one of the most honored filmmakers of all time. He had received an Academy Award nomination for Best Director and his picture, THE LAST PICTURE SHOW

251

Peter Bogdanovich.   Photo courtesy of Eddie Brandt's Saturday Matinee.

(Columbia, 1971), was nominated for seven more awards.
No one had heard of such potent beginner's luck since 1942,
the year Orson Welles' CITIZEN KANE (RKO, 1941) was
nominated for Best Director, Best Actor, and Best Original
Screenplay.

After the dust settled on the Academy Awards, THE
LAST PICTURE SHOW had claimed only two Oscars: one
for Cloris Leachman, Best Supporting Actress; one for the
powerful supporting performance given by Ben Johnson, ex-
stuntman and Western supporting actor. Leachman and Johnson repeated their Best Supporting honors when they received
British Academy Awards. Bogdanovich and author Larry Mc-
Murtry shared the British award for Best Screenplay.

The film industry was in a period of transition during
the late 'sixties. These were the years when the last of the
industry's founders began to retire and the studios began to
ease into the momentarily more profitable business of real
estate and inventory liquidation. When Bogdanovich arrived
in Hollywood he seemed to promise a way out of the industry's
decline by a return to the traditional story-telling virtues of
John Ford or Howard Hawks. Bogdanovich was an historian
who said the Golden Age of American filmmaking ended in the
early 'fifties. He was now going to make pictures like those
produced during the 'thirties and 'forties. He had a complete
collection of Film Daily Yearbooks and a coded file of over
6,000 3 x 5 index cards with his notes on films, both classic
and undistinguished. He had started the file when he was
twelve years old. For a moment, it appeared that Bogdanovich might lead American filmmaking to its greatest glories.

In TARGETS (Paramount, 1968), his first picture, he
plays a movie director named Sammy Michaels. "All the
greatest movies have already been made," Michaels says.
Bogdanovich wrote and directed the lines he spoke in TAR-
GETS. Ten years later, when Ryan O'Neal played a movie
director in NICKELODEON (Columbia, 1976), he very nearly
read the same line.

Bogdanovich was an unlikely maverick when he came
to Hollywood, but a maverick nevertheless, an outsider with
an insider's knowledge. His sense of Hollywood was historical,
almost mythological. L.A. was larger and colder than the
Hollywood he had recorded in his histories. "God," he was
to write for Boris Karloff, in TARGETS, "what an ugly town
this has become." TARGETS was disillusioned, the death of

Hollywood made literal, its villains represented sprawl, decay, and the infamous Southern California smog. A lot of the fun had disappeared; there was a hidden charge for the region's sun and mobility.

Most of the men Bogdanovich admired had already stopped making pictures. Allan Dwan made his last film in 1961, Raoul Walsh and John Ford finished theirs in 1964 and 1966 respectively. Some of them were officially retired. Others were still talking about their new projects in 1977. Only Howard Hawks finished a film after Bogdanovich moved West. None of the older directors was still working when he received his first Oscar nomination.

Bogdanovich found himself a late immigrant, a passenger to a Hollywood which no longer existed. He was one of the last of the first generation filmmakers, one of the last young men to get up and "go West." By temperament, Bogdanovich might have worn the white gloves of European immigrants like Fritz Lang and William Dieterle. By inclination, his pals were the two-take directors of the old breed. His contemporaries were hippie aristocrats who had grown up in Hollywood or studied at prestigious film schools. He felt closer to men in their seventies and eighties than to his comrades under thirty. After he made TARGETS, Bogdanovich was regarded as an admirable quirk, the only American critic who had managed to follow the directing path. Bogdanovich's first films contained set-ups with old movie posters, theatres, television and film clips. His characters seemed to be more concerned with the past than the present and their strongest emotions were loss and regret. They were sentimental. Lost opportunities were everywhere; nothing in the future ever looked or felt so good as the movies and memories of the past.

Bogdanovich is a self-admitted artist now that it has become more fashionable, and perhaps more healthy, to admit to hack-work. "I never use a second unit director," he once said. "I think it's lazy. I think there's only one place to put a camera, and if you use a unit, that can be off. I've let somebody else shoot the shot, when I had to do something for another shot, but I've always placed the camera and blocked it off. It's not a big deal but I always make sure that the shot is going to be the way I want it. Orson Welles said that a director is a man who presides over accidents, and I think he's right. Anything can happen. If you're not there when an accident occurs you might miss something."

After the release of TARGETS, Bogdanovich gleefully pointed out references to other motion pictures and other directors in his work. It was as if he were introducing a dinner party in his home with five or six of the greatest American film directors seated around his table. It was also a tip of his hat and cigar that may have cursed him for the rest of his career. "Somebody called me up," he told Martin Rubin, in The Director's Event (Atheneum, 1970). "They said, 'Didn't you work on the script for THE WILD ANGELS?' I said, 'Yes, how did you know?' He said, 'Well, it has a line that's right out of RIO BRAVO [Warner's, 1959].' I was also trying to do the chase in HIGH SIERRA [Warner's, 1941] and I failed.

"You don't have to invent new words to be a great writer," he went on, "and the same holds true for the vocabulary of motion pictures. Hopefully, a style of my own will emerge. I want to make the kind of pictures where the direction has meaning and is not just showing off. I want every shot and camera angle to have meaning or not be there.

"A movie is not just a movie. It exists in time. There were thousands of movies before it and there will be thousands more after it. You must have perspective to judge movies, just as you would any other work of art. The movies are only fifty or sixty years old, so there's not that much to know."

Bogdanovich eventually became tired of being measured by the success of his derivations. "It didn't hurt me in terms of success," he once told me when I interviewed him in 1977, "but it hurt me in terms of the nonsense that was written about me. I was just blabbering on about something then. I think the real reason I said those things was because I was young, and I was sort of amazed at my success and embarrassed by it. I was particularly embarrassed by the fact that I was getting lots of work offers and that people like John Ford and Howard Hawks were not. It seemed to me that I said those things as a way of repaying a debt, or acknowledging a debt. There were good people who were still living who were being ignored. I didn't really mean it to be taken as a kind of homage.

"They tend to jump on you in this business when you get past a certain age. Then they think that you're over the hill and you can't hack it any more. I don't think that's necessarily true. Buñuel is in his seventies and he's made

some wonderful pictures. I think Jack Ford could have made
a picture for the last--he didn't make a picture for about ...
nine years before he died ... I think that for about six of
those years he certainly could have made a picture. I didn't
want to take a job away from anybody, I just thought these
people should have been working. My comments were totally
misinterpreted by the critics. They simply thought I was
acknowledging some elaborate form of theft. Well, we all
steal. Hawks stole from Ford, Ford stole from Griffith,
and Griffith stole from David Belasco, so there's no such
thing as anything original. You bring your personality to
work, to bear on something, and it's either going to work
or it's not!

"Of the eight movies that I've directed, I think that
only half of them were things that I really wanted to make,
when I thought I must make it. The other ones were chances
that came up and I figured, 'Why not?'--and I was interested
in them when I made them. I did the best I could and I
think I made some pretty good pictures.

"Generally speaking," Bogdanovich went on, "I have
a whole bunch of projects. I'm interested in making any good
story, and I have about twelve or thirteen things I'm working
on, in various forms, in my mind. I'll do them as it seems
to be the right time. Comedies are my favorites. They're
more fun to make than anything else. They're tougher to
make but they're more rewarding. I don't see how I could
make a picture that didn't have a lot of comedy in it. I don't
think I've ever made one that didn't. I've spent the last seven
months thinking about what I want to do next. I'm interested
in a lot of different things and I've been trying to figure out
what I really want to do. I've seen one or two good screenplays but those are few and far between. Most of the pictures
I have in mind are things that I've decided I want to do, books
or movies. You know, ideas can come from anywhere. A
script usually needs to be redone."

The afternoon interview proved nothing so much as it
confirmed the axiom that things change in Hollywood. A few
months after the meeting Bogdanovich was rushing between
the television cameras into a church to attend Howard Hawks'
funeral. He was again writing a column in Esquire.

"Everybody's got a lot of advice," Bogdanovich had
said during our interview, "they're always saying, you ought
to do this, or you ought to do that, or you need a hit, or you

need a big picture, you need a little picture, you've got to
work with a star, you shouldn't work with a star, and everybody's got their own opinion. I don't want to rush into anything.

"When you've had a few successes, you can say the
stupidest thing in the world, and people think it's clear. When
you've had a few flops, you can say something perfectly reasonable and they look at you as if they had no idea what you
were talking about."

Bogdanovich henceforth wants to make motion pictures
that are different from anything he has made in the past. "In
one sense," he said, "I think I'm ready to make pictures now,
more than I ever was before!"

II

Peter Bogdanovich was born 30 July, 1939, in Kingston,
New York. His parents had fled the Nazis in Europe. Bogdanovich learned to speak Serbian before he spoke English. Even
after he fell in love with the movies, his father refused to
allow a television in their apartment. By the age of fifteen,
Bogdanovich had decided he wanted to be a movie star and he
began to take acting lessons. Later he studied in a Stella
Adler acting class with Warren Beatty. He failed an algebra
examination, left high school without a diploma, and began
sitting in on a Columbia University film history course taught
by Cecile Starr. Brian De Palma was another member of the
class. "They all shared the dream of becoming great directors," Starr recalled, "but Bogdanovich and De Palma seemed
to hold onto the dream while the other students were too easily seduced by reality. They kept the dream pure. If anything or anyone was going to make filmmakers of them, it
would be destiny and themselves alone."

In 1956 Bogdanovich saw CITIZEN KANE and decided
he wanted to direct motion pictures. He wrote a screenplay
about returning home after watching THE GRAPES OF WRATH
(20th-Fox, 1940) and TOBACCO ROAD (20th-Fox, 1941). In
1960 he co-produced and directed an off-Broadway production
of The Big Knife starring Carroll O'Connor. In 1961, his
favorite play during a season of summer theatre in Phoenicia
was Ten Little Indians, based on an Agatha Christie mystery.
Prophetically, Bogdanovich said he was influenced in his directing by Hawks and Welles instead of René Clair, the French

director who had directed one of the film versions of AND
THEN THERE WERE NONE (20th-Fox, 1945).

In 1962 Bogdanovich wed Polly Platt, a stage designer.
Between stints on stage, Bogdanovich was writing for film
magazines and for the program notes of film societies and
the New Yorker Theatre. He was also helping the New Yorker's owner, Dan Talbot, prepare his schedules. As a result,
the New Yorker was one of the first theatres in the U.S. to
revive classic American motion pictures. Bogdanovich began
to write monographs for the Museum of Modern Art: Orson
Welles, in 1961; Howard Hawks, in 1962; Alfred Hitchcock,
in 1963. He considered himself more a popularizer, he said,
than a critic.

Among Bogdanovich's friends were Andrew Sarris and
Eugene Archer, the latter a fourth-string reviewer on the
New York Times. "It was Gene's masterplan," Bogdanovich
wrote, in a 1978 issue of Esquire, "and he was full of dark
and Byzantine masterplans--to bide his time writing cleverly
veiled notices and occasional features until Bosley Crowther,
the number one reviewer, miscalculated and lost his position,
or retired, or was murdered by some producer. In the meantime, Gene didn't want to blow his cover. As a revolutionary
in the citadel of traditional film criticism, he couldn't write
for the conventional journals, like Film Comment here, or
Movie in England. Instead he inspired and indoctrinated dis-
ciples to carry the word through the underground, preparing
for the day he could surface and exert his influence publicly,
sway the taste of the taste-makers and then the nation and,
like those Frenchmen before him, eventually make his own
movie.

"... Andy Sarris, his chief disciple, and I, a junior
initiate, used to sit around the gray, windowless upstairs office of the New Yorker listening to Gene expound on the relative merits of Ford and Hawks, the superiority of Hitchcock
over Antonioni, or Samuel Fuller and Frank Tashlin and their
influence on Godard, the genius of the later Welles, the like-
ability of Tay Garnett and Allan Dwan, why Gary Cooper was
better than Paul Muni or why later Rossellini was more personal than early Rossellini, the sublime Renoir, Mizoguchi,
Ophuls, and so on late into the night."

Bogdanovich compared Archer to Montgomery Clift, a
romantic character who once stopped at the theatre with Mrs.
Walter Huston. "They were both," Bogdanovich said, "unac-
knowledged leaders."

He introduced himself to Clift, who was watching his performance in I CONFESS (Warner's, 1952). It was after a car accident during the filming of RAINTREE COUNTY (M-G-M, 1957). "Those breathtaking eyes," Bogdanovich wrote, "now looked out from behind a mask that could only approximate what his face had been.

"His huge image on the screen must have seemed to mock him. He turned away and looked at me sadly. 'It's ... hard, you know.' He said it slowly, hesitantly, a little stunned. 'It's very ... hard,' he said. I nodded. He looked back at the screen.

"When the picture was over, he and Mrs. Huston came out of the theatre. I was standing outside. He waved to me gently and they got back in the Rolls Royce and it was driven away. He made only one film more before he died five years later, at the age of forty-six--a lost poet from Omaha, Nebraska, the most romantic and touching actor of his generation."

In 1975 Bogdanovich returned to New York for the opening of AT LONG LAST LOVE (20th-Fox, 1975) and an interview with the Village Voice. "Why isn't Andy here?" he asked Jon Carroll, a Voice writer who thought the director looked tense and tired.

"Why isn't Andy Sarris here?" Bogdanovich asked again. "I figure that it's either that Andy hated the picture and wanted to give me a chance to defend myself publicly, or that he loved the picture and wanted to give me some more publicity."

His instincts seemed to point towards the first possibility: "I don't learn anything from reviews," he said. "And I know so many of the critics, and they know me, that it becomes kind of unpleasant, a friend attacking a friend."

It was an accurate statement: seldom had so many reviewers used the word "disaster." "You may believe it or not," Sarris wrote, "but to me the arrival of a bad movie represents a bit of bad news. And when I know the people involved even slightly, the reporting of this bad news becomes very painful.... My judicial sentence on this occasion requires my draping a black hood over my head. By now it's hardly news that AT LONG LAST LOVE is generally regarded as a monumental miscalculation.... In short, AT LONG

LAST LOVE can serve as a pincushion for every taste and distaste."

Fifteen years before this, Bogdanovich had planned his first trip to Hollywood after he requested an assignment from Robert Silvers, an editor at Harper's magazine. Silvers gave him limited encouragement and a letter of introduction. For a man who had never received a high school diploma, Bogdanovich must have been a remarkably self-possessed twenty-year-old. He used the letter to schedule interviews with Alfred Hitchcock, Billy Wilder, Gordon Douglas, John Sturges, Jerry Lewis, Jack Lemmon, Dean Martin, Cary Grant, Laurence Harvey, Walt Disney, Richard Brooks, Mark Robson, Angie Dickinson, and William Wyler.

Nine months later, Bogdanovich wrote a seventy-page journal about his two-week stay in Hollywood. Silvers read it and suggested cuts but it was still rejected. Dwight Mac-Donald sent the manuscript to the Atlantic Monthly. Again, it was rejected.

"One evening at a dinner that preceded a press preview of Howard Hawks' HATARI! [Paramount, 1962] I was seated next to a handsome Southern gentleman who said he was with Esquire," Bogdanovich wrote, in Pieces of Time (Arbor House, 1974), a collection of his articles. "We got into a discussion about movies, during the course of which I believe I insulted him and his taste about fifteen times.... As we were leaving the restaurant, I asked him what it was he did at Esquire. 'Managing Editor,' he said. It was Harold Hayes.

"A week later I phoned him. 'Hi,' I said, 'I'm the fellow that insulted you all through dinner last week.' He remembered me. I told him the history of the article I'd done and asked if he would like to see it. He would, he did, and another ten days later he called me. 'Hi Buddy,' he said. 'Hey, we're going to buy that piece and we want you to go on to Hollywood and do another one for us right away.' It was the beginning of many good things for me."

In 1964 Frank Tashlin urged Bogdanovich to move to Hollywood. When he arrived in L.A., a mutual friend introduced him to Roger Corman at a screening of one of Corman's pictures. Corman asked Bogdanovich if he wanted to write for pictures. Yes, he said, he did, so he and his wife Polly Platt began collaborating on a World War II story called THE CRIMINALS.

In 1965 Corman asked Bogdanovich to work as assistant to the producer on THE WILD ANGELS, which was scheduled for six weeks of shooting. Bogdanovich began researching locations. A week and a half before the starting date,
he volunteered to rewrite the script.   Later, he shot and
edited second-unit footage. Bogdanovich's six-week commitment became twenty-two weeks of work.   "It was done on the
run," he said.

Originally, the picture starred George Chakiris.   When
Chakiris quit, Peter Fonda, a supporting player, took the lead,
and Bruce Dern took over Fonda's role.   Corman used members of the Hell's Angels as extras.   "THE WILD ANGELS
was eventually finished," Bogdanovich said.   "If you'll look
carefully you can see me getting beat up by the Hell's Angels.
You see, I was always with Roger, and they hated Roger, so
they hated me, too.   During the final fight scene, we needed
more extras, so Roger said, 'Run in there!' Well, they tried
to kill me--they really did.   I fell to the ground, and they
murdered me."

Bogdanovich shot the opening sequence.   "I think it
begins with a baby in a crib," he said.   "Then Peter Fonda
comes in on a motorcycle.   He's riding down to see Bruce
Dern, down at the oil rigs.   I shot all that stuff.   That's what
Roger wanted, but I set up the shots and did them.   That was
the first thing I ever directed in a picture."

Bogdanovich accepted a third assignment from Corman
after they finished THE WILD ANGELS (American International,
1966).   Corman had bought a Russian science fiction picture,
STORM CLOUDS OF VENUS, which American International
pictures had agreed to distribute if Corman could put some
women in it.   Bogdanovich directed new footage at Leo Car-
rillo State Beach with a group of blonde alien women lead by
Mamie Van Doren.   Then he mixed his film with the Russian
material, receiving credit for the revised picture under the
name Derek Thomas.   It took five days of shooting and several
months, until the end of 1966, to finish VOYAGE TO THE
PLANET OF PREHISTORIC WOMEN (American International,
1969).   For one thing, a red star on the side of one of the
spaceships had to be painted out.   Another problem was the
story; the plot was fuzzy.   First, Bogdanovich gave the women
thought waves.   When the story still didn't make sense, he
wrote and read a narration for one of the astronauts.   The
Russian cosmonauts and busty prehistoric women were never
able to meet, of course, but were limited to sultry gazes
towards their counterparts' horizons.

Corman, who directed an average of three or four
pictures every year, had also hired, at one time or another,
Jack Nicholson, Robert Towne, Dennis Hopper, Bruce Dern,
Robert DeNiro, David Carradine, Sylvester Stallone, Monte
Hellman, Martin Scorsese, and Francis Ford Coppola. "The
reason Corman gave us jobs," Bogdanovich said, "was a combination of things.   In part, it was his personality, and his
commitment to filmmaking.   He also knew that if he used
young people he wasn't going to have to pay us very much.
He gives you a chance and he takes a chance.   I might just
as easily have turned out to be a bust."

After he finished THE RAVEN (American International,
1963), starring Vincent Price, Boris Karloff, Peter Lorre,
and Jack Nicholson, Corman decided to make another film
with the same sets, again with Karloff and Nicholson.   The
result of the hasty inspiration was a barely comprehensible
picture called THE TERROR (American International, 1963).
It was one of the artistic low points in Corman's career,
though according to Nicholson, Corman did little of the directing himself.   Nicholson said Coppola, Monte Hellman,
Jack Hale, and Dennis Jacob directed parts of it and that he
himself directed the final scene.

THE TERROR was finished at a pace which still left
two days on Karloff's contract.   Corman decided to make a
third feature.   He figured he could recycle twenty minutes
from a flooding scene in THE TERROR, shoot two more days
with Karloff and release another quick, cheap picture.   He
needed someone to film another hour of film with a separate
cast so he gave Bogdanovich $125,000 and told him to write
and direct a picture starring Karloff.   Polly Platt helped her
husband come up with the story.   The day before shooting
began, she learned she was pregnant.

Bogdanovich and Karloff became friends, prompting
Karloff to work for three extra days during the twenty-five-
day shooting schedule.   In Dear Boris (Knopf, 1975), Cynthia
Lindsey remembered helping Edie Karloff talk her husband
into leaving the sets long after his own scenes had been completed.   There was obviously not enough time on Karloff's
contract to shoot an entire picture with him, nor, during his
later years, was he capable of much exertion.   For his part,
Bogdanovich was unenthused about using the footage from
THE TERROR.   First, he thought he could cast Karloff as a
heavy.   Instead, he chose Tim O'Kelly, a blond, bright-faced
boy to play a spic and span, composed, efficient, and method-

ical mass murderer. He calmly sits behind a drive-in movie
screen and shoots at the audience in their cars.

Karloff considered TARGETS, as the film was titled
upon release, his last serious performance. It suggested
the roles he had played in the past. Basically, he played
himself: a shuffling, elderly actor named Byron Orlock, who
has spent the last five years moving from studio to studio,
working with producers like Monte Landis (Marshall Smith),
who says, "If not for me, the only place you'd be playing is
in wax museums."

Bogdanovich, who was twenty-eight, said, "TARGETS
contains two kinds of horror, the kind represented by Boris
Karloff and the senseless kind so prevalent today--a man
walks into a beauty shop and kills six people or climbs a
tree and starts sniping away. There is something in the way
we live today that fosters it. We live in a more impersonal,
more mechanized, plastic age, and I feel that all this must
play a part in such inhuman snipings. In the past, people
were killed, usually by strangulation or by a knife. Now a
machine does it for you. The horror of modern killing is
that you can kill somebody and not get blood on you--not physically stained."

Sam Fuller and George Cukor read the script for
TARGETS after Bogdanovich finished the first draft. Both of
them suggested improvements. Bogdanovich remembered Fuller's suggestions: "He doctored it," he said, "not by sitting
down and writing, but by pacing up and down and telling me
things. It was very helpful. The scene at the end, when
the killer shoots at the movie screen, and the Oriental girl
as Karloff's secretary, were his ideas. It was mostly the
scenes with Karloff where he helped."

The many autobiographical elements which appeared
in TARGETS were drawn from both Karloff and Bogdanovich.
It could be, in fact, the record of the making of TARGETS
or any other ambitious, low-budget horror flick. Critics applauded its violent moments but its most moving scene was
when Karloff and Bogdanovich watched scenes from CRIMINAL
CODE (Columbia, 1931), one of Karloff's first featured roles.
"Hey," Bogdanovich said, "CRIMINAL CODE! I saw it at the
Museum of Modern Art! Howard Hawks made that ... he
really knows how to tell a story!"

The scenes between the two men were filled with rev-

erence and double takes.   Bogdanovich passed out in Karloff's
hotel room, then shuddered when he woke beside his host.   It
was a reaction the equally inebriated Karloff considered absurd.
A moment later, Karloff spied his reflection in a mirror and
flinched.

Though it romanticized the motion picture business,
TARGETS satirized the low-budget quickies on which both
Bogdanovich and Karloff had been working.   Even Karloff, a
consummate professional, appeared to relish the opportunity.

The blend of filmmaking with the horrific was not a
unique idea.   The relationship between real and theatrical
horror was one which had intrigued movie makers for many
years.   As television grew more ubiquitous, it tried to mo-
nopolize the conflict between fact and fiction, and nearly every
backlot was found to have monsters and deranged propmen
haunting its sets.   It seemed that whenever the heroic leading men of monster and horror films weren't looking for diamonds or exotic medicines, they were looking for new night-
club acts or film stars with two heads.   Karloff had entered
the subgenre in FRANKENSTEIN 1970 (American International,
1970), when he played an ambitious, but low-budget, scientist
who dispatches nearly half a Hollywood production crew before
he finishes building his monster.

TARGETS opened with the scenes from THE TERROR.
Sammy Michaels sits in a screening room with Orlock, producer Monte Landis, and their assistants.   "Somebody kept
me up until four in the morning," Michaels says.

"Work of art," Landis decides, at the end of THE
TERROR, "very great piece of art!"   He speaks to an actor's agent over the phone: "Who remembers him?   For that
money I could get Sandra Dee or Pat Boone!"

Michaels says he has a new script for Orlock, a
dramatic feature.   If he doesn't want it, Michaels will offer
the script to Vincent Price.   Orlock says he'd rather retire.
"I couldn't play a straight part," he says.   "I've been doing
the other too long.   No one is afraid of a painted mask."

The scenes with the murderer and his collection of
guns were almost all action, so much so, in fact, that O'Kelly's
character remains a cipher, virtually nameless and mindless,
a felon who does not frighten quite so well as if he were given
an added dose of characterization.   The first of many emo-

tionally blank characters in Bogdanovich's films, he remained
a lone nut without past or future, surrounded by the good,
suburban life--golfclubs, binoculars, a piano, bottles of Pepsi,
a sports car loaded with weaponry, and Baby Ruth bars. If
he is a tragic hero, his great flaw is simply that he lives in
a home where guns and bullets are prized. Most reviewers
praised the sets more highly than they did the actors.

Beyond the film's title and its rough equation between
people and targets, there was no explanation for O'Kelly's
murders. The boy says he gets "funny ideas." He must
make a dramatic, deadly act before his blood petrifies from
inertia.

TARGETS showed that Bogdanovich was better at setting
a scene that at leading his audience to a conclusion. Con-
clusions were provided during post production when the distributor appended a message about gun control to the credits:
"Why gun control?" it asked. "Why did a lunatic sniper kill
or maim eleven innocent victims in Texas on 3 June, 1966?
Why were over 7,000 Americans slain or wounded by gunfire
in 1967? Why in 1968, after assassinations and thousands of
more murders, has our country no effective gun control law?
This motion picture tells a story that sheds a little light on
a very dark and a very deep topic."

The satirical elements of TARGETS were sapped by
the solemnity of its topic and by a conscientiously respectful
attitude towards the art of filmmaking. Bogdanovich spent
so much time filming the preparations of a projectionist at a
drive-in that TARGETS began to look like an educational film.
Bogdanovich's norm, his return to the common after the horror of the killings, lay in the direction of new illusions. The
illusions, TARGETS suggested, are the causes and perhaps
the solutions to the problem of violence in America. When
the ancient Karloff disarms the young sniper it is not a realistic solution to the violence, but the triumph of fantasy over
life. For two seconds, Karloff, the legend, towered over
Karloff, the actor.

Bogdanovich finished TARGETS in 1967 but found no
distributor until Paramount released it in mid-1968, opening
it in New York and Chicago to test audience reactions.

Bogdanovich's earliest critics suggested he might be
best directing action. Renata Adler, in the New York Times,
called TARGETS "a rhapsody to shooting people." "People

are picked off one after another," she wrote, "as impersonally
--and this is the point--as satisfyingly as cans were shot down
in a row, earlier in the film, at a shooting range. This is
the extraordinary thing: the perspective in the film is almost
entirely the perspective of the gun, things are seen through
the crosshairs on the gun sight, and one does not want O'Kelly
to miss. It turns out that the covergence between gun and
film is ideal.... This is a perfect affinity."

After TARGETS Bogdanovich continued in a scholarly
bent, producing articles and both writing and directing a documentary on John Ford, DIRECTED BY JOHN FORD. This
was to have been the first in a series of films on veteran
American directors financed by the California Arts Commission and the American Film Institute. Ford, a man of few
words, gave Bogdanovich two pieces of advice: "Have fun
and make sure your pictures make money." He said he
thought Bogdanovich had done a good job on a dull subject.
Clips of the film were shown during an A.F.I. tribute to
Ford.

Bogdanovich left Corman and began to work on several
projects which were later put into production by other directors. He taught a course on American Film at UCLA and
interviewed Orson Welles on the set of CATCH-22 (Paramount,
1970). He also hoped to produce and direct a film for Cinema Center Films based on The Looters, by John Reese. He
had already written a script. "I'm going to try and make a
movie that never lets up," he said. "No build up, start right
out with a fifteen-minute bank robbery, then no let-up.

"By the way, they originally wanted Don Siegel to direct but couldn't get him, so he recommended me, which was
a great compliment. I'll have a Siegel quality." Later,
Siegel changed his mind; he made the picture with a new
script and released it as CHARLIE VARRICK (Universal, 1973).

"What I'm most excited about," Bogdanovich said, "is
a project on Hollywood from 1909 to the present. It's about
a Dwan-Griffith-like figure: great instinctive genius done to
death by the system."

Bogdanovich also went to Italy, where he worked with
Luciano Vincenzios and Sergio Leone on DUCK YOU SUCKER.
It was to be Leone's first crack at producing another director.
Then Bogdanovich quit and Leone directed the project. "He'd
seen TARGETS," Bogdanovich said. "It didn't work because
he kept trying to tell me how to direct the picture."

"Most of our time was taken up with plotting," Bogdanovich wrote, in New York magazine.   "Sergio would begin
each new sequence with a rush of English and much acting,
all of which he did in the middle of the room accompanied by
dramatic gestures.... He and Luciano would look at me for
a reaction, which early in these conferences I would attempt
to make one of enthusiasm, but which invariably moved into
something closer to exasperation.   After all, it had always
been my assumption that a director planned out his own sequence of shots. "

Later, Leone tried to produce two more pictures.
"After a while," Bogdanovich continued, "circumstances again
forced Leone to take over, though finally, I'm afraid, that's
what Sergio wants; if the picture then turns out to be a bomb,
he has the excuse that it was not really his plan to make this
one.... When all those critics and people say you're good
and you don't really believe it, at some point perhaps the
thought of being found out becomes overwhelming and you
would rather retire undefeated than face failure. "

Three or four of Bogdanovich's friends, including Sal
Mineo, had urged him to read The Last Picture Show (Dial,
1966) by Larry McMurtry, a story about the coming of age
of a young man in Texas.   "I didn't read it for a long time,"
Bogdanovich said.   "Finally, I did read it, and I thought it
would make an interesting picture.   Bert Schneider had just
finished co-producing EASY RIDER [Columbia, 1969] and he
wanted to make a picture with me.   I told him about Picture
Show, he read it, he got the rights, and we made it. " Schneider
had formed BBS Productions in partnership with Bob Rafelson
and Steve Blaumer.   Their first picture was FIVE EASY
PIECES (Columbia, 1970), directed by Rafelson.   When Bogdanovich started THE LAST PICTURE SHOW, two more BBS
pictures, DRIVE, HE SAID, and A SAFE PLACE, were in
post-production.

The Last Picture Show had been the third of McMurtry's
novels.   The first, Horseman, Pass By (Harper & Row, 1960),
was filmed as HUD (Paramount, 1963), starring Paul Newman.
The second, Leaving Cheyenne (Harper & Row, 1963), had
been bought by Warner's and scripted several times, including screenplays by Don Siegel and Robert Altman.   In 1974
the book was finally filmed as LOVIN' MOLLY (Columbia,
1974).

Bogdanovich had decided to make the picture in Mc-
Murtry's home town, Archer City, Texas, where McMurtry's

mother played a small part but his father refused to make an
appearance. Archer City was a town brought into being and
then nearly abandoned by oil. In 1971, all but 100 of the
city's 1,700 population belonged to one or another of the city's
churches. It was a dry, alcohol-free city where bumper stickers read "God Bless America."

Bogdanovich's second daughter was born shortly before
he began production. While he was in Texas his father passed
away and his marriage began to fall apart. After an attempt
at reconciliation, he and Polly Platt were divorced in 1972.

"I changed a lot of things from the book," Bogdanovich
said. "All the records and all the television and all the movies that were dealt with, that was all me. I added all that.
I picked things I liked from what was going on at the period.
I used RED RIVER [United Artists, 1948] because it was a
story about Texas in the romantic era when it was filled with
adventure and hope. It made an interesting contrast with the
story, which was essentially the end of the West.

"I used recordings of the period. I just looked for
records. On TARGETS, we couldn't afford to get anybody
very good. We just got everything we could pick up, but
they weren't recorded for the picture. They were just records which I found I could get for free. On THE LAST PIC-
TURE SHOW and PAPER MOON [Paramount, 1973], we had
to pay for them, but we got some great music. PICTURE
SHOW is the only picture that I can think of that had two
soundtrack albums released on two different labels. We had
a lot of music. PAPER MOON was also put out on an album
which I supervised."

Bogdanovich and Polly Platt liked THE LAST PICTURE
SHOW more than its author. "Peter Bogdanovich hired me to
collaborate with him on the screenplay of my third novel,"
McMurtry wrote in an early column for American Film. "At
this point I was so ignorant of film mechanics that I supposed
the only way to get from one scene to the next was by means
of a cut. My initial step-sheet for THE LAST PICTURE
SHOW offered the director an unbroken sequence of quick cuts.

"Both of them had been too stunned by their first visit
to the desolation that is Archer City to believe that real people could ever have lived there. They accepted the town, but
only as a kind of extension of my imagination, and while they
had a notion of how teenagers growing up there in 1953 might
have behaved, it was largely a literary notion."

"Texans really thought I'd captured their state," Bogdanovich said. "It was shot in Texas, the writer was from
Texas, and almost all the actors, except the leads, were
from Texas. Ben Johnson was from Oklahoma, so he was
from close by. I'd met him when I was doing an article
about Ford. He didn't want to make the picture--I had to
drag him into it kicking and screaming because he thought
there were too many words. Luckily, I had some help from
Mr. Ford. He helped me talk him into it--we took turns.
Johnson was reluctant because he'd never played anything like
that. He didn't think he could do it. I thought he could.
We shot all his stuff at the same time, so he only worked
on the picture for ten days.

"I wasn't looking for stars. Basically I was just trying to cast the parts. Jeff Bridges came in to read for Sonny
Crawford and he seemed right for Sonny's friend, Duane. He
gave me a clue as to how the part ought to be played. If you
can find an actor who, in a sense, gives you a clue as to how
to direct the part, or how to play the part, you know that he
is probably the right one for it. It was just in talking with
him that I noticed this. It was the same with Cybill, and
later, for Madeline Kahn, in WHAT'S UP DOC? [Warner's,
1972]. Simply by talking to her, she gave me an idea of how
the part ought to be played. She was so funny, that woman.
It's usually something that they have in life, in normal conversation, that makes them right. I don't spend any time
wondering if they have star quality or not. You can tell if
they do, but that usually develops later. I can usually tell
if the camera is going to be friendly to them or not. Casting is really a matter of instinct: what you need in a person
and what you think you can get out of them.

"We replaced one person on PICTURE SHOW before
we started to shoot. In a couple of places, I'm sorry about
people who I didn't fire, because they weren't good enough or
they were hard to work with. There were one or two of them
but I won't say who!"

Despite an effective performance, one of those Bogdanovich wished he'd replaced was undoubtedly Timothy Bottoms, who played Sonny. It was Bottoms' second motion picture. Like Jeff Bridges, Bottoms was twenty-one. Later,
when his brother visited the Texas location, Bogdanovich cast
him as a retarded boy named Billy.

"Tim had these extraordinary eyes which looked as if
they carried the sorrow of the ages in them," Bogdanovich

said. "The truth of the matter, when you got to know him
better, was that he was just feeling sorry for himself. But
it looked at first, and I think, in the movie, as though he
was feeling sorry for the world. His eyes had an epic sorrow. I thought he would be good for the picture.

"I told Bert Schneider 1 wanted to shoot it in black and
white when we were in pre-production. We had already spent
three months working on it. I guess he agreed with me or
was trying to please me. He pushed it through with Columbia.

"Schneider liked the picture right away. Later, I found
out that when we started, he didn't really think it was going
to be very good. He didn't even like the script, but he thought
I liked it, and that maybe it could make a good picture. He
believed in me and it was a cheap picture to make. That's
a good producer!"

Polly Platt was again Bogdanovich's costume and set
designer. For the costumes, she bought 700 outfits from an
auction at the M-G-M studio. "Most of our costumes you've
seen in some old M-G-M film," Bogdanovich said, as he paced
about in the pants worn by John Wayne in THREE GODFATHERS
(M-G-M, 1948). "Cybill Shepherd's jeans, for example, were
first worn by Debbie Reynolds in I LOVE MELVIN [M-G-M,
1953]!"

Bogdanovich kept the pants. Later, he told an interviewer they gave him respect and recognition--"the only trouble
was that I couldn't sit down in them--unless it was on a
horse."

Emotionally, THE LAST PICTURE SHOW appeared to
be Bogdanovich's most heartfelt, most committed motion picture. Even more than TARGETS, it was a film about loss.
It opened with a flat Texas street photographed in black and
white by Robert Surtees. The road was so desolate, the
town so rutted, that Bogdanovich turned to Hank Williams for
his score. In the photography and in Williams' ballads there
is a sense that this community, as well as its citizens, are
flimsy, transient creations.

Behind the opening credits, Timothy Bottoms sits in
a pickup with broken windows in a made-up Texas town called
Anarene. Outside, leaves are mixed with dust and wind.
Billy, the retarded boy, wears a Cub Scout hat and sweeps
the streets as if he was trying to hold back nature's anarchy,

to stop it from pouring over the boardwalks of this city.   In
McMurtry's book Billy carries his broom everywhere: "...
He swept out the pool hall in the mornings, the cafe in the
afternoons, and the picture show at night, and always, unless
somebody specifically told him to stop, he just kept on sweeping, down the sidewalk, on through the town, sometimes one
way and sometimes another." Bogdanovich added to the broom
a bit of business with the hat, a device which still managed
to fill out a character who has no dialogue.

Bogdanovich's rendering was nearly a literal translation
from the novel, including much of the original dialogue. During shooting, he found that the scenes were playing longer than
anyone had expected. He started to cut.

In what remained there was a rich rendering of adoles-
cence. Sonny and his friend Duane are poor football players
and equally fumbling lovemakers. They smuggle liquor into
Christmas parties, take their sex on squeaky bed frames, and
pull chewing gum from their mouths before they kiss. They
take turns with their pickup, hanging their girl friends' bras
on the battered rear-view mirror. In school, their classmates
pass notes and I, The Jury; they mess one another's hair and
watch dogs fornicate outside their window during a discussion
on Keats. Nearly all the characters are doomed by their
conflicting drives towards sex and security.

Anarene is a small town. A waitress says that no one
can sneeze without someone offering them a handkerchief. All
the characters sneeze, repeatedly. Instead of leaving town
they remain, along with their failures and lost opportunities.
They are never able to forget their emotional hurts.

Before production started, Bogdanovich had said he
was going to try and show the decline of Archer City by the
deterioration of its movie theatre. After its casting, THE
LAST PICTURE SHOW became a more resonant film, a metaphor for America's failing imagination.

Bogdanovich helped Ben Johnson extend the kind of sensitivity which he had shown during appearances in RIO GRANDE
(Republic, 1950) and SHANE (Paramount, 1953). Bogdanovich
used these romantic proportions as effectively as he manipu-
lated the career of Karloff in TARGETS. In both instances,
the authenticity the actors brought to their roles gave the productions an integrity they might have otherwise lacked.

"Movie stars form a kind of twentieth-century myth-
ology," Bogdanovich told Digby Diehl, a writer for the L.A.
Times, "--they are the Greek gods to us.   Each one of them
has a different aspect of human character, and each one of
them has his different world which he inhabits up there in
Olympus.   It's the same with a fascinating personality which
has been magnified a hundred times on the screen, and who
has been created by countless directors and writers.   He becomes this sort of fascinating creation.   What does it matter
what he was really like or not?   It's the art that's created
in its own way.   The star's life in toto is a kind of work of
art--a sculptured artifice of its own kind.   That's really the
iconography of the screen: those people."

The underlying theme of filmmaking was woven into
the story of two boys' growth, from innocence to the kind of
desolation mirrored by their home town.   Their town is shabby
and their lives lack definition.   Their elders are anesthetized
by TV and Scotch.   The only entertainment in their city is the
Royal Theatre, a failing business.

Sam the Lion, played by Ben Johnson, is the only man
who is able to bridge the gap between the mythic West and
the early 'fifties.   He is a man who looks and sounds like an
elderly Shane who has finally settled in their town.   On the
screen, he is a supporting character.   In the subtext, which
McMurtry began to develop in the last drafts of his screenplay, Sam the Lion is the sun around which the rest of Bogdanovich's ensemble revolves.

When the boys return from a trip to Mexico--sick and
covered by sombreros--the pool hall is closed.   Sam the Lion
is dead, a death which saps what little vitality remains in the
town.   Like bodies without gravity, the characters begin a spin
towards oblivion.

Ben Johnson earned his Academy Award in the most
respectful, moving scene in the picture: when Sam takes
Sonny and Billy fishing at a water tank containing no fish.
His speech, reminiscent of those by Karloff in TARGETS,
sets the tone for THE LAST PICTURE SHOW.   Without the
force of his reading, the sentimentality of the script shines
through: "You wouldn't believe how all this has changed,"
he says.   "The first time I saw it there wasn't a mesquite
tree on it, or a prickly pear cactus.   I used to own this land.
First time I watered a horse at this tank, was more than
forty years ago.   I reckon the reason I always drag you out

here is just because I'm just as sentimental as the next guy when it comes to old times.... Old times.... I brought a young lady swimming out here once, more than twenty years ago. It was after my wife had lost her mind and my boys were dead...."

·"Being a decrepit bag of bones," he says, "is what's ridiculous. Getting old."

In McMurtry's novel, the last movie playing at the Royal Theatre was THE KID FROM TEXAS (Universal, 1950). By switching the scheduling to RED RIVER Bogdanovich played with his own enthusiasms and sense of retrospection. In RED RIVER, the cattle wranglers whooped and hollered and sang. Sonny could almost taste the dust and the smoke; he could almost see the frosty breath of the cattle. Then abruptly, the film within a film was over.

"As empty as he felt or as empty as the country looked, it was too risky going out into it," McMurtry wrote, "--he might be blown around for days like a broomweed in the wind." In the novel the theme of emptiness frames the story. Somehow, Bogdanovich managed to take this contemporary crisis of faith and make it look as traditional, and steadfastly American a conclusion as the nation-building of RED RIVER.

Many reviewers had remarked upon Bogdanovich's use of black and white film. (Orson Welles had suggested black and white to Bogdanovich.) He shot test footage in both black and white and in color. He decided the color was "too pretty." "People think black and white will hurt a picture on television and they think it will hurt it abroad," he said. "I don't think there's any proof of that--I don't think the public cares. Black and white certainly helps the actor. Color is distracting, it tends to putrify. It has to be very carefully handled.

"I recut PICTURE SHOW and all my pictures for television. If I don't do that, somebody else will screw it up. They took fourteen minutes out of PICTURE SHOW. I looked at it, and I said, 'You can't do that!' They said they didn't know how to leave it in, so I said, 'Let me try it.' I recut it, and we got some of the actors to come in and we dubbed-- we changed the dialogue and ended up cutting only four minutes out of the picture. ABC was thrilled because it meant they had more commercial time. They gave me a big present and we were all very happy. The picture was still not as good as it was in theatres, but it wasn't as bad as it was in their version.

"In a couple of places I think I recut it better. We
also cut PAPER MOON. We didn't do much, just ten seconds, or thirty seconds."

THE LAST PICTURE SHOW premièred at the 1971 New
York Film Festival and opened the first Los Angeles International Film Exposition at Graumann's Chinese Theatre. Robert Aldrich, George Cukor, Robert Wise, John Huston, George
Stevens, and Samuel Fuller were among those who attended.

The back-seat, motel room sex in THE LAST PICTURE
and a four-second shot of frontal nudity earned the picture an
R rating. City police in Phoenix, Arizona, forced a drive-in
theatre to withdraw the picture. They said to clip the scene
or end the engagement. The department's action was taken
to court, where its obscenity contention was rejected. The
court likened the scene under attack to the painting "Septem-
ber Morn."

THE LAST PICTURE SHOW became a hit and the Los
Angeles Times sent their writer Charles Hillyer to Archer
City, where some of the residents still hid McMurtry's novel
from their children. "Many residents of this drab, dusty
North central Texas town are furious about THE LAST PIC-
TURE SHOW," he wrote. "The movie filmed here, suppos-
edly 'lays bare the secret transgressions of an entire com-
munity'--namely Archer City.

"What bothers the 1,700 townspeople is that the film
is filled with nudity and it portrays the town as populated with
men and women of low moral character--another Peyton Place."

Hillyer wrote that the streets and sidewalks of Archer
City closed at 9 P.M. "The producers of the film told everybody in town THE LAST PICTURE SHOW was going to be a
family movie about small town life," John B. Addams, the
principal at Archer City High School for eleven years, commented. "They said they would not be filming the dirty parts
of the book, that the picture's worst possible rating would be
GP. North Texas people still accept you at your word. Well,
we were taken in and lied to.... And to think we let that
Hollywood crowd use our school to film some of the scenes.
Our band appears in what we now learn is an extremely dirty
movie."

Hillyer also interviewed Frank McDaniels, a former
Texas Ranger who still remembered the days when Bonnie and

Clyde hid out in the city. "The film company spent $150,000 in this town," he said. "Who the hell cares what the movie was about! Some of the old gals around here are belly-aching about a bad image in Archer City. I tell those women they probably were doin' the same things mentioned in the book when they were in their prime."

According to McMurtry's mother, "THE LAST PICTURE SHOW is going to win Oscars whether people like it or not!"

Bogdanovich was asked to take over both THE GETA-WAY and A GLIMPSE OF TIGER while THE LAST PICTURE SHOW was still in a rough cut. Sue Mengers, his new agent, favored the latter, which had been in production with Elliott Gould and Kim Darby before it was shut down. Barbra Streisand had taken over the production. She asked for Bogdanovich and was willing to accept Ryan O'Neal as her co-star.

Bogdanovich didn't like the script. He thought it was half-drama and half-comedy. Streisand thought a dramatic motion picture would be nice; something with the tone of THE LAST PICTURE SHOW would be just fine. Bogdanovich wanted to make a comedy. He called in the screenwriting team of Robert Benton and David Newman, who had written BONNIE AND CLYDE (Warner's, 1967). According to Benton, Bogdanovich said he wanted to direct a remake of BRINGING UP BABY (RKO, 1938). They completed the first draft of their story in a week and a half. After they finished a second version, Bogdanovich called in Buck Henry, who took another two weeks to finish the screenplay.

"It was fun working with Peter," Newman said, "because we'd all spent our lives watching the same movies, and all our reference points were the same."

A GLIMPSE OF THE TIGER was shelved and WHAT'S UP DOC?, which replaced it, became Bogdanovich's most profitable picture. "A screwball comedy," its ads asked, "Remember them?" Critics remembered the comedies, and they also remembered Bogdanovich's quotable participation in the auteurist revival of Hollywood directors. They put two and two together and came up with their headlines.

"A Hawks comedy?" many said, "with a Bogdanovich byline." Bogdanovich was an archivist. Streisand was playing Hepburn and her co-star Ryan O'Neal was playing Cary Grant.

WHAT'S UP DOC? took off on the wrong foot, with a combination press and sneak preview in New York. Vincent Canby, of the New York Times, was one of the reviewers who couldn't find a seat. Pauline Kael called the picture a "fac-simile" in The New Yorker. "It's too early in the history of movies for this feeding off the past," she wrote, "and, as it is, there's almost nothing left; TV has picked those bones clean. It's the tragedy of TV that instead of drawing upon new experiences and fresh sources of comedy it cannibalizes old pop culture. When movies do the same now, they aren't even imitating movies, they're imitating TV."

Peter Bogdanovich demonstrates to Ryan O'Neal how he wants Barbra Streisand kissed in WHAT'S UP DOC? (Warner's, 1972). Photo courtesy of Eddie Brandt's Saturday Matinee.

Peter Schjeldahl's piece in the New York Times was titled "Why Is Watching WHAT'S UP DOC? Like Eating Cel-ery?" "The fact which almost everyone agrees on--is that there is scarcely a character, a situation or a gag in this film that hasn't appeared in some form in some other movie of the remote or recent past," he wrote. "... The predicta-

bility of the punchlines is so wearing that one finds oneself
practically reciting them along with the actors.... The really
haunting fact about WHAT'S UP DOC? is the feeling we get at
a certain point that this movie is not actually a movie at all,
that it is some kind of simularum of a movie, a celluloid
zombie. "

Bogdanovich still bristled in 1977 at the suggestion that
WHAT'S UP DOC? was a remake. "A remake?" he asked.
"Not in any way. How would you say that?"

"The tone, the pace, and what you said at the time,"
I said. "A Hawks comedy?"

"Yeah," Bogdanovich replied, "I said that in interviews
at the time, that it was inspired by BRINGING UP BABY,
which led everybody to believe that I had meant that it was
a remake of BRINGING UP BABY. If you see the two pictures together there are only about three jokes that are the
same. They also have the same basic premise: a girl chas-
ing a guy, but that's a pretty standard comic device."

WHAT'S UP DOC? was a love triangle. Like TARGETS
and THE LAST PICTURE SHOW, it was organized around a
series of subplots, some of which were considerably more effective than others. One of them had something to do with a
jewel heist; in another Michael Murphy lugged around a suitcase with papers marked "Top Secret" while voicing concern
about the public interest. O'Neal has his musical rocks and
Streisand her laundry. Here's the gag: the characters all
check in at the same hotel and all their suitcases look the
same. After a breathtaking chase, WHAT'S UP DOC? herds
more than a dozen supporting characters into a courtroom administered by Liam Dunn.

Bogdanovich's characters never become quite as likeable as he would have wished them to be, primarily because
so much of the film is so good-naturedly familiar. Perhaps
it was the two weeks of rehearsals that gave WHAT'S UP
DOC? a look of calculation. Even a cursory acquaintance
with television's Late, Early, and Late Late Movie Shows,
however, should have been enough to give an audience a sense
of déjà vu. Actually, WHAT'S UP DOC? was a collection of
styles and scenes, not a remake but an eclectic style seldom
seen in the past. The undertones, the references and asides,
they all had to do with other motion pictures. Consider the
characters: Howard Bannister (O'Neal), a musicologist who

blathers about early man's relationship with igneous rock;
Judy Maxwell (Streisand), an aggressive, equally eccentric
doyen with an encyclopedic mind; High Simon (Kenneth Mars),
Bannister's rival; Frederic Larrabee (Austin Pendleton), a
short philanthropist.   Though all of these characters are similar to those in a Hawks comedy like BRINGING UP BABY,
one of them was actually a broad parody of critic John Simon.
On balance, the gags and casting in WHAT'S UP DOC veered
closer to the comic theories of Mack Sennett, Leo McCarey,
and Buster Keaton.

Whatever the reactions of critics, the picture was a
success, bringing in $165,398 at Radio City Music Hall, the
biggest single grossing day in the Hall's history.   Bogdanovich,
O'Neal, and Streisand were each offered a million dollars to
make a sequel.   The stars agreed but Bogdanovich refused.
"It was simple," he said.   "I said no.   I said, 'What's the
sequel going to be?   It's not going to be the same thing all
over again.   What's the point of doing that?'   I had an idea
when they asked me for a sequel.   I said, 'Well, we could
call it That's All, Folks!   The picture could begin with Barbra
on an airplane, leaving San Francisco, and the plane crashes,
and they both get killed, and that's the end of the picture.   I
didn't know what the hell to do....   That's All, Folks.

"WHAT'S UP DOC? was fun to make almost all the
way through.   Streisand was really wonderful with me, and
I really enjoyed working with her.   I like her a lot.   She's
a cute girl, but she wasn't a movie star to me, certainly not
a superstar.   She was just a nice, interesting girl.   She didn't
want to make WHAT'S UP DOC?   She was another one who
was dragged kicking and screaming through the picture.   She
thought we were going to do something else, and I suppose I
tricked her.   She'd make trouble occasionally about things
that she didn't think were funny, and I'd just laugh at her.
She'd ask me what I was laughing at and I'd tell her she was
cute.   She wouldn't know what to say to that.

"She really wasn't sore when it was all over.   She
made more money on WHAT'S UP DOC? than on any picture
she made until A STAR IS BORN (Warner's, 1977).   She made
about three million dollars.   She would have made more but
she sold her piece for a big hunk of money.   She would have
made twice that much, but she didn't believe in the picture."

After WHAT'S UP DOC? Warner's signed Bogdanovich
for three more films: a Western named STREETS OF LA-

REDO, THE APPLE TREE, from a John Galsworthy story,
and a third film about the early days of filmmaking. Before
the casting of STREETS OF LAREDO fell through, Bogdanovich had made a trip to the Dallas Film Festival, where he
paused at the Governor's Mansion long enough to ask the State
to build a facsimile of the city of Laredo circa 1870. Gavin
Lambert was working on the screenplay for THE APPLE TREE,
a project Bogdanovich said he'd been interested in since he
was sixteen years old. "It was quite a good script," Bogdanovich said, "but I just didn't want to make it. Like many
beloved projects, you want to do it for so long that by the
time you do get to do it you just don't want to make it any
more. It's almost as though you'd made it already and there's
no longer any challenge left."

Eventually, Bogdanovich left his Warner's contract without directing any of the films which had been proposed.

Paramount asked Bogdanovich to make a picture from
Addie Pray (Simon & Schuster, 1971) by Joe David Brown, a
story about two con artists during the Depression. Earlier,
John Huston had considered making the picture with Paul Newman and his daughter. Paramount gave Bogdanovich a first
draft script. He didn't like it. He read the book and decided
he liked it even less; nevertheless, he agreed to the project.

Shortly after he began preparing ADDIE PRAY, Bogdanovich signed on as a member of Paramount's Director's
Company with Francis Ford Coppola, William Friedkin, and
three Paramount representatives. They were to make twelve
features during a period of six years. Bogdanovich also hoped
to produce a film for Orson Welles through the arrangement.
He went on to make PAPER MOON (Paramount, 1973) and
DAISY MILLER (Paramount, 1974) for the company. Coppola
made THE CONVERSATION (Paramount, 1974) and Friedkin
was working on THE BUNKER HILL BOYS before the group
dissolved.

Bogdanovich was unhappy with the Addie Pray title so
he changed it to PAPER MOON, then he wrote a scene to
justify the new title. Orson Welles told him the title was so
good he shouldn't make the picture. Later, when the novel
was re-released, its title was also changed.

Bogdanovich remembered the flat, lonely backroads of
the Midwest he had traveled during his drive to California and
he moved the Southern setting of the book to Kansas, where

Moses (Ryan O'Neal) and Addie Pray (Tatum O'Neal) short-
change shopkeepers, steal bootleg whiskey, and sell Bibles
to newly bereaved widows. Addie, who may or may not be
Moses' illegitimate daughter, picks up the tricks of the con-
game trade with ease, smoking, cursing, and splitting up a
romance between Moses and Miss Trixie Delight (Madeline
Kahn), a carnie floozie. As in THE LAST PICTURE SHOW,
nearly all the minor characters appeared well-suited; both
Tatum and Miss Kahn were nominated for Best Supporting
Actress during the 1973 Academy Awards.

PAPER MOON was Bogdanovich's most painstaking
period piece to that point. Once again, the music in the
picture was among its most effective qualities. Bogdanovich
borrowed recordings by Tommy Dorsey, Ozzie Nelson, Jack
Benny, Hoagy Carmichael, and many others from Rudi Fehr,
head of Warner's editing department. Laszlo Kovacs returned
to his second Bogdanovich production as director of photography
on the grainy, black and white film.

Perceptive critics, aided by Bogdanovich's own remarks, were able to detect the influences of John Ford in
THE LAST PICTURE SHOW, and no one could miss the footnotes to earlier movies which were tacked all over WHAT'S
UP DOC? By the time PAPER MOON was released, many
critics seemed to prefer watching the movies Bogdanovich suggested, rather than the films he was actually producing. Bogdanovich felt heckled by those who refused to discuss his motion pictures on their own terms. "Vincent Canby, in probably
his lowest, lowest moment, said PAPER MOON was inspired
by LITTLE MISS MARKER [Paramount, 1934]," Bogdanovich
said. "I don't know if you've seen LITTLE MISS MARKER,
but about six months after PAPER MOON came out, I ran it,
because I'd never seen it, and it had nothing to do with PAPER
MOON, except that he's sort of a racing tout, kind of a con
man, and she's a little girl. But the relationships are totally
different, and Tatum is the antithesis of Shirley Temple; she's
doing almost the opposite of what Shirley Temple was doing."

Bogdanovich read another review which suggested he
was trying to copy Frank Capra. "I just wanted to blow up
the magazine," he said.

Contrary to his audiences, Bogdanovich felt it was
really a sad story. "It's a story about a little girl whose
father can't commit himself on any level," he said. "He
doesn't really love her at all; he uses her as much as he can;

and when he gets his balls cut off, he wants to deny her.
She's smarter than he is at every turn. But she's at a dis-
advantage because she loves him. "

      At first Bogdanovich was unsure whom he could use as
the girl. He had cast Ryan O'Neal when Polly Platt suggested
Tatum. Bogdanovich met Tatum on the beach at Malibu and
immediately decided she was right for the part. It won her
the Oscar for Best Supporting Actress. "It was hard to work
with her," Bogdanovich said, "because she was only eight
years old and she didn't have any idea what the hell we were
doing, and for half the movie she could have cared less. I
just had to keep Ryan from killing her. He'd shout: 'Goddamn it Tatum, will you learn your lines? I'm not going to
do it again. We've done it twenty-eight times. I did five
thousand Peyton Places and I never went through anything like
this. '"

      Tatum was a hit, and despite a series of announce-
ments that she was going to retire and become a "normal"
child, she continued to make pictures. By 1976, she was
the only woman on the list of the top ten box-office attrac-
tions. She had received $16,000 for her part in PAPER
MOON. When Bogdanovich hired her again, for NICKELOD-
EON, her fee had escalated to $125,000.

      Later, Bogdanovich was asked to make a sequel with
Tatum and Mae West. There was certainly a lot of material
that was still left from Addie Pray. "I said no to all that
stuff," Bogdanovich said. "I didn't see any future in it. It
was stupid. Mae West is marvelous but she's already done
her stuff. I didn't want to kind of ... prop her up there.
She's done her best things. I had a chance to do something
good with Karloff because he hadn't done any serious work in
a long time. I was even able to use that in my story. But
there was nothing that I was going to make with Mae West
that was any better than what she'd already done. "

      Though praised by critics and public alike, there were
those who reserved their applause. Penelope Gilliatt took
issue with the romantic depiction of the father-daughter team
of swindlers and the implication that it is all right to cheat
the foolish or wealthy. In particular, she disliked Tatum's
comic pimping of Trixie Delight. The O'Neals are so cute
that their crimes pale, so cute that the audience desperately
wants them to embrace one another. Sentimental but successful, the film resembled THE KID (First National, 1920) more
than any film ever made by Shirley Temple.

Next, Bogdanovich decided to direct two pictures starring Cybill Shepherd, who had been taking singing and opera
lessons since THE LAST PICTURE SHOW. Another picture
was to have been BUGSY SIEGEL, for the Richard Zanuck/
David Brown producing team. Shepherd had suggested the
project after she read a book on Siegel--she wanted to play
the part of Virginia Hill, his lady. Ryan O'Neal could play
the gangster.

Since his early successes, there seemed to be no limit
to what a dedicated, energetic director like Bogdanovich could
attempt. He pushed until he discovered boundaries; first
DAISY MILLER, then AT LONG LAST LOVE seemed to fall
outside those boundaries.

Appropriately enough, DAISY MILLER was about an
American girl who scandalizes European society with her
brusque Americanism and her propensity for flirtation. Henry
James had written two versions of the story, in 1878 and 1909.
Bogdanovich used material from both editions.

Bogdanovich filmed the novel with an Italian crew on
the same locations where James set his book--Vevey, Switzer-
land, and Rome, Italy. Inevitably, Shepherd's performance
was attacked. Cloris Leachman and Barry Brown were also
considered unsuited for their parts. Duilio Del Prete, Mil-
dred Natwick, Eileen Brennan, and James McMurtry, the son
of Bogdanovich's former collaborator, fared better.

Initially, Bogdanovich expanded on the story with Frederic Raphael, his screenwriter, adding dialogue and new incidents. Then Bogdanovich decided he'd gotten too far away
from the basic story written by James. He felt the material
in the book was better than the new story he had helped write.

"The script we used is very faithful to the book," Bogdanovich told an American Film Institute audience. "People
don't always realize that almost all the dialogue in the picture
is by Henry James. It's a good story, and I think the film
is well made. Some people find it difficult to accept a character like Daisy Miller in such a milieu. If I were telling a
Western with the same basic plot--an Eastern girl comes to
the West, she doesn't understand the way you're supposed to
behave, people don't understand her--nobody would have any
difficulty at all believing the character. After all, the picture
is set in the same period most Westerns are set, 1875 or
1880. But the minute you take this chattering American girl,

sophisticated, highbrow, artistic, pretentious--some people
find it hard to believe.   Still, that's essentially the point of
Henry James' story.   If you'll read it again, you'll find that
she's described as being crude, vulgar, annoying, naive, flir-
tatious--everything we tried to do in the movie."

DAISY MILLER and THE CONVERSATION, directed by
Coppola, were the kinds of pictures that seemed best fitted
for The Director's Company had it continued.   Both were designed for minority tastes, though the political content of THE
CONVERSATION was sure to give it immediate attention.
Bogdanovich's picture could not so readily find its audience.
If anything, the admirers of Henry James appeared to attack
DAISY MILLER.   Though it was true, perhaps overly true to
the book, it was impossible for Bogdanovich's picture to capture the subtlety of James' words.   Instead, Bogdanovich filled
his motion picture with striking, evocative photography and effects.   It was the kind of picture, many felt, that could have
enjoyed modest but lengthy engagements had it been directed
by a Frenchman and imported from Europe.

DAISY MILLER was certainly not a project designed
for the audiences of WHAT'S UP DOC? and PAPER MOON.
It was like "trying to make high drama out of mere social
graces," Jay Cocks wrote in Time.   "It is a little like trying
to wring a sonnet out of a bill of fare."   Vincent Canby called
it an unexpected triumph.

Bogdanovich's next picture, AT LONG LAST LOVE
(20th-Fox, 1975), was potent ammunition for those who most
deeply mistrusted his abilities.   He had decided to make a
new musical set in New York during the 'thirties and formed
around twenty-four Cole Porter songs.   The singing was going
to be direct recorded, Bogdanovich decided, without overdub-
bing or lip syncing.   It was probably the first time a musical
had been made in this fashion since the early 'thirties.   Before AT LONG LAST LOVE was released the number of songs
it contained was cut to sixteen.   Two complete songs and
parts of three others were cut after they had already been
filmed.

Bogdanovich made up a plot to fit the songs.   "In the
Hollywood musicals I grew up with," he said at the time, "I
was always restless for them to skip the plot and get to the
numbers.   I'm trying to remedy that by making the songs
themselves the scenes."   As a result, the film is nearly
plotless.   AT LONG LAST LOVE would have no sense of

realism, Bogdanovich said. He wanted to shoot it on studio
lots to make it look like an artificial New York. He was
filming in color but he wanted all the sets and costumes to
be in black and white.

"I am making this movie," he told a reporter, "because
I had fantasies of starring in a musical when I was a child."

According to Hollis Alpert, in Saturday Review, "...
so Bogdanovich wrote, directed, and produced AT LONG LAST
LOVE, and it demonstrates nothing so much as how easily a
fellow can be deluded by his evaluation of his own brilliance.
With no experience in writing a musical, he wrote one. With
no experience in directing a musical, he directed one. With
no experience in producing a musical, he produced one."

Many of the production numbers were as cheerfully
literal-minded as the layouts for one of the Fleisher Brothers'
bouncing ball cartoons. In the cartoons, the redundancy of
lyric and image was charming; in Bogdanovich's live-action
musical the effect appeared much more heavy-handed.

Bogdanovich divided his cast into two pairs of lovers,
including Eileen Brennan, John Hillerman, Madeline Kahn,
Cybill Shepherd, and Duilio Del Prete. Initially, Bogdanovich
wanted Elliott Gould for his male lead. Instead, he cast Burt
Reynolds. Reynolds, a beefy, good-looking action star, had
already appeared as a starring or supporting player in four
or five television series when Bogdanovich hired him. Reynolds was a leading man with pretensions. He wanted to play
new roles where he wouldn't have to fight, jump over cars,
or defer to chases. He wanted to direct. He said he'd
waited twenty years to make AT LONG LAST LOVE. It was,
he said, a "Cary Grant-type" role. "When Bogdanovich approached me to do song and dance it was not like jumping
from square one to square two," he told the New York Times,
"it was like jumping from square one to square eighty-nine.
It was a terrible mistake because we all sank together. My
audience, which is a big audience, let me know right away
that they don't want Burt Reynolds to sing and dance. They
practically picketed the theatres, it was frightening.... I'm
not going to take the entire blame for AT LONG LAST LOVE.
I think Peter and Cybill should share some of it. Ironically,
I came out with better reviews than anybody else, but that's
like staying afloat longer than anybody else when the Titanic
sank. I still drowned."

Notices on the picture were almost universally sour, so much so, in fact, that Bogdanovich felt called upon to apologize for it when he praised the contributions of his direct recording sound team in a Hollywood Reporter advertisement: "All this was to prove the perhaps lame-brained theory of the director that musicals ought to be done entirely live. Whether he was right or wrong is beside the point." The film, in effect, was more an eccentric, technical feat than a successful entertainment. It was hustled through post-production to make a Radio City Music Hall opening in early March, 1975.

Like WHAT'S UP DOC?, AT LONG LAST LOVE was a mosaic, a pastiche of musical and comedy turns, a triumph of style over content. This time, the result did not hold up. It was not going to be "campy," Bogdanovich had said. Unfortunately, he delivered an uneven picture that was, in fact, campy. How else could one explain the project--to make a meticulously prepared musical starring two people who are not singers--if not to say it was "campy," an esthetic of absurdity. Who, besides Bogdanovich, wanted to see Burt Reynolds and Cybill Shepherd sing, dance, shave, and brawl?

"Nobody ever saw the complete version of AT LONG LAST LOVE," Bogdanovich told me. "I recut it under a tremendous amount of pressure. They thought it would be better in a shorter version. I regret the cuts that were made. First of all, the picture opened with about eight or nine minutes out of it that I thought ought to be in it.

"First, I cut nervously and under pressure. I convinced myself it was the right thing to do and I did it. Then it opened and it got terrible reviews. The studio dropped it-- they just wrote it off. They took a six-million-dollar loss while it was still playing at the Music Hall. They also asked me to cut some more out of it, so I took another five minutes out. I returned from a trip to Europe, I went to see it, and I thought it was just ... horseshit. I came back, and because I had it in my contract, I said, I don't consider this to be a finished picture and I want to put the stuff back. I paid for it myself because they had lost money. I had the stuff put back into the negatives, 16 and 35, though no prints were struck. That period had passed, but it's there, at least, in the negative. You can rent it from Films, Inc. , and get the complete version, and I think it will be more complete on television, than when it was released."

Robert Chartoff and Irwin Winkler had made a deal

with Columbia Pictures to develop and produce STARLIGHT
PARADE, an original story by W. D. Richter.   It was a
comedy about the early days of filmmaking, and it was longer
on gags than on characterization.   The Chartoff-Winkler team
went on to hire Bogdanovich as director and Bogdanovich began rewriting and casting the picture.   He planned to shoot in
black and white, and to star Cybill Shepherd.   When both
choices were vetoed, he cast Jane Hitchcock, a friend of
Cybill's, and also a model, as a young, near-sighted silent
star.

     For several weeks, STARLIGHT PARADE was on the
edge of cancellation due to what were called serious artistic
difficulties between Bogdanovich and Columbia.   For one thing,
the studio thought the script was too long.   After their differences were settled, Columbia decided to insure their investment by making it a co-production with British-Lion.   Under
a new title, NICKELODEON (Columbia, 1976), the production
continued to be plagued by uncertainties.   The première was
delayed and the opening night relocated so that the picture
could be held for recutting.   When this was completed, Columbia charged a nickel's admission and opened it at four-
hundred theatres as a benefit for the American Lung Association.

     After the disastrous reception accorded AT LONG LAST
LOVE, NICKELODEON returned to touch so many of Bogdanovich's winning bases that it should have been his come-back
picture.   Again, there was a chemistry between O'Neal père
and Tatum, who was given card lessons for the picture by
magician Mark Wilson.   NICKELODEON resonated with the
laughs from old comedies: here was a gag à la Hawks, here
one from Keaton, and here was another gag, the suitcase
switch, from WHAT'S UP DOC?   Though sure-fire, the gags
were often hasty and inappropriately timed.   The film also
included fights, falls, a balloon chase, and a long clip from
THE BIRTH OF A NATION (Epoch, 1915).

     Though all of Bogdanovich's pictures had reflected his
background in film study, in none of them was this connection
made so explicit as in NICKELODEON.   Both theme and stars
were part of the Bogdanovich "family."   Sam Fuller made an
off-stage phone call and Fuller's wife, Christa Lang, appeared
as a dancer.   The rest of the cast included Burt Reynolds,
Ryan O'Neal, and Tatum O'Neal.   John Ritter was a newcomer
whom Bogdanovich had attempted to cast six years earlier in
THE LAST PICTURE SHOW.

Peter Bogdanovich with his two stars in NICKELODEON (Columbia, 1976), Ryan O'Neal and Burt Reynolds (in wig). Photo
courtesy of Eddie Brandt's Saturday Matinee.

        Much of NICKELODEON was dramatized history, in-
cluding patent wars, old-fashioned, open-air motion picture
stages, and a stirring recreation of the première night of
BIRTH OF A NATION.   Bogdanovich was working with his
most inspiring, magical subject, but it was a sense of magic
only intermittently translated to the screen.   As he moved
closer to his models, Bogdanovich made a film which was
least like those which Hawks, Ford, Dwan or Walsh might
have made.   NICKELODEON was like a picture frame--its
climax was THE BIRTH OF A NATION.

        At its best and most true, NICKELODEON chronicled
the celebrity of a group of ordinary people, not artists, but
craftsmen who were happy enough to find jobs.   Occasionally,
the self-consciousness of 1976 crept in, as if this were Bogdanovich's special present for the American Bicentennial.
After a long buildup, the plot evaporated.   Its funniest moments occurred before its two main characters even met.
After their meeting, the whole cast wises up and gets serious;
unfortunately, they become artists, and NICKELODEON gets
bogged down in the romantic professional entanglements of

characters who were never particularly well developed in the
first place. NICKELODEON is dramatic, but not dramatic
enough; historical, but not historical, tragic, serious or romantic enough. It tries to be funny but Bogdanovich never
allowed it to become a full-fledged comedy. The women's
roles, in particular, suffer. Jane Hitchcock, whatever her
newly found talents may have been, is never able to overcome
the poverty of her part. Stella Stevens' role was diminished
by late revisions of the script and editing, so that her relationship with O'Neal and Ritter is never made clear. Bogdanovich cut the scenes of the romantic triangle because he
thought they were too rough. Later, even after NICKEL-
ODEON's release, Bogdanovich was still considering cutting
a scene where Stevens leaves Ritter, O'Neal, and the rest
of the independents to rejoin a studio boss played by Brian
Keith, a role originally intended for Orson Welles.

        The earliest scenes in NICKELODEON were galvanic,
and not only because of the overwhelming volume of gags.
Both O'Neal and Reynolds fall, quite literally, into the motion
picture business. Reynolds is a horseman who can't ride,
O'Neal is a lawyer who can't argue.

        O'Neal played Leo Harrigan, a boisterous opportunist,
in the comic style of WHAT'S UP DOC? and PAPER MOON.
As in the earlier films, O'Neal was an unlikely comedian.
After three pictures with Bogdanovich, all of them comedies,
he had still created no recognizable comic persona, and he
had played very nearly the same character in every picture.
Things happened to him, but very seldom was he an active
agent himself.

        After joining a film company and writing a script or
two, Harrigan takes a train from New York to Cucamonga,
California, where the company's crew has been waiting for
their director to sober up. He takes the advice offered by
Ritter, that "any jerk can direct," makes up a plot on the
spot, and prepares a scene with a rattlesnake. The snake
(which is really only a trick snake, since its poison sacs
have been removed) bites him. It is a trick they play on
every new director, and a trick that was actually played on
Allan Dwan when he entered the business.

        Bogdanovich was afraid the scenes from THE BIRTH
OF A NATION were running too long so he cut the homecom-
ing of Henry B. Walthall. "I'm sorry I had to cut that," he
told me, "but it was just too long. It was amazing that we

got away with it as it was. This huge picture just sort of
stops while we do this set-piece about the opening of THE
BIRTH OF A NATION. "

    Bogdanovich also considered making PICTURE PALACE,
a sequel to NICKELODEON covering the years between 1919
and 1929, with all the same characters except Reynolds, who
was going to be killed during the First World War. "The
second picture seemed to evolve from the first," Bogdanovich
said. "I don't imagine that it will ever get made, but maybe
I'll make something about that period. That's when they
started to make good pictures. See, the part I covered in
NICKELODEON was really about the period when they weren't
making anything special. "

III

    So ends the first half of Peter Bogdanovich's career
as an historian, a filmmaker, and sometimes both at once.
Two years after his voluntary exile from theatre screens he
returned from four months of shooting SAINT JACK in Singapore. Again, spirits were high among those with an interest
in Bogdanovich's future. AT LONG LAST LOVE and NICKEL-
ODEON were in the past. SAINT JACK seemed destined to
become a come-back, if for no other reason than because
Bogdanovich's stock had fallen so low. He had been riding
a streak which had drawn to its close. What Bogdanovich
needed now was to become selfish, to seek an affirmation of
purpose in his own work of the past. He needed to find new
sources of inspiration so he could throw away his footnotes.
SAINT JACK might be the beginning of this.

    Bogdanovich made it possible, perhaps not altogether
unconsciously, for his audience to consider NICKELODEON
the close of a period which began with TARGETS. He was
ready for something new, for a turning away from the past
in deference to the present. Bogdanovich seemed already to
have made every kind of movie which he wished to make when
he entered the industry. He had clung to a sort of boisterous
innocence longer than most, plumbing his fantasies instead of
the shrewd sense of story and effect of which many observers
believed him capable.

    It is immensely difficult to change a theme once you
have spent half your life arguing, polishing, and living that

theme. No less, however, seems to be required from Bogdanovich at the close of the 'seventies.

Bogdanovich's worst problem has been that he has
simply stopped telling stories. In attempting to stretch the
boundaries of film, as well as his own boundaries, he has
lost sight of one of the American film's requisites--he has
shed the basic building blocks of story-telling. There is no
question that Bogdanovich has made mistakes. What is more
pressing is the hope that he has made the right mistakes, so
that his failures will finally allow him to make up for lost
ground. The lines he spoke in TARGETS taunted him for
more than ten years--"The best pictures have already been
made."

Despite what may have been unarguable evidence to the
contrary, if any filmmaker can make the kind of spectacular
resurrection which our entire society seems to want, it is
Bogdanovich. As he enters the second half of his career, it
appears that, yes, perhaps he can learn to integrate the divergent elements of his background. He can use his knowledge of the past to help us move into the future. Just once,
instead of lending the creative dissonance of the 'seventies to
a character from another era, one of Bogdanovich's characters
could say, "We're going to go out and make the best movie
ever made." Certainly, Bogdanovich can find better stories;
to do any less would be to misplace his talents.

In weathering failure and frustration, in finally reaching an end to fantasies he began with, there is hope that
Bogdanovich might begin to compete with his contemporaries
instead of with the dead--he might begin to speak again to the
needs of today. He might help lead us to a second, maybe
even a third, act in American filmmaking. He might again
look like the man who was sent to lead American filmmaking to
greater heights. One thing is sure: he looks like a survivor.

PETER BOGDANOVICH

A Film Checklist by Vicki Piekarski

Director

1.   TARGETS (1968). P: Paramount. C: Boris Karloff,
       Tim O'Kelly, Nancy Hsueh. Color. 90m.

2.   THE LAST PICTURE SHOW (1971). P: Columbia.
        C: Timothy Bottoms, Jeff Bridges, Cybill Shepherd.
        118m.

3.   WHAT'S UP DOC? (1972). P: Warner's. C: Barbra
        Streisand, Ryan O'Neal, Kenneth Mars. Color. 94m.

4.   PAPER MOON (1973). P: Paramount. C: Ryan
        O'Neal, Tatum O'Neal, Madeline Kahn. 102m.

5.   DAISY MILLER (1974). P: Paramount. C: Cybill
        Shepherd, Barry Brown, Cloris Leachman. Color.
        91m.

6.   AT LONG LAST LOVE (1975). P: Twentieth Century.
        Fox. C: Burt Reynolds, Cybill Shepherd, Madeline
        Kahn. Technicolor. 118m.

7.   NICKELODEON (1976). P: Columbia. C: Ryan
        O'Neal, Burt Reynolds, Tatum O'Neal. Metrocolor.
        Panavision. 121m.

Martin Scorsese.   Photo courtesy of Columbia Pictures.

Chapter 9

MARTIN SCORSESE

By Bella Taylor

I

The debut of the independently-financed, brilliant MEAN
STREETS (Warner's, 1973) marked Martin Scorsese's arrival
as a major new director on the American scene. Despite a
relatively short filmography, which nonetheless spans an eclectic variety of styles and genres, such momentous films as
ALICE DOESN'T LIVE HERE ANYMORE (Warner's, 1974) and
the tumultuous TAXI DRIVER (Columbia, 1976) have earned
the director the attention and respect accorded an original
artist of importance. Often mentioned in connection with the
"New Hollywood," the film school-educated generation of young,
successful directors which includes Francis Ford Coppola,
George Lucas, John Milius, Peter Bogdanovich, and Steven
Spielberg, Scorsese stands stylistically and substantively apart
from this new breed. Regarded by the industry and critics
alike as a highly-personal, idiosyncratic New York filmmaker
who has never really "gone Hollywood," he has dramatized the
urban experience and the frustrations of individuals living the
alienated lives of our modern times. His films have none of
the neat, glossy symmetries of myth and romance manufactured in the fantasy factories of the movie capital. No one
lives happily ever after in a Scorsese picture; there are no
harmonious plot resolutions, only tentative solutions at best.

Upon meeting him, one is immediately struck with the
inexplicable notion that he looks and acts like the creator of
a Scorsese movie. A small, wiry, fragile-looking man, his
dark, bearded appearance seems darkened further by the sullen expression fixed on his face. He is an odd combination
of New York "seen-it-all" cynicism and a wistful, idealistic
innocence that infuses his movies with the tensions of both
pessimism and hope. Dressed in jeans and a black T-shirt,

293

he could have just walked off the streets of Little Italy, the
benighted ghetto of his youth where he saw a brutish, treacherous side of life that is the basis of his artistic vision.   His
"black," brooding presence fits the somber, moody tones of
his pictures.   The director moves and expresses himself with
the high-strung, nervous energy that is reflected in his hyper-
active, intensely wrought filmmaking style.

        He brightens when the conversation turns to movies and
music--his twin passions.   Speaking in a soft, breathless
flurry of words, Scorsese's rapid-fire speech can barely keep
up with the quick intelligence of his mind.   An ardent film
buff, his talk invariably turns to a favorite movie, a cherished
scene or a glowing reference to an admired director.   His own
pictures often pay tribute to the cinematic styles and conventions, as well as the artists that have inspired him.   "I will
always have things about movies in my movies," he asserts.
"I love film ... it's my whole life and that's it."   Despite
his look of frailty, Scorsese's strong-willed assertiveness
leaves little doubt that he possesses the authority of a director who can compel people to do his bidding.   It is clear that
the full strength of his personality drives him to explore the
complexities of his own behavior and instincts.   His own quest
for self-understanding is the force that shapes his art.

        Scorsese is drawn to creating cinematic character stud-
ies that are extensions of his own persona.   The characters
in his movies grapple with the problems that trouble him,
they mirror his anxieties and, often, their moral dilemmas
echo his Catholic sensibilities.   He notes, "If my films aren't
quite autobiographies, there are certain feelings in the characters which I identify with ... if I were disinterested in the
characters or couldn't relate to them, I couldn't make a film
about them."   His protagonists are cut from the whole cloth
of common experience; they are average, unremarkable people,
steeped in personal guilts and loneliness.   Charlie of MEAN
STREETS: J. R., the central figure in WHO'S THAT KNOCK-
ING? (Brenner, 1969), and TAXI DRIVER's Travis Bickle
exist in a state of psychic entrapment.   Incapable of resolving their moral and emotional conflicts, they battle innate
frustrations within the arena of their relationships.   Violence
is often a temporary outlet for the mounting tensions that are
beyond resolution.   If Scorsese's perceptions are keyed to the
darker elements of human nature, the grim realities portrayed
in his movies are tempered by the humor and compassion he
exhibits for his characters.

The director's intense, hyper-kinetic energy characterizes his style. (Critic Peter Cowie observed, "The common filament in Scorsese's movies is energy, an energy so
impetuous, and yet so robust that it finally resolves the physical and spiritual tensions of his world.") It is a style which
reflects his compulsive drive to stalk those magical conver-
gences of time, place, and human interaction in order to catch
that bit of filmic serendipity that will shine with truth. Journalist Guy Flatley commented, "His scenes throb with crude
life, his camera seems nervous, almost hysterical, jumping
here, darting there, as if there may not be time enough to
capture the beauty or ugliness of the moment."

In a corporate Hollywood, increasingly dedicated to
serving up cinematic "fast food" for mass consumption, Scorsese is that rarest of creatures--an American auteur. His
movies are among the most personal bodies of work in contemporary cinema. Retaining a continuity, unified by the director's vision, his pictures explore similar characters and
themes which are altered and expanded upon with each suc-
cessive film. Most importantly, his films resonate with the
compelling urgency and drama of an artist reaching into himself to try honestly to examine and represent fragments of
his own psyche on the screen. "It's really too early to talk
about me in terms of style," he says, "but I suppose you can
say my movies are similar to me, to the way I am as a person ... and my rhythm and pacing reflect the way I think and
talk and move."

Martin Scorsese's earliest childhood memory, as he
tells it, is of sitting in a movie theatre seeing Roy Rogers
and his horse leaping over a log. It is as if the moving image of the horse leapt straight into his heart and initiated a
passion that fired his very sense of being. He recalls, "When
my father asked if I knew who Trigger was, I said it was
something on a gun. He told me Trigger was the horse's
name. When he asked if I wanted to come back and see a
movie the following week, I could hardly contain my excitement as I said, 'yes.'" The trailer was the first in a virtual litany of films in the memories of which he exults.

The son of Sicilian parents, Scorsese was born in
Flushing, New York in 1942. His father, a garment worker,
had briefly moved his wife and son to the Queens area from
the troubled tenements of Little Italy. The family's modest
means forced them to return to the congested, darkly sinister

streets of the Italian ghetto on Manhattan's Lower East Side.
Within this insular conclave of dingy tenement buildings and
grimy, maze-like streets, the surreptitious rites of organized crime were practiced alongside the sacred rituals of the
Catholic Church. The harsh contradictions of these divergent
strictures would inform the conflicts of the Scorsese protagonist in his semi-autobiographical films, WHO'S THAT KNOCK-
ING AT MY DOOR? and the tumultuous MEAN STREETS.

A small, sickly child, Scorsese was often forced to
stay in bed with severe bouts of asthma, a malady which can
disable him to this day. While he waves off the mythic proportions of the young suffering artist scenario, he candidly
admits that his illness left him with the solitary sense that
he was somehow different, set apart by nature from others.
Scorsese's cinematic contemplations of death and violence may,
in part, originate from the intellectual dalliances with death
that the chronically ill engage in. The director's parents
were extremely protective of their ailing son, and their over-
bearing concern for the state of his health probably enforced
an identity of the weak, damaged invalid of limited energy.
Perhaps this accounts for the seemingly compulsive, almost
manic energy level at which Scorsese works. A complete
workaholic, who functions naturally at a high-pitched, frenetic
pace, he seems tenaciously bent on outrunning the limited
time he feels is his.

The young Scorsese spent many days of his childhood
in the sole company of his imagination. "It's only beginning
to dawn on me," he remembers, "how lonely I was as a kid.
My parents worked, and I came home from school at three
o'clock and sat at the kitchen table making up stories on my
drawing board, or watching TV or escaping to the movies.
Not being able to be physical on the same level as the other
kids, not being able to play ball or to fight. So I went off
in the other direction, as chronicler of the group, trying to
be a nice guy to have around." As chronicler, Scorsese took
to recreating the films he had seen, drawing elaborate renderings of them.

In a Film Comment interview with Marjorie Rose, he
remembered, "The first thing I ever did was work with comic
frames, not strips, because I couldn't flip them. I put them
through a piece of cardboard from which I'd cut a hole for the
screen. I'd slip the pictures through individually. I did that
from the time I was eight until I was thirteen. I colored them
all in. It was a big production. At twelve, I did the costumes

from QUO VADIS; I drew the pictures from the screen. I
copied the pillars, even the pillars. And sometimes, I'd
copy the small pictures, 'B' pictures, which were small
screen, which I'd transfer to a 3 x 4 box; I'd draw them
black and white, in ebony pencil, and, sometimes, I'd color
them in sepia. Occasionally, I'd copy a television show like
Danger. And the spectators were in Scope. If the small
pictures were in 3 x 4, the Scope would be, maybe, 3 x 6.
And I'd have credits, such as 'Hecht and Lancaster Presents....' Sometimes, I'd even do 3-D; every once in a
while, I'd paste a gun coming out of the frame, especially
with low-budget, sepia-tone Westerns. But then I threw those
out because my parents discovered them, and they must have
thought I was cutting out paper dolls or something."

If a common theme of Scorsese's pictures is that of
the outsider straining for the recognition of a hostilely indifferent environment, it is because the director identifies himself with the plight of the "outsider." Writer Guy Flatley
observes, "The dominant characteristic of all of Scorsese's
films, and the trait which sets him honorably apart from the
majority of his movie-making peers in this time of gimmickry
and exploitation, is his preoccupation with people, with the
things we can discover about them and the things which remain a mystery. And the people to whom he is most fanatic-
ally drawn are the misfits, the losers, and the loners. His
zeal for documenting the struggle of the alienated individual
against an oppressive society undoubtedly stems from his own
youth, in New York's Little Italy, from the spiritual suffocation so harshly mirrored in MEAN STREETS, with its semi-
autobiographical rendering of an aimless Italian-American
drifting from mass to Mafia to barroom and back again, a
potentially whole man torn apart by religious guilt and hand-
me-down bigotry."

In an interview with Flatley, Scorsese acknowledged,
"I look for a thematic idea running through my movies, and
I see that it's the outsider struggling for recognition. Charlie,
in MEAN STREETS, is an outsider and so are Teresa and
Johnny Boy. Johnny Boy was going to blow up the whole system. And Alice is an outsider and, above all, Travis Bickle,
the taxi driver, is an outsider. In Scorsesean film vernac-
ular, the loneliness of the overlooked and anonymous every-
man is tantamount to an act of psychic violence. In TAXI
DRIVER, Travis Bickle would be driven to reflect and answer
this psychic violence with physical violence.

Scorsese's loneliness can certainly be understood in
the context of the conditions of his youth. Deprived by ill-
health from participating in the often fractious activities of
his peers, he sought refuge in his love of film, in music, and
in his strong faith in the Church. These passions provided
sanctuary to this lone inhabitant, who felt himself otherwise
apart and a stranger to the world of his peers. Film, no
doubt, offered the young Scorsese a transcendent dimension
by which to soar above the oppressively hostile landscape of
his youth. It provided a wonderful outlet for fantasy to the
boy whose young world was claustrophobically inhibited by illness, loneliness, and the grim privations of lower-middle-
class life in the gray urban grids of New York's tenement society. He speaks elatedly of his weekly visits to the movies,
revelling in the memories of the films of his youth like a man
happily re-living the best moments of his life. His recollections of the important films which helped to expand the bounds
of his imagination and aesthetic awarenesses were shared with
the writer, Behrouz Saba.

"I remember very vividly, when I was on the bus, on
my way to see Sam Fuller's first film, I SHOT JESSE JAMES
[Lippert, 1949]; I couldn't wait to see it. I remember being
very disappointed too, because STAGECOACH [United Artists,
1939] was re-released, playing only two days. Monday and
Tuesday everybody worked, we were a working family, and
nobody was able to take me to see the film. Sam Fuller's
films influenced me so greatly; PARK ROW [United Artists,
1952], PICKUP ON SOUTH STREET [20th-Fox, 1953], these
are some of the strongest things I've ever seen. Later I
saw FORTY GUNS [20th-Fox, 1957], which is my favorite.

"One of the greatest experiences was seeing THE AD-
VENTURES OF ROBIN HOOD [Warner's, 1939] re-released
in color. Another great moment is my mother taking me and
a bunch of kids to see RED RIVER [United Artists, 1948]. We
walked in at the middle of the film and were disappointed because we realized that it wasn't in Technicolor, but we loved
every minute of it. I remember seeing DUEL IN THE SUN
[Selznick, 1947] and hiding my eyes near the end of it when
they shoot at each other. It turned out to be one of my favorite films ... also THE FOUR FEATHERS [United Artists,
1939) and THE DRUM (United Artists, 1938] by Zoltan Korda.

"I very much liked the Westerns. John Ford is my
very favorite director, I love all of his films ... THE
SEARCHERS [Warner's, 1956] became one of my favorite

films. I began to develop a critical awareness when I realized that most of these films were made by the same people. There was usually John Wayne in the movie, Maureen
O'Hara, and Henry Fonda.

"Then in the early 'fifties, I started to go to movies
by myself or with my friends; I saw a lot of American 'B'
films. We'd see a Bing Crosby and on the bottom half would
be 99 RIVER STREET [United Artists, 1953], Phil Karlson's
first film. I remember seeing BAMBI [RKO, 1942], and on
the bottom half of the bill was OUT OF THE PAST [RKO,
1947] with Robert Mitchum, one of the classics of film noir.
Then came ON THE WATERFRONT [Columbia, 1954], then
EAST OF EDEN [Warner's, 1955] and GIANT [Warner's,
1956].... In 1958, I began to discover foreign films ... LA
GRANDE ILLUSION [French, 1937], Ingmar Bergman's THE
SEVENTH SEAL [Swedish, 1956]. The British films became
very important to me ... Michael Powell is a favorite of
mine. I saw a variety of genres, and I lived them over and
over again."

Beyond the weekly visits to the movies, Scorsese developed an abiding love of music. His tastes are eclectic
and he exhibits a wide-ranging knowledge of the subject. At
any time, he is as likely to be listening to La Traviata as to
the Sex Pistols! His animated conversation is peppered with
references to music from which he draws metaphors to discuss his work. Scorsese's familiarity with it was bred initially by his parents' tastes, which were not limited to grand
Italian opera. "I've always been interested in music. My
father introduced me to the big bands and the music of people like Django Reinhardt, which influenced me to do NEW
YORK, NEW YORK [United Artists, 1977]. We always lis-
tened to music ... popular music, jazz, even Country/West-
ern. My mother used to listen to Hank Williams on Sunday
morning. They had a feeling for all different types of music."

Scorsese's ardent passion for music inspires and in-
forms the spirit and content of his films. In MEAN STREETS
the music provides an undercurrent of commentary on the
characters and elucidates their psychological conflicts. The
soundtrack reflects and augments the tension between Italian
tradition--symbolized by the opera and folk music heard at
the Feast of the San Gennaro festival--and contemporary values, mirrored through the use of raucous rock and roll. In
her glowing review of the film, New Yorker film critic Pauline
Kael perceived the score as "the background music of the

characters' lives--and not only the background, because it
enters in. It's as if these characters were just naturally
part of an opera with pop themes. The music is the electricity in the air of this movie; the music is like an engine that
the characters move to.... In Scorsese's vision, music and
the movies work within us and set the terms in which we per-
ceive ourselves. Music and the movies and the Church. A
witches' brew. " The raw-edged sensuality of the rock and
roll music track of WHO'S THAT KNOCKING... ? underscored
the buoyant energy and rough sexuality of the young men. In
ALICE DOESN'T LIVE HERE ANYMORE, the strident, hard-
driving strains of Mott the Hopple and Leon Russell conveyed
the building domestic tensions in the Hyatt household. The
director's musical conceptualizations are a vitalizing presence
in all his films. Beyond the musical and cinematic references
which appear in them, the often refrained thematic nature of
his pictures can be understood in light of his religious upbringing.

Raised as a religious Catholic, Scorsese adhered de-
voutly to Church dogma, taking it very literally. He aspired
to the priesthood for a long time and entered a preparatory
seminary where a combination of course failures and "misbe-
havior" led to a premature leavetaking from the school. He
went, however, to the parochial high school, Cardinal Hayes
in the Bronx, and subsequently applied but failed to gain admission to Fordham University. Disaffection with the Church
began when he noticed the disparities between religious dicta
and their practice. While he has never gotten over the rituals
of Catholicism, his disenchantment with the Church is the result of his perception of its all too mortal nature. Speaking
to interviewer Saba, Scorsese explained the causes of his dis-
illusionment. "The Church tells you, for example, that you
can't eat meat on Friday. For a while, I was going to be a
priest and I really adhered to that. 'Mortal,' they told you,
'it would be a mortal sin.' After a while I found out that this
was really a Church-made law, that there is nothing about it
in the Bible.

"Then I found out other things. I started to become
involved with films; there were a lot of films on the old condemned list of the Church; all of Max Ophuls, Jean Renoir and
Bergman films were on the list. They told me that I could
go and see them because of my work, but the masses shouldn't
see it. What is the difference between me and them? I come
from the masses.

"They started to make little distinctions. Once you
start to make little distinctions, there is something wrong
with the policy. Later on, when the rules about eating meat
on Friday were taken out, people started to realize the differences between the man-made laws and the God-made laws.
How dare they talk about 'mortal sins' in regard to man-made
laws? You're eight years old, you eat meat by mistake on
Friday and say, 'I'm going to die tomorrow.' The sense of
guilt is tremendous."

Despite his angry sense of "the betrayal of the ideal"
that led to a repudiation of the Church, Scorsese admits that
Catholicism has been a major influence on his life and realizes that it will always figure prominently in his art. He
says, "Being a Catholic is a seminal force in my work as an
artist." Writing about the director in her book, Hollywood
Renaissance (Barnes, 1977), author Diane Jacobs observed,
"... even more than visceral violence, religion, in the sense
both of ritual and of an absolute power, is more vital to
Scorsese than to any of his fellow directors. For him, the
Church is unquestionably also a propagator and false appeaser
of guilt. When I asked Scorsese what remained the strongest
legacy of his strict Catholic upbringing, he replied unequivo-
cably, 'Guilt, a major helping of guilt, like a lot of garlic.'"

Scorsese's vestigial Catholic sensibilities manifest
themselves in the conceptions of his film characters. The
Scorsesean protagonist aspires to a purity of spirit in a
scabrous world where such ideals can never be fully actual-
ized. He appears unable to resolve and mediate the spiritual
conflicts incurred by the warring terms of transcendent morality and the exigencies of earthly survival. His inability to
achieve psychological resolution is a source of pain and visceral frustration which in a Scorsese film will explode into
anarchic violence. Analyzing the director's work, writer
Peter Cowie noted, "his male protagonists suffer regularly
from intimations of sainthood, only to be chastened and even
brutalized by the everyday struggle to survive."

In WHO'S THAT KNOCKING...?, the protagonist, J.R.,
cannot have sexual relations with the woman he loves, feeling
that without the sanctions of wedlock, they would be dishon-
ored. He is blindly outraged when he learns that the girl is
not a virgin. Despite the fact that her "deflowering" was the
result of a brutal rape, he cannot forgive her. His unyielding
contempt for her destroys the possibility of their relationship.

It is clear that the bonds of religion seem to militate against
emotional and sexual fulfillment. Guilt seems firmly entangled
with all thoughts of desire and personal gratification.

Deeply-held religious guilt also torments Charlie in
MEAN STREETS. Scorsese refers to him as a "false saint."
He explains, "The whole idea of the film was to make a story
of a modern saint; you know, a saint in his own society, but
his society happened to be gangsters. It should be interesting
to see how a guy does the right thing; that's the old phrase
they use, 'the right thing,' in a world [where] if somebody
does something wrong, you've got to break his head or you
shoot him. It's as simple as that. He became a character
who refused to acknowledge that, and eventually did the worst
thing he could do--he put everything off, put all confrontations
off, until everything explodes." Travis Bickle in TAXI DRIVER
is another failed saint. His fixation with the moral filth of
New York appears to be the distorted psychological response
of a man repressed by religious interdiction. He seeks re-
demption from his own unclean thoughts by his efforts to
"save" a child prostitute. Says Scorsese, "[Travis] is a guy
who sets out to save people who don't want to be saved and
ends up hurting them. In the end, the prostitute is safely
ensconced in the bosom of her family and miserable, and
thanks to our hero, a lot of people are dead."

The sudden outburst of violence is a usual element in
a Scorsese film. The director seems drawn to exploring its
causation, and his cinematic enactments of physical brutality
are shudderingly real. Scorsese notes, "Violence has always
been a pretty scary thing for me, but I'm fascinated by it,
especially by the aimlessness of it. It's always erupting
when you don't expect it, particularly in a city like New York.
You're sitting in a restaurant, eating, and suddenly a car
crashes through the window and you're dead. When we were
scouting locations for TAXI DRIVER up by Lincoln Center one
day, the ballet had just let out and a number of women were
crossing to catch a bus. Suddenly a big guy walked over to
a very old lady and punched her in the mouth.... The guy
just turned around and walked away. Senseless violence. Yet
if you got into that guy's head--into his character--who knows?"

The omnipresence of incipient violence in an urban environment of concentrated hostility and frustration, obviously,
made an indelible mark on the young Scorsese. Petty hoods,
derelicts, gangland killings, and the bigotry that is bred into
ghetto inhabitants were the everyday presences in his young

world. Within the dark shadows of the grimy tenements,
these menacing elements would often ignite into paroxysms
of violence. Perhaps, as a result, Scorsese's work is almost compulsively consumed with the pathology of violence
in a pressure-cooker world of thwarted dreams, destructive
relationships, and oppressive loneliness. As one critic put
it, "He is an artist preoccupied with human perversity and
the violence lurking beneath a veneer of complacency."

New York City is the inspiration, the "feel," if you
will, of a Scorsese film. Its dark human perversities, its
sweltering hostilities and the grim primal terms of survival
in its "rat race" have shaped Scorsese's "reality." ("I go
back to New York, a concrete island, and find it totally un-
natural; it's total madness. Yet I am a product of that and
I feel at home there.") Witnessing the brutalities and indig-
nities suffered by the people in the tenements, Scorsese learned
at an early age man's capacity for inhumanity towards his
fellow man. It is a nightmarish world recalling the most
horrific, surreal renderings of Hieronymous Bosch. "There's
something extra-violent about New York. Growing up in the
neighborhood, we used to go to school in the morning, carrying a little briefcase, going to Saint Patrick's school around
the corner. We lived a block away from the Bowery and
there were always the drunks, the bums beating each other
up with bottles. There was blood all over the street and
you'd just step by. I mean, that was normal. Then there
was rivalry between the Neapolitans and Sicilians and Cala-
brese. There was rivalry between all three against the ones
that lived on the East side and the West side. Even down to
buildings. They got into rivalries between buildings. It was
always crazy that way."

Mistrust, poverty and the fear that stalks the ghetto
found their outlets in irrational hatred of "outsiders" and in
random acts of mindless cruelty. "It's the ghetto that creates prejudice," asserts Scorsese. "I can remember when
I was five years old and my brother was twelve, we were
walking down the street one day and, suddenly, we saw a big
crowd of people. They were standing around a man who had
fallen, and his head was bleeding. My brother took a look
at him, and then he turned to me and said, 'Oh, he's only
a Jew.' And that is one of my earliest memories."

The Mafia presides in the dirty, decaying streets of
Little Italy. While the Syndicate's nefarious dealings are an
ominous presence pervading the streets of Little Italy, its

operations are nonetheless an interwoven part of the community's way of life. It is accepted as an established way of doing business, an entrenched institution in the best traditions of our free enterprise system. Its wholesale control of the area has transformed it into a gangland fiefdom. It is a treacherous environment where venality, cynicism, and the constant danger of mayhem "naturally" thrives in bizarre counterpoint to the Catholic tenets its inhabitants were raised to believe.

Scorsese recalls, "In my neighborhood you dealt with the 'organization'--I don't like to call it anything else--which is stronger than the government, the Church, and the police. The government is a joke and the police are even a bigger joke, because the 'organization' runs them. We knew that as kids; it was common knowledge. As a kid, I knew, if a gangland shooting was to happen, a cop would come and tell me to go home. He knew because he was in on it, he turned his back--that's how he was in on it. Then after the shooting, he would go back and say 'Okay, what happened here?' That's what I mean, I don't mean that the cops came to shoot people. They used to work together; 'private discussions,' they called it. MEAN STREETS shows that organized crime is similar to big government. They're both machines."

It was not until Scorsese entered New York University that the idea of a vocation in filmmaking presented itself as a possibility. The Greenwich Village school was virtually a universe away from the comparative "heart of darkness" of his neighborhood. Within its sanctuary, he would be initiated into the new perspectives and refinements of culture--it would be the means of his "escape" from the fierce world of his youth, a world he would return to only in his films. The first member of his family ever to attend college, Scorsese originally planned to study English, but switched to film study after a momentous introduction to a film history course. The director remembers his film school days with great fondness. In speaking with him, one is struck by the passion he exudes for the study of cinema. "It was a marvelous time to be in film school--the timing was perfect.... It was 1960, and I started to make my first film in 1963; it took me three years to get to make a picture. In those three years, there was not only the French New Wave, but the Italian New Wave; we got hit with everything."

Films such as Godard's BREATHLESS (French, 1959), Alain Resnais' HIROSHIMA MON AMOUR (French, 1959),

Truffaut's JULES ET JIM (French, 1961), Olmi's IL POSTO
(Italian, 1961) and I FIDANZATI (Italian, 1962) were stunningly
original works that challenged the very conventions of filmmaking.   They set the way for a whole new generation of
filmmakers who would be dazzled by their seeming free-
spirited, innovative, and personal approach to cinematic exposition.   Truffaut's 400 BLOWS (French, 1959), one of
Scorsese's favorites, and particularly his SHOOT THE PIANO
PLAYER (French, 1960), had a monumental impact on student
filmmaking.   ("The audacity of that film just took off and
soared....") These movies inspired the students to a new
sense of the unlimited potential of filmmaking art.   However,
at times, their work was too heavily influenced by these New
Wave directors and their films were too self-consciously deriv-
ative. Scorsese's first feature, WHO'S THAT KNOCKING...?
suffered from his eagerness to emulate the styles of this exciting vanguard of foreign film directors.

Most importantly, film school facilitated the director's
access to expensive camera equipment with which to learn
filmmaking skills.   Further, it provided the opportunity to
deal with professors and students with whom he would collaborate on his later film projects--people such as Mardik Martin, the screenwriter who co-wrote MEAN STREETS with
Scorsese and later worked on NEW YORK, NEW YORK with
Earl MacRauch; Haig Manoogian, Scorsese's professor and
mentor, who helped produce WHO'S THAT KNOCKING...?;
Richard Coll, his long-time friend, who worked on some of
the director's early shorts and idd the photography on WHO'S
THAT KNOCKING...?; Michael Wadleigh, with whom Scorsese
collaborated on the production of WOODSTOCK.

Assessing the value of his film school experience,
Scorsese agrees that it was beneficial in permitting access to
the technology of filmmaking, but he concludes, "No matter
what you've learned in terms of dramatic structure and all,
you ultimately make a film on your own. No school can teach
you how to make a film.   In other words, you have to know
who you are, or you can't really have your films mean anything to you or to anyone else. Knowing who you are is a
major necessity, and once you've fulfilled that requirement,
you've got to make a picture the best way you know how and
you can't really think in terms of how to make it palatable
for everyone."

Scorsese received a master's degree in film and, in
1963, wrote and directed his first movie, a nine-minute, 16mm

short called WHAT'S A NICE GIRL LIKE YOU DOING IN A
PLACE LIKE THIS? The short, produced by the New York
University Department of Television, Motion Picture and Radio
Presentations, is an off-beat, humorous little tale about a
writer whose difficulty with writing leads to such various dis-
tractions as an inordinate fascination with a painting. His
obsession with it leads to his eventual transformation and im-
prisonment within the painting. It is a highly-original, amusing film replete with visual jokes--one that Scorsese describes
as "an exercise in style. I was very interested in the new
form at that time--the New Wave films were a big influence.
I primarily wanted to see if I could make a film without one
match cut, and use all sorts of techniques--stills, slow motion, fast motion. And at the same time, I wanted to do a
kind of take-off on a horror-horror story where the character
winds up in a negative situation--he winds up drowning in his
own picture. I guess the chief influence for the film was
Mel Brooks. His cartoons, THE VIOLINIST [United Picture
Artists, 1962] and THE CRITIC [United Picture Artists, 1963],
and Truffaut's JULES AND JIM and SHOOT THE PIANO PLAYER
gave me the feeling that I could do anything I wanted in film."

     Scorsese's next New York University-produced short
was IT'S NOT JUST YOU, MURRAY! (1964), a snappy tongue-
in-cheek parody about an Italian gangster and his crazy relationship with his best friend. The fifteen-minute, 16mm black
and white film was written and directed by Scorsese. In 1968,
Time magazine, in a feature on college movie makers, called
the film perhaps "the best university movie ever made."
MURRAY! also won the Edward L. Kingsley award.

     A free-wheeling spoof, the short is a humorously com-
pressed extravaganza which was filmed in 65 different locations with 45 costume changes and included a play within a
film motif! The director even makes a deferential nod to
Fellini's $8\frac{1}{2}$ (Italian, 1963), in the form of a parody of the
famous circus scene in that Italian masterpiece. According
to Scorsese, the relationship between Bob Hope and Bing
Crosby in the famous road pictures was the prototype of the
relationship between the characters in MURRAY! "MURRAY
has a lot of influences--THE ROAD TO ZANZIBAR [Para-
mount, 1941], the roaring 'twenties; a lot of it was also based
on people that I knew, some people in my family. MURRAY
was also inspired by Mel Brooks, I thought the 2,000-year-
old man was fantastic."

     In both short films, Scorsese reveals a puckish sense

of humor one does not usually associate with him. However,
typical of his "dark side," the characters in these comedies
are in less than humorous situations: Murray is a gullible,
ingenuous schmoe who is constantly duped by his best friend,
and the protagonist in NICE GIRL is a restless neurotic who
is undone by his obsessions. It is clear upon viewing these
two shorts that Scorsese is a spirited, highly original director
who has an instinctive facility for the pyrotechnics of filmmaking. He demonstrates an assured vitality in his use of
a moving camera. The cinematic verve of these shorthand
character studies can be attributed to the director's deft execution of pacing and his fine command of visual imagery.

Although Scorsese denies any interest in politics, his
1967 short, THE BIG SHAVE, was a filmic metaphor for the
United States' involvement in the Vietnam War. The five-
minute award-winning color film was made with the support
of the Belgian Cinémathèque. Upon his submission of an outline of the script for THE BIG SHAVE, the director received
a grant from the Palais de Beaux Arts in Brussels, which co-
sponsors the famous independent or underground film festival.
The grant, one of a hundred given, was an award of ten roles
of agva color film.

Scorsese refers to his short as "a brief American
nightmare." He explains, "It was made in 1967-1968; the
Tet offensive was on in Vietnam. A blond-haired, blue-eyed
guy comes into a white-tiled bathroom which resembles a tor-
ture chamber, and he proceeds to shave himself to death. In
this daily morning ritual, an American is cutting his own
throat without realizing it. The guy keeps shaving until he
is covered with blood--it's sort of surreal, he doesn't die,
he just stands there with blood all over the place. Imagine
waking up every morning--you put that goddamn razor to your
face and then visualize stretching that, making it into a horror
thing, like the film is. It becomes funny. The song that is
heard, the Bunny Berigan standard, 'I Can't Get Started' [I've
been around the world and set revolutions in Spain. . . . '], was
meant to emphasize the irony between now and a very naive,
young America--it was an America I missed and was sorry
for. I knew in 1967 we were in big trouble."

THE BIG SHAVE caused a sensation at the Knokke Experimental Film Festival and won the Prix de l'Age d'Or. It
was seen at other film festivals and was chosen as the short
to appear with Godard's surrealistic satire, WEEKEND. When
THE BIG SHAVE was shown at the New York Film Festival,

it stirred a tumultuous response. Commenting on the controversial nature of the short, Scorsese observed, "If you see
the film with a large crowd, 10,000 people, it splits the
crowd down in half. Half of them start booing and hissing,
the other group starts laughing and applauding. People first
think it's a joke, but then they realize it's not. When I gave
Francis Ford Coppola a print of the film, it became the movie
they showed when company came, whether it was their old
Italian aunt or the famous director, Antonioni. I met Antonioni, three years ago in Cannes. He said to me, 'I like your
film, THE BIG SHAVE.' I asked, 'Where did you see it!'
And he said, 'the Coppola house.'"

     As a graduate student at N.Y.U., Scorsese wrote the
script for his first feature, WHO'S THAT KNOCKING AT MY
DOOR?, a film which would take three years to complete and
would appear in several incarnations. It was a difficult time
for the fledgling director. Married, and with a newly-born
daughter, Scorsese remembers, "I didn't care about money
at the time; all I wanted to do was work in film. My parents
helped me financially. It was a shameful thing, but I didn't
care. I was prepared to do anything I had to, and that's what
broke up my first marriage." In the meantime, his short
films had won numerous awards and had gained him much
favorable attention. Scorsese felt ready to direct his first
"big movie."

     He would turn to the streets of Little Italy for the
subject of his premier film dramatization, WHO'S THAT
KNOCKING...? (the title comes from the 1958 hit rock song
by the Genies). Scorsese intended the film to be the first
student film shot in 35mm, black and white stock. "I wrote
it first in a very obscure way. Richard Coll shot the scenes
in 35 ... therefore, all the scenes with the guys are in 35.
It was then called BRING ON THE DANCING GIRLS [this was
the original title of WHO'S THAT KNOCKING...? and Zina
Bethune was not in the film]. Harvey Keitel was in it and I
shot some scenes with another girl--but nobody understood it!
It was an hour and ten minutes long and nobody understood it.
It was a mess, a disaster! We put it away until my old professor, Haig Manoogian, encouraged me to work on the film
again."

     Scorsese was urged to fix up the script and develop
the relationship between the boy and the girl. New scenes
were shot in 16mm and blown up to match the original 35mm
of the film. Zina Bethune was chosen to play the part of The

Girl, and Manoogian offered his services as producer of the
film. It was to be his first feature. "Joseph Weill, Haig
and his wife, Betzi, got $5,000, and I proceeded to shoot
for another two weeks in 16mm. Then the film was re-named,
I CALL FIRST. It was shown in 1967 at the Chicago Film
Festival, and Roger Ebert, the film critic, gave it a great
review. It was taken very seriously, but I couldn't get it
released."

In 1968, the director joined his friend, Richard Coll,
who was making commercials in Europe. Coll had encouraged
him to try his hand at commercials too. While there, Scorsese
helped work on the screenplay of Pim de La Parra's OBSES-
SIONS (1968). Eventually, he heard word from Manoogian
that I CALL FIRST could not be sold without a nude scene.
Joseph Brenner, of Joseph Brenner Associates, a distributor
of "porno" movies, wanted to "go legit" and was willing to
distribute the Scorsese film on the condition that a nude scene
was included.

Scorsese agreed to the inclusion of a nude segment,
but his professional commitments required that he stay in
Amsterdam. Therefore, he had Harvey Keitel fly to the
Netherlands. "We got a bunch of girls and shot this crazy
nude scene with Harvey. There was a building there that
looked like something out of the Bowery. I shot and cut the
footage, and Dick Coll did the lighting. Then I put the Doors'
song, 'The End,' over it." The scene, a highly-erotic "masturbation fantasy," conveys dark, aggressive overtones to suggest that J.R.'s (Harvey Keitel) Catholic upbringing is in conflict with the fulfillment of his sexual desire. Says Scorsese,
"He can't face the fact that he needs women. Therefore, after
he achieves orgasm, in a sense, he rejects it. On the soundtrack, you hear the Doors chanting, 'Kill, kill, kill....'"
The scene is charged with sexual tension, and a surreal sense
of disorientation is evoked by a perpetually moving camera.
To convey J.R.'s emotional turmoil, the camera is constantly
panning, producing, at times, a sensation of confused spinning.

After six months in Europe, Scorsese returned to the
United States with the nude segment. It was edited into the
middle of a scene that had already been filmed. "The whole
scene goes white, and people think the film broke. Then a
big eye comes into the scene. I figured if we were going to
stop the film that way, let's stop the film completely. And
in a way, at that point, I did it in anger because I felt the
film was already so choppy as it was. We had no exposition,

no establishing shots.   You don't know who people are, you
don't know what's happening.   The picture was done over such
a long period of time that there's no transition between scenes.
You have no idea where people are.   The only thread of it is
the characterization.   It was very heavily influenced by all the
New Wave movies and Kenneth Anger's SCORPIO RISING (America, 1964).   As it turned out, it took three years to finish,
and finally we called it, WHO'S THAT KNOCKING AT MY
DOOR?   It was released in New York in 1969 and shown at
the Carnegie Hall Cinema."

   Scorsese refers to WHO'S THAT KNOCKING...? as an
"experimental" film and, at its best, it virtually surges with
the gleeful energy of cinematic inventiveness.   Analyzing the
film in her book, Hollywood Renaissance, Diane Jacobs describes Scorsese's style as "replete with nouvelle vague and
Cassavetes influences....   [His characters] drive the obliga-
tory New Wave cars and find headlights and skylines and old
Westerns dazzling."   The hand-held, off-beat rhythms of the
movie impart the spontaneous, naturalistic look of cinéma
vérité.   We are treated to a breathtaking visual vocabulary
of pans, zoom-ins, peculiarly angled shots and straightforward
closeups.   Scorsese's itinerant camera appears always on the
move, good-naturedly nuzzling the characters as it swings by.
While the film is stylistically self-conscious, it displays in
good measure Scorsese's cinematic "sure-footedness," and his
unmistakable ability to elicit dramatic tension through the very
placement of his camera.

   WHO'S THAT KNOCKING...? is an evocative mood
piece which faithfully renders the aimless, bored activities
of a post-adolescent group of young men living in the Italian
neighborhood of Scorsese's childhood.   The protagonist, J. R.,
is gamely caught up in these passing rites of early manhood,
brooding, dawdling, and carousing with his jobless friends,
whom he prefers to regard as being "between positions."
Their world, as the Time film critic pictures it, is one
"where Cadillacs park conspicuously in front of tenements
and the guy taking his grandchildren down to the corner for
a lemon ice is the No. 1 professional murderer on the East
Coast."

   Scorsese is most comfortable in depicting the gruff
bantering camaraderie among men.   We see their goading,
rough-housing ways, as they attempt to relieve their boredom
and frustration in the spiritually suffocating urban spaces of
the ghetto.   Dark, smoke-filled bars, narrow tenement hall-

ways, dirty alleys, and cramped apartments are the physical
appurtenances of this urban landscape. It is the stock catalogue of Scorsesean metaphors for the psychic claustrophobia
out of which violence often erupts. The young men's nervous
energy is underscored by the director's vertiginous camera
which benignly stalks them, articulating their uneasiness and
ebullience as they engage in their puerile, teasing games. In
one memorable scene, J. R. and his friends are at a party
for which two prostitutes have been hired. As the youths
wait to take their turns with the women, the camera pans
widely, spiralling back and forth, stylistically reflecting their
anxious, aggressively boisterous sexual play.

WHO'S THAT KNOCKING...? is a loosely-constructed
narrative whose plot-line revolves around J. R. 's pursuit of
The Girl (that is how she is referred to in the credits), vaguely
acted by Zina Bethune. She is the least well-conceived of all
Scorsese's heroines. Says Jacobs, "Even more than MEAN
STREETS, WHO'S THAT KNOCKING...? is uncomfortable with
its women. Like Coppola, [Scorsese] is uneasy with the concept of woman. He has knocked her off the pedestal, but is
still wary of playing around with her."

The Girl is portrayed as a vision of blonde, ethereal
purity, an untouchable ideal destined to be tainted as, inevitably, she becomes the object of J. R. 's sexual desire. It is
a Catholic Catch-22 that deifies only the virginal woman encouraging male contempt of her if she yields to his sexual
passions. As J. R. puts it, "the difference between a 'broad'
and a 'girl' is you use one for convenience while you marry
the other." This seeming irrationality is derived from the
Catholic conscience, best set forth by Scorsese himself: "I
grew up in a culture where women were separate; and the
madonna-whore dichotomy encouraged fear of them, distrust,
and because they didn't seem like real human beings, difficulty in relating to them." Thus, the character of The Girl
is underdeveloped, more symbolic than a full-blooded, three-
dimensional human being. We never get to know her--what
she does or where she comes from. Because one cannot
identify with her, the emotional impact of the break-up of her
relationship with J. R. is undermined by our lack of involvement with the character.

The film has many stirring sequences, particularly a
lovely meeting staged on the Staten Island ferry, where J. R.
"courts" The Girl. It is a marvelously breezy, improvised
scene that conveys the nervous spontaneity of chance romantic

encounter. The camera pans unsteadily around The Girl, ex-
tracting the undercurrent of uneasiness characteristic of first
meeting. The point of rapprochement is none other than film
buffery. J.R. and The Girl come together over mutually fond
recollections of scenes from the movie, THE SEARCHERS.
J.R. affirms his passion for Westerns, proclaiming, "If everyone loved Westerns, the world would be okay." In the manner of the French New Wave directors, Scorsese chose in
this way to pay tribute to his favorite director, John Ford,
and celebrate his abiding love of Westerns. (He regards THE
SEARCHERS as a film of "pure poetry," and his affection for
the picture compelled him to include a clip of the fight scene
between Jeffrey Hunter and Ken Curtis in his movie, MEAN
STREETS.)

One of the most stunning visual set pieces in the movie,
WHO'S THAT KNOCKING...?, is an explosively violent rape
scene. The brutally realistic action is filmed in a car. (It
marks the director's first use of the car as a symbol of emotional alienation and repression--a prosaic, modern day pressure-cooker. His employment of the car in the film as a
site of violent action pre-figures such signature scenes in
MEAN STREETS, TAXI DRIVER, and NEW YORK, NEW YORK.
Of course, the taxi in TAXI DRIVER is the physical metaphor
of Travis Bickle's psychic isolation, and Alice's most frustrating confrontations with her son occur in the family station
wagon in ALICE DOESN'T LIVE HERE ANYMORE.) A scene
of overpowering, realistic impact, the rape sequence all but
lunges out of the screen. Filmed partly in slow-motion, it
presaged Sam Peckinpah's utilization of that method for the
depiction of grossly violent action.

The segment is shown as a flashback in time as The
Girl tells J.R. of the assault. Interestingly, it is J.R.'s
conception of the rape that we see on the screen. The rape
sequence is repeated in slow-motion a number of times--a
visual enactment of J.R. mentally lingering on the violation
which he perceives as The Girl's act of betrayal. Although
he loves her, J.R. is morally outraged by her loss of vir-
ginity. His anger is no less abated by the fact that The Girl
has been involuntarily "deflowered" by a vicious assault.
J.R.'s inability to mediate between his Catholic conscience
and the mitigating facts of reality destroys the relationship.

WHO'S THAT KNOCKING...? proved to be a noteworthy
debut for Scorsese. It gave every evidence that the director
was an original talent with a uniquely personal vision which he

could translate stunningly into film art. Most notably, he
demonstrated a distinct flair for directing and an instinctive
eye for placing his peripatetic camera. His camera all but
moves with the irrepressible abandon of a swooping bird,
strongly attesting to the spirited vitality of an expansive creative energy. While the film communicates an invigorating
inventiveness, it suffers ultimately from the distracting,
spliced-together incongruencies of divergent style and tone,
no doubt attributable to the protracted amount of time it took
to make the movie. The resulting loss of cinematic momentum diffuses the overall dramatic thrust of the picture.

The critics hailed the film as an excitingly original
first effort by a young director. The Time film critic remarked, "The whole of the picture is less than the sum of
its parts, many which abound with vitality and cinematic innovation. Scorsese choreographs his camera movements with
an exhilarating, easy grace, and his dramatic use of rock 'n
roll surpasses similar efforts in THE GRADUATE [United
Artists, 1967] and EASY RIDER [Columbia, 1969]. WHO'S
THAT KNOCKING.... ? ... introduces a young director who
just may turn out to be one of the brighter talents of this
eager generation." Newsday proclaimed the picture to be
"a highly original film of great worth and sensitivity ... a
very profound film in the way that MEDIUM COOL [American,
1969] and EASY RIDER express and create ideas about a
certain aspect of modern life." Most concurred that the film
was a fresh, accurate evocation of the mores of a certain
sector of the youth scene. Unfortunately, the film, which
cost $35,000 to make ($6,000 of which were student loans),
was poorly distributed and hardly seen. Its release in Los
Angeles under the title J.R. proved fortuitous, however,
since Roger Corman got a chance to see it there. The famed
"B" movie producer's favorable impression of the film would
eventually lead to his offer of a picture deal with Scorsese.

II

In 1968, Scorsese began directing THE HONEYMOON
KILLERS (American International, 1969). However, his affiliation with the project was short-lived. He was taken off
the film over a conflict of ideas with the movie's writer,
Leonard Kastle, who eventually took over its direction. According to Scorsese, the film retains the "National Enquirer
look," a concept which he originated for the picture. He admits in retrospect that perhaps he "didn't know enough" at the

time. "I learned a lot from working on the film. I hadn't
been taking cover shots ... but I laid out the entire way the
movie should be done in terms of black and white photography.
Some of my footage is in the film, but I never saw the whole
movie. Leonard Kastle was the man who should have directed
it in the first place. It was his baby."

Meanwhile, Scorsese was asked to join the faculty of
New York University's film department. His teaching schedule
was periodically interspersed with his work on various film
projects. He also put in a brief six-week stint as a film
editor for CBS. His most notable professional association
at this time was his involvement on the production of the
famous rock documentary, WOODSTOCK (Warner's, 1970).
He served as assistant director and supervising editor on the
film record of the 1969 celebratory "love-in," rock festival
which took place in the small country hamlet in upstate New
York.

As an instructor, Scorsese taught film production,
acting classes, and film criticism. During his three-year
teaching affiliation with N. Y. U. , he demonstrated a marked
predilection for using American movies as a basis for instruct-
ing his classes. "I threw out all the film normally shown for
some of these courses ... WILD STRAWBERRIES [Swedish,
1957] and NIGHTS OF CABIRIA [Italian, 1956], which are
great films, and instead, I showed EL DORADO [Paramount,
1967], THE SEARCHERS, JOHNNY GUITAR [Republic, 1954],
THE NUTTY PROFESSOR [Paramount, 1963], THE BAND
WAGON [M-G-M, 1953], THE BIG HEAT [Columbia, 1954],
and FORCE OF EVIL [M-G-M, 1948], one of my favorite
films. I definitely emphasized American movies--I grew up
on them! You can mention European films in class.... You
can read various books about them, but I wanted my students
to see what these foreign films' influences were. I would say
to them, 'Don't be snobs. Don't miss seeing American pictures. It's one helluva history we've got here. ' Because
filmmaking is very much an American art form. "

In 1970, Scorsese worked as a production and post-
production supervisor on the New York Cinetracts Collective
feature, STREET SCENES. The seventy-minute documentary
movie, which centered on public reaction to the American invasion of Cambodia, was, in Scorsese's words, "a guerrilla-
type film, using black and white, as well as color film with
very few cuts. " (Francis Ford Coppola contributed some film
stock after Scorsese sent him a letter of request.) Most of

the documentary was shot by students and friends of the director. He notes, "I always make it very clear that while
the film was my idea, I didn't shoot most of it. I only filmed
one small segment of it, but, of course, edited it along the
lines of what I wanted it to say." Scorsese shot only the last
sequence in the film. "I used footage that showed nobody
knew what to do, neither radicals nor conservatives. Everybody was yelling at everybody, and the picture ends in the
middle of an argument because that was when the film literally ran out! I just left it that way. I thought, 'Perfect,'
it was God-sent."

The project was fraught with troubles and difficulties.
Some of those shooting the picture were physically struck and
their cameras smashed amidst the fray of the furious political
demonstrations that were triggered by the invasion. The director recalls that making STREET SCENES was one of the
most "unpleasant experiences" of his life. ("In fact, that was
the time I was hit by a really bad asthma attack; I started
taking cortisone and I haven't stopped since.") For his work
on the film, he was condemned by left and right alike, as
well as by some of the students who shot footage for the film.
They objected that the documentary was not "political" enough,
and that their "side," in particular, was unfairly portrayed.
The director was also criticized for making the film an "entertainment piece," because of his typically spirited use of
rock and roll music on the soundtrack. According to Scorsese,
he utilized the intensely frenetic music of the rock groups
Canned Heat and Blind Faith to echo "the madness and fury"
of the political debates.

Like many artists, Scorsese deplores the brittle,
humorless provincialism of the politically-minded. He detests
the dogmatic thinking of those who can only see the "rightness" of their cause. "I wanted to show the humanistic,
rather than the political, nature of the issue. All I wanted
to show was that no side had the answer. At the end, all
we saw was utter hopelessness ... not futility, but the im-
potence of the people. They were sitting around and just
arguing and arguing."

STREET SCENES received a poor review from the
Film Society Review, which called it the "worst example of
student filmmaking." (Scorsese, answering the criticisms,
retorts "Of course the camera work was shaky--the kids were
getting beaten on the head!") Ironically, the negative review
was written by a former student of the director's. As a

result, the documentary was hardly distributed, although it
was shown at the New York Film Festival and some other
festivals. Scorsese does not include STREET SCENES in his
film credits because he claims it was done as a community
service. No doubt, the frustrating experience of working on
the movie contributed to his decision.

    Scorsese's increasing professional involvement in num-
erous film projects began to interfere with his full-time teaching responsibilities at N.Y.U. Eventually, he was forced to
leave the school and decided to try his chances on the West
Coast. It was just a matter of time before anyone who was
serious about working in movies would find himself in the film
factories of Hollywood. Indeed, in 1971, California beckoned:
producer Fred Weintraub requested Scorsese's services on the
floundering rock documentary, MEDICINE BALL CARAVAN.
The director and his film school colleague, Mike Wadleigh,
had formerly worked for Weintraub on the film, WOODSTOCK.
Commenting on the project, Scorsese explained, "Fred needed
somebody to salvage MEDICINE BALL CARAVAN, which was
shot in three gauges--35mm Techniscope, 16mm and 8mm.
It was nine hours long, and nobody knew what was happening!
It had absolutely no continuity. Weintraub brought me to
L.A. and said, 'Try and see what you can do.' I thought I
would be there for two weeks, and I've been there ever since."

    Editing the rock and roll documentary proved to be a
grueling experience, but while working in Los Angeles Scorsese met Roger Corman. The producer had seen WHO'S
THAT KNOCKING...? under the title, J.R., when it had
opened at L.A.'s Vagabond Theatre. (The theatre distributor
didn't like the title WHO'S THAT KNOCKING...?) The movie
had garnered favorable reviews, and Corman liked it. He
offered Scorsese directorial work on the sequel to BLOODY
MAMA (American International, 1970). Excited at the prospect of directing a "costume movie with guns," Scorsese eag-
erly accepted Corman's proposition. The producer promised
to send him the script for the picture, BOXCAR BERTHA
(American International, 1972), in the following few months.
In the meantime, Scorsese finished editing MEDICINE BALL
CARAVAN, and subsequently found work editing the soundtrack on John Cassavetes' MINNIE AND MOSKOWITZ (Universal, 1971). Cassavetes, Scorsese's trusted friend and mentor,
had loved the young director's debut feature film. He would
later prove instrumental in encouraging Scorsese to resume
work on his dormant film project, MEAN STREETS.

When the script Corman had promised to send failed
to arrive at the designated time, Scorsese became concerned
that Corman might be just like the many producers who never
followed through on their "big deal" pitches.   But the script
eventually arrived; it had been delayed by Corman's marriage,
for which he'd taken time off.   He was, of course, different
from most producers.   Heralded as the king of the "B" movie,
Corman and American International Pictures had helped many
young directors, Francis Ford Coppola, Brian De Palma, and
Peter Bogdanovich among them, on their maiden outings.   His
production company was a well-oiled, successful movie-mill
that spun out formularized film fare at a fast and profitable
rate.   Characterizing Corman's modus operandi, Scorsese
says, admiringly, "He's a tough guy, meaning he knows what
he wants and he gets it ... and he knows how to go about
getting it.   Roger's films make money because of the speed
and the economy with which they are shot.   And I love his
films ... as a kid, when I used to see his name on a film,
we'd go to see it immediately.   He's one of the best, but
he's underrated in America--just alone, what he has done
for other filmmakers is amazing."

On the set of BOXCAR BERTHA, Scorsese quickly
learned the Corman formula.   Brisk efficiency is of the essence.   "You learn what's essential to a scene, how to get
it quickly shot.   Roger came down to Arkansas, marched
onto the set, made an angry face, stirred up the crew and
got them to work a little harder.   Granted, you have to play
within the limits of whatever the game is ... every fifteen
pages, I had to have a flash of nudity or some sort of nudity
because that was the year for it.   You had to do it.   Violence here and there, a car chase, etc.   But we shot the
film in 24 days for $650,000, and it made a profit.   I got
$5,000."   Scorsese got much more in filmmaking experience.
He received a beneficial opportunity to film on location, and
he learned how to work expeditiously on a conventional genre
picture scripted by a writer other than himself.   Significantly,
it gave the director the chance to practice the pyrotechnics
of cinematic "bloodletting."   He got plenty of practice indeed.
The movie is a virtual showcase of the "I'll blow you away"
variety of gun play.

BOXCAR BERTHA is a violent exploitation film set
in the languorous Depression South.   The screenplay was
adapted by Joyce and John William Corrington from the autobiography of "Boxcar" Bertha Thompson.   The plot revolves

around Bill Shelley, a labor radical, a "Joe Hill" type of
character, played with poker-faced stoicism by David Carradine. He teams up with Bertha (Barbara Hershey), a newly-
orphaned, doe-eyed gamine, and together with a powerfully-
built, black "faithful" (Bernie Casey) and a ne'er-do-well,
itinerant Yankee gambler (Barry Primus), they unite to bring
the "bad guy" railroad boss to his villainous knees. The
movie chronicles the rock 'em, shoot 'em up exploits of this
rag-tag little crew of robbin' hoods as they steal from the
railroad to give to the union. When the union rejects the
group's ill-gotten "contributions," they embark on a life of
mindless mayhem, ostensibly for the hell of it. Eventually,
the gang's motives prove too indefensible, as their actions
become little more than identifiable with those of mechanical
wind-up dolls. (Scorsese admits he fumbled the plot-line,
and acknowledges, "there's a point in the film where you lose
track of the characters' motivations.")

The group's reign of terror is treated as a perfunctory
matter--a couple of murders is all in a day's work. Rather,
we are asked to regard empathetically the whimsical abandon
with which the four take to a life of spirited anarchy. This
proves increasingly difficult to do as their trail of crime becomes progressively cluttered with corpses. The runaway
ride of these guileless "merry men" comes to a grotesque
halt when the railroad's henchmen catch up with them and
nail poor Bill Shelley to the side of a train car. This ludi-
crous attempt to portray the Carradine character as a Christ
figure would be laughable where it not for the grisly depiction
of his crucifixion. This brutally-rendered crucifixion scene
is the final discrediting blow to a movie whose raison d'être
is to frolic in the gory antics of gun play.

Scorsese admits BOXCAR is a formulary exploitation
film that was planned to highlight violence. To be sure, the
movie's story line is an untidy excuse to frame the action-
packed tableaux of this blood and gore extravaganza. A couple
of sensual love scenes are thrown in to avoid, pardon the expression, overkill. While the picture has all sorts of political,
sociological, and religious allusions, their import is obscured
amidst the blood spattering. As one critic put it, "There is
scarcely a moment from the time of the opening air crash
that one form of carnage or another is not occurring; and the
film gyrates with the cadence of a shooting gallery."

The picture did receive some favorable reviews. Los
Angeles Times critic Kevin Thomas stated, "What is most

(impressive about BOXCAR BERTHA is how 28-year-old director Martin Scorsese, in his first Hollywood venture, has managed to shape such familiar material into a viable film.')
Los Angeles Herald Examiner's Bridget Byrne praised the
performances of the actors and credited Scorsese's direction
as tipping "the film out of the conventional exploitation field
of cliché plot and easy violence into a bizarre never-never
land all of its own. A combination of self-mockery and madcap high spirits creates a mood which is chaotic and indeci-
sive but never dull.... Scorsese's casual camera work is
somewhat self-indulgently trippy; but the macabre result is
rather intriguing. Vitality compensates for amateurism." But
ultimately, one would have to agree with the views of Variety,
which declared, "Whatever its intentions, BOXCAR BERTHA
is not much more than an excuse to slaughter a lot of people.... There's hardly a pretense toward justifying the carnage."

The movie is skillfully mounted and leaves no doubt
that Scorsese is a highly competent director who can embel-
lish the "meat and potatoes" fare of a genre stock piece with
his own special touches. The director's bent towards using
an interpretive camera was again in evidence in several sequences. A card game segment is a particular example of
Scorsese's kinetic camera work. Relating the camera set-up,
he explained, "When Barry Primus was trying to pull a fast
one with the cards, you see him smiling sleazily--the camera's
kind of sleazy, sliding against the edge of the table. What I
was looking for was to give a kind of psychologically unstable
feeling to the audience regarding those characters." The
lovely romantic interludes between Carradine and Hershey,
which are well done, are the only "pastoral" sexual love
scenes that appear in any Scorsese film. The Arkansas back-
woods locales are effectively used to evoke the hard-bitten,
demoralizing days of the Depression.

Although BOXCAR's characters are roughly-drawn,
the film offers some fine performances by the Carradines--
fils et père. The elder Carradine delivers a delightfully
campy performance as the wicked railroad boss. Bernie
Casey is a powerful on-screen presence who invests his character with a quiet dignity that is moving. Barry Primus is
amusing as a cowardly Yankee gambler, out of his depths in
the rural, redneck South. (Scorsese claims identification with
the Primus character, "who is very much like me stuck in
the milieu of Arkansas ... I didn't know what to do, the cows,
the guns--I felt out of place!")

BOXCAR BERTHA seems to deviate from the thematic
and environmental elements normally associated with Scorsese.
He is insistent, however, that the picture reflects some of
his personal views. "Otherwise," he staunchly maintains, "I
couldn't have made the film. The conception of this film has
a lot to do with movies. It was my impression of the films
of the 'thirties ... that's why the whole opening is in black
and white. You see people's faces come out and their names
are under them like in 'thirties movies. I love the genre,
and I felt I was really making a film about films. I found
the union element particularly fascinating. Mostly, I attempted
to show the characters as people acting like children, playing
with violence until they start getting killed--then they're stuck
in a real game, a life and death game. I used the element
of surprise violence to emphasize that. When you least expect it, things are destroyed, people are killed--that's very
important to the picture."

Scorsese was scheduled to do one more picture for
Roger Corman, I ESCAPED FROM DEVIL'S ISLAND, which
was to be shot in Costa Rica. However, he never worked
on the film. After a screening of a rough cut of BOXCAR
BERTHA, John Cassavetes took the director aside, and attempted to dissuade him from making exploitation films. He
was a great fan of WHO'S THAT KNOCKING...? and felt it
held great promise as a laudable example of personal filmmaking. Scorsese, thereafter, decided to take up a script
he and screenwriter Mardik Martin had written in 1966. After
numerous rejections, they had shelved the piece, initially entitled SEASON OF THE WITCH. In 1972, Scorsese began re-
writing the script which would be the basis for MEAN STREETS.

In the period of 1972-1973 Scorsese worked as a film
editor while he re-wrote the screenplay for MEAN STREETS.
He was involved with editing a movie on roller derbies called
THE UNHOLY ROLLERS (American International, 1972), produced by Roger Corman. The picture was directed by Vernon
Zimmerman, an old Scorsese acquaintance, who had also been
a winner of the Prix de l'Age d'Or some years ago. According to Scorsese, the film was highly underrated and hardly
seen by anyone. The director also worked as one of two editors on the documentary, ELVIS ON TOUR. He recalls that
it was a most difficult time. "I was about to cast MEAN
STREETS and the people affiliated with ELVIS ON TOUR were
under pressure. They wanted me to do more than I could.
It was while working on that project that I realized that I
couldn't do films for other people anymore."

III

χ MEAN STREETS is the most personal work of all of Scorsese's films. It was the picture he had to make. The director readily admits that the movie is semi-autobiographical in nature .. χ its making represented a purging of his ambivalent feelings towards the cultural "ghetto" of his unbringing. He expressly likens the work to an allegory of his experiences "trying to make movies, trying to achieve success...." All that Scorsese couldn't fit into WHO'S THAT KNOCKING...? "spilled over into MEAN STREETS." The screenplay for the film, which he had started in 1966, was shelved until the director completed BOXCAR BERTHA. A former film professor advised Scorsese to forget the screenplay because, in his words, "Nobody wants to see films about Italian-Americans." (It was the year just before The Godfather [Putnam's, 1969] was published.) After resolving to work solely on his own projects, he began to restructure the screenplay, drawing from neighborhood incidents and characters he had known as a youth.

Plans for the picture really got off the ground when Scorsese met Jonathan Taplin, the 26-year-old road manager for The Band and pop idol, Bob Dylan. Taplin was interested in financing a film. His favorable impression of the director's earlier work and the MEAN STREETS screenplay led to an agreement whereby he raised the initial $300,000 for production of the film and became its producer. The remaining $200,000 in production costs were obtained through deferment. (According to Scorsese, the Canadian Film Institute gave his script a high rating, and therefore provided the director with complete use of its facilities--screening, processing, developing, and answer print. Payment was to be forthcoming a year after the film was completed.)

The movie's extremely limited budget required that it be produced expeditiously within a compressed shooting schedule. Scorsese's experience working with the highly efficient production crew on BOXCAR BERTHA proved fortunate. Their established ability to minimize production costs and their capacity for "fast-forward" work made MEAN STREETS possible. To facilitate speedy production, Scorsese was advised that most of the film would have to be shot in Los Angeles. At first, the possibility of shooting a movie so totally germane to the New York experience in a city as different as Los Angeles seemed absolutely inconceivable. But convinced that it was his only viable option, the director shot background foot-

age and exteriors for a short period in New York. The
movie, in his words, was filmed like a jigsaw puzzle. In a
1975 interview with the Fellows of the American Film Institute, Scorsese described a bit of the cinematic synthesis by
which Los Angeles and New York sites were melded to evoke
the ambience of the latter.

"I shot the car crash in downtown L. A. at night. All
the other exteriors are New York. Even the beach in New
York, because the water looks different at Staten Island than
it does out here. . . .   All the interiors are L. A. , except the
hallways. The hallway stuff is very important because we
couldn't find a hallway to double. We shot these literally
where the film actually takes place. In fact, we were working
out of the woman's house who was the mother of the boy Robert De Niro was portraying. But we only shot six days in
New York. We kept stretching it to get more the New York
feeling. The best I could do was put the people in the middle
of the buildings and let the buildings do all the talking.

"When De Niro is shooting his gun off the roof, the
roof is New York because you see the Empire State Building,
but the window is Los Angeles. When David Carradine gets
shot in the bar, the guy falling in the street is actually in
New York; that was a double--we shot that first. We blocked
out his face just right so that he falls and hits the car. The
rest of the scene was shot in Los Angeles. At one point,
Jon Voight was going to be in the picture. The night in New
York that we discovered he wasn't going to be in it, I went
right back to Harvey Keitel, and he did it that day. The
[footage] you see of Harvey walking through the feast was
done right at the spur of the moment, when I said that he
was going to be the lead. I got him a coat at Barney's and
we went. That was the way it was."

Scorsese calls MEAN STREETS "a very sloppy film,"
even though every frame was carefully planned on a storyboard. But to adhere to its fast-paced shooting schedule,
there was not time to look at rushes. Often, Scorsese could
only nominally supervise the shooting of a scene, relying on
his second-unit cameramen to follow through on his directions
while he shot another scene at a different location. "Every
picture was on a storyboard so we knew what we were doing
in terms of the camera. I'd lay out all the storyboards and
[the crew] would juggle all the pictures. Scenes were shot
out of sequence. Not only that, but within one scene [we
were] shooting three lines that were in the middle first. It's

Martin Scorsese (center), directing Robert De Niro (left) and
Harvey Keitel in MEAN STREETS (Warner's, 1973).

very hard for the actors, but it worked. It was the only way
we could get the picture done on time."

Besides ten days for rehearsals, the entire movie was
filmed in a remarkable 27 days! Filmed at a breakneck pace,
its hectic shooting regime is reflected in the abruptness and
the frenetic intensity of some of the scenes. Says Scorsese,
"It a miracle the film got made. MEAN STREETS showed
such a frenzied energy level because we were frenzied! You
can imagine how I directed that picture: running around the
set screaming, yelling, pushing. Often, I had to keep the
crews until midnight, and we still didn't have time for such
rudimentaries as establishing shots. When I see the film
today, I think, 'How the hell does an audience know where
these characters are?'"

While MEAN STREETS is, perha
cinematic conventions, its rough-edged
invigorating camera work of Kent Wake
ingly original movie.   The limitations
verged beneficially to foster bold inno
matic focus in making the film.   In
rector's work appearing in the Inter   ter
Peter Cowie commented, "There is,   ce
to MEAN STREETS, a throbbing, pain   s
not only Scorsese's personal tensions but also   es
of filmmaking itself. ... "

Stylistically, the picture combines the naturalistic camera movements of cinéma vérité with the more formalistic
approaches to cinematic storytelling. (The prominent hand-
held camera ambiences enhance the raw-nerved intensity of
the characters' confrontations.) The awkwardly angled vantages
and the unsteadiness of Scorsese's camera techniques serve
to accent the threatening malevolence and the insidious tensions of this stiflingly confined society. A memorable example of the jolting realism compelled by his visual style is
a boisterous drunken party scene held in a bar.   The subjective camera tilts and sways with the intoxicated revellers,
and suddenly reels, disoriented, when the celebration erupts
into a violent fracas.

Characteristically, the director encouraged his actors
to improvise.   The "spontaneity" of their filmed responses
and the hand-held camera visual effects lend a semi-documentary feel to the picture. Of the actors, Scorsese says, "The
principals in the cast are from Manhattan or Brooklyn and
were familiar with the 'neighborhood' environment I was intent
on depicting.   Originally, I had considered using well-known
actors like Voight or Bruce Dern, but decided to go with unknowns."   Many of the exteriors were shot in the very streets
and tenements where the director was raised, and footage of
the traditional San Gennaro festival, in progress at the time
of the film's shooting, is interspersed throughout the movie.
Scorsese also used extras who were members of the community. Their presence, as well as the employment of actual locations, imbues the film with a spirit of authenticity recalling
the very sights and sounds of the Lower East Side ghetto.

A trademark of Scorsese's films--his inspired use of
music--is shown off to stunning effect in MEAN STREETS.
The hard-driving, urgent rock and roll songs of the late 'fifties and 'sixties convey the sensual raucousness of the young

Charlie's affair with Teresa provides yet another example of his unwillingness to commit himself to anyone. Teresa is in love with Charlie and wants him to move with her to an apartment uptown. (She is the one character in the film who wants to escape the narrow mentality of the ghetto.) It is evident that he intends to stay, but he strings her along, remaining noncommital about his decision. He keeps Johnny Boy similarly in tow, proffering his help, but doing nothing more than putting his best face forward.

The unfriendly convergence of time and fate forces Charlie's hand. In the picture's most harrowing sequence, he precipitously takes Teresa and Johnny Boy "out of town." As they drive on the bridge to Brooklyn, it is clear that they are headed for the darkly alien terrain of an implacable destiny. In the best traditions of film noir, the chilling night seems about to engulf them. There is no escape from the wrath of the ghetto--Michael and his hired hit man (played by Scorsese, himself) are following close by. The tension builds to a fevered pitch and explodes in a wrenchingly convulsive segment when the assassin fires, shooting Johnny Boy in the neck and hitting Charlie in the hand. The car careens and hits a hydrant, spouting water everywhere. The three are thrown out into the shudderingly cold, wet shadows of an alley. Johnny is seen crazily running away, like a wounded animal; Charlie, on his knees, holds his wounded hand upward in supplication, an expression of solemn revelation on his face. In the distance, sirens are heard as the film shifts back to Charlie's uncle watching television and returns to the lively celebrants at the festival. It is an ironic evocation of the heritage that has led to Charlie's grim fate.

MEAN STREETS received a full complement of critical acclaim. It was hailed as a cinematic tour de force. Kael pronounced it a "true original of our period, a triumph of personal filmmaking.... It's about American life here and now.... Every character, every sound is rooted in the streets." The picture's gritty, naturalistic rendering of a young Italian-American generation relegated to its criminal legacy was lauded for its unromanticized, honest representation. The film is indeed an unglamorous, scruffy image of small-time hoodlums and their mundane, workaday involvements in petty racketeering. It is a gangster movie worlds away from the mythologized gloss of THE GODFATHER (Paramount, 1972). MEAN STREETS made the critics "Ten Best" list of 1973 films. Robert De Niro's performance as Johnny Boy received superlative praise; he was declared a major acting "find," comparable in stature to the young Marlon Brando

and James Dean.   The National Society of Film Critics and
the New York Film Critics Circle named De Niro their choice
for best supporting actor.   The film's level of acting was
generally cited for its outstanding quality.

        The independently financed picture was distributed by
Warner Bros.   Despite the critical kudos it inspired, the
movie was not very successful at the box office.   A combination of the film's reputation as an "arty," New York-oriented
movie and the distributor's inability to come up with a "saleable" image made it difficult to sell.   The film was poorly
distributed and its exposure to the public was very limited.
Although the disjointed rhythms of the film and the vertiginous
motion of its expressionistic camera work renders it, at
times, difficult to follow, (MEAN STREETS' stunning originality
and its raw-nerved intensity distinguished Scorsese as a director with a uniquely personal vision)   The picture scored as a
dazzling hit at the New York Film Festival.   The director was
greeted as a significant cinematic talent, one of the most
promising filmmakers of his generation.

                              IV

        After receiving widespread critical accolades for the
direction of MEAN STREETS, Martin Scorsese became the
hot new director to watch.   He was inundated with scripts to
consider, but most were disappointingly trivial versions of
gangster-type pictures. The director wanted the challenge of
working on a movie project that varied distinctively from the
films that he was associated with. — In his words, "I wanted
to practice my craft, practice making different types of films
and different ways of working with other types of actors."
For her part, actress Ellen Burstyn was in search of a new
young filmmaker who could demonstrate a novel approach to
a script she was interested in doing.

        The two "found" each other on a tip from Francis Ford
Coppola.   Upon his suggestion, Burstyn screened MEAN
STREETS and loved it.   After her success in THE EXORCIST
(Warner's, 1973), Warner Bros. wanted the actress to star
in a movie property owned by David Susskind.   Part of her
agreement to star in the picture hinged on her right to choose
a director and retain script approval.   Her positive impression of MEAN STREETS compelled her to offer Scorsese the
script idea for ALICE DOESN'T LIVE HERE ANYMORE.   "I
was very impressed with MEAN STREETS," said Burstyn.

"The level of acting was consistently high all the way through, not just the leads. It was a movie with a life and a reality of its own. I thought Scorsese would be perfect for ALICE, which needed to be roughed up. I wanted to make it the story of women today, with our consciousness as it is now, not a Doris Day film."

The director was instinctively attracted to the plight of the characters sketched out in the rough copy of the screenplay. When he met Burstyn, their discussion of the film's premises led to an amicable agreement of how the characters and their situations should be portrayed. Scorsese describes the picture as being about "emotions and feelings and relationships and people in chaos. . . . [It] was something very personal to me and to Ellen at the time. We felt like charting all that . . . and showing people making terrible mistakes, ruining their lives and then realizing it and trying to push back when everything is crumbling--without getting into soap opera. We opened ourselves up to a lot of experimentation."

ALICE DOESN'T LIVE HERE ANYMORE marks Scorsese's entry into the proverbial "big time" of filmmaking. It meant the passage from independently-financed, small-budget movies to studio-sponsored productions, complete with name stars. WHO'S THAT KNOCKING AT MY DOOR? had cost $35,000 to make; ALICE was produced on a budget that exceeded $1.6 million; the spectacular "red opening" sequence that was shot on a Hollywood set cost $85,000 for one day's shooting alone. The larger budget permitted the director the luxury of more rehearsal time in which to experiment with the actors. He was also able to shoot a lot more footage than on any previous film he'd directed. (His original rough cut was three hours and sixteen minutes. It was eventually edited down to its present running time of one hour and 53 minutes.) Scorsese's first big "Hollywood" picture was filmed in eight weeks, almost entirely on location in Tucson.

The film's production crew consisted of many women in key staff positions: Sandra Weintraub was associate producer, Toby Carr Rafelson was named set designer, and Marcia Lucas was assigned as film editor. Ms. Rafelson had previously worked with her husband, the director Bob Rafelson, on FIVE EASY PIECES (Columbia, 1970), and Ms. Lucas joined hers, George Lucas, on the production of AMERICAN GRAFFITI (Universal, 1973). As film editor, Ms. Lucas recut the whole picture under Scorsese's supervision. Of the editing, he says, "In my first experience working with an

editor, I wanted one with whom I could work, because I cut
some of the scenes myself." (He relied on these women and
the members of the cast to help provide insights into the female characters and to verify their reactions.) "There was
a great deal of improvisation, and when a line of response
rang false, these women were free to criticize and suggest
alternatives."

Scorsese felt challenged by the prospect of directing
a movie whose protagonist was a woman. He welcomed the
opportunity to explore the frustrating conflicts he had encountered within his own relationships. "The film dealt with women,
and I wanted to better understand my relationships with women
--the whole male/female thing. I really believed in the story;
I knew what Alice was going through." ALICE centers on a
woman's search for her own identity, apart from the man in
her life. "The women I had been with had made it clear they
wanted recognition for themselves, and not just for their association with me. It was a very personal thing to me to
make a film about such a person." The director was pleased
by the challenge to work with actresses, particularly those
who had been in the business for years. The pleasure he
derived from working with Ellen Burstyn is exemplified in
his comment that "Ellen is the movie. The way Alice reacts
is the way Ellen does. I received a lot of input on the character from her. The film is practically a documentary of
her!"

Known as an actor's director, Scorsese values the
natural dramatic instincts of those performers "who are receptive to structured improvisation--those who are spontaneous
in relationship to their own acting style." He asserts, "I
think 80 per cent of a film's success comes from good actors,
assuming your script is good. And I've been lucky. Mine
have been good and intelligent." (His heavy reliance on actors' feedback in creating a role has led to his penchant for
working with many of the same people in his films.) What
amounts to a Scorsese repertory company includes performers like Robert De Niro (some regard him as the director's
alter ego), Harvey Keitel, Jodie Foster, Barry Primus, and
numerous character actors appearing variously in most of his
movies. Speaking of the director's relationship with his actors, Keitel says, "Marty lets actors bring their own human-
ity--their eccentricities, their humor, their compassion--to
a role. You know you have freedom, and you know something
always pops up."

Scorsese is always ready to include "whatever pops up" and integrate it into the action of the film. His distinct predilection for improvised acting and screenwriting techniques derives from his wish to capture "the flavor of immediacy to changing feelings of the moment." The script for ALICE was left open-ended to accommodate the director's tendency to extemporize. He explains, "I like to meander, as they say, within a structure. It's very often thrown at me as a criticism, but to me, it means character. For me, it means atmosphere." Robert Getchell's screenplay was shaped to incorporate the dialogue improvised by the actors. Their improvisations were often videotaped during the two-week rehearsal period and throughout the shooting of the film. The tapes were given to the screenwriter to re-work into new dialogue for inclusion in the script. According to Scorsese, for him, the very essence of the filmmaking experience is getting a good "script, the casting, and achieving a give-and-take relationship with the actors."

Whereas directing MEAN STREETS involved the native terrain of his own background, working on ALICE meant dealing with relatively new territory. While the director drew often on the collaborative efforts of the cast and screenwriter, Getchell, to "make a picture that was as true to women as possible," he nonetheless set the tone of the work and retained control of its flow and direction. ALICE has the unmistakable markings of a Martin Scorsese film: the exuberant use of an ambulatory camera, filmed action inspired by the impulse of the moment, a jarring, unconventional utilization of music, honest observations of the idiosyncrasies of human behavior, and the naturalistic portrayal of violent action.

Thematically, the picture is an extension of the concerns of his former films. Once again, his protagonist is trying to do "the right thing," find "the right way" to self-fulfillment within the constraints of her responsibilities to others. Characteristically, it is the action of Fate that is the impetus for change in her life. In a Film Heritage interview with writer F. Anthony Macklin, Scorsese commented on the effect of Fate on Alice's life. "I understand a person being trapped; I understand a person being taken away from the trap, not of her own accord, but by God's will. The finger of God comes down, the truck crashes (her husband is killed in the accident). Because if she left her husband, it would be a different story, and then I really wouldn't be interested in it. It would have to be a person thrown out on

her own, out into the wilds, and that's the kind of thing that
interested me about the whole piece. "

Scorsese, the film buff as director, loves to include
tributes to Hollywood movie conventions in many of his films.
ALICE DOESN'T LIVE HERE ANYMORE opens with a stunningly crafted, sepiadrenched prologue, inspired, he says,
"by movies like THE WIZARD OF OZ [M-G-M, 1939], DUEL
IN THE SUN [Selznick, 1946], EAST OF EDEN [Warner's,
1955], and GONE WITH THE WIND [M-G-M, 1939]." The
segment pays homage to William Cameron Menzies. "He was
always the magic of movies," Scorsese declares. The scene
shows a misty, red-hued studio sunset going down over a Wizard of Oz-like Kansas farmhouse. The dreamy, flamboyant
sequence represents Alice's idealized vision of herself as a
child in Monterey, wistfully hoping to become a singing star
like Alice Faye (who is heard singing "You'll Never Know"
on the soundtrack accompanying the prologue). Since her idol
exists in the world of movies, Alice relates her own goals
within the fantasy imagery of Hollywood. The director felt
the motif for the prologue was an interesting way to evoke a
flashback that reflects the illusory nature of Alice's impossible
dream of becoming a singer. The film follows her adventures
on the road to the "promised land" of Monterey, illustrating
throughout the ironic disparity between her whimsical conceptions of the ideal and the rougher, intractable reality of her
situation.

ALICE, like Scorsese's other movies, is a contemplation of an individual's struggles within the confining grip of
inhibiting relationships. The film delivers stirring portrayals
of the emotional half-life of people in oppressive marital situations. Alice is initially viewed as a woman who has totally
submerged her own identity within the ministering roles of
housewife and mother. The shaky, sharply-angled camera
perspectives infuse the "family scenes" in the Hyatt household with a pervading tone of disquieting uneasiness. Alice
is the very model of the timorous, middle-American, middle-
class housewife whose standard offerings of homey pies and
favorite foods do very little to improve her husband's generally sullen humor. In a notable sequence which characterizes
the estrangement between Alice and her husband, the restless
quiet of a family dinner is disrupted by a mischievous prank
played on them by their rascally son (Alfred Lutter). The
undercurrent of tension erupts as the husband's ire zeroes
in on Alice, and the obtusely angled camera vantage emphasizes her obsequious, cowering stance before what is made

to be seen as his towering presence. The director presents
a totally unsentimental view of family life--hollow domestic
rituals and actions have replaced the genuine human interactions of people who cannot relate to each other even though
they are related.

     ALICE DOESN'T LIVE HERE ANYMORE is a bitter-
sweet comedy-drama about different relationships: Alice's
frustrating marriage to her irascible husband, the rambunc-
tious contention with her smartalecky son, the binding, tender
trust she shares with her best friend, Bea (Lelia Goldoni),
her affair with a young, teasing, bulpine stud (Harvey Keitel),
and the volatile courtship between Alice and the "rancher-
prince" (Kris Kristofferson) she falls in love with. The free-
wheeling, sometimes disjointed motion of the movie seems
propelled by the very mercurial dynamics of relationships
themselves. The film's thin story-line is a fixed point from
which Scorsese diverges in his amoeba-like digressions, playing cinematic variations on a paltry theme. Reflecting the
quick-silver currents of human interactions, his camera stops
in a capricious aside to ponder a sudden moment's fury, and
lurches impetuously to mirror the abruptness of the characters' shifting moods. The shape of the movie is that of a
pastiche of brief character sketches--quick, pungent glimpses
of the idiosyncrasies of people in their relations with each
other. These incisive moments of character revelation are
like a bright filagree which frames and illuminates the different facets of Alice's personality. The director's "meandering," openended film techniques give ALICE its distinctive look.
Describing his style, one critic observed, "Scorsese makes a
virtue of ... quickness, short cuts, fast fades, deliberate in-
consistencies--the hell with linearity...." The result is a
collage-like portrait of a woman who is determined to "find"
herself. The dimensions of her character are set forth in
discursive cinematic passages that reveal more often by al-
lusion than by action or narrative.

     As Alice sets out on her journey to self-realization,
Scorsese's itinerant camera seeks her out, charting the diverse turns and detours her odyssey takes. "Right away I
felt we should keep the camera moving because the picture
was on the move," he states. "I was trying to capture a
number of characters (particularly Alice) who were really
very much in a state of confusion and never really settled.
So the camera is always kind of shifting around, moving
around, slightly sliding. When it does stop, they are usually
in scenes of stability." Almost from the beginning, the film's

camera work visually communicates a sense of gentle upheaval
and restive motion.

In one of the movie's most novel visual expositions,
the physical point of view shifts from the Technicolor vignette
of Alice as a child to a tracking shot along a street in So-
corro, New Mexico. The camera seems to be flying along
the road looking for the grownup Alice, moving towards her
modest tract house and espying her through an open window.
The crashing strains of the hard rock sound of Mott the Hoople
are heard over the tracking shot and serve to build a tension
that characterizes the discordant ambience of the Hyatt household. The young Alice's spunky resolve to become a singer
has been pre-empted by an early marriage in which she is
seen reduced to the position of unhappy referee between her
irritable husband and their infuriatingly precocious son. Her
marriage provides her with little more than physical security,
but it is clear that Alice accepts her frustrating marital life
as one that is almost ordained; she would have never abandoned
her home to seek a more fulfilling existence had her husband
not been killed.

Left suddenly widowed, Alice rediscovers the dream of
her youth. She has never really worked at a job except for
a brief stint as a cafe singer in Monterey before her marriage.
In one lyrical scene that perfectly evokes Alice's uneasy excitement at the prospect of rekindling her fledgling "career,"
she is seen sitting at her piano practicing her repertoire.
Dressed in a gay pink gress, as the sun pours in on her, she
softly sings the Rogers and Hart song, "Where or When," the
wistful ballad about déjà vu which beautifully conveys the
dreamy spirit of her mood. The camera pans 360 degrees
around Alice as she sings, and the action transmits the whirling elation of an individual inspired by her fantasy. But just
when we're ready to slip into the warm syrupy complacence
of Hollywood wish-fulfillment, Scorsese, characteristically,
puts the situation in its proper, unsentimental perspective:
Alice, whose voice is thin and pretty shaky, gets up from the
piano and ironically snorts, "Well, it ain't Peggy Lee!"
Alice's self-deprecating wit, her resilient stamina and her
honest self awareness are revealed as the admirable qualities
that will really get her by. It is evident that Alice has very
little chance of becoming a singer of professional calibre, but
the director benignly regards the value of her ideal as the
very necessary inspiration that will orient the direction of
her newfound path.

Myths and dreams are amusingly, but compassionately, punctured in the film. The optimistic expectations for her future are almost immediately undercut by the tedium and frustrations of the car trip. Tommy is constantly on the verge of car-sickness, and his bratty impatience and peevish whining turns Alice's "rites of passage" into a maddening trial. The characterization of Tommy is reminiscent of the manic recalcitrance of Johnny Boy in MEAN STREETS; the perverse zeal with which he recounts the same joke over and over again practically drives Alice to distraction. Alfred Lutter's superb comic timing and his unstudied performance create a role that has an uncanny naturalness. The story about the great gray gorilla which he repeats in the car was a joke which he knew and he actually plagued the director with his innumerable re-tellings. At times, the mother/son routines in the car are almost too vaudevillian and seem a little forced. But the relationship between Tommy and Alice is a strangely unconventional one, with the precocious young son at times acceding to a position of dominance with regard to his mother. Despite his childishness, Tommy already has the natural authority of a male and his irreverent attitude towards Alice emulates the relationship he has witnessed between his mother and father   Theirs, the core relationship of the film, is seen to undergo the changes wrought by the fluctuating tides of their life on the road.

As Alice faces the responsibilities of fending for herself and her son for the first time in her life, it is clear that she relies on Tommy's dependence and support to embolden her. She is thrust into the relatively inhospitable circumstances of finding work along the way in order to raise funds for the trip to Monterey. In a stylistic play of light and shadow, Alice makes her way in and out of the glare of the Tucson sun and into the cool, shadowy darkness of the bars where she auditions as a singer. Scorsese, who had demonstrated a mastery in depicting the spiritual claustrophobia of urban settings, does equally well at portraying the harsh confining spaces of the sun-baked, small-town desert locales of Arizona and the stupefying monotony of highway travel. These stark, insipid vistas of "blue collar" life in the Southwest project a well observed spirit of listless provincialism characteristic of the area. The lovely audition sequence again attests to the director's instinctive capacity for communicating ineffable emotional experiences in purely visual terms.

Discussing the reasoning behind the 360-degree panning

of Alice at the piano, with writer Steve Howard in a Filmmakers Newsletter interview, Scorsese detailed his conceptions for the camera movements: "At first in the audition,
the camera moves toward her and down and then comes up
from behind and goes in towards her. I felt the constant
circular movement should be a feeling of whirling as the camera began to move around her, because by the end of the audition, she has gotten a little more confidence and she's flow-
ing and going with it ... so everything is into her and not
away from her and we are drawn to her. She's in her own
world, and all the camera sees is her, until it almost becomes like her mind."

     As she confronts the harsh realities of making a living,
Alice is plunged into a new working-class world of cheap motel rooms, dreary bars, and the hot, stifling chaos of Mel's
diner, where she works as a waitress. As a single woman,
removed from the relative security of her home, Alice's loneliness and work as a "cocktail lounge" singer leaves her vulnerable to the advances of a young stud whose boyish charm
hides his mentally unbalanced temperament. Her affair with
Ben leads to the movie's most violent scene, a Scorsese signature piece which again shows off his talent for filming action sequences. The director's utilization of hand-held camera
techniques augments the frightening actuality of the melee as
Ben breaks into the tiny motel room and, in a fit of blind
rage, brutishly descends on his waifish, pregnant wife (Lane
Bradbury) who has gone to plead with Alice to leave her husband alone. He kicks her out and threatens the terrified
Alice with similar violence if she doesn't "behave." Harvey
Keitel's performance as the dangerously disturbed lover is
alarmingly realistic. To effect an unconsciously apprehensive
feeling on the part of the audience, Scorsese had the hand-
held camera move all in one take, panning over everything:
"It gave a very uneasy, almost documentary, effect and it
was done in order to create tension."

     The film veers from its often naturalistic renderings
to a bit of Hollywood mythic gloss when Alice chances upon
the handsome, rancher/fairy-tale prince who can take her
away from the drudgery of the demeaning jobs she has had to
take. Kris Kristofferson's natural easy-going charm makes
David the kind of man who would melt the steelly conviction
of any ardent feminist. However, Kristofferson's character
seems a bit too movie-ideal to be real. Warm and supportive
of Alice's ambiguous goals for self-realization, he's willing
to give up his own ranch and lifestyle to follow her to Mon-

terey. Although Alice has resolved to shape an independent
existence, whereby she would never again "live through another
man," her love for David forces her to admit to herself, "I
don't know how to live without a man." In a sense her odyssey has brought her to this essential bit of self-understanding
--her need for the love of a man. Scorsese admits, "I can't
live without a woman ... we all need other people."

   While all of his films deal with the inherent conflicts
and turmoil of relationships, the writer Diane Jacobs observes,
"Scorsese's characters are uneasy within relationships, but
hopeless without them. His characters need each other on
very basic and profound levels.... [He] is mostly concerned
with the struggle for freedom within the relationships, and not
at their expense." The director permitted himself to express
an optimism in ALICE which he rarely exhibits in any of his
other movies. "I wanted the film to end happily--I guess for
my own good because I hope that people could get together
sometimes.... Once Alice begins to understand a little more
about herself as a person, she may have a chance at having
a better relationship with a man." But, characteristically,
Scorsese is committed to as honest a reflection of life as
possible--rather than a "they lived happily ever after ending"
with the lovers going towards the sunset, the movie closes
with Alice walking down some unknown street, arm-in-arm
with her son, Tommy. Their relationship is the most important one in the picture. This last scene, shot with a long
lens, gives the movie a tentative feeling. Says the director,
"The walk represents their future. I wanted it to look dif-
fuse, disjointed, uncertain."

   While ALICE sparkles with a surging vitality born of
its eager inventiveness and cinematic experimentation, the
overall emotional impact of the film is somewhat weakened
by its inconsistencies of style and tone. The incompatibility
of Scorsese's semi-documentary style and his fanciful semi-
parodies of old-movie conventions particularly muddles the
intelligibility of Alice and David's relationship. The portrayal
of the interactions between the two progresses unevenly from
the joltingly realistic rendering of their break-up argument at
the ranch to the romanticized version of their reconciliation.
Alice and David reunite in the midst of the crowded, noontime
hubbub of Mel's diner; the scene where they kiss and embrace
as the restaurant's patrons cheer and applaud them is something straight out of the romance comedies of the 'thirties.
In this case, the juxtaposition of such disparate stylistic perspectives clouds the import and significance of the events. It

further conveys an uncertain tone that might well reflect the director's own perplexed feelings towards Alice's plight and his confusions with respect to male/female relationships. The film critic Myron Meisel opined, "One gets the sense that Scorsese's feelings are too complex for his ideas."

Certainly the development of Alice and David's relationship is treated in overly broad terms; it is presented in a slick, cursory way which highlights the director's stylistic flourishes while fudging over the substantive heart of the matter--the problems and conflicts inherent in their coupling. The exposition of the central theme of the film--Alice's quest for self-realization--is sometimes obfuscated amid the razzle-dazzle of Scorsese's bravura digressions. The conflict which arises out of her dependence on the love of a man, at the same time that she craves the independence of her own career, is not clearly explored. To those critics who claim that the picture's "feministic" premise is contradicted by its ending (they regard the film as an old-fashioned romance that is up-dated with modern idioms, since Alice, as in old movie plots, is precipitously dumped off into a relationship, as if that were the only natural thing for her to do), Scorsese responds, "I wanted to make a picture about a person who is a woman and not the other way around. Sure it's about a woman learning about herself--which is why it's been associated with woman's lib. But it's about people first and women second; it's not meant to be rhetoric or polemic. This film deals on a basic human level."

ALICE DOESN'T LIVE HERE ANYMORE is Scorsese's pastoral film, a movie that succeeds as a commercial entertainment vehicle while retaining a major degree of artistic integrity. A vivid cinematic picaresque, it offers several rousing vignettes of Alice and the "colorful" people whom she meets on her journey. Although uneven at times, it is a film of memorably privileged moments: the parting between Alice and her best friend, Bea, touchingly enacted by Lelia Goldoni; a confused Alice confiding to the foul-mouthed, randy waitress, Flo, cramped in the tiny outdoor bathroom adjoining Mel's diner--Diane Ladd gives a delightful performance as the cursing, salt-of-the-earth Flo whose folksy wisdom and lusty wit provide the film with some of its most uproarious segments-- while the spacedout Olive Oyl-looking waitress, Vera (Valerie Curtin), is left alone amidst the hilarious tumult of the diner's lunchtime trade and is practically lynched by the irate customers whose orders she constantly mixes up; Tommy and the low-voiced Audrey (Jodie Foster) getting drunk on cheap wine

while she talks about her "weird" mother who turns tricks
for a living.

ALICE is finally a buoyant comedy which, despite its
Hollywood "sheen," displays the special attention to detail that
characterizes Scorsese's "small" pictures. The movie received
generally favorable reviews that unanimously praised the superb level of acting of the movie's performers. Ellen Burstyn's spirited, multi-dimensional characterization of the good-
humored, resilient Alice was roundly lauded and she won the
Academy Award for Best Actress of the year for her performance in the film. ALICE was the "sleeper" movie of 1974,
drawing large audiences and racking up solid totals at the box
office. The picture was a landmark film of sorts, initiating
a revival of interest in "women's pictures" as a bankable commodity for the film industry. Its financial success established
Scorsese as a director whose talents could be applied to commercial ventures. As a result, his star rose in the Hollywood firmament, which can always be counted on to take the
latest winners of the risky movie stakes to its bosom.

In the midst of shooting ALICE DOESN'T LIVE HERE
ANYMORE Scorsese was asked to do a short on the subject
of Italian immigrants and their lives in this country. It was
to be one of a series of documentaries, produced under the
auspices of the National Endowment for the Humanities, focusing on the different ethnic groups that emigrated to the United
States and their contributions to our culture. The television
series honoring the bicentennial was called The Storm of
Strangers.

At first the director did not believe he could fit the
project into his busy schedule, but his interest in making the
short prevailed. He called in some of the crew members who
had worked on MEAN STREETS to help film the informal interviews with his parents in their New York apartment. He
asked screenwriter Mardik Martin to write and organize the
scripting of the questions that were to be asked. The short
documentary took six hours to shoot and has a running time
of 48 minutes. The resulting film, ITALIANAMERICAN, is
an effectionate look at Italian-American culture, featuring the
director's parents, Charles and Catherine Scorsese. ITAL-
IANAMERICAN is a straightforward, casual documentary that
has the intimacy of a gathering of family members at the
dinner table rehashing the proud stories of their heritage. It
affectingly captures the unpretentious, engaging spontaneity of
his parents as they relate the often humorous tales of their

struggles in the poor Italian ghettos of New York. The short
was well received and in 1974 won a New York Film Festival
award. Scorsese is proud of ITALIANAMERICAN, a film
which turned out to be a labor of love. Of the movies he
has made, it remains one of his personal favorites.

V

        No one was quite prepared for the tumultuous reception
that greeted the 1976 premier of TAXI DRIVER. The film
garnered widespread critical acclaim, although many critics
withheld their total "endorsement" because of its graphic depiction of a bloody shootout. Perhaps one of the most controversial pictures of the 'seventies, TAXI aroused a furor
of debate, polarizing critics and audiences alike into differing
camps: those who regarded it as a formidable artistic work
of integrity, and those who viewed it as a gross exploitation
film which glorified violence. Of course, the controversy
which swirled around the movie fanned public curiosity and
attracted large audiences. It was generally agreed, however,
that the film had a deeply provocative and disturbing effect on
almost everyone who saw it. Speaking of its devastating impact, one critic put it rather succinctly when he said, "Viewing TAXI DRIVER is like being on the receiving end of a
giant mugging...."

        There is no doubt that the cinematic portrayal of a
psychotic ex-Marine who attempts to assassinate a political
candidate struck a deep nerve. An America which had been
so roughly jolted out of its political innocence by the horrific
succession of assassinations in the 'sixties flinched in guilt and
resentment at the depiction of its violence-prone culture in
TAXI DRIVER. The harrowing account of the psychological
deterioration of a lonely "outsider," ignored in a brutishly
indifferent society, was yet another uncomfortable reminder
of the receding humanity of our troubled times. While some
in the audience were indignant at having to experience the
nightmarish existence of a psychopathic killer, others were
keenly moved by the humanistic rendering of TAXI's troubled
protagonist. More than a delineation of the sociological etio-
logy of an assassin, the film peers directly at the darker
corners of human nature and suggests that the urge towards
violence may be an increasingly natural response in a moral
universe divested of human values. Such revelations angered
and troubled many people viewing the film. But as media
proliferation of stories on crime and mayhem attests, we are

Martin Scorsese's cameo appearance in TAXI DRIVER (Columbia, 1976) with Robert De Niro. Photo courtesy of Columbia Pictures.

alternately terrified, repelled, and absolutely fascinated by the violent calamities that abound in our society. At the bidding of deep-seated urges, we are all drawn to the tales of human tragedy. As TAXI proved, while many were deeply discomfited by it, and some infuriated by the graphic depiction of bloody shootouts, few among us could avert our eyes.

Martin Scorsese found himself quickly in the center of the growing controversy surrounding the movie. Word spread rapidly that TAXI was the hottest movie in town. The film and its director became the focal point of widespread media coverage; major metropolitan newspapers like the New York Times ran important feature articles on Scorsese. He was sought by the TV talk-shows to appear as a guest. Columbia Pictures, the movie's distributor, ran full-page ads everywhere reprinting Pauline Kael's entire glowing review of the film. Similar distributors' ploys utilizing Kael's accolades in advertisements on behalf of Bernardo Bertolucci's LAST TANGO IN PARIS (United Artists, 1972) and Robert Altman's NASHVILLE (Paramount, 1975) helped boost their popularity

and their revenues. All the media hoopla attracted movie-
goers and TAXI broke movie theatres' house records during
the first day of its showing. It was a glorious validation for
the makers of a movie the so-called Hollywood "pros" pre-
dicted would be a definite loser.

    After the success of ALICE DOESN'T LIVE HERE
ANYMORE, Scorsese achieved recognition as a director who
could score well at the box office. He could easily have
maintained this positive momentum by choosing film properties conceived for popular consumption. But as is his wont,
he sought work on those movie projects that provoked his
personal interest. "Success is mainly a matter of chance,"
he states. "To play it safe, you can take less risks. If I
played it safe, it wouldn't be hard at all to stay on top. All
I'd have to do would be to direct the best properties of the
year. But that's wrong for me. You should make the pictures you want to make, and also those that you will learn
from. "

    Screenwriter Paul Schrader had a difficult time getting
anyone interested in his script about a schizophrenic cabbie
whose psychological deterioration leads to his assassination
attempt on the life of a political candidate. Director Brian
De Palma read the script and suggested the screenwriter show
it to producer Michael Phillips. Phillips and his partners,
wife Julia Phillips and actor-turned-producer Tony Bill, were
at once interested in the property. They promptly optioned
it for their production company in 1972. But production on
TAXI would be delayed. Bill/Phillips Productions were already committed to producing two other projects--STEELYARD
BLUES (Warner's, 1973) and the picture that would turn out
to be the hugely successful, Academy Award-winning movie,
THE STING (Universal, 1973). In the intervening time, they
chose Scorsese to direct the picture, convinced, after screening MEAN STREETS, that he was the perfect choice for the
film.

    Few pictures could have been more ideally suited to
Scorsese's artistic sensibilities than TAXI DRIVER. He intuitively identified with the despair and isolation of a strange,
bewildered misfit lost in the maddening shuffle of an indifferent
city. Schrader's modern-day horror story of human alienation
could readily be translated by the director whose own bleak
vision of life and brooding temperament were well known
through his work. Scorsese, whom one critic dubbed "the
virtuoso of urban Angst," had revealed in MEAN STREETS

that he could portray the sinister soul of New York. He was
familiar with the sordid recesses of the city where daily
scenes of human degradation are played out. Scorsese was
eager to work on a picture that dealt with the feverish fantasy
world of a psychopathic cab driver who resorts to acts of violence to escape the desperate anonymity of his existence.

Explaining his interest in the film's subject matter,
he insisted, "I knew TAXI DRIVER was going to be a kind
of exorcism for me. I had to make that movie. I emphasize
'had to.' Not so much because of the social statement it
makes, but because of its feeling about things, including
things I don't like to admit about myself. (I'm not into vid-
eotaping my life, but in a way I am trying to put certain
things about myself on canvas." His instinctive compassion
for TAXI's hapless protagonist, Travis Bickle, determined
his wish to direct the film. "I know this guy Travis," he
says. "I've had the feelings he has, and those feelings have
to be explored, taken out and examined. I knew the feeling
of rejection that Travis feels, of not being able to make relationships survive. He wants to be recognized for something,
but he has nothing tangible to be recognized for, except himself. Nobody pays any attention to him; he's got something to
say, something to do, but he doesn't know what it is. I know
what it can feel like to be angry like that." He adds, "You
can't keep making pictures like ALICE, which was really an
experiment for me, without making pictures like TAXI which
are directly connected to things inside your head."

Despite warnings from industry "mavens" that a depressing movie about an insane killer would do poorly at the
box office, Scorsese, De Niro (he was signed to play the role
of Travis Bickle), and the producers felt deeply committed to
making the movie. Said producer Phillips, "It was an unusual
picture because everyone involved with it was motivated by
wanting to make a good film, rather than motivated by personal career considerations." Remarking on the controversial
nature of the film, Julia Phillips discussed the producers' interest in the difficult screenplay: "We all know about these
events ... about Charles Whitman who killed 15 people [from
a Texas university campus tower], Lee Harvey Oswald, Sirhan
Sirhan, and Arthur Bremer [the film is purported to have
been influenced by the diary of Bremer, the man who shot
presidential candidate George Wallace]. The senseless violence. And everyone asks, 'Why does it happen?' This film
explains why. (It explores the dark side of all of us.') Everyone connected with the picture felt so strongly about the im-

portance of doing the movie that they were willing to produce
it at a commercial sacrifice. Said Schrader, "We all wanted
to do it, and were willing to do it for nothing if we had to.
As a matter of fact, we did do it for virtually nothing."

Scorsese acknowledged, "TAXI DRIVER was probably
one of the biggest risks I'd ever undertaken. It was a question of its commerciality. If this picture didn't do well, there
are always ways it could hurt you. (It doesn't mean I wouldn't
get to do other films, but it could mean I'd experience more
problems with freedom.) The film was made to get certain
things off our chests. 'We all did it for certain prices to
keep the budget as low as possible, so we all knew what we
were getting into. We were quite honest about making it for
our own reasons, but, still, it was a big risk for me." He
later confessed his total astonishment at the film's resounding
popularity and financial success.

There were difficulties with getting the film made from
the very start. It was hard to "sell" the picture. Besides
the controversial nature of the material, neither Scorsese,
De Niro, nor Schrader was well known enough at the time to
be considered "bankable." They received an offer of $500,000
to do the picture for Warner Bros. Although they were intent
on keeping the budget low, the producers knew the movie
could not be made with so little money. Columbia, and its
president, David Begelman (the studio had rejected it several
times), eventually decided to finance the risky property. The
film came in on a slim budget of less than $2 million.

TAXI DRIVER was scheduled to go into production in
the summer of 1973. But filming was postponed because
many of the principals were working on other projects. It
was not until June of 1975 that production on the film commenced. The delays proved beneficial in the long run. In
the intervening time, the producers had scored impressively
with THE STING, De Niro had been hailed as the most impressive American actor since Marlon Brando for his performance in GODFATHER II (Paramount, 1975) (he won the
Academy Award for Best Supporting Actor for his role in the
picture), and Scorsese had triumphed soundly with ALICE.
"The studio wound up raising the budget in accordance with
everybody's rise in stature, and what they believed to be the
viability of the film, but it was still a low budget movie,"
noted Phillips. One thing was certain: Scorsese's, De Niro's,
and the producers' dedication to the film definitely vitalized
its prospects.

Besides its director, TAXI's major shaping force was its screenwriter, Paul Schrader. He had a direct hand in the casting and the selection of Scorsese to be its director. TAXI DRIVER is semi-autobiographical in nature, based on a particularly difficult episode in the writer's own life. Disconsolate during a period when his professional career was going badly, the fledgling screenwriter (he was a former film critic of the L.A. Free Press) suffered a severe bout of deep depression. He had very little money, his marriage had broken up, and his personal life was in shambles. Sleeping much of the day, Schrader took to drinking heavily and wandering aimlessly through the sleazier parts of town. Memories of this torturous period of time was the source of his screenplay. Says Schrader, "I was looking for something like the metaphor of the cab driver to express the loneliness and the agony I was feeling. He just came to me. Here's someone who moves through the city in a steel coffin, moving around the city like a rat through the sewers." He wrote the script in 1972. Since then, Schrader has become one of the most sought-after screenwriters in Hollywood. Something of a "Wunderkind," he had written and sold six screenplays by the age of 29. He has gone on to write the scripts for Sydney Pollack's THE YAKUZA (Warner's, 1974), Brian De Palma's OBSESSION (Columbia, 1976), and HARDCORE (Columbia, 1978), the movie he wrote and directed, starring George C. Scott.

Expounding on the concept for the film's protagonist, he adds, "I intended to dramatize the all too human condition of loneliness, a human being who moves through the crowd, jostled, brushed aside, ignored, or abused, hassled or pandered, but who somehow is utterly untouched by any of it because of his own secret world of fantasy and his inability to communicate with his fellow humans. In short, a lonely man, aching to be noticed, recognized, and loved, but unable to attain it." Indeed, Travis Bickle is a man consigned to move aimlessly like a soul in limbo. He ferries passengers throughout the city, people who barely acknowledge him and see him as little more than an extension of the cab's mechanism. Surrounded by people, he is nonetheless inextricably apart, overlooked by all. He is always on the outside looking in, the means by which others make connections while he remains "unconnected." Ever the voyeur, he overhears the dark confidences of his passengers, but cannot share them; through his rear-view mirror he watches their intimacies while he remains shrouded in anonymity, unable to engage anyone.

According to Schrader, the other influences for his

script were Jean-Paul Sartre's Nausea (1939) and Dostoyevsky's
Notes from the Underground (1866).   The film also follows
stylistically the formats Schrader observed in the films of
Ozu, Carl Dreyer, and particularly Robert Bresson, whom
he admires and wrote a book about.   "I wanted to find a new
context for the hero from Europe," says the intellectual
Schrader.   "When he is put in America, he becomes younger,
less intelligent, and violent."   Like Travis, he is prone to
act out his frustrations in aggressive acts towards others,
whereas his European or Japanese counterpart turns inward
and harms himself.   He observes, "We have a tendency to
act out our personal problems on other corpses.   I wrote a
character going crazy in a linear pattern until he gets very
schizophrenic.   When the pressure gets too great, this young
man decides that the only answer to life is to kill or try to
kill a presidential candidate.   This film is continental in feeling, but American in action."

          TAXI DRIVER was shot entirely in New York during
its typically humid, sweltering summer months.   Shooting occurred throughout the city amidst crowds--the hubbub of congested streets in the garment district and Times Square--and
in the snarled traffic of cab-choked streets in Manhattan.
They were plagued with a bout of rainstorms that delayed
the shooting, but, overall, the filming and editing were done
very quickly.   To abide by a studio deadline, the picture was
placed on a speeded-up editing schedule.   "The studio wanted
the film out fast and we agreed to try to get the movie to
open by a certain date, which meant that I had to edit the
picture to get a rough cut in four weeks--like a Roger Corman
movie, meaning your editor's working while you're shooting,"
Scorsese explained.   "It was insane, to have to do it on a
picture like this!" he exclaims.   The director worked with
three editors plus three assistants.   He believes the editing
process is so vital that a director should take part in it.   He
sat in on every cut and cut a few scenes himself.   "Editing
is harder than the shooting," he explains, "but I enjoy it ...
for me, it is where you really create the picture ... you can
actually see the thing come alive."

          In terms of visual style, TAXI DRIVER differs dra-
matically from any of Scorsese's other pictures.   There are
few of the jump cuts, the uneven pacing, the gritty documentary, cinéma vérité shooting style, or any of the impulsive
digressions that characterize his other films.   TAXI is a
more formalistic, controlled film which displays greater linear
continuity than any of his former work.   The picture has a

sophisticated, sleeker look that reflects the confident guiding
hand of a director whose mastery of the medium is evident.
Most distinctively, hand-held camera shooting techniques were
out. In an interview with journalist Ann Powell, the director
noted, "I've always done a lot of hand-held camera shots ...
but in TAXI there's not one hand-held shot. It's all tied
down. We even had dollies inside the cab. Sometimes I was
planning a shot I had seen in my head, a shot I had visualized
as a hand-held shot, but I had to give it up. The subject
matter is so strong in TAXI that the camera movements don't
have to take over ... we shot it simpler." He added that
making the film helped him think consciously of pacing: "It's
the first script that I've worked on that has a direct movement. Travis feels one way ... he does this; he does that
and then something leads him to something else."

The subjective camera technique represents Travis'
vantage of the city and the people he observes; we see through
the point of view of his ever-narrowing, "disconnected" eyes.
Says the director, "Certain segments of the picture were shot
slightly off-speed, slightly off-edge and a little paranoid; for
example, the camera will always move in the opposite direction you'd expect. That's just to throw you a little off, the
way Travis does, because he's full of contradictions. Also,
many of Travis' close-ups aren't at the usual frames per
second--they're at 36, which makes them a little slower,
more deliberate and off-kilter than the rest." But Scorsese
has not abandoned the fluid, constantly moving camera motion
that is one of the trademarks of his cinematic style. Rather,
as writer Powell describes it, he has "abstracted the camera's
motion. The camera movement in TAXI is a kind of motion-
less movement." The dynamism, the personal intensity, and
the raw power that are endemic to his other films epitomize
the physical qualities of TAXI, qualities he admires in the
work of director Sam Fuller. Speaking of his influence,
Scorsese acknowledges, "The director I feel closest to is
Fuller: his camera movement, his aggressiveness, and the
emotional and physical impact of his films."

Scorsese impressively represents the dark, distorted
interior world which Travis inhabits. While it is nearly impossible to portray cogently the idiosyncratic mysteries of a
mentally-deranged individual, the director and cinematographer
Michael Chapman were remarkably compelling in their ability
visually to externalize Travis' psychotic view of things.
Travis' New York is rendered as an infernal vision of human
depravity and spiritual suffocation. His cab is conceived as

a claustrophobic ferry that moves damned souls across the
fetid river Styx. In the film's opening shot the cab, moving
in slow-motion like a sinister hearse, goes through a column
of erupting steam. It seems like smoke welling up from the
subterranean depths of hell. The ominous, nerve-chilling
strains of Bernard Herrmann's richly evocative score herald
our entry into a world of eternal night. Herrmann, the veteran composer who wrote the music for CITIZEN KANE (RKO,
1941), PSYCHO (Paramount, 1960), and THE BIRDS (Universal, 1964), died immediately after completing the score for
TAXI DRIVER. He was especially good at expressing psychological disorder with his dissonant music. The city is filmed
in surreal, daemonic hues--baleful faces are bathed in the
phosphorescent glow of neon lights. The pimps, prostitutes,
pushers, and street people are grotesqueries of human corruption, demon wraiths that inhabit the dark shadows of the night.
In Travis' view, the city is "an open sewer. Sometime, a
real rain's gonna come and sweep all this scum off the street,"
he tells himself.

"New York is a whole character in TAXI DRIVER,"
says the director. Scorsese utilizes to perfection its protean
attributes. We are shown a city of kaleidoscopic contradictions. From the garish, neon-lit porno theatres of Times
Square offering the furtive pleasures of "dirty sex," the cab
moves to the temperate, blue-suited world of Columbus Circle
where the presidential candidate's campaign office is head-
quartered, and on to the garbage-strewn, crime-ridden streets
of the decaying ghettos--the seething frustrations of its inhabitants fill the air with menace (there is a rather blatant characterization of blacks as violent-prone people; Travis regards
them as threatening figures of evil), and then to the comparative "safe haven" of tree-lined streets where the wealthy live
in their austerely elegant townhouses. Scorsese knows the
darkest corners of the city, the sense of danger, the fear and
desperation that stalk its streets. Illuminated in the reddish
glare of the street lights, he transforms it into a surreal underworld that mirrors Travis' distorted, paranoid vision.

Newsweek art critic Jack Kroll best describes the director's depiction of the city: "Scorsese's verminous New
York is a descendant of Baudelaire's 'anthill' Paris, Eliot's
'unreal' London, the nightmare Berlin of such German films
as Fritz Lang's M [Germany, 1931]. In this vision the great
modern city is the crossroads where fenced-off forces break
loose and collide. The overworld and the underworld embrace
each other in a dance of mutual lusts that can only lead to

violence." The director wanted to reveal particularly the malevolent ambience of the city, the alienation and anger of people whose lives are warped by poverty, racism, and moral anarchy. He will assure you that he loves the city, but he points out, ("There's a definite craziness to New York--there's something foreboding and threatening about being here. Sometimes, I find myself shooting the camera over somebody's shoulder, for example, because it gives you a feeling that you are stalking somebody, that something bad can happen, that somebody can jump at you at any second. It's what growing up in the city is like.") He adds, "You know what I wanted to do with TAXI DRIVER: open up with a shot of a maniac black man, stoned or drunk, howling at the goddamned sky ... he comes down the street, raging right toward Travis, but he doesn't even see him, he's raging at the sky, cursing God. That's what New York's about to me and that's what the film's saying."

Scorsese has drawn a sexually-charged ambience whose enticements incite Travis' mounting unease and frustration. His psychological problems are seen to originate in part from the neurotic perversion of his sexual urges. Critic Joseph Gelmis observed, "The film is, in terms of the sexually repressed Travis, an orgasmic violence looking for a place to happen. It is one long build-up to a getting-it-off massacre." Through the iridescent swirls of the city lights refracted in the raindrops of Travis' windshield, he watches the scantily clad women in their summer shorts and halter tops. The sensual velvet black of the night, the flashing images of human carnality and the sultry blues of Herrmann's music evoke a seething, pulsating undertow of erotic allure. But Travis is an "outsider," a voyeur who can have no part of this action. And so he rails against it, reviling the "filth" and obscenity of the "dirty" sex that is bought and sold in the sleazy Times Square district. But he is drawn to the raffish world of porno theatres, sex parlors, and sordid neighborhoods where whores and pimps peddle their wares. He is willing to take his fares to the "unsafe," squalid tenement areas, teeming with the urban poor sweating in the steamy city summer. These sights of human degradation "feed" Travis' anger; he revels furtively in them, channeling his feelings of loneliness and sexual inhibition into a growing visceral hatred. In viewing scenes of "ugly" sex, he can justify his own sexual deprivation. "Since the movie deals with sexual repression," Scorsese explains, "there's a lot of talk about sex, but no sex, no lovemaking. A lot of brothels, but not even a nude scene. If the audience saw nudity, it would work like a re-

lease valve, and tension that's been building up would be dissolved.   The valve in TAXI DRIVER is not released until
Travis finally lets loose and starts shooting."

     The stifling claustrophobia of Travis' existence grows
as his frustration mounts and his emotional alienation intensi-
fies.   He moves in a sleepless torpor from the dark anonymity of his cab to the darkness of all-night porno movie theatres, and returns to his cell-like room where he confesses
to his diary, "Loneliness has followed me my whole life everywhere."   He seems cast adrift in limbo, like a soul condemned
to roam ceaselessly, never taking hold of anything.   We know
very little about Travis--where he comes from, who his family is, or what has caused his problems.   This further rein-
forces the almost "alien" quality of his being.   The question
arises whether we can ever really "know" or understand the
Travises amongst us.   When he signs on to become a cabbie
(he is suffering from insomnia and wants to occupy as much
of his time as possible and he settles on driving a cab), Travis
appears so disoriented that he seems, indeed, to be re-enter-
ing a society that he has been apart from for a long time.
Common references, like the word "moonlighting," appear
foreign to him and he has difficulty communicating with people.   There is evidence that Travis is an ex-Marine who may
have been to Vietnam.

     Robert De Niro's performance as the troubled Travis
Bickle is a remarkable rendering of suggestive characterization.   It has always been extremely difficult for an actor to
portray the psychic torments of the mentally deranged, so
that we can comprehend or relate to such a character.   De
Niro does not play the role to get "sympathy" for the character; his is a starkly realistic revelation of an estranged misfit who unravels psychologically before our eyes.   He draws
a portrait of isolation, restrained hostility and loneliness with
facial expressions, the look in his eyes, and his gestures:
the glazed, vacant stare on his face as he sits with the other
cabbies in the Belmore cafeteria, unable to talk with them;
the eerie, twisted smile he shows as he speaks to the Secret
Service man who has spotted the would-be assassin in a crowd
listening to the candidate; and the obssessive intensity with
which the glassy-eyed Travis almost ritualistically practices
drawing his guns in preparation for the shooting.

     As Travis becomes more unhinged, De Niro plays him
as if he is in a trance, offering only hints of the mysteries
that have contorted this damned hackie's mind.   The actor

However, he is the one member of the group who makes his
living by comparatively honest means. In one of the most
bizarre sequences in the movie, Tony sits inside the cage
of his pet lion in the back of his bar, trying to persuade the
beast to lick him. It is an example of the many off-beat
touches in the movie which hint at Scorsese's wry sense of
humor. Johnny Boy is Scorsese's most perfect prototype of
the embodiment of a compulsively anarchic spirit. He is depicted as a maddeningly reckless gambler, who displays an
almost demented irresponsibility. Ruled by a manic, self-
destructive energy, Johnny flouts the accepted code of behavior. He is a character conceived to be a direct contrast to
Charlie. As played by Robert De Niro, his gleeful insou-
ciance has a compellingly winning charm.

Within the oppressive tinderbox of their neighborhood,
the group indulges its chronic idleness in the gloomy, lurid
spaces of bars, pool halls, and alleys. We witness their
nightly rituals: the macho camaraderie they engage in, typified by the laying on of the hands; their drunken revels, how
they deal with the "broads" from uptown, and the gleeful way
they work their scams. All the while, the camera's uneasy
motion emphasizes a foreboding sense of danger which per-
meates their world. This pervasive threat of violence is exemplified in a brutal scene depicting a violent killing in Tony's
bar. A man (David Carradine) is suddenly gunned down in a
gangland shooting by a young hood trying to score points with
the Syndicate. He is unceremoniously left to die in the gutter,
while the bar is hastily closed down to avoid any further
trouble. It is apparent that the grim stakes of their treacherous transactions hold the young men poised on the edge of
some inevitable catastrophe.

Charlie courts disaster when he gets involved in Johnny
Boy's problems. However, it serves his needs to keep Johnny
Boy dependent on him. Scorsese likens Charlie to the Phar-
isees: "They used to give money to the poor and blow trum-
pets so everybody could watch them do it." This entangle-
ment forces Charlie to confront himself with the choice between "sainthood" and his ambitions. While he cannot forsake
Johnny Boy, he refuses to risk incurring his uncle's disfavor
with a plea for his help. It is the only viable solution, but
Charlie is emotionally stalemated, his guilt-tormented conscience vying with his practical aspirations. His uncle dis-
approves of Johnny Boy and his epileptic cousin, Teresa
(Amy Robinson), and has cautioned Charlie to disassociate
himself from them.

ambitions.) Seeking advancement in the ranks of the Syndicate
(he is being considered to take over a restaurant whose owner
can no longer afford the "payments"), Charlie barely breaks
stride between kow-towing to his Mafia boss uncle and genu-
flecting in atonement before God.

Charlie's Catholic upbringing has left him obsessively
guilt-ridden, with a religious-bred fear of divine retribution.
Throughout the film, he holds his hand near a flame to con-
jure up the fires of Hell.   (Says Scorsese, "Putting your
fingers in fire was something they used to make us do on religious retreat to help us imagine the pain of Hell.") He had
developed a personal "arrangement" for his repentance; in one
of his adjurations to God, he affirms, "Now when I do something wrong, I just want to make up for it my way." Scorsese
explains, "The voice-over was the whole business of his
[Charlie's] relationship with God, his own way of looking at
things.   And also his guilt. He would go to confession but
he wanted to deal with things in his own way, so he would
never really....   No matter where he goes, he's lost."

Primarily, Charlie is a product of his society, a
hustler, concerned with getting ahead against the day-to-day
odds of survival. "You don't make up for your sins in Church,
you do it in the streets...," he says. At the same time, he
importunes God to believe his honest intention to "do the right
thing." Fearful of sustaining the loss of heaven, as well as
more earthly real estate (the restaurant), Charlie steers an
expeditious course of self-interest. Currying favors with
those "in power," he is intent on making as few waves as
possible. He's ostensibly everybody's friend, but his kind-
nesses to them are an extension of his own self-serving goodness. "Charlie likes everybody, everybody likes Charlie ...
fuckin' politician," Johnny Boy taunts.

MEAN STREETS' secondary characters represent varying degrees of adjustment to this corrupt ghetto life. There
is Michael (Richard Romanus), a vulturous hood, who thrives
in this degenerate environment. Nattily attired in dark busi-
nessman's suits, Michael is a ruthless loan shark, operating
with the efficiency of an accountant balancing his ledgers.
But he is as apt to turn coldblooded executioner when he cannot collect from his delinquent "clients." (Johnny Boy's inability to pay the debt he owes Michael is the suspenseful
focal point on which the film's plot hinges.) Tony (David
Proval) is a genial bar owner; his friendship with the others
involves him by association with their scabrous lifestyle.

men's nighttime "play." The songs exist as a primary source
of identification with Scorsese's own youthful experiences. A
song like "Be My Baby" is played almost as an anthem sig-
nifying the contemporary environment of this second generation
of Italian young men. ("'Be My Baby' by the Ronettes was
the song ... I mean that's 1963 or 1962 in New York. We
used to hear that late at night. There was always a social
club stuck in the back of some building, and that song was
always playing, echoing in the streets.") The strains of im-
passioned opera music, heard at the San Gennaro festival,
evoke the influence of "old world" traditions on the characters' lives. Scorsese's skilled use of music as a thematic
undercurrent of the action is a distinctive characteristic of
all of his films. It serves to vitalize his movies, and calls
forth the very sense of the times in which its characters live.
In MEAN STREETS, the music is an electrifying presence
that excites as it entertains the viewer.

Scorsese's films are wholeheartedly conceived as
"character studies." The director does not adhere simply
to the linear dynamics of mapping out a plot line; rather, the
discursive course his movies follow is ideally suited to prob-
ing the psychology of its characters. The essence of the
filmmaker's work can be traced to his instinct for the cinematic revelation of his characters--it is the very impulse that
shapes his art. But if his movies resonate with a special
intensity of feeling, an almost visceral urgency, it is because
they are invested with Scorsese's own soul-searching efforts.

In devising the thematic concepts of his pictures, he
indicates, "I always start with a person, not a statement.
The structure of the film comes out through the people. You
start with a character and then put him through scenes, through
conflicts, that illustrate your theme. Then the character
grows, in a positive or negative way. The main thing is that
I have to believe in that person, I have to feel a lot of things
that the character feels. If I don't feel that the characters
are very much like me, I can't really make a film about
them."

MEAN STREETS' themes are articulated in the interplay between the protagonists, Charlie (Harvey Keitel) and
Johnny Boy (Robert De Niro). Their interactions (and the
film's movement) have the improvisational vitality of jazz-
like progressions. The movie's nominal story-line serves to
frame their "free form" encounters. "The film's structure
is achieved mainly through the scenes with Charlie and Johnny

Boy, the variations on what they're saying," Scorsese points out. "Some people think it's just repetition, but it's not, it's intensity, less intensity, then more and more. It's like a musical theme. In [the movie], there is no basic plot really; the people of the movie are the story. It deals with their strong relationships and high-pitched emotions, these second-generation Italians caught in a complex web of personal entanglements in the cloistered world of New York's Lower East Side."

Scorsese depicts the "mean streets" of Little Italy as a sinister, subterranean enclave, which is so isolated as to exist alone in a tiny corner of the universe. The film's darkly lit pastiche of narrow hallways, shadowy alleys and dingy tenements portrays a claustrophobic environment, seemingly enshrouded in eternal night. Within the confining bounds of this benighted place, the director draws montage-like portraits of four young men enmeshed in a society where the laws of institutional crime prevail. Unquestioningly, the group is governed by its terms of survival; they appear almost predestined to accept. "Somebody does something wrong, you've got to break his head or you shoot him."

In her highly laudatory review of MEAN STREETS, Pauline Kael aptly describes these characters as "Mafiosi loafers, small-time hoods (good Catholics who live at home with their parents) who have more in common with the provincial wolf pack of Fellini's I VITELLONI (cadging, indulged sons of middle-class families) than with the other ethnic groups in New York City. And these hoods live in such an insulated world that anyone outside it--the stray Jew or black they encounter--is as foreign and funny to them as a little man from Mars."

Despite the pervasive tensions of their malevolent environment, the four exhibit the torpor of damned souls cast adrift in stagnant moral waters. Their actions seem strangely pre-determined by the code of behavior dictated by the Church and the Syndicate. It is as if their individual thoughts and values are virtually pre-empted by these incongruent strictures. Charlie Cappa's characterization is conceived to illustrate an individual trying to "make it" within the contradictory imperatives of Church and criminal "estate." A junior league Mafioso, he is a collector for his Uncle Giovanni's (Cesare Danova) loan shark operation. Charlie, according to Scorsese, is a "would-be saint," aspiring in religious terms to spiritual purity within the parameters of his rather unholy temporal intuitively becomes more mechanical in his moves and gestures as Travis metamorphizes into a killer; at this point his performance conveys the hollow soul of a programmed automaton. In one of the film's most chilling sequences, De Niro stares straight at the camera, his gaze fixed hypnotically as he points the gun straight at us, addressing a make-believe adversary. De Niro is so unnervingly real as Travis, there is a startling sense that he and the character have merged as one. Chicago Sun-Times film critic Roger Ebert noted, "Scorsese's style selects details that evoke emotions, and that's the effect he wants.... He goes for moments from his actors, rather than slowly developed characters. It's as if the required emotions were written in the margins of their scripts. Robert De Niro, as Travis Bickle, is as good as Brando at suggesting emotions even while veiling them from us...."

In the earlier part of the movie, Travis is still attempting to make some "connection," to link up with someone. He tries to converse with a girl selling candy at the porno theatre, but he is awkward, and she rebuffs him. When he sees Betsy, a blonde, all-American goddess in white, he perceives her as an apparition of purity. Cybill Shepherd is perfectly cast as a coolly reserved, sorority queen-type who accepts a "date" with Travis out of curiosity rather than real interest. After all, Travis is clearly different from the college and business men this darling of well-heeled metropolitan society is accustomed to. Scorsese explains, "When I went to the university, I met girls who were blonde almost for the first time. As a kid, I had literally only known dark-haired girls. But the girls at NYU were blonde, sweet-looking, intelligent, wore pleated skirts and spoke proper English. Maybe a non-Latin type would have cast a dark-haired actress as the girl Travis idolizes in TAXI DRIVER, but I wanted Cybill Shepherd."

Scorsese utilizes slow-motion to convey Travis' idealization of Betsy. She is seen walking towards her office; she is a campaign worker for presidential candidate Charles Palantine (Leonard Harris). Moving in slow motion, her hair blowing ethereally in the breeze, she is a vision of white, wholesome loveliness. We hear the voice-over of Travis writing in his diary: "She comes out of this city which is like a filthy sewer. She's alone. Nothing can touch her." The director's Catholic background is clearly a point of reference for his explanation of Travis' feelings for Betsy. "When Travis falls in love with a woman, he can't admit he

wants to make love to her. That's forbidden. What he feels
for her is like a masturbating fantasy of the Blessed Virgin.
We have here the image of the woman as something she's not
... as a goddess, and Travis' problem of not being able to
relate the goddess to the whore, not being able to deal with
both. Travis becomes obsessed with this woman, but she's
only a fixation, something he can worship."

There is a religious implication in the guilt, sexual
repression, and excessiveness of Travis' moral outrage toward the society he finds himself in. Schrader admits, "The
problems that the character has--his obsessiveness--stem
from religion taken to the extreme." The screenwriter's own
strict Dutch Calvinist background, no doubt, was a significant
influence on his conceptualization of Travis. He attended a
divinity school and was prohibited by religious interdiction
from going to the movies--they were regarded as evil. Schrader
didn't see his first movie until he was 18. The religious
connotation extends to Scorsese's perception of Travis as a
"Latter-Day saint whose mission, in his mind, is to clean up
the whole stinking mess. He has the energy of a saint, and
he could have been one in a different context." Travis can
be viewed as another one of Scorsese's "failed saints," who
perversely commits evil in order to eradicate evil.

Travis' pathetic efforts to strike up a relationship with
Betsy are obviously doomed. She is merely intrigued with
the intensity and the enigmatic qualities of the strange young
man. When he takes her to a porno movie on their first
date, she is instinctively frightened and repelled by such an
aberrant gesture. While it is difficult to believe that Travis
would not know better than to take Betsy to a porno movie,
Scorsese insists it indicates the degree of Travis' innocent
unsophistication. When she refuses to have anything more to
do with him, Travis is humiliated, but persists in trying to
reach her. In what the director personally regards as one
of the film's most important scenes, Travis is shown attempting to call Betsy from a pay phone in the sterile vestibule of
a building. Betsy, on the other end of the line, is apparently
telling him she never wants to see him again. The camera
dollies away from Travis and focuses on the long, empty corridor. Scorsese explains that the sequence (reminiscent of
Antonioni) is meant to keep us from seeing the pain of Travis'
unbearable rejection. The director received some negative
criticism from critics who felt the stylized segment was too
salient and drew attention to itself.

In his grief and anger, Travis retreats further into himself. In an improvised sequence, Travis tries to confide his incipient desire for vengeance to fellow cabbie Wizard, a self-styled hackie-philosopher (Peter Boyle, who plays the role of Wizard, wanted to do the cameo performance because he has such great regard for TAXI DRIVER's script). But Travis has grown so introverted, he can barely communicate with anyone. He speaks in a strange, halting way. Confused by his thoughts, he can hardly find the words to express what he is thinking. "I've got some bad ideas in my head," is all he can muster in his conversation with Wizard. In the much-talked about "Alka Seltzer" shot, Scorsese attempted to represent the seething agitation of Travis' mind. We see him sitting with the other cabbies at a cafeteria. He is totally distanced from them, staring into his glass of Alka Seltzer. Scorsese zooms into the glass of bubbling seltzer; the screen is filled with the tiny explosions of carbonation. The Godard-like shot, says the director, symbolizes "the closing-off of Travis' universe. The Alka Seltzer says something about his pain, he's taking all these pills, he's ruining his body. His physical pain mirrors his mental anguish." It is also a metaphor for the growing tensions, the repressed anger Travis is feeling. "The shot is a forewarning that trouble is brewing, that something is going to explode."

As Travis grows more despondent, he languishes in his dingy room, subsisting on stomach-killing, bizarre combinations of food--candy, soda, old bread with brandy poured over it--and watching soap operas and writing in his diary. The room is filled with rotting flowers, those which Betsy refused to accept from him. They evoke a sense of death and decay. His smoldering rage begins to ignite; he burns the desiccating flowers and, while watching television, pushes the set over, causing it to explode. Betsy's rejection has concentrated all of his discontent and resentments past the point where he can "absorb" them any longer. His spurned affection for her has given way to hatred and a desire for vengeance.

Violence, as an outcome of thwarted love, is a theme reiterated in a lacerating scene which takes place in Travis' car. A passenger insists that Travis drive him to a corner where he can watch the silhouettes of a man and woman embracing in the window of an apartment building. The passenger (Scorsese himself plays the role; he was replacing the actor set for the part, who was hurt in an accident) is a

cuckolded husband whose wife is having an affair with a black
man (they are the silhouettes in the window). Choking back
his jealous rage, he describes how he is going to mutilate
his wife with a . 44 magnum gun. Travis just stares at the
man through his rear view mirror, never saying a word to
this demented stranger, who is gleefully confessing his horrid
intentions. The idea of getting a gun has been planted in
Travis' mind in the exchange and this scene frighteningly pre-
figures his own brutal retaliation on a world that has spurned
him. Scorsese's sizzling performance is nothing short of ter-
rifying. He looks like a possessed demon with his black blazing eyes and swarthy appearance. The nervously quick, jazz-
like progressions of his speech are the fiercely intense incan-
tations of a deranged man. The rhythmic way he talks suggests a sexual urge which is to be released through violence.
Referring to Scorsese's captivating performance, one critic
noted that his acting had such scalding intensity that it all
but burned a hole in the screen.

Travis sets out to assassinate Palantine and ritualistically works at a rigorous regimen of physical fitness and
practice shooting. He becomes like an ascetic, enacting sacred ceremonies for this "transcendent mission," a mission
to which he is totally given up, and which now defines his
existence. There is nothing political about his motives to kill
the presidential candidate; he is totally ignorant of Palantine's
political views. The candidate is caricatured as an urbane
man of privilege who is clearly not "one of the people."
When, by chance, he gets into Travis' cab, he is seen to
be as "out of touch" with the people as Travis is. The film,
however, does not really try to make a political statement.
He is merely "transferring his fixation from Betsy to her
boss, Palantine," claims the director. "At this point he
could be fixated by anything. The focus of his violence is
almost arbitrarily a political candidate." Perhaps killing the
one person he knows is so important to Betsy may be a way
of "killing" her too.

Writer Diane Jacobs observed, "Violence is endemic
to Scorsese's world--not just in the eye-for-an-eye sense of
Coppola's Sicilian justice, but as an expression of frustration
and, ultimately, a perversion of the love impulse.... Violence as release of pentup frustration is ... explored in TAXI
DRIVER, where love of Betsy is visually transmitted into love
of weaponry. Travis' affection for guns, like Hedda Gabler's,
borders on the pornographic, but it is significant that neither
his interest in killing nor his potential for violence surfaced
until after all hope of winning back Betsy was lost."

The assassination sequence is masterfully handled; the criss-crossing of close pans to wide pans of the crowds waiting to hear the candidate builds the tension and sets the scene for some erratic action.   The camera cites Palantine as if he is being seen through the eye of a gun.   Finally, the camera locates Travis; his appearance is startling.   He has shaven most of his head into a bizarre Mohawk Indian haircut.

Earlier in the film, Travis comes across Iris, a 12-year-old prostitute, whom he is trying to "rescue" from her pimp, Sport (Harvey Keitel).   Revolted by the degeneracy of her living circumstances, he steadfastly tries to convince her to return to her parents.   Before his planned assassination effort, he sends her money to go home with.   While Iris is moved by Travis' concern, she does not want to leave Sport, who is shown to be loving towards her.   Critic Jack Droll likens Travis to Dostoyevsky's "underground man, who was the 'real man of the ... majority' whose tragedy lay in his 'self-torture, the consciousness of what is best and the impossibility of attaining it.'   Travis has an ideal of beauty and goodness.   As with Dostoyevsky, this ideal is embodied in woman, in Travis' case two women, two polar opposites. Betsy is a blonde vision, an 'angel' who floats untouched above the filth and mess of the city.   Iris is a 12-year-old whore, the child who's been corrupted by that filth.   Poor crazy mixed-up Travis tries to win the immaculate Betsy with dirt (he takes her to a porno movie) and save the tainted Iris with virtue, trying to persuade her to go back to her parents."

In one of the picture's "softer" moments, Sport calms an anxious Iris, allaying her doubts about his love for her. He takes her in his arms and dances with her, crooning softly, "I only wish every man could know what it's like to be loved by you."   They dance in the candle-lit glow of the room.   (The clusters of candles burning all around the room where Iris "turns tricks" ironically recalls the ambience of a religious sanctuary.   It may just be an instinctive gesture by the Catholic Scorsese.)   While it is an outlandish "romantic" scene, it is nonetheless very affecting.   Jodie Foster, in the part of the child-prostitute, projects an uncanny blend of world-weary wisdom and the naive innocence of a child. Dressed in hot pants, flimsy top, wide-rimmed hat, and poised precariously on high heels, she is an unlikely cross between a klutzy tomboy and Lolita.   Speaking with Travis over breakfast at a diner, she parries effectively his entreaties that she leave Sport.   A hard-nosed survivor educated in the streets, she has the maturity to see right through Travis, although she spreads layer after layer of jam on her bread like the child that she is.

Harvey Keitel invests the role of Sport with such an oddly winning charm that we aren't wholly repelled by the depravity of his character. Long-haired, tight muscled (he has one long-nailed pinky finger that is painted with red nail polish), he looks like a gypsy street punk. In a superbly improvised confrontation between him and De Niro, their spontaneous interaction generates a tension that is altogether realistic. When his plan to shoot Palatine "misfires," Sport becomes the object of Travis' unvented fury. Out to wreak vengeance on the degenerate world that has shunned and tormented him, he explodes in a nihilistic frenzy. He is determined to smite the dragons of indecency, inhumanity, and loneliness--but most of all, he wants to obliterate himself. There is a climactic shoot-out as Travis guns down Sport, and then proceeds to kill four other people in the dingy "house of sin" where Iris and the other prostitutes "conduct business." The killing spree is grimly graphic--fingers are shot off, there are close-ups of spurting blood as the bullets make their contact. The M.P.A.A. threatened to give the film an "X" rating, so Scorsese desaturated the color of the blood from a vivid red to a murky brownish-red color. An overhead tracking shot (one of the few objective camera sequences in the movie) moves lingeringly above the mutilated bodies, the blood-stained walls and stairwells of the hotel, and out into the streets where police cars and curious crowds are gathering. The sequence is reminiscent of the sensationalistic crime coverage of city tabloids. Scorsese remarked, "TAXI DRIVER is a Daily News horror story!"

The camera draws away from the site of the disaster, seeming to signal the grim finale of the film. But surprisingly, the movie continues and cuts to an epilogue. The coda that follows wryly proclaims Travis' "resurrection." We learn from on-camera newspaper clippings that Travis, who was shot in the melee, has incredibly survived the inferno, and, more amazingly, has been hailed as a hero. It appears that some of the men he killed in the whorehouse were wanted criminals. In a voice-over, we hear Iris' father reading from a letter he has written (shown on the screen) to Travis thanking him for saving his daughter, Iris, and sending her back home. In the next sequence, we see Travis taking up where he left off; he is picking up fares in Manhattan when he coincidentally happens upon Betsy. Her interest in the "hero" of so much media fanfare is obvious, but Travis barely acknowledges her as he drops Betsy off at her destination. The almost "pastoral" segment registers a becalmed "return to normality" feeling that seems to signify that Travis has

been pacified. However, we see a reflection of a strange
look in his eyes in the cab's rear view mirror, and we are
left to wonder if Travis has indeed spent all his fury.

Unfortunately, the inclusion of the epilogue dilutes the
overall impact of this searing human drama. The coda ending is literally anti-climactic and serves to muddle the import
of the film. It is an artificial postscript that deviates from
the intimately subjective purview of the film and turns the
movie into an ironic fable with a jokey twist ending. (Scorsese
and Schrader mean to imply that the morally twisted society
which has warped Travis is only capable of recognizing him
after he has committed this sick act of self-proclamation.
While society's bestowal of hero status upon Travis stretches
credibility, Scorsese seems content with drawing such a par-
allel. "The ending is Travis' triumph," the director admits.
"It is the way the real world perceives what he has done as
opposed to what he really did do. And the real world, which
always excluded him, finally accepts him...."

Conferring sainthood upon a schizophrenic man whose
misguided fantasies compel him to destroy the "destroyers"
almost threatens to romanticize mental illness. It seems
almost to imply that schizophrenia is a "social" disease" created by society itself. Equating mental illness with social
protest certainly reflects too many logical inconsistencies and
is a facile form of sociologizing. However, Scorsese admits
that Travis is pictured as a "mad saint, like Savonarola, who
was burned at the stake." "I respect Travis," he says, "but
I wouldn't want to be him or spend much time with him. He's
got a noble ambition that has become twisted. This picture
is structured like a messianic blood sacrifice. After all,
St. Paul was definitely a sociopath. Charles Manson? Two
thousand years ago he would have had a nice following. At
one point, during the shootout, Travis looks and seems like
King Kong to me, holding off the planes. My intention was
to be as graphic as if I was making a Christ movie."

Many critics complained about the implausibility of
the tacked on, mock-ironic ending, and of its inference that
society has accepted Travis as a hero. The movie was
roundly denounced for its overly vivid, "sensationalistic" depiction of the brothel bloodbath. Some accused the director
of glorifying the bloodletting, while others criticized him for
a seeming advocacy of violence as a natural response to the
frustrations of living in a brutally inhumane world. Despite
the controversy, it was generally agreed that the film was a

powerfully drawn, riveting account of one man's psychological breakdown. Scorsese and cinematographer Chapman have done a masterful job in drawing the grotesquely haunted vision of a psychotic killer. Scorsese asserts the film avoided making any moral judgments, and he vehemently denies that its purpose was to justify the carnage in the wake of Travis' actions.

"Certainly you don't condone or excuse any of the violence," he insists. "You just present it. I didn't use slow-motion during any of the killings because I think violence should be shown as being ugly and awful. At least, that's how I see it and how I must present it." He adds, "I hate violence. But as much as I hate it, I know that it's in me, in you, in everyone, and I want to explore it. My personal feeling is that anybody is capable of going over the edge like that."

Despite losing control of his ending, Scorsese has created a film of hypnotic beauty and monumental power. The vivid Expressionism of its imagery, the deft execution and dynamic creativity of his filmmaking techniques, the superb acting and the incredibly potent impact of TAXI DRIVER make it one of the most memorable films in contemporary times. The film was showered with accolades, winning four Academy Award nominations and receiving the Golden Palm Award for Best Picture at the Cannes Film Festival in 1976. It was chosen as one of the year's ten best films by the National Society of Film Critics and by most of the major metropolitan newspapers in the country. The movie was a resounding box-office hit and Scorsese was identified as one of America's most important and original filmmakers.

VI

Given Scorsese's enthusiasm for the musical films from the 'thirties and 'forties, it was perhaps inevitable that he would try his hand at one of his own. NEW YORK, NEW YORK was it. Because of his previous successes, the picture had the highest production budget of any of his films. Scorsese did it as a period piece, opening in the year 1945, the year the Second World War was ending, the era of the big bands, starting with a Tommy Dorsey swing broadcast. Robert De Niro was back as the lead, this time playing a musician who very much wants success. Liza Minnelli played a singer, the girl with whom De Niro falls in love and whom he finally marries.

This is where the typical musical film from the 'forties would have ended, but in Scorsese's film it is almost where the story begins. De Niro's character is at best questionable and at worse repellent. The marriage to Minnelli does not work out. There are scenes of excruciating domestic pain, haranguing, even physical violence. The tonneau of an automobile is still seen as a "pressure cooker": De Niro and Minnelli have one of their most vicious fights in the back seat of a car. Whereas critics had complained about Scorsese moving his camera when De Niro in TAXI DRIVER was on the telephone trying to patch up his relationship with Cybill Shepherd, in NEW YORK, NEW YORK Scorsese did a reverse and kept the camera on De Niro all through an anguished conversation between De Niro and Minnelli. However, despite the elaborate trappings of a period piece and a seemingly conscious effort to evoke cinematic nostalgia, the ingredients of film noir did not blend with a musical and the film proved over-long, meandering, and tedious.

Martin Scorsese was supposed to take time off between the grueling 22-week shooting schedule and editing of NEW YORK, NEW YORK. But workaholic that he is, the director decided to "rest" in perhaps the only way he is most comfortable with--gearing up to do yet another film. Having worked on WOODSTOCK, MEDICINE BALL CARAVAN, and ELVIS ON TOUR, Scorsese had long wanted to direct his own rock film. His spirited passion for music and his predilection for working in the documentary form converged auspiciously in the making of THE LAST WALTZ. In the director's words, the opportunity to work on a rock documentary was "like going home again. I like to do documentaries while I do features, to keep my hand in. That's when you get back to roots. And on THE LAST WALTZ ... there are roots there too. The songs mean very strong things to me."

In an article appearing in New York's Village Voice, writer Terry Curtis Fox observed that the director's involvement in the rockumentary "was not just work; it was a special kind of anchor. Scorsese's love affair with rock and roll, his commitment to music as a form, is at least as deep and abiding as his love and commitment to film. He has always used music in his films, knowing just what the kid would listen to in ALICE DOESN'T LIVE HERE ANYMORE, manipulating the track of TAXI DRIVER with disc-jockey ease. The cultural conflict in MEAN STREETS is most directly expressed as a war between two styles of music, Italian and rock."

The period between the making of NEW YORK, NEW YORK and the release of THE LAST WALTZ proved a particularly difficult time for Scorsese. The former film had received mixed critical reviews and, despite heavy promotion, did not do as well as expected at the box office. He had also experienced a disappointing first theatrical outing as director of the stage play, The Act. Starring Liza Minnelli, the play was a direct spin-off of their collaboration in NEW YORK, NEW YORK. The Act did poorly on the road, and Scorsese was replaced by veteran Broadway director Gower Champion. The break-up of his second marriage, to writer Julia Cameron, soon after the birth of their daughter, was a particularly harsh blow to the director. Working on THE LAST WALTZ would prove to be like "therapy" for him. "It was the only thing that held me together," he stated.

THE LAST WALTZ is a record of the last concert appearance of The Band, one of the 'sixties' most respected rock groups. Perhaps, because they could no longer bear to tempt the Fates, The Band had decided to quit the road after sixteen years of playing in dance halls, bars, dives, concert halls, arenas, and stadiums. They no longer wanted to try their luck on the glory-hungry road that was littered with so many of rock's casualties--Janis Joplin, Jimi Hendrix, Jim Morrison, and Elvis Presley. Since their first concert as The Band had been at San Francisco's 5,000-seat Winterland auditorium, they felt it was only fitting to hold the celebration of their final concert there. Initially, the group wanted a video-cassette of the performance as a souvenir, but when they considered having a film made, Scorsese was the logical choice to be director. The link was Jonathan Taplin, The Band's former road manager and the producer of Scorsese's MEAN STREETS.

Scorsese was immediately attracted to the project. He felt that The Band's farewell appearance at Winterland on Thanksgiving of 1976 was a cultural event deserving cinematic treatment. Preparation for the film took three weeks and most of it was shot in one day. "We went in thinking, we'll document The Band's last concert and maybe we'll get something, maybe we won't. Then when the footage came back and we looked at it on the KEM, I just said, 'Wow ... we've got a movie.'" The director had assembled a constellation of celebrity cameramen to shoot the film--Michael Chapman, the director of photography, Laszlo Kovacs, Vilmos Zsigmond, and others. Conceived as "an opera," the production had unusually grandiose trappings. Scorsese recounts, there was

"a Strauss orchestra and a set built by Boris Leven, set designer on NEW YORK, NEW YORK, and chandeliers, two of
which were from GONE WITH THE WIND. The whole concert
was mixing William Cameron Menzies and a Visconti/Cocteau
kind of effect.

"It was a seven-hour concert, so my idea of shooting
in 35mm was hard to do because the camera ran out faster
and overheated a good deal. But it worked out better because
the visuals were quite good. Then I shot about four days'
documentary over a period of three to five months, and then
we just intermixed them. It's almost like a record album."
The documentary was one of the first films to use an incredible 24-track recording system. This highly-complex system
was a sound editor's headache, and the formidable editing job
contributed to a delay of the film's release. The final print
is in voluptuous four-track Dolby sound.

Scorsese prepared a scrupulously intricate 200-page
script which gave specific camera movements for every lyric
and every chord change to convey the color and shading of all
the different moods of the music. As one critic aptly noted,
"If Scorsese's fiction films have musical structure, THE LAST
WALTZ, with its meticulous script and pre-planned camera
angles, was constructed in the same manner as his narra-
tives." Besides recorded footage of the concert, the director
had three beautifully mounted set numbers filmed at an M-G-M
sound studio. He conducted rather awkward interviews with
The Band's members, and segments of them are interspersed
throughout the movie. Scorsese agrees that he is, in his own
words, "the world's worst interviewer," and the interview
fragments do, indeed, slacken what is otherwise an energetically
paced and exciting musical experience.

Rather than portray the free-wheeling love-fest between
rock stars and concert audiences that is so common in most
concert films, Scorsese's cameras were fixed solely on the
performers. We never see the concert audience, we can only
hear it. The full thrust of the movie is tilted to focus on the
music and the musicians. In his conception for the film, the
director set out to capture the intense communion of performers in concert. "Being a layman, I was interested in how the
musicians reacted to each other on stage. There are so many
films out today that call themselves 'musicals,' but they don't
deserve the name. They're imitating playing music. They're
not really playing it. The thing I wanted was the excitement
of the performance."

In one sense THE LAST WALTZ is a paean to the
music that grew out of the political and sociological turmoil
of the 'sixties.   The music of such song writer/performers
as Bob Dylan, Van Morrison, Neil Young, Joni Mitchell, Eric
Clapton, and, of course, The Band is featured in this nostalgic and highly personal documentary.   But at its best, the
film offers a breathtakingly close vantage of the rock performer's turbulent idyll, magnified in the glare of the concert spotlight.   In tightly held shots, the camera achieves
an enthralled intimacy with the musician caught up in the or-
giastic rites of performance.   Intense emotional expression
characterizes all Scorsese films, and THE LAST WALTZ is
particularly enlivened by the director's high-strung sensibilities.   Keenly attuned to the sharp-pitched energies of the
concert experience, Scorsese's cameras registered the gal-
vanic excitement of the rock performance and almost mag-
netically relayed it to the viewer.

As we are drawn in closer, both the spiritual exalta-
tion and the physical intensity of the performer becomes a
shared reality.   The Band's lead guitarist, Robbie Robertson,
who was also the movie's producer, commented, "The film
is the first time you get a real view of what happens on stage,
what goes on between the musicians.   You can see we're not
up there just giggling and wiggling.   Performing can be very
painful.   In each song, you put your whole body into it.   You
don't save it up.   That's why I think of concerts as being like
prize fights.   By the time you get to a certain stage, it almost becomes individual rounds.   You have to keep telling
yourself you can make it to the end."

THE LAST WALTZ is a compelling reflection of
Scorsese's love of music and the painstaking diligence with
which he marshals his film projects.   It is a joyously appreciative contemplation of the larger-than-life image of the
rock performer "enshrined" in the mythic world of the concert
stage.   Critics hailed the movie as a captivating concert film
that far transcended past examples of the genre.   Robert Hil-
burn, the Los Angeles Times critic, lauded the director's
ability "to capture the shades of urgency, joy, and physical
ordeal of musicians.... It's his purist approach to the rock
concert that gives THE LAST WALTZ its power and dignity.
To compromise would have destroyed it."   Film critic Myron
Meisel observed, "Martin Scorsese ... can never be impersonal and this elaborate fantasy is anything but a 'rockumentary'.... The choreographed camera renders the concert a
genuine occasion for beauty.   THE LAST WALTZ shows, yet

again, that a film artist can make his feelings known just by
the way he points (or moves) his camera."

Scorsese shows a definite predilection for making documentaries.   Since THE LAST WALTZ, he has completed yet
another one--AMERICAN BOY, a film about one of his close
friends and associates: Steven Prince (he played the role of
the gun salesman in TAXI DRIVER).   According to the director, the film deals in part with the tumultuous idyll of the
'sixties as it is reflected in Prince's own colorful experiences.
"The picture is about America and being on the road, rock
musicians, drugs ... and it's the story about his family."

In the works are plans for an upcoming movie on the
life of the prizefighter, Jack La Motta, starring Robert De
Niro.   Making a film, which he describes as focusing on the
ascetic world of the fighter--"he's like a monk or a priest"--
will be "like going home again," he exudes.   Asked about his
plans, there is talk of a proposed picture on underworld gangs
in New York.   He adds, "I think I may want to get away from
big budgets. ... "   He acknowledges his dilemma over favoring
the production of pictures in which he has personal interest
and the need to stay commercially viable.   "I love blockbuster
films, but I tend to make a much more personal sort of picture.   I'm trying to figure out how to keep doing that in a
way that still makes commercial sense.   I'm trying hard to
erase that conflict because if you do one just for commercial
reasons, you can really find yourself not wanting to get up in
the morning to shoot the scene.   And then what the hell do
you do?   How do you do the scene?   Just take a master and
a close-up and medium shot and that's it?   There's no soul
behind that.   And if there's no soul behind it, you can forget
it!"

Martin Scorsese's films are spirited with the fierce
intensity of an artist caught up in a determined struggle to
comprehend the nature of his own being, and, in turn, illu-
minate the greater expanses of the human psyche.   Ask him
what the role of the artist is, and he seems embarrassed to
consider defining himself in the context of such a weighty
philosophical question.   Filmmaking is simply what he wants
to do, he will say--or, more aptly put, has to do.   He waves
aside the grander implications of his work and states plainly,
"I'm not a prophet, a seer, a politician, or a philosopher.
I'm just not able to articulate that way.   I can only be articulate in the choice of films that I choose to make, the choice
of characters I choose to deal with in my films.   There's no

direct social commentary in the movies I make. No, there's
none of 'this is what's happening, isn't it horrible, here's
what can be done about it.'   My films depict a state of mind,
a state of being.   And the characters in them are those that
I can believe in.   I have to feel a lot of the things the characters feel because, eventually, they become almost inter-
changeable with me.   If I can't relate to the characters, I
can't make a film about them."

      Perhaps the most we can ask of any artist is that he
communicate with his audience out of a sense of personal conviction and the desire to be honest about what he portrays.
Scorsese is that kind of a filmmaker, one who finds it extremely difficult to compromise his insights and his own vision. He acknowledges that all he is trying to do is represent reality as he truthfully perceives it.   His movies are
character studies of individuals with whom the director shares
problems, concerns, anxieties and hopes.   He has no taste
for the false flourishes, the romanticized heroes, or the idealized situations that most of us see portrayed in the movies.
He wants to understand Charlie and Johnny Boy in MEAN
STREETS, Alice, Travis Bickle, and Jimmy Doyle in NEW
YORK, NEW YORK--why their relationships fail, why they
are angry, lonely, afraid. In rendering the small interior
dramas of their lives, Scorsese provides honest glimpses of
himself, the person he wants most to understand.

      The humanism that pervades his films is derived from
the basic compassion Scorsese feels for his characters.   There
are no real "bad guys" in his movies.   We are made to come
to terms with the wholeness of each of his protagonists, and
see them in the light of their hopes and ideals, all the while
we are privy to their mistakes, their anguish and the wrongs
they are capable of inflicting upon others.   In coming to know
them, we are brought closer to ourselves.   "One of the biggest satisfactions," says Scorsese, "is seeing an audience re-
act to the picture and knowing that you've gotten through to
some people, you've made them feel something, you've made
them understand something about themselves maybe, about you,
I guess about life in general.   Pictures like TAXI DRIVER
or ALICE cause people to relate to themselves in all kinds
of different ways."   He pauses and adds soberingly, "But they
still keep missing each other.   I don't know, I don't have the
answers.   It's disturbing, but then life is so very disturbing."

      Scorsese is not stopped by such bleak thoughts nor his
dour purview of life.   With every prospective project, he can

be counted on to give himself up totally in dedication and
fervor. If it is a fervor almost approaching frenzy at times,
Scorsese admits he is driven by a compulsive need to work
and to outrace that loudly ticking clock that signals the limits
of his mortality. About his future, he will state, matter-of-
factly, "I'm going to be very careful about choosing what my
next films will be because I'm convinced I have very little
time left--physically, I just believe it. And I've got to do
what's important to me. I don't want to do a movie unless
it furthers me not only as a filmmaker, but as a person, and
unless I can say what I want to say with it. "

MARTIN SCORSESE

A Film Checklist by Bella Taylor

Director

1.   WHAT'S A NICE GIRL LIKE YOU DOING IN A PLACE
       LIKE THIS? (1963). P: New York University Depart-
       ment of Television, Motion Picture and Radio Presen-
       tations. C: Zeph Michaelis, Mimi Stark, Sarah Brav-
       erman. 16mm. 9m.

2.   IT'S NOT JUST YOU, MURRAY! (1964). P: New
       York University Department of Television, Motion Pic-
       ture and Radio Presentations. C: Ira Rubin, Sam
       DeFazio, Andrea Martin. 16mm. , 35mm. blow-up.
       15m.

3.   THE BIG SHAVE (1967). C: Peter Bernuth. Agfa
       Color. 16mm. 6m.

4.   WHO'S THAT KNOCKING AT MY DOOR? (1969).
       (Earlier versions: BRING ON THE DANCING GIRLS
       [1965], I CALL FIRST [1967], and J. R. [1970]). C:
       Harvey Keitel, Zina Bethune, Lennard Kuras. 90m.

5.   BOXCAR BERTHA (1972). P: American International
       Pictures. C: Barbara Hershey, David Carradine,
       Barry Primus. DeLuxe Color. 88m.

6.   MEAN STREETS (1973). P: Warner's. C: Robert

De Niro, Harvey Keitel, Amy Robinson.   Technicolor.
110m.

√7.   ALICE DOESN'T LIVE HERE ANYMORE (1974).   P:
        Warner's.   C: Ellen Burstyn, Kris Kristofferson,
        Harvey Keitel.   Technicolor.   112m.

8.   ITALIANAMERICAN (1974).   P: National Communica-
        tions Foundation.   C: Charles and Catherine Scorsese.
        16mm.   Color.   45m.

√9.   TAXI DRIVER (1976).   P: Columbia.   C: Robert
        De Niro, Cybill Shepherd, Jodie Foster.   Color.
        Panavision.   112m.

10.   NEW YORK, NEW YORK (1977).   P: United Artists.
        C: Liza Minnelli, Robert De Niro, Barry Primus.
        Technicolor.   Panavision.   155m.

11.   THE LAST WALTZ (1978).   P: United Artists.   C:
        The Band, Bob Dylan, Joni Mitchell.   DeLuxe Color.
        Panavision.   115m.

Chapter 10

ROMAN POLANSKI

by Jon Tuska

I

Some years ago in a magazine article I had occasion
to use the word "aloneness" and a reader wrote to advise me
that there is no such word in the English language. Technically that reader was correct. Latin had no word for aloneness save solitudo, and the closest the ancient Romans came
to using it in the sense I meant was when Cicero commented
"in animi doloribus solitudines captare": in anguished souls
solitudes are captured. Modern French is of little help because, should you wish to describe aloneness, you must be
satisfied with either isolement, which merely means loneliness, or solitaire, which denotes a recluse; although didn't
Proust say, "Nous sommes irrémédiablement seuls"? The
tractable German language, which has permitted so many who
have written in it to commit nearly unpardonable abuses,
comes nearest perhaps with Alleinsein, the state or condition
of being alone.

Could it be that language in the Western world has had
little necessity to describe an almost universal sense of being
alone since the first century before Christ until the twentieth
century after Him? Maybe it is so. Maybe only in the most
extreme anguish is solitude captured. If, like Dr. Johnson,
I could write my own dictionary, that would be the definition
I should give for aloneness; and aloneness comprises the inner
lexicon of all of Polanski's films.

Prior to our meeting in Paris in the spring of 1976 at
the Studios de Boulogne, I had been to Chartres. It was a
good thing, not because Chartres today is so much like it was
during the Middle Ages with its majestic cathedral and its
medieval dwellings, but because it brought to mind Bernard

369

Roman Polanski as a hoodlum in CHINATOWN (Paramount, 1974).   Photo courtesy of Eddie Brandt's Saturday Matinee.

of Chartres, who wrote in the twelfth century that we have
nothing that we are not given, and because in this century
we have chosen to reject all that we have ever been given
so as to exist in a self-imposed vacuum amid feelings of indeterminate loss.

Polanski was in the midst of dubbing his most recent
film, LOCOTAIRE (THE TENANT), into English. The scene
projected on the giant screen was the one where Polanski
climbs the stairs alongside Melvyn Douglas while he is being
told how to act properly in Paris. Up the stairs, backwards,
up the stairs, backwards, up the stairs--each time some new
effect was added; each time the bands indicating the sound
track running on the screen beneath the picture frame took on
different markings; shapes are sounds. Polanski was giving
directions in French and with every success, every "Bon!"
from Polanski and triumphant murmurs of endorsement from
the technicians, a feeling of eerieness stole over the sequence,
not visual save on the track, but aural, suggestive, macabre.
Up the stairs, backwards....

After a time, Polanski walked over to where we were
sitting opposite the control panel.

"Parlez-vous français?" he asked.

"Oui," I said, "mais ma compagne ne le parle pas."

"Will you have a cigar?" he asked, picking up a box
of Havanas.

"Non, merci."

"This is my new picture," he said, turning to Vicki.
"It is about a man who comes to live in Paris. He becomes
a naturalized French citizen. But the French, they do not
accept him. He is made to feel an outsider. He may be a
French citizen, but he is not French. And his mind, he is
beginning to lose his mind."

He left the sentence hanging and resumed working. Up
the stairs, backwards. I began to think that Polanski and
Douglas would never make it; then they did. Douglas opened
the door to his apartment. A clock began to chime. "Dix
heures!" Polanski proclaimed, followed by a "Bon!" Suddenly,
backwards, up the stairs, backwards, up the stairs.

Time passed and while it did I thought of how fondly

the French had once treated Polanski, in his early years as
an international director; of the respectful portrait of him
which had been drawn in Cahiers du Cinéma in February,
1966.   Now, quite the same as the character Trelkovsky whom
he was portraying in the film, Polanski was a naturalized
French citizen.   After all, he had been born in Paris, of
Polish parents, on 18 August, 1933.

"Have you ever had couscous?" Polanski asked, pop-
ing up again into our midst.

"No."

"It's a dish from Northern Africa.   Come, I know a
restaurant nearby.   Try some."

He escorted us out of the editing room.

"Posters all over Paris are announcing the opening of
LOCOTAIRE," I told him as we made our way along a narrow
passageway.

"Yes, but the French critics don't like it.   It was entered at Cannes, one of the two French entries.   I don't give
interviews.   That was a mistake.   In France, you must give
interviews, or you'll pay for it.   I'm paying for it now."

We began descending a long flight of steps.

"Did you ever interview Adolph Zukor?"   Polanski
asked me, pausing at the midway landing.

"Yes.   He was nearly a hundred and had what I thought
to be an incredible memory."

"Let me tell you a story."   We resumed our descent.
"When I was at Paramount in New York, I would see him every
day at lunch time.   He always hid his mouth with his hand,
as if he didn't want anyone to see that he was shoveling the
food in, you know?   When he had a mouthful, he would take
his hand away.   Every day one of the publicity people would take
me over to his table and introduce me.   'Mr. Zukor, this is
Roman Polanski.   He is directing a picture for us.'"

Polanski giggled light-heartedly as we came out into
the grayish light of day.   It had been raining.   Water ran in
the streets.

"And every day he would nod at me as if we were meeting for the first time. 'Good,' he would say, 'that's good.'"

We paused in the middle of the sidewalk at the studio entrance. It seemed as if it might rain again.

"This way," Polanski directed. "It isn't far."

I felt a drop or two of rain. Some lines of Rilke's, memorized long ago, came back to me:

> Regnet hernieder in den Zwitterstunden,
> wenn sich nach Morgen wenden alle Gassen,
> und wenn die Leiber, welche nichts gefunden,
> enttäuscht und traurig voneinander lassen;
> und wenn die Menschen, die einander hassen,
> in einem Bett zusammen schlafen müssen:
>   dann geht die Einsamkeit mit den Flussen ...
> [Raining down in the hour of twilight,
> as all the streets turn toward the dawn,
> and when bodies, sad in unfulfillment,
> disillusioned leave one another,
> and when, hating each other, they must sleep
> together in one bed:
>   then loneliness merges with the rivulets ...]

"What's wrong with him?" Polanski asked Vicki.

"Oh, nothing," she quipped. "It's just that he spent several hours yesterday walking around Paris trying to find a bottle of Scotch, and when he found one, it was of the lowest grade and cost him a hundred francs."

"This is Paris, you must remember," Polanski said, laughing.

Once we arrived, Polanski held the door. We were shown to a booth. Polanski ordered couscous. We had whiskey; he had wine.

We had with us a book of screenplays from Polanski's first three feature films. There were many candid illustrations of him directing.

"Have you seen this?" I asked him.

"No," he said, taking the book at once and avidly paging through it, intrigued by the illustrations. "You know," he said after a time, "it is strange, I was so unhappy when I made these pictures, but when I look at these photographs, I feel nostalgic."

"I understand from John Huston," I said, "that you were responsible for changing the ending of CHINATOWN [Paramount, 1974]?"

"Yes," Polanski said, putting down the book.

"Keep it," Vicki said.

"When I was given the script," he said, acknowledging the gift as he spoke, "it was about 250 pages. Many of the characters were unfilmable. I worked on the script for eight weeks just to get rid of unnecessary characters. The script had it that Huston died at the end. I didn't want that. I wanted him to live."

"Why?" Vicki asked.

"Because there is no justice in the story. You want the audience to be perturbed because justice isn't done. Hollywood likes to tease the audience, but the hero always comes along at the end and kills the bad guy. It's not that way, and I didn't want to film it that way. I wanted Huston for the role of Dunaway's father. He was perfect. And Nicholson. The script was rewritten with him in mind. Ask Bobby Evans at Paramount to show you the original script I was first handed. You wouldn't believe it."

Couscous was brought. Polanski gave instructions in how it was best seasoned.

"Now what do you think?"

We both nodded our accord.

"Don't go anywhere else in Paris but here," he cautioned.

"The detective loses in the end," I said, changing the subject.

"Well, he had to lose, didn't he? Detectives are losers

to begin with.   Theirs is a dirty business, peeping and spying, getting photographs of what people do in hotel rooms.
That's not a profession.   A detective is a loser. "

"What amazes me about the film," Vicki remarked, "is
how little violence there is in it. "

"Yes," Polanski nodded vigorously, "and the critics
attacked it, saying it was full of violence.   But there is none
really.   Violence shouldn't be drawn out.   It's there in the
scene where I cut Nicholson's nose.   It happens so fast, you
aren't aware of it; then it's over.   That's how violence is.
They want to cut that scene when they release the film to
television.   Even when Dunaway gets shot, the violence is
quick.   Audiences like sensations.   So if you have to include
violence, if it's quick, it is also sensational. "

When we were nearly finished eating, Moroccan tea
was served, in glasses, drawn from a samovar which was
brought to our table and left there.   For a moment at least,
Polanski seemed at home in Paris.   Polanski, for whom life
was being constantly at work, or skiing, or exercising fran-
tically, or going to bed with women, was comfortable.   He
stretched out in his booth seat.

"CHINATOWN didn't have a very happy ending, " I
taunted him.

"Happy endings make me puke, don't they you?"

"But audiences like happy endings. "

"I don't believe in giving people what they want, or
what they think they want.   When I was little I saw OF MICE
AND MEN [United Artists, 1939].   That didn't have a happy
ending, did it?"   He knew I hadn't been serious, but he per-
sisted.   "Think about successful stories.   They're usually unhappy.   Happiness doesn't give you intrigue, no suspense;
and if you don't have conflict, you don't have a movie. "

"Can I ask you something?" Vicki said.

"Anything dear.   You can ask me anything. "

"What's WHAT?"

"What?"

"WHAT? What is WHAT?"

"What? Do you mean WHAT? Oh, WHAT?!" Polan-
ski broke into laughter and drew himself together in his seat.
"WHAT? Dear, WHAT? is like a rondo. You know? Tra-
la-la-la, tra-la-la-la, and then la-la, and then it comes back
again, Tra-la-la-la, tra-la-la-la. WHAT? is a rondo."

"Rondos don't make any sense. They are rondos.
That's all. It's a theme you keep coming back to, that repeats. I wanted to do a movie that was like a rondo."

It was time to go. Polanski threw two hundred francs
on the table and we walked out of the restaurant. His spirits
were jubilant. He began to whistle as we walked; or, I should
say, while we walked and he skipped along the curb.

I thought about Howard Hawks' TO HAVE AND HAVE
NOT (Warner's, 1944), the way he gave the story a happy
ending and allowed Humphrey Bogart, one man supposedly
alone, to triumph over his situation. The Harry Morgan
character Bogart was playing had nothing to do with Hemingway's character, as Hawks well knew, and as he had often
confessed to me.

> "A man," Harry Morgan said, looking at them
> both. "One man alone ain't got. No man alone now."
> He stopped. "No matter how a man alone ain't got
> no bloody f---ing chance."
> He shut his eyes. It had taken him a long time
> to get it out and it had taken him all his life to
> learn it.

That was how Hemingway had written it in the 1937
novel. He had told how Harry Morgan had to lose his boat,
because in life, when somebody wins, somebody else has got
to lose. And lying on the deck of his boat, gut-shot and
bleeding to death, Harry Morgan lost his freedom and his
self-reliance, and was even losing his life. When Paramount
filmed ISLANDS IN THE STREAM in 1977, with George C.
Scott in the starring role, Denne Bart Petutclerc ignored the
third part of Hemingway's posthumous novel and went back to
Harry Morgan's story from TO HAVE AND HAVE NOT, but
for the fade ... for the fade he went back to Howard Hawks!

John Huston altered some of the stage play dialogue
when he came to film KEY LARGO (Warner's, 1948). Edward

G. Robinson, holding Bogart, Lauren Bacall, Claire Trevor,
and Lionel Barrymore hostage, is asked by Barrymore what
he wants. "He wants more," Bogart answers for Robinson.
"Yeah," Robinson agrees, taken with the idea. "That's what
I want. I want more. More!"

"Will you ever get enough?" Barrymore asks him.

Robinson is perplexed. "I don't think so," he says.
"I haven't yet. "

In CHINATOWN, Jack Nicholson confronts John Huston.
The bond issue has gone through. The people of Los Angeles
will be paying to irrigate land in the valley owned by Huston.
It will make Huston another fortune.

"How much money do you have?" Nicholson asks Huston.

Huston shrugs his shoulders.

"A million dollars?"

Huston nods agreement.

"Ten million?"

Huston again agrees.

"Well, then," Nicholson asks in exasperation, "why
are you doing it?"

"Because," answers Huston, "you have to think of the
future. "

Criminal corruption, by the time CHINATOWN was
made, was more than synonymous with the American political,
judicial, and law enforcement systems; it was, in fact, in-
digenous to the American way of life. The "future" for Huston in the film is possession of his daughter/granddaughter
whom he incestuously conceived with Faye Dunaway, his screen
daughter. Jack Nicholson would prevent that future from happening; he would have Huston brought to justice. Dunaway and
the daughter/granddaughter are about to escape from their
hiding place in Chinatown. Huston arrives there with Nicholson. Nicholson's men were supposed to wait for him there,
but the police have shown up in the interim and now Nichol-

son's men are handcuffed. When Dunaway makes a break for
it, she is shot through the eye by a plainclothes policeman.
Huston embraces his daughter/granddaughter and leads her
away from this terrible sight.

"He owns the police," Nicholson is warned when he
would struggle and object.

"As little as possible," he mutters beneath his breath.

"C'mon Jake," his men comfort him. "It's Chinatown."

As I watched Roman Polanski skipping along, it occurred to me that at that very moment, in the States, the
story of his wife's brutal murder was being televised for a
vast viewing audience.

"CHINATOWN didn't have a very happy ending," I
said again.

Polanski moved back onto the sidewalk and walked
beside us.

"When people leave a theatre," he said, "they shouldn't
be allowed to think that everything is all right with the world.
It isn't. And very little in life has a happy ending." He
stopped in his tracks and faced us. "And CHINATOWN was
a popular film, wasn't it?"

"You needn't be so smug about it," I said. "All you're
saying is that you were lucky--once--and got away with telling
the truth."

We were at the entrance to the Studios de Boulogne.
Polanski put his arm around me.

"Let's go back inside and work on LOCOTAIRE, shall
we?"

II

"Tiefdenkende Menschen," Nietzsche wrote in Menschliches, Allzumenschliches, "kommen sich im Verkehr mit
anderen als Komödianten vor, weil sie sich da, um verstanden
zu werden, immer erst eine Oberfläche anheucheln müssen."
[Deep thinkers always appear in intercourse like comedians

because in order to be understood they must first simulate
a superficies.] Polanski, who used to remark, "I am not a
pessimist, I am just serious," had sufficient provocation to
simulate a comic superficies at eight years of age when he
was left to his own resources. His parents had returned to
Poland in 1936 and, following the Nazi invasion, they were
among those placed immediately in Auschwitz, intended as
participants in Hitler's "letzte Auflösung" to the Jewish question. "My father cut the wires," Polanski recalled, "and I
was off." After Roman's escape, the elder Polanski was removed to Mauthausen, and survived; his mother remained at
Auschwitz and was gassed.

Picking berries in a field one day, Roman was sighted
by a group of German soldiers. For amusement they used
his frightened, scampering figure for target practice. Roman
was shuttled from family to family. While playing in an abandoned bomb shelter, he was set upon by a Polish thug and
nearly murdered. The beating he received required that a
steel plate be set in his skull cage. He remained longest
with a Catholic peasant family in the village of Wysoka.

When questioned as to the probable traumatic effects
of this separation from his parents and his nomadic existence,
Polanski was inclined to attach little significance to it. "The
real source of human character," he said, "is genetic and
what you've experienced in the first three years of your life.
I was raised with gentleness and care and love." He was
addicted to movies at an early age, especially Disney cartoons,
Jeanette MacDonald musicals, and Errol Flynn in THE AD-
VENTURES OF ROBIN HOOD (Warner's, 1938), which he saw
twenty times. He didn't break that record until he saw Laurence Olivier's HAMLET (Universal, 1948) twenty-four times.
"Even when the Nazis showed anti-Semitic propaganda films,"
he remembered, "I'd be glued to the barbed wire. There
was a magic about movies, though I was fully aware of the
content."

The peasant family in Wysoka converted Roman to
Catholicism during the war. "They were great people," Polanski said, "even though they couldn't read or write. Having
to do farm chores made me think for myself." Polanski exchanged Catholicism for Marxism at twelve with the arrival
of the Red Army. "They were the avengers who brought us
freedom," he said, much as any Pole would have said of Na-
poleon a century before when the French liberated Poland
from Russia.

When Roman's father was released from confinement, he enrolled Roman in a technical school where he studied to be an electrician, while resuming his former job as manager of a plastics factory. Roman became bored and, at fourteen, began acting in local theatre groups. Later he worked his way into films, appearing first in a compilation film made by students, entitled THREE STORIES, and in Andrzej Wajda's first important production, A GENERATION, in 1954. Once his father remarried, Roman asked to move out and live on his own. His father understood and agreed to finance him until he found a suitable vocation. Polanski enrolled in art school at Krakov and studied graphic arts and sculpture. His Marxism evaporated commensurately with his disinclination to enter military service. At twenty, encouraged upon gradua- tion by a professor, Polanski underwent the grueling ten-day examination required of applicants to the Polish National Film Academy in Lodz, hoping to be accepted as an acting student, but instead, because of his previous technical training, he was accepted by the directing school. Polanski's early color ex- perimental film, THE BIKE, was left unfinished, but he did complete BREAK UP THE DANCE in 1957. TWO MEN AND A WARDROBE was filmed in 1958, his third year at Lodz, and was his first student film seen outside Poland.

Polanski felt that dialogue had little place in a short film and therefore concentrated on telling visually the story of two men who emerge from the sea carrying an old-fashioned wardrobe. No one wants any part of the men or their burden. When a girl is about to be molested by a gang of thugs, she sees their reflection in the wardrobe mirror and runs to safety. In retaliation, the thugs fall upon the two men and beat them up. Polanski cast himself in a cameo role as one of the thugs. Finally, in despair, the two men decide to re- turn to the sea, still carrying the wardrobe between them.

In making the film, Polanski adhered to Flaubert's admonition, "il ne faut jamais conclure." He has never really retreated from that principle, nor has he done much to change his orientation since this early propaedeutic exercise. The music for the picture was composed by Krzysztof Komeda who, until his death in 1968, composed the music for nearly all of Polanski's films. "Though symbolically one regards the two men as a single entity," Ivan Butler wrote of TWO MEN AND A WARDROBE in his book Roman Polanski (Tan- tivy, 1970), "in actual fact they at least have the companion- ship of each other, a friendship that stands all the strains of their dilemma, and which later solitaries ... will not know."

In 1959 Polanski's diploma work consisted of THE
LAMP, never seen outside Poland, and WHEN ANGELS FALL,
the latter occasionally blocked with one or another of his features in American art theatres. WHEN ANGELS FALL tells
of an old woman who works as a matron in a public lavatory.
Her present is filmed in black and white, whereas her memories of the men in her past, the cavalry man who seduced
her, the son to whom she gave birth, the death of her lover
during a war (with Polanski in a bit part), are filmed in color.
She is constantly reminded of the present through the sordid
incidents happening in the urinal until, magically, her lover
comes crashing through the skylight in the form of an angel
with comic wings and a wired-on nimbus, setting her free in
death.

"She is moving, that old woman," Polanski was quoted
in the February, 1966 interview for Cahiers du Cinéma. "In
life too, she was moving. I found her in a home for the aged.
She was ninety or ninety-two ... I no longer know, but she
was old, old.... So old she no longer had any wish, and
when we paid her, we saw that money no longer meant anything to her. One day, I asked her what she was going to
do with the money. She thought it over. She said in the
end that she was going to buy sugar. I told her: 'But you
have much too much money for sugar!' She said: 'Oh yes,
wait ...' and she thought. Then she said 'All the same I am
going to buy sugar.' She kept to that. And that too was
moving, for one said to oneself that in that institution they
must not give them enough sugar for their coffee, the beasts!
... She had glimmers, the old woman. Things came back,
but one understood nothing of them. She saw a costume and
that said something to her. She spoke then of the Russians
who had come in eighteen hundred and something, but what
she said had neither beginning nor end. It was pieces that
came back to her. Little pieces of her life that nothing linked
together, but all that moved me enormously, for she was exactly the character of the film. And she was always sitting,
pensive, never saying anything...."

In 1960, his training completed, Polanski worked for
a time for Kamera, one of Poland's eight production companies, assisting French director J. M. Drot on a series of documentaries and Andrzej Munk, a Polish director he very much
admired, on a feature. Then he went to France, where he
stayed for nearly eighteen months. During this time he helped
write, and then directed and appeared in, a sixteen-minute
short film, LE GROS ET LE MAIGRE (A. P. E. C. , 1961), in

which he portrayed a servant tyrannized by actor André Katelbach playing his peasant master. If the Germans and the Russians had taught him nothing else, they were adept instructors
in the meaning and exercise of power in the modern world.

Polanski returned to Poland in 1961. He married
Polish film actress Barbara Kwiatkowski (whose screen name
was Barbara Lass). The marriage ended in divorce in 1962.
Polanski has frequently declared that if when given two lovers,
as La Rochefoucauld once put it, "il y a toujours un qui aime
et un qui se laisse aimer," he was the one who did the loving. I suspect that this experience merely confirmed, rather
than shaped, his view of women.

"Niemand tritt ins Leben ohne Voraussetzungen," C.
G. Jung reminds us in his essay "Die Lebenswende," the
turnings of life (contained in Volume VIII of the Gesammelte
Werke, Rascher Verlag, 1967). "Diese Voraussetzungen sind
gelegentlich falsch, sie passen nicht auf die äusseren Bedingungen, denen man begegnet. Oft handelt es sich um zu
grosse Erwartungen oder um Unterschatzung der ausseren
Schwierigkeiten oder um unberechtigten Optimismus oder um
Negativismus." [No one enters upon life without assumptions.
These assumptions are occasionally false, arising not from
the external situations which one encounters. Often it is a
matter of too great expectations or an underestimation of external difficulties or unjustified optimism or negativism.] We
are all prone to such assumptions, engendered by temperament, or perhaps by some primordial and hidden psychic pre-
disposition. The aging process, if it isn't excessively hindered
by neurosis, should in time divest us of at least some of the
more untenable of our assumptions. But what are we to make
of the notion that women are by nature promiscuous and unfaithful? I do not think that we can attribute this accurately
to the category of unconscious assumptions about life which
are more or less present at birth.

Presumably the idea for KNIFE IN THE WATER (Contemporary, 1962) came from Jakub Goldberg, an assistant
director working for Kamera at the time and a friend of Polanski's whom Roman cast as one of the two men carrying the
wardrobe in his earlier short film. To collaborate with him,
Polanski chose Jerzy Skolimowski, a younger man who was
just beginning the five-year course at the Lodz Film School.
The two men locked themselves away in Goldberg's room and
came up with a script that Polanski subsequently credited
more to Skolimowski than to himself. Kamera accepted the

screenplay for production and Polanski went about casting it.
Of the three parts called for in the script, only that of Andrzej
was assigned to a professional actor, Leon Niemcyzk. To
play Andrzej's wife, Polanski spent days at the Warsaw swimming pool, interviewing talent in and out of the water. He
finally came up with Jolanta Umecka, a music student, who
seemed to fit his idea of the kind of woman he needed. The
role of the young man who seduces Umecka was given to Zygmunt Malanowicz, a drama school student.

Production proceeded at a snail's pace--much of the
story taking place aboard a boat in the Polish lake region--
with Polanski sometimes getting ten seconds of film a day,
sometimes nothing. To evoke a performance from the old
woman in WHEN ANGELS FALL, Polanski had plied her with
chocolate bon-bons. To overcome Umecka's anxiety before
the camera, Polanski resorted to a similar device, feeding
her chocolate biscuits; as her tension increased, so did her
eating, and the curves restrained by her bathing suit became
more opulent. Production was halted half-way through the
film when rumors concerning orgies in the boathouse reached
Warsaw. Only after the most vehement denials did it resume.

There are two stories in KNIFE IN THE WATER. The
primary story is the Oedipus conflict played out between an
older man and his young wife when a hitchhiker intrudes on
their lives and proceeds to sexually challenge the older man
and finally succeeds in seducing the wife. The knife carried
by the hitchhiker, which he can use dexterously, is obviously
symbolic of his youthful sexuality. There is a reversal, in
that it is the hitchhiker who is supposedly murdered by the
older man; but this is only a sham, and while the husband
is ashore the hitchhiker rejoins the wife who is isolated on
the boat, and she welcomes his sexual advances. The secondary story is the tedium of conventional bourgeois married
life and the pointlessness of existence, for all three of the
characters, in which sexual interest conflicts with possessive-
ness.

Upon release, the picture won rave reviews and, after
being shown at the New York Film Festival, was even nominated for an Academy Award. Polanski found himself famous, virtually overnight, and began referring to himself as
"the great Polanski"--and meaning it. What impressed critics
about KNIFE was its intense concentration, and they delighted
in the opportunity afforded them to dissect the Freudian undertones; some went so far as to read in it an ambiguous political

statement. Certainly Poland's Communist Party leader,
Wladyslaw Gomulka, felt this way when he condemned the
picture for depicting decadent behavior. The upshot was that
Polanski, although acclaimed, was unable to secure further
employment. While the preference for theme over story has
long been a Slavic proclivity, KNIFE IN THE WATER, viewed
objectively today, is a trifle dull if the political implication
of depicting social ennui behind the Iron Curtain is not taken
into account; certainly it had much to do with the film's popularity in the West.

There appears to be some dispute about Polanski's
next film into release, the short, MAMMALS, which won the
Grand Prix at Tours. Polanski claims that it was filmed
before KNIFE and edited after KNIFE was completed; most
other sources state that MAMMALS was the only prospect
Polanski had after KNIFE. It was financed privately by Wo-
jciech Frykowski, the son of a Polish black-market king.
The film, photographed against a dazzling background of white
snow, was a parable about two men who bicker so much between themselves that they are unable to help each other
across the frozen wastes.

In a way, because of the Grand Prix, you might think
MAMMALS an auspicious beginning for Frykowski as an independent film producer, only it didn't work out at all as he
surely expected it might. He followed Polanski to the United
States, was readily absorbed into the Southern California drug
culture, and was there on Cielo Drive in Sharon Tate's "love
house" when the Manson "family" struck. Shot, repeatedly
slashed and stabbed, thought by his assailants to be Roman's
"younger brother," he staggered out onto the front lawn,
screaming "Help, help, somebody please help me!" The
drugs and the dreams in the smog-laden City of the Angeles
ended abruptly for him as, in the words of one of his assassins, "then we finished him off."

In 1963 Polanski accepted an offer to direct the Amsterdam episode of the film LES PLUS BELLES ESCROQUERIES
DU MONDE. His collaborator on the screenplay was Gerard
Brach and their similar temperaments and sense of humor
(or, better put, their sense of comédie noire) made the association one of long standing. Together they adapted a novel
by Georges Bardawil for the screen, directed by Jean Léon
and released under the title, AIMEZ-VOUS LES FEMMES?
It dealt with a cabal of Parisian cannibals who serve pretty
girls as the haute cuisine at their get-togethers.

Polanski and Brach shared an apartment and arrived at their cinematic ideas through animated discussions which were followed by Brach writing the scenes in French. It would begin over chess at breakfast. They would talk. Brach would then retreat to his room to write while Polanski busied himself making telephone calls. Later, Polanski would ask Brach to recite what he had written and they would decide if it should be kept, altered, or discarded. They assembled a script out of scenes they felt they would like someday to see in a film and called it WHEN KATELBACH COMES, and then KATELBACH, and finally CUL-DE-SAC. Polanski could find no backers for the project and many producers refused even to read the screenplay.

Gene Gutowski, a producer in England, was so impressed with KNIFE IN THE WATER that he invited Polanski to come to London to direct REPULSION (Compton-Cameo, 1965). Polanski alleges that the film was based on a published story, but, even if it was, the scenario Polanski and Brach wrote in French was sufficiently undiluted "Polanski" to deserve the credit the two of them were given for an original screenplay. REPULSION starred Catherine Deneuve, who had begun her film career in earnest in Roger Vadim's LE VICE ET LA VIRTU in 1962. Initially she wanted to marry Vadim but, due to his reluctance, settled for having a child by him out of wedlock instead. "Her hair was dark chestnut," Vadim recalls in his book Memoirs of the Devil (Harcourt, 1975), "shoulder length. Her figure was slender, the shy and discreetly perverse adolescent figure of a Colette heroine.... She liked to laugh but went through life with an air of gloom."

I asked Polanski if the Deneuve character in the film was supposed to have Lesbian tendencies, as suggested by some critics at the time. "Not at all," he said. "She murders men out of a fear of sex. She's not a normal person to begin with; hence the photo of her at the end. She's a homicidal schizophrenic, yes, but not a blood-thirsty monster. The opposite is true. She is innocent. She's just fascinated by sex, by her sister's boy friend's things in the bathroom."

After a somewhat moody build-up, Deneuve "flips out" and murders one of her male admirers and the landlord before she is discovered by her sister and her sister's boy friend cringing beneath her sister's bed. The highpoint of the film, according to its admirers, is the development of Deneuve's disintegratory hallucinations. It is on this basis that comparisons are drawn between REPULSION and Hitchcock's PSYCHO (Paramount, 1960).

Columbia Pictures acquired distribution rights for the United States and, as a sales tool to excite general interest among exhibitors and the public, leaked the rumor that in those scenes where Deneuve fantasizes that she is being raped (she appears to enjoy the second, anal, rape more than the first one administered vaginally; but this may be due to Polanski's dark humor), because Polanski is a fanatic for realism he was supposed to have filmed the sexual act in progress and lighted the participants' figures so as to cast revealing shadows on the wall.   It was a lie and it did nothing to counteract the disappointing American box office.   Internationally, however, REPULSION did much better.   European critics tended not only to overlook the heavy-handed special effects, but they seemed to ignore that in making Deneuve's descent into insanity so subjective an experience, Polanski drew it as more alienating than empathetic (the German word Mitleid, meaning literally "suffering along with," would probably be more apt).   Which is unfortunate, because it is Mitleid Polanski needed most of all to put across both the character and her situation.   As it stands, REPULSION shocks without ever evoking human involvement; we are as much outsiders from Deneuve's personality as she is from those around her.

"I do not mean there are no neurotics in Poland," Polanski told Cahiers du Cinéma, talking about REPULSION, "but no doubt there are fewer of them; in any case neurosis is not expressed that way!   What is the reason?   Maybe the solitude is less great there than elsewhere....   In any case, I wanted to show precisely a certain kind of disorder and not another.   Therefore I had to do so where that disorder existed."

The reader might think that the British would object to Polanski's saying that he had to have an English setting for Deneuve's breakdown; but not at all.   Most British critics seemed to concur with Ivan Butler that "the entire atmosphere of a peculiarly English mode of existence is caught with a fidelity and accuracy astonishing in a foreign director."

What is impressive to me about REPULSION is Polanski's use of sound to heighten every significant visual effect; indeed, it is the accompanying sounds which make the visual effects significant.   Polanski can at times become so enraptured with visual content that he utterly forsakes story, drama, or character, as he did subsequently when filming MACBETH (Columbia, 1971), but his sense of the dramatic power of sound never deserts him.   When he was interviewed by film

students at the American Film Institute in Los Angeles--the
interview appeared in Dialogue on Film in August, 1971--
Polanski took pains to illustrate how a composer working at
a piano, by means of rigorous trial and error, comes to com-
pose a faultless melody. I was affected by that same quality
in him while I was in Paris listening to his dubbing THE
TENANT.

The success of REPULSION was such that, in association with Gutowski as the producer, Polanski could proceed
with CUL-DE-SAC (Compton-Cameo, 1966). For me it is the
first film he made up to that time that proves consistently
entertaining; the characters and the comédie noire situation
in which they find themselves never slacken. Donald Pleasence, later a nasty heavy in several Hollywood films, was
cast in the lead as George, a man who leaves his first wife
to live in a secluded castle with a second, younger, more
beautiful wife whom he genuinely loves and who is unfaithful
to him; it ends with George sitting, bereft, on a rock in the
midst of a promontory, calling out in his aloneness the name
of his first wife. Françoise Dorleac, Catherine Deneuve's
older sister, soon to die in an automobile crash while vaca-
tioning with Deneuve, plays the second wife (we never see
the first one). Neither Pleasence nor Dorleac were in accord
with Polanski's interpretation of their relationship. "She went
for his money, of course," Pleasence once remarked, "but
she liked him as well. This was an area where Roman and
I disagreed. He was absolutely adamant that she did not find
George attractive in any way."

The most amusing character in the film is Lionel
Stander, who is splendid portraying a bumbling American gangster disrupting this idyllic, medieval romance (one-sided, according to Polanski) between Pleasence and Dorleac. "Of
course she is bored," Pleasence went on, "but Françoise
wanted the character to be more two-dimensional, whereas
Roman wanted her to be simply sluttish. I don't think he
ever really liked her performance very much, though I myself thought it was great."

What came to affect Polanski's view of women--although
not permanently, to be sure--was meeting Sharon Tate prior
to making his next picture, THE FEARLESS VAMPIRE KILL-
ERS (M-G-M, 1967). Martin Ransohoff was the executive
producer on the picture, acting as liaison between M-G-M
and the film's producer, Gene Gutowski, with Polanski directing from the script he had written with Gerard Brach. Sharon

Tate was working at the time in another Ransohoff/Filmways
production and Ransohoff wanted Roman to use her in VAM-
PIRE KILLERS. Polanski was first introduced to Tate at
one of Ransohoff's parties.

"I thought she was quite pretty," Polanski said later,
"but I wasn't at that time very impressed. But then I saw
her again. I took her out. We talked a lot, you know. At
that time I was really swinging. All I was interested in was
to fuck a girl and move on. I had a very bad marriage, you
know. Years before. Not bad; it was beautiful, but my wife
dumped me. So I was feeling great, because I was a success
with women and I just like fucking around."

Once Sharon Tate was dead, the police investigators
questioned Polanski about their relationship; they had married
on 20 January, 1968. Shortly before his official interrogation,
Polanski had given a press conference at which he verbally
chastised reporters for stories carried in the press about
marital rifts, orgies (some of which had been videotaped at
the "love house" and found by the police), and the use of
drugs. Even though Sharon Tate had had a reputation as a
woman of easy virtue at the time Polanski met her, he never
regarded her that way. To the press, he called her "beautiful," and "a good person," and now that she was dead, stated
that the "last few years I spent with her were the only time
of true happiness in my life...."

"I remember," Polanski told the police, "I spent a
night--I lost a key--and I spent a night in her house in the
same bed, you know?" It was while they were working together on VAMPIRE KILLERS. "And I knew there was no
question of making love with her. That's the type of girl she
was. I mean, that rarely happens to me! And then we went
on location--it was about two or three months later. When
we were on location shooting the film, I asked her, 'Would
you like to make love with me?' and she said, very sweetly,
'Yes.' And then for the first time I was somewhat touched
by her, you know. And we started sleeping regularly together.
And she was so sweet and so lovely that I didn't believe it,
you know. I'd had bad experiences and I didn't believe that
people like that existed, and I was waiting a long time for
her to show the color, right? But she was beautiful, without
this phoniness. She was fantastic. She loved me ... she
was a fucking angel. She was a unique character, who I'll
never meet again in my life." (Emphasis appears in the
original police transcript.)

Yet, however much Sharon Tate affected Polanski off-screen, she did nothing to alter his view of women in VAM-PIRE KILLERS or in any of his subsequent films. According to Freud in his essay "The Most Prevalent Form of Degradation in Erotic Life" (contained in Volume IV of the Collected Papers, Basic Books, 1959), "a fully normal attitude in love" comes about when the "two currents of feeling have to unite--we may describe them as the tender, affectionate feelings and the sensual feelings...." Not only does this never happen in any of the male/female relationships depicted in Polanski's films, but women are always pictured merely as flat, one-dimensional sources of sexual gratification. The exception is the Deneuve character in REPULSION, who becomes a castrating, murderous female, but in her sexual obsession she is related in spirit, if not expression, to all of Polanski's other major female protagonists.

M. Esther Harding, who identified libido with the "daemon of sexuality," related in her book Psychic Energy: Its Source and Its Transformation (Princeton/Bollingen, 1973) that "a human being who is still identified with the daemon of sexuality is able to live his sexuality only on an auto-erotic level. This is true whether the impulse finds its outlet in masturbation or whether it leads him to sexual relations with another person of either his own or the opposite sex. For as the interest and desires of the individual in this stage of development are concerned solely with his own sensations and bodily needs, his sexual instinct still lacks that degree of psychic modification which necessarily precedes any real concern with the object. Therefore almost any partner will serve for satisfaction on this level, provided the necessary stimulus is present to set off the physical mechanism of detumescence. Consequently, persons in this stage of development are usually promiscuous and fickle, and at times may be driven by a veritable daemon of desirousness, seemingly without regard for either the requirements of relationship or the fundamental decencies. To a man on this level, a woman is nothing but a sexual object, and one woman can be substituted for another with the greatest ease."

There is an additional factor to be taken into account. "Whatever the deeper motives are for a woman's promiscuity," Theodor Reik wrote in The Need to Be Loved (Farrar, Straus, and Giroux, 1963), "her behavior is inevitably accompanied by a loss of self-esteem and results in contempt for herself as an individual and for her sex. It corrupts her self-image when she is degraded to the position of a sexual object of the

male. No woman with a high opinion of herself as a person
and as a member of her sex will drift into promiscuity except
in utter despair or under the pressure of dire need of money.
The demoralizing effect of promiscuity is akin to that of a
man who sells himself into slavery."

        Hence Françoise Dorleac's objection to the way Polan-
ski insisted she portray Pleasence's wife. Polanski's heroines
have no integrity because they are made to appear contempti-
ble. Polanski's pursuit of a promiscuous life-style can only
bring him into contact with promiscuous women; this limita-
tion at once explains the lack of change in his on-going cinematic images and the characteristic sluttishness associated
with all his major female characters.

        VAMPIRE KILLERS had an original running time of
128 minutes. It was shaved under Ransohoff's supervision
for the American version into a 98-minute picture. Polanski
was so incensed at such arbitrary treatment that he demanded
his name be removed from the credits. This M-G-M and
Ransohoff's Filmways company refused to do.

        Intended as a satire on vampire films (although it es-
capes me how any film in this genre can be regarded as anything less than a satire), whether as comedy or parody VAM-
PIRE KILLERS is in the vanguard. It is dull at times, when
Polanski becomes infatuated with visual imagery, but it was
his first color film and perhaps he can be excused for luxur-
iating in it. This is especially true if we acknowledge Polanski for showing us scenes never photographed before, such as
the Jewish vampire who isn't affected in the least by having
a crucifix thrust in his face, or the fagelah vampire who is
quite taken with Alfred, played by Polanski, arguing for sexual tolerance even in the realm of the occult.

        "I think he put more of himself into VAMPIRE KILL-
ERS," said Dennis Slocombe, cinematographer on the picture,
"than into any other film. It brought to light the fairy-tale
interest that he has. ... The figure of Alfred is very much
like Roman himself--a slight figure, young and a little de-
fenseless--a touch of Kafka. It is very much a personal
statement of his own humor. He used to chuckle all the way
through."

        Between writing CUL-DE-SAC and REPULSION, Brach
and Polanski wrote a script titled CHERCHEZ LA FEMME,
telling the story of a divorced American dentist who is weary

of American women and embarks on a series of adventures
through Europe in quest of a more congenial wife. It was
translated into English by Larry Gelbert. Polanski and Gutowski had formed a production company, Cadre Films, and intended this to be their second production after their joint-
venture with Ransohoff's Filmways and M-G-M on VAMPIRE
KILLERS. However, the dispute over the cutting of KILLERS
culminated with M-G-M acquiring the CHERCHEZ screenplay
(still unproduced) and Polanski personally signing a three-
picture contract with Robert Evans, then head of world-wide
production at Paramount after that studio's take-over by Gulf
& Western. There was nothing in Evans' background, from
his being rescued from haberdashery by Norma Shearer to
play her first husband Irving Thalberg in MAN OF A THOUS-
AND FACES (Universal, 1955), to Darryl Zanuck's having
Henry King cast him as the toreador in THE SUN ALSO RISES
(20th-Fox, 1957), to explain how he suddenly emerged in such
an important executive capacity. Nor was his tenure very
long. With the failure of Polanski's THE TENANT (Paramount, 1976)--although his fall was unrelated to it--he was
ousted and went into independent production.

When Ira Levin's novel Rosemary's Baby (Random
House, 1967) was still in galleys, Levin's Hollywood agent,
Marvin Birdt, sent a copy of it to Alfred Hitchcock and a
second copy to horror exploitation film producer and director,
the late William Castle. Castle was excited and told Birdt
he wanted to purchase screen rights, but Birdt's asking price,
a quarter of a million dollars, was too steep for Castle. After some haggling, Castle acquired the rights for $100,000,
plus an additional fifty thousand if it became a bestseller, and
five per cent of the net profits.

Robert Evans telephoned Castle and had him come over
to the Paramount lot in Los Angeles. Paramount wanted to
finance and distribute. Evans introduced Castle to Charles
Bluhdorn, the mastermind behind Gulf & Western. Bluhdorn
negotiated terms with Castle and they agreed on a figure of
$250,000 and fifty per cent of the net profits. Neither Evans
nor Bluhdorn had read the novel, but Bluhdorn wanted Roman
Polanski to direct it, probably at Evans' instigation. Castle
wanted to direct ROSEMARY'S BABY himself, but he agreed
to at least meet with Polanski.

Polanski frequently gives people a poor first impression and it was no different with William Castle. "On my
first meeting with Roman Polanski," Castle recorded in his

autobiography, Step Right Up (Putnam's, 1976), "I took an
instant dislike to him. A short, stocky man, dressed in the
Carnaby Street fashion of the time, he seemed cocky and vain,
continually glancing into the mirror in my office. I had made
up my mind that he would not direct ROSEMARY'S BABY. I
asked him to sit down, which he declined. He insolently
faced me, legs spread apart. It was useless trying to make
small conversation with him, so I decided to make the meeting brief and get rid of him."

Yet, in spite of Castle's resolve, Polanski, who had
read the book, talked so intelligently and knowingly about how
to treat the property that Castle changed his mind and called
Bluhdorn at Paramount after the meeting to tell him so. In
fact, while discussing the novel, Castle had found Polanski
"fascinating, brilliant, and wonderfully receptive." Polanski
returned to London, completed a first screen treatment, and
sent it on to Castle. He then telephoned Castle from London,
told him he would be arriving in a week and said he would
appreciate it if Castle would help find a house for him to rent
somewhere near the ocean. His fiancée, Sharon Tate, would
be in touch with Castle. When Castle met Sharon, he found
her "beautiful," with an "unaffected simplicity." Castle told
her he had located just the house for her and Roman, Brian
Aherne's home, which he was willing to lease since he was
going to Europe. When he showed it to her, Sharon enthused,
"Roman and I will be so happy here."

ROSEMARY'S BABY (Paramount, 1968), with its story
of an innocent girl impregnated by the devil and living in New
York City surrounded by a cult of devil-worshippers, was the
picture Polanski made when he was his happiest, the story of
a diabolical conception while he and Sharon, having married,
conceived a child together. It was filled with the tensions,
suspense, suspicions, and hopelessly trapped feeling so typical
of Polanski's European cinema, but added were strong logical
and narrative story elements, a well-made plot if you will--
very uncharacteristic of Polanski's previous films. Once it
was released, public response was spirited, and there were
numerous crank threats sent to Castle, obviously inspired by
the Satanism depicted in the film. Castle had his problems,
certainly, fighting the crackpots and kidney stones at the same
time.

Polanski achieved a degree of intimacy in ROSEMARY'S
BABY that was new, chiefly by having the camera follow Mia
Farrow rather than having her walk toward the camera or

away from it or in front of it. If anything, the dream sequence was far more compelling than similar scenes in RE-
PULSION. Polanski has in fact studied his own dreams ex-
tensively in working out his films. "The fact that the dream
is frightening," he told the students at the American Film
Institute, "is because the subject of the dream is frightening....
I think the main thing about dreams is that everything constantly changes. Dreams are not static, and when you look
at someone's face, his face imperceptibly changes. Like you
start talking to your father and before you even realize, he's
already Nixon for some reason. The other thing about dreams
is that you are not aware of the background unless it plays
some important role in the dream. When there is someone
talking to you, you don't remember the background exactly.
So in trying to translate a dream to a film, I try to make
this background so that it is not so prominent, except when
it has some particular meaning."

The Polanskis kept changing houses until 12 February,
1969, when they moved into the house on Cielo Drive. Sharon
had never really been a star. Her semi-nude photograph,
taken by Polanski, had appeared in the March, 1967 Playboy.
Polanski was fond of dressing her to look like a little girl
and her innocence in the photographs taken of them at the
time surpass anything in Mia Farrow's projection of innocence
on screen in ROSEMARY'S BABY. Sharon so much wanted
to have her baby that she had not told Roman about it until
it was too late to abort. She hid the dissensions in her marriage, caused by Polanski's philandering, and frequently told
at her own expense the story of how Roman had once driven
through Beverly Hills and, spotting a pretty girl walking
ahead of him on the sidewalk, had yelled out, "Miss, you
have a bea-u-ti-ful arse." Only when the girl turned to look
at him did Roman realize it was Sharon.

Sharon's assailant, a girl named Susan Atkins, claimed
in talking to the police that by driving a knife into Sharon she
was expressing her love for her. Sharon had pleaded to the
Manson gang when first they seized her and the other four at
the Cielo Drive home early that night in August, 1969, to
spare her for the sake of her baby. Had there been time,
Susan had hoped to cut the dead baby out of Sharon's corpse.

The violent and brutal world which most Americans
prefer not to see, and which Polanski had been recording on
film, suddenly came to life and tapped him on the shoulder.
Polanski, after his press conference and the police interro-

gations, hid out at Paramount studios. When William Castle
visited him, Polanski, who had been out of the city during the
time of the tragedy, met Castle with tears in his eyes.
"Sharon," he said, "my poor Sharon ... and our baby."

The murderers will soon be eligible for parole. The
public quickly forgets. Yet for Polanski the after effects
have been unceasing. With the passing years, Sharon has
come increasingly to symbolize purity; his veneration of her
memory is unbounded.

Let me quote again from Nietzsche's Menschliches,
Allzumenschliches: "Mit Personen," he reflected, "deren die
Scheu vor dem Personlichen fehlt, muss man nicht umgehen
oder unerbittlich ihnen vorher die Handschellen der Konvenienz
anlegen." [One should not associate with people who lack shy-
ness about what's personal, or inexorably put the handcuffs of
convenience on them beforehand.] Because of the anguish in
his life, Polanski continues to be dogged all his days about
how he must feel about it, while in print he has become the
subject of pseudo-psychoanalytic speculations. Yet the most
moving part of this drama is not Roman's mourning, nor his
perplexity, nor the public invasion of his privacy, but rather
the senseless death of Sharon herself, who, in those last
months, despite everything, was totally devoted to her marriage
and her baby. Her bloody crucifixion reveals barbarism to
be as much a constant in human affairs as the failure of judicial systems to administer anything even dimly approaching
justice.

III

Before the last World War the late Sir Thomas Beecham
made a recording with the London Philharmonic of Act IV of
Puccini's La Bohème (Columbia MM-274), with Lisa Perli as
Mimi and Heddle Nash as Rodolfo. Just why he didn't record
the entire opera--the performance was singularly well-done--
I do not know. It wasn't until Arturo Toscanini's broadcast
of La Bohème from February, 1946 (Victor LM-6006), with
Licia Albanese and Jan Peerce, was released that a comparable performance became available (Toscanini, after all, premièred the opera in 1896).

It is in the fourth act that Mimi stumbles into Rudolfo's
garret, dying of consumption, and the two of them lyrically
sing of their past love, which had once brought them so close

and then drove them even more irresistibly apart. "Che
gelida manina ... Se la lasci riscaldar!" Mimi quotes Rodolfo as saying, remembering the first time they met. It is
this line at the conclusion of VAMPIRE KILLERS that Polanski
gave himself in the character of Alfred, commenting to Sharon,
"Your tiny hand is frozen..." before she sinks her vampire's
fangs into his neck.

   The last stage performance we saw of La Bohème was
at Covent Garden, the soprano singing Mimi competent but
disgracefully overweight. Vicki objected. "How are we honestly to believe Mimi is wasting away from tuberculosis when
she comes bouncing on stage at a hundred and fifty pounds?"
she asked. It was as ridiculous in its way as Lady Macbeth
in Polanski's version, in her night of guilt and sorrow, before
her suicide, surrounded by murmurs concerning her madness,
walking to and fro bare-assed in her bed chamber, her slender body lithe, youthful, sensuous, her red nipples erect with
excitement (or reacting to the drafts on the set). Polanski
went still farther in his conception of MACBETH when he presented the weird sisters as ugly hags engaging in their Cory-
bantic antics in the nude. According to Polanski, he had studied Shakespearean literature and staging exhaustively, always
taking "the explanation that was the most visual, that was the
most useful for our cinematographic adaptation. I also tried
to translate to a visual whatever was possible, because often
the language is so archaic that half the house doesn't understand what it's all about, but they shake their heads as they
don't want to appear stupid." It escaped Polanski's notice
that nearly every high school student in the United States has
read MACBETH and knows what it's about.

   In 1969, after Sharon's murder, Polanski scripted and
co-produced with Gene Gutowski A DAY AT THE BEACH, an
Anglo-Danish production directed in Denmark by the Moroccan
director, Simon Hesera, and based on a Dutch novel by Heere
Heresma. Polanski had hoped to follow ROSEMARY'S BABY
with THE DAY OF THE DOLPHIN, based on the Robert Merle
novel, but the assignment fell instead to Mike Nichols. Polanski had intended to make a film about the life of Italian
violinist and composer, Niccolò Paganini. He had plans to
make a film based on the ill-fated Donner party which, en
route to California, got snowed in and resorted to cannibal-
ism, reminiscent of AIMEZ-VOUS LES FEMMES?

   Instead, he made MACBETH. He was under a strain.
Shakespeare wasn't the least squeamish about blood-letting on

stage, but it was due to his perspicacity as a dramatist, and
not reticence, that he decided to have the rape and murder of
MacDuff's wife and children take place off stage.   Polanski
insisted on introducing it vividly into his film and made it
incredibly gory.   Unfortunately, the eruptions of violence and
the luscious, gorgeous photography are all his MACBETH has
to offer.   Polanski had no feeling for the primitive sublimity
of Shakespeare's English.   There is so little emotion of any
kind that Polanski's MACBETH might well be an adaptation of
a play by Jean Racine.   When Lady Macbeth stands on a par-
apet and demands:

> Come, you spirits that tend on mortal thoughts,
> unsex me here; and fill me, from the crown to
> the toe, top-full of direst cruelty.

she has in the Polanski version merely the insouciant placidity
of Racine's Bérénice when she reflects stoically:

> Je l'aime, je le fuis; Titus m'aime; il me quitte.
> Portez loin de mes yeux vos soupirs et vos fers.
> Adieu.   Servons tous trois d'exemple à l'univers.

> [I love him, I flee from it; Titus loves me; he would
> be quit of me.   Take your sighs and your armor far
> from my eyes.   Farewell.   All three of us serve
> as examples to the universe.]

Bald language with no expression cannot tell us what the characters feel, nor what motivates them to act as they do, although Shakespeare can always make us feel more than Racine
can.   Having had to struggle during my teens reading Martin
Luther's Bibel when German was not my native language, I
recognize the problems this assignment must have presented
Polanski just in the effort to familiarize himself with Eliza-
bethan English, but in Shakespeare as in St. Jerome's Vulgate,
the King James Bible, or Luther's Bibel, words must carry
the strongest emotional and dramatic conviction, for they arise
from it as well as give expression to it.

St. Jerome was so fond of Cicero's polished and controlled Latin that his contemporaries accused him of covert
paganism, but when he translated the Bible he made language
serve his cause completely, and his Latin achieved a power
and grandeur of evocation, a poetry and sensuousness that
pressed words to their limits and beyond.   Polanski, in trans-
lating MACBETH to the screen, never had his characters

assault the heavens, as indeed they must; he satisfied himself
with pretty images and hollow words. His version can rival
neither Orson Welles' for Republic in 1948 nor Maurice Evans'
later British production.

Nor was Polanski's next undertaking any more successful. D Major!--the key in which Mozart composed such ex-
quisite Unterhaltungsmusik, the key of the K. 136 Divertimento,
the second flute concerto, the "Coronation" piano concerto,
two string quartets, a string quintet, so many serenades, the
"Haffner" and "Prague" symphonies, and that minor masterpiece, the Sonata for Two Pianos which was formerly performed
with such élan and introspection by Robert and Gaby Casadesus
in their concert engagements and which they recorded some
years ago in a brilliant performance (Columbia ML-5046). It
may be "bloss eine kleine klassische Bewegung" in the Mo-
zartian oeuvre, but I delight in it. Polanski does too, and it
was no accident that D Major was the key he chose for WHAT?
(Avco-Embassy, 1973).

Remember the scene at the end of La Traviata when
Violetta, filled with the sudden strength of dying, whispers
(voce sotto) to the Germonts and her servant, "È strano!"
and the Germonts, straining forward toward where she lies
on her sofa, enquire, "Che?" There is no word in Italian
opera so rich in associations. Polanski knew it, and so did
the audience; but that is as far as the audience could go. Beyond that, only Polanski and Gerard Brach knew what was going on in WHAT?, a Carlo Ponti production filmed in Italy.
Nor did anyone much care, apparently; the idea was to get a
Roman Polanski film to follow in the wake of the success of
ROSEMARY'S BABY.

Polanski was back at the pool side, this time in Rome,
interviewing some forty girls, in and out of the water; he
finally chose Sydne Rome, one of the first to be interviewed.
She was to play "the girl" in WHAT?, to run around an Italian
seaside villa with her naked breasts flapping, pursued by roués
and social decadents, because, for Polanski, she symbolized in
her appearance and personality something typically American.
When she sits down before the piano--ah, it was Mozart, in
D Major!--not once, but twice, she asks her accompanist:
"Haven't we gone through this before?" Like the D Major
sonata, the film also has its introspective and melancholy
moods, juxtaposed with the vigorous, absurd, almost silly
gaiety. Polanski went a step beyond FANTASIA (RKO, 1940)
and set a story to music, rather than music to a story. He

cast himself as Mosquito, a zany character flitting among such
comédie noire characters as the old philosopher, impotent
with age and dying, who can expire in ecstasy thanks to Rome
spreading her legs over his face so he has one last look at
that organe du transport délicieux; or the amorous couple un-
dulating beneath an animal skin with their minimal dialogue:
He: "Take." She: "Give." He: "Take." She: "Give!"
They sigh, I believe, when he does, and she does.

What amusing nonsense when writing about it, but it is
rather boring when viewing it.   When I saw WHAT? again at
a re-issue house, the audience (fully aware of Polanski's more
recent difficulties) laughed harder at the trailer for THE TEN-
ANT than at WHAT?, with its narrative overlay announcing that
"No one does it to you like Roman Polanski!"

"I am sexually obsessed?" Polanski confided to Cahiers
du Cinéma.   Ralph Bellamy had no doubt about that when we
lunched together.   "He's a brilliant director," Bellamy said,
"and a perfectionist.   You will go through a scene again and
again until you hear this chuckle from behind the cameras.
Then you know that Polanski liked it, that he got what he
wanted.   I was offered John Huston's role in CHINATOWN.
I turned it down.   I was sent a script that didn't look at all
like the picture when Polanski finished it.   It read like a
porno film.   They had me in an incestuous situation already
on the third page!"

CHINATOWN is Polanski's most effective film, probably
because in it, more than usual, he was compelled to stick to
a strong plot-line.   "Whenever I was trying to do something
interesting," he admitted, "I realized that it was a vain effort and I was going against the grain.   It looked as though
I was trying to jazz up certain things, so I just abandoned
that approach and made it a straight suspense story."   I imagine that's why it worked as well as it did.   Polanski has never
outgrown his love for the ambiguous and, whatever his dedication to discipline, he has always reacted disparagingly when,
in conversation, I have told him of my preference for the
compactness of the French in their penchant for a well-made
plot.   Yet it is to ROSEMARY'S BABY, which closely adhered
to Ira Levin's novel, and to CHINATOWN that Polanski owes
his popularity with American audiences.   These films have,
in fact, so enhanced his reputation as a commercial filmmaker
that it is easy for some critics to overlook that, notwithstand-
ing, he is a European, with a European's sensibility and a
deep inner commitment to European culture and European

music. When he completed CHINATOWN, he went to Rome
to direct a stage performance of Alban Berg's atonal opera,
Lulu. When he completed dubbing THE TENANT in Paris,
he went to Munich to direct Verdi's Rigoletto for the stage.

I have mentioned the universal promiscuity of Polanski's
female characters. They exist for the sexual pleasure of the
male characters. This is no less true of Isabelle Adjani (who
was much better utilized by François Truffaut) in THE TEN-
ANT, the last of Polanski's credits to date, than it was true
of Jolanta Umecka at the beginning in KNIFE IN THE WATER.
For the Deneuve character, her descent into insanity is sexualized, as is Lady Macbeth's descent. Women, in Polanski's
view, are as driven to be sexual objects as men are desirous
of having them be sexual objects; they are also capable of
little more, save murder, or inducing another to murder, or
being unfaithful. Faye Dunaway in CHINATOWN is sexually
exploited by her father, is obviously promiscuous behind her
husband's back, and is of no use to Jack Nicholson's J. J.
Gittes other than as a convenient sexual partner. She is totally without depth. Rosemary is a sexual object for Satan
and, in her pregnancy, is of sexualized and diabolical significance for the others; at the fade she accepts her fate.

John Alan McCarty, in an article titled "The Polanski
Puzzle" for Take One (Vol. 2, No. 5), makes the claim that
"the theme of isolation is, in fact, the nucleus of all of Polanski's films." This is true enough, as far as it goes, but
McCarty does not get to the root of the sense of isolation.
It is quite obviously sexual in origin. Male characters seem
to be concerned either with material possessions or sexual
conquests. The middleaged husband in KNIFE IN THE WATER
regards his young wife as among his belongings, like his sail-
boat and his late-model car. The young hitchhiker is only
interested in sexually experiencing Umecka's body before moving on; in Polanski's lexicon, he "just likes fucking around."
The boy friend of Deneuve's sister in REPULSION is unhap-
pily married but has no intention of getting a divorce; the
sister exists solely as a sexual distraction. Deneuve, unwilling to accept this role of a sexual object, retaliates, but amid
fantasies which would make her retaliation ultimately a lie.

The male characters in CUL-DE-SAC may be searching
for something, but it becomes evident that it is not to be
found in the company of a female and is so ambiguous that
we are no more certain of their motivations than we are of
Treklovsky's identification with the former female tenant of

Roman Polanski as Trelkovsky in THE TENANT (Paramount,
1976).   Photo courtesy of Eddie Brandt's Saturday Matinee.

his apartment in THE TENANT.   It might seem that Gittes
in CHINATOWN is questing for truth, but if he is, he is easily quieted through cynical despair at the ineradicable corruption of the social order of which he is a corrupt part.   More
than sixty-five per cent of the film had to be shot on indoor
sets to give it the illusion of a period piece, but whether the
setting is medieval Scotland, Southern California in the 'thirties, or present-day Paris, the corruption and indifference of
society remain essentially unassailable.   In VAMPIRE KILL-
ERS, the occult has been eroticized, for the sake of humor
to be sure, but the vampires prey on ordinary mortals just
as men and women use one another sexually for obscure and
dubious ends.   In these terms, the hot pursuits of VAMPIRE
KILLERS are not really unrelated to the males sexually pursuing the females, above all Sydne Rome, in WHAT?

        I would truthfully like to say in Polanski's behalf that
when these images of men and women interacting together are
juxtaposed, they somehow constitute a commentary on the human condition, but I cannot.   I do not think it is possible

even to comment that Polanski's films are a study in the vicissitudes of neurosis, because they strive to be something more than a catalogue of psychopathologies. Moreover, because Polanski is who he is, his films cannot be said to exist even secondarily as vehicles for sheer entertainment.

The conclusion to which I am drawn is not one represented in Polanski's oeuvre by conscious design; rather, the isolation most of his characters experience is based, as I have already hinted, in their hopeless promiscuity which, because of its regressive and infantile character, never permits any of them to rise to the occasion of a stable human relationship, much less enter upon the difficulties and challenges of maintaining such relationships. The essay of Freud's to which I referred earlier, "The Most Prevalent Form of Degradation in Erotic Life," instructs us that "unrestrained sexual liberty from the beginning leads to no better result. It is easy to show that the value the mind sets on erotic needs instantly sinks as soon as satisfaction becomes readily obtainable. Some obstacle is necessary to swell the tide of the libido to its height; and at all periods of history, wherever natural barriers in the way of satisfaction have not sufficed, mankind has erected conventional ones in order to be able to enjoy love." Polanski's characters, for the most part, exist without such barriers, and therefore in a self-imposed vacuum which can know nothing of love and from which, seemingly, there is no escape.

We had all promised to see one another again when we parted in Paris, but when the opportunity arose, in March, 1977, Polanski having come to Hollywood to work on a screenplay for Columbia Pictures, it had to be postponed. On 11 March, Polanski was arrested in his suite at the Beverly-Wilshire on six charges dealing with rape, drug-abuse, and sodomy. The victim, a thirteen-year-old girl, had presumably accompanied Polanski to Jack Nicholson's Woodland Hills home the previous day, while Nicholson was out of the city, and the two had been observed by John Huston's daughter, who agreed to turn state's evidence provided a drug-possession charge against her was dropped. On 30 March, Polanski was indicted in Los Angeles Superior Court on all six counts, but by 9 August this was reduced to a single charge of statutory rape. Polanski was ordered by the court to undergo examination and mental tests to be administered by two court-appointed psychiatrists (despite all the evidence to the contrary, courts appear to believe that modern psychiatry is an exact science capable of precise measurement). By this time Polanski had

been taken off the Columbia project. Executives at Columbia
were fond of telling jokes about the "Polanski affair," such
as that his latest picture was to be titled "Close Encounters
of the Third Grade," after the new Steven Spielberg picture
they were about to release, CLOSE ENCOUNTERS OF THE
THIRD KIND (Columbia, 1977), and that the theme song to
this opus would be "Thank Heaven for Little Girls."

Anatole France once remarked ironically that the majestic equality of the law is such that it forbids the rich as
well as the poor to steal bread or to sleep under bridges.
In CHINATOWN, Polanski had a character comment about
John Huston's screen character, "Sue people like that and
they're likely to be having lunch with the judge who's trying
the case." Polanski was identified in the public mind not
with an underdog but with the rich and influential, although
the judge who later withdrew from the case had such antipathy
toward him that it is doubtful that they would ever likely be
in each other's company anywhere save in a courtroom. The
public disregarded the fact that the victim, to use the
judge's words, "was not unschooled in sexual matters,"
and met Polanski with moral opprobrium. Even when I
mentioned to various parties who were familiar with the
case that more than one beloved and venerable screen personality had cruised around Hollywood High School for the last
twenty-five years seeking young girls looking for sexual experiences "with the stars," I was met with comments such
as "He was stupid, that's all," or "He shouldn't have got
caught." Americans, it would seem, have always expected
the human race to conduct itself according to a moral standard
neither they nor anyone else could maintain, but that has never
prevented them from, externally at least, imposing the sever-
est strictures on those unfortunate enough to have been found
out.

In the interim Dino De Laurentiis hired Polanski to
direct a remake of THE HURRICANE (United Artists, 1937),
originally directed by John Ford. Polanski having been forbidden by his attorneys to see or talk to anyone before the
bargaining with the district attorney's office was concluded,
the first time I spoke to him was on the telephone prior to
our lunching with him at the Brown Derby in Beverly Hills,
near De Laurentiis' office. He sounded, if anything, sadder
than I could recall his ever having been. To reporters he
was more stoical: "I'm used to grief," he said. "This is
a trifle." Then he was on the front page again, this time
for grabbing a news photographer's camera and smashing it

when the photographer had attempted to snap his picture while
he knelt at Sharon Tate's grave.

He was half an hour late and his secretary had telephoned to apologize and assure us he was on the way.   He
appeared nervous and harried as he entered the front door,
and Vicki walked at once to him to guide him back to the
table we had reserved.

"You look like you could really use a drink," I said
as he slid into the booth.

"No, definitely not a drink," he said, fumbling with
a packet of Antonio y Cleopatra cigars.   I held out my lighter
and he puffed at the cigar, finally taking the lighter tremblingly
into his own hand to get the cigar going.   "I'm hung over,"
he confessed.   "It's the first time since last Christmas, when
I went back to visit friends in Warsaw."   He grinned.   "Going to Poland always makes me want to drink, you know?
Vodka.   Sit around and talk and drink vodka."

"Have a drink," I urged.   "It'll settle your stomach."

"What are you drinking?"

"Bloody Marys, but take my word for it, they're
awful."

"A Coke.   I'll have a Coke."

The waiter took our order.

"You seem so upset," I said.   "Last time we spoke
you were very happy."

"Happy?"

"Yes.   In Paris.   You were happy in Paris."

He nodded to himself as much as he did to us.   "That
was a happy time, wasn't it?"

The drinks arrived and we decided from the menu.
"Maybe," I suggested, "you should try a Bromo-Seltzer and
a couple of aspirins."

"Gaghch!"   He shook his head vehemently.   "Bromo-

Seltzer!" He settled on chicken soup and ground sirloin.
"This place is so noisy," he complained, looking around the
dining room.

"Don't blame us. You wanted to come here."

"Well, yes, I haven't been here for years. It brings
back memories."

"The food could be better. The only person I know
who eats here regularly is George Raft. He has a table in
the back dining room."

"George Raft? Who's he?"

"He used to play gangsters, especially at Warner
Brothers. You know who Alban Berg and Franz Kafka are,
and not George Raft? Watch the late movies."

"Yes, I know. There are so many movies on at night
out here. I've been watching them every chance I get."

"Good, because we have a movie question for you.
Vicki and I saw THE TENANT again and we figure you didn't
tell the whole story, did you? Trelkovsky is so fascinated
by the girl who was the previous tenant in his room and is
driven to suicide out of guilt...."

"Yes," Roman interrupted, gazing at us pensively.

"We felt that perhaps he drove her to suicide," Vicki
interjected. "Maybe he even pushed her out of the window
himself and that's why she screams when he comes to visit
her in the hospital. Like CRIME AND PUNISHMENT."

Roman was shaking his head in despair. "You must
have your Hollywood plot, mustn't you? Trelkovsky is just
a hypersensitive person. When you're dealing with a hypersensitive person, you don't have to look for all manner of
explanations. You always want to explain everything. Trelkovsky imagines he contributed to her death because he is
sensitive. People who are lonely seem eccentric ... you
see them in every big city walking down the street muttering
to themselves."

"The French didn't like the film," I said.

"That had nothing to do with the plot ... it had to

do with the French. I took them seriously, you see. You
can make fun of a working man or a priest, but you must do
it with tenderness. They like to laugh at themselves, but not
if you do it critically. I was trying to show the typical
French middle class."

      Lunch was served. Polanski began nervously to spoon
soup.

      "Why are you here?" he asked. "Why didn't you stay
in the East?"

      "I hate California!" Vicki said.

      "It wasn't the smog that attracted us," I said. "But
places get bad. This place has gotten bad."

      "Yes, yes," Polanski nodded. "The only way is if
you have a house, you know, and have a few friends over.
Then it's nice here ... but not if you don't have your own
place."

      "People magazine," I said, "quoted you as saying that
if you could live your live over again, you wouldn't."

      "No, I wouldn't."

      "Why not? You have money."

      "Money," he said scathingly.

      "Yes, money. And you're making pictures, some of
them very good pictures."

      "Money is overrated." He pushed his empty soup cup
aside. "You tell me? If you could live your life over again,
would you really want to? You'd want to make a change here
or there. I mean, with no changes? If I balance the good
things that have happened to me with the bad, there's been
more bad, and the bad has been more painful."

      "And the good things?"

      "You want my life?" he demanded accusingly. "Here!"
He held out his cupped hands to me. "You want it? Take
it! Me? I wouldn't live it over again."

      On 19 September, 1977 the psychiatrists' reports were

in their words, that Polanski was not a "men-
__d sex offender." He was granted a stay of
_____ns to complete work on HURRICANE, after which
he was ordered to report to the state prison at Chino, California, for ninety days of additional psychiatric study; but
the stay proved insufficient. When the time came for Polanski
to report to the prison authorities, he and De Laurentiis arrived at an amicable agreement whereby Polanski surrendered
the picture.

After only forty-two days at Chino the psychiatric staff
had prepared their reports, requesting straight probation based
on their findings that Polanski had no psychiatric problems
and was not in need of psychotherapy. The judge announced
prior to Polanski's next hearing that, despite the reports, he
felt jail time was called for. Polanski, before he could be
sentenced on 1 February, 1978, fled the United States to his
apartment in Paris. It was a most prudent move for him to
have made. In the treaty between the United States and
France, statutory rape is not an offense subject to extradition.
"There is too much at stake," Polanski told reporters in
Paris. "Please have sympathy with my problems."

I must caution those who have not lived in Southern
California that the liberality often associated with it is very
much a falsehood. There is a drive to absolute political
power there comparable to that of any totalitarian state. It
isn't merely that in recent times the state has produced leaders like Richard Nixon and Ronald Reagan; it goes deeper
than conservatism. On the front page of the Los Angeles
Herald-Examiner carrying the report of Polanski's flight,
officials were quoted in Los Angeles as saying: "We've got
the dogs out. The hounds are on his trail." Adjacent to
this report was an article telling of a South Los Angeles man
who had his neck broken as a result of a dispute with a policeman who arrested him for jaywalking with his two-year-
old grandson. In Southern California it is the order of the
day that the citizen must be made to realize that government
and law enforcement are absolute authorities that can be met
only with abject submission. We know. That's why we no
longer live there.

Perhaps in retrospect Namatian, the Gallic senator
to Rome, said it best when he surveyed the ruin of his age:
"ordo renascendi est crescere posse malis"--which, literally
translated, means a "rebirth of order can spring from misfortune," but which I once saw more freely rendered as "it

is the law of progress to advance by misfortune." I prefer the latter in this context because Roman Polanski is ultimately an artist and a free spirit whose greatest challenge remains to function creatively by means of his art, so as to survive the nearly intolerable injustice with which life continually assails him, as it does all of us, and which quite possibly only art can ever surmount. There is no question but that the spectre of what happened in Los Angeles will haunt him for some time and might even curtail his mobility as a director.

On the title page to James Fenimore Cooper's The Deerslayer, a novel of 1841, are imprinted the words:

What Terrors round him wait?
Amazement in his van, and Flight combined,
And Sorrow's faded form, and Solitude behind.

Roman Polanski isn't the first artist who, behaving contrary to the official government position, first in Poland, then in Southern California, has been singled out for punishment, the more severely to be sure than were he not an artist. Nor will he be the last, even though fifty years from now his plight may seem only ridiculous, or, in his words, "a trifle." And maybe not in fifty years. On the "Weekend Update" portion of the satirical NBC show, Saturday Night Live, Polanski, wearing a beard, was shown, presumably in Paris, addressing a little girl, with a comedienne commenting, "Polanski claims they are just friends." He has passed into folk culture, and for all the wrong reasons. But Rilke's lines, which occurred to me in Paris, are perhaps more appropriate to his inner state than all the humor at his expense would allow.

ROMAN POLANSKI

A Film Checklist by Vicki Piekarski

Director

1. ROWER (THE BIKE) (1955).

2. ROZBIJEMY ZABAWE (BREAK UP THE DANCE) (1957).

3. DWAJ LUDZIE Z SZAFA (TWO MEN AND A WARD-

ROBE) (1958). P: Polish Film Academy. C: Jakub
Goldberg, Henryk Kluba, Roman Polanski. 15m.

4.   LAMPA (THE LAMP) (1959).

5.   GDY SPADAJA ANIOLY (WHEN ANGELS FALL) (1959).
C: Barbara Kwiatkowska, Jakub Goldberg, Henryk
Kluba.

6.   LE GROS ET LE MAIGRE (THE FAT AND THE LEAN)
(1961). P: Claude Joudioux/A. P. E. C. C: André
Katelbach, Roman Polanski. 16m.

7.   SSAKI (MAMMALS) (1962). P: Lodz. C: Henryk
Kluba, Michal Zolnierkiewicz, Roman Polanski. 11m.

8.   NOZ W WODZIE (KNIFE IN THE WATER) (1962). P:
Contemporary. C: Leon Niemczyk, Jolanta Umecka,
Zygmunt Malanowicz. 94m.

9.   LES PLUS BELLES ESCROQUERIES DU MONDE (THE
BEST SWINDLES IN THE WORLD) (1963). P: Ulysse/
Primex/Lux/Vides/Toho-Towa/Caesar Film Productie.
D: Claude Chabrol, Ugo Gregoretti, Jean-Luc Godard,
Roman Polanski. C: Nicole Karen, Jan Teulings,
Arnold Gelderman. Polanski's episode is A RIVER
OF DIAMONDS.

10.   REPULSION (1965). P: Compton-Cameo. C: Catherine Deneuve, Yvonne Furneaux, John Fraser. 104m.

11.   CUL-DE-SAC (1966). P: Compton-Cameo. C: Donald Pleasence, Françoise Dorleac, Lionel Stander.
111m.

12   DANCE OF THE VAMPIRES (American title: THE
FEARLESS VAMPIRE KILLERS: PARDON ME, BUT
YOUR TEETH ARE IN MY NECK) (1967). P: Metro-
Goldwyn-Mayer. C: Jack MacGowran, Roman Polan-
ski, Alfie Bass. Metrocolor. Panavision. 107m.
(In America 98m.)

√13.   ROSEMARY'S BABY (1968). P: Paramount. C: Mia
Farrow, John Cassavetes, Ruth Gordon. Technicolor.
137m.

14.   CHINATOWN (1974). P: Paramount. C: Jack

Nicholson, Faye Dunaway, John Huston.   Technicolor.
Panavision.   131m.

15.   LOCOTAIRE (THE TENANT) (1976).   P: Paramount.
C: Roman Polanski, Isabelle Adjani, Melvyn Douglas.
Eastmancolor.   125m.

FILM RENTAL GUIDE

For readers who may be inclined to view many of the motion pictures discussed in these pages, the following film rental companies are listed with their addresses. The list is scarcely exhaustive except for the films of the directors covered in Close-Up: The Contemporary Director, most of which are available from these sources:

FILMS, INC.
1144 Wilmette Avenue
Wilmette, Ill. 60091
Attn: Allen Green
(for 20th-Fox, M-G-M, Cinerama, and RKO)

SWANK MOTION PICTURES
201 S. Jefferson Avenue
St. Louis, Mo. 63166
Attn: Ray Swank
(for Columbia, Warner Bros. , National General, and American International)

JANUS FILMS
745 Fifth Avenue
New York, N.Y. 10022
Attn: Bill Becker
(for most foreign films)

PARAMOUNT PICTURES NON-THEATRICAL
5154 Marathon Street
Hollywood, CA 90038
Attn: Chuck Cromer

UNIVERSAL SIXTEEN
445 Park Avenue
New York, N.Y. 10022
Attn: Gene F. Giaquinto
(for Universal films and Paramount films prior to 1948)

UNITED ARTISTS SIXTEEN
769 Seventh Avenue
New York, N.Y. 10019
(for United Artists films and Warner Bros. prior to 1948)

MACMILLAN/AUDIO-BRANDON
34 MacQuesten Pkwy. South
Mount Vernon, N.Y. 10550
Attn: Myron Bresnick
(for most vintage Columbia films and selected foreign films)

CONTRIBUTORS

JACOBA ATLAS has been a film critic for The Los Angeles Free Press and a contributor to Ampersand, Women and Film, Film Comment, Rolling Stone, Los Angeles Magazine, and Melody Maker. Currently she is writer/associate producer for the Rona Barrett portion of the television show Good Morning America. Working on her doctoral dissertation on the pre-1935 efforts to unionize the American motion picture industry, she has also been a guest lecturer at UCLA, Immaculate Heart College, University of California at Northridge, and at Long Beach.

PAUL FRIZLER is a lecturer and professor in film, popular culture, and popular literature at Chapman College in Orange County, California. He has recently written and directed his first feature-length theatrical motion picture, GETTING WASTED.

VICKI PIEKARSKI is the Associate Editor of the Close-Up on the Cinema series. She is Co-Editor-in-Chief of The Westerns: An Encyclopedia of Western Fiction, Film, Radio, and Television, to be published by McGraw-Hill Book Company in 1981, and co-author of The Frontier Experience: A Study Guide to the Life and Literature of the American West, to be published by The Greenwood Press in 1982.

BELLA TAYLOR is a free-lance writer living and working in the Los Angeles area. Her appearance in this volume marks her debut in writing film history/criticism.

JON TUSKA is the General Editor of the Close-Up on the Cinema series. He is the author of several books on American social culture, among them The Filming of the West (Doubleday, 1976), which he is currently revising into two volumes, and The Detective in Hollywood (Doubleday, 1978). He has been special film consultant for Images of Indians (PBS, 1980) and among his forthcoming books are Hollywood

412

Filmmakers and In the Cage: A History of American 'Film Noir'.

DAVID WILSON is the Research Editor of the Close-Up on the Cinema series. He is currently a contributor to The Los Angeles Times and is at work on a history of stunt work and second unit direction in Hollywood films.

INDEX

415